Huntington Library Publications

American Fiction

1774-1850

A CONTRIBUTION TOWARD A BIBLIOGRAPHY

BY

LYLE H. WRIGHT

SECOND REVISED EDITION

THE HUNTINGTON LIBRARY
SAN MARINO · CALIFORNIA

1969

PUBLISHED WITH THE ASSISTANCE OF THE
UNION PACIFIC RAILROAD FOUNDATION FUND

PRINTED IN U.S.A.
BY ANDERSON, RITCHIE & SIMON : LOS ANGELES

CONTENTS

v

INTRODUCTION

THE first revised edition of this bibliography was published about twenty years ago. Since that time many librarians, collectors, bookdealers, and this compiler have been on the lookout for new material. Through these efforts, one hundred and forty-three new titles have been accepted as within the scope of this work, and scores of new editions have been added.

Seven titles listed at the end of the Chronological Index as "N. D." have now been assigned dates: Numbers 69, 151a, 299, 442, 1319, 1345, and 1797. And also noteworthy, of the many new editions added, eight are earlier than previously recorded: Numbers 108b, 133a, 161a, 337a, 1695a, 2069a, 2093a, and 2303a.

The Appendix has been eliminated from this revision. Virtually all of the titles listed therein have been located, and those which qualified have been incorporated.

The original numbering has been retained. An "a," "b," "c," etc., appended to a number designates a new title or edition. The one exception to this is the first entry, which has been assigned the number −1.

An anonymous title entry, for which authorship is now established, adds that information in a note (see No. 215). The title also appears under the author's name as an unnumbered entry.

It so happens that the last entry, Number 2772, of the previous edition is again the last one here. If the entries had been renumbered for this revision, however, they would have approximated 3,500.

Since the scope of the bibliography and the procedure of its compilation have remained unchanged, the introductory material to the previous edition is herewith reprinted with very little alteration.

This bibliography lists American editions of prose fiction written by Americans and published between 1774 and 1850. The few foreign-born authors who are included claimed the United States as their home. Anonymous works have been retained when it was not readily determined whether they were of foreign or American origin.

At the time work was begun on the first edition of the bibliography, it was intended to list only novels, romances, tales, and short stories. Shortly thereafter, records had accumulated for many items of fiction which could not be classified in any one of these categories. Investigation established the fact that such material had been overlooked; consequently, much of it was lost to students of American literature. The scope of the work, therefore, was broadened to include fictitious biographies, travels, and sketches, allegories, tract-like tales, and other writings of similar nature.

A large proportion of the tract-like tales were written by authors interested in one or more of the various social reform movements organized in the first half of the nineteenth century. Charles Burdett's prefatory statement in *The Elliott Family; or, The Trials of New York Seamstresses* (New York, 1845), fiction written to promote the improvement of the factory girls' lot, offers a contemporary reason for this type of literature: "I have perhaps committed an error in weaving a story with such a subject: but I felt well assured that a dry detail of facts, however well authenticated, would be, if read at all, forgotten too soon for any advantage to accrue by exciting public sympathy to those whose advantage I had in view. . . . It has not been written for the sake of writing, but with the simple wish, that through the statements it contains, public attention may be aroused to the true condition of the seamstresses of New York."

In general, it has been intended to omit annuals and gift books, publications of the American Tract Society and the Sunday School Union, juveniles, Indian captivities, jestbooks, folklore, anthologies, collections of anecdotes, periodicals, and extra numbers of periodicals. The last two mentioned include such items as Cooper's "Le Mouchoir" in *Brother Jonathan*, Extra Sheet, XXII; Poe's "[The Balloon Hoax]" in *The Extra Sun*, April 13, 1844; Whitman's "Franklin Evans" in *The New World*, II, No. 10, Extra Series, No. 34; and the tales in the *New Mirror* and *Boston Notion*. It has also been intended to omit essays; however, as Arthur Hobson Quinn says in his *American Fiction* (1936), such works as Mitchell's *Reveries of a Bachelor*, included in this bibliography, represent "the border line between fiction and essay." Likewise, some stories written "for young people" and "for youths of all ages," included in this work, are border-line juveniles.

Authorship of several formerly anonymous and pseudonymous entries has been established. A few titles in the earlier edition have been deleted as they have been since identified as American reprints of foreign fiction, usually of English origin.

The bibliography was compiled to serve as a guide to the books of American fiction rather than as a complete bibliographical description of them. The compiler has seen the majority of the titles, but rarely has he examined more than one copy of a title. Consequently, variations between copies are seldom noted, and in only a few cases are distinguishing points of issues brought out. This statement applies to the two-volume works that were also issued as two volumes in one. Bibliographies and lists by others have been used freely, with acknowledgment wherever practicable. No effort has been made to locate all copies extant, but only those in the twenty-two libraries listed on pages xvii and xviii. The two private collections listed in the census of the previous edition, designated "Mr. JTB," for James T. Babb, and "Mrs. RCT," for Mrs. Robert Coleman Taylor, are now located at Yale and the University of Virginia respectively. The private collection of C. Waller Barrett has also been presented to the University of Virginia.

MECHANICS OF COMPILATION

Entries   The books are entered under the author's name, when known; otherwise, by titles, unless unidentified pseudonyms or authors' initials appear.

Titles   Some titles have been shortened, and authors' names and quotations appearing on the title pages have been omitted. Omissions are indicated by ellipses. The use of the abbreviation "anon." for anonymous, following a title, indicates that the author's name does not appear on the title page. The abbreviation "pseud.," following a name that is on the title page as the author, is self-explanatory. These two abbreviations are given only in the first-described editions and do not necessarily apply to later editions. Punctuation and capitalization have not followed the original titles.

Imprints When more than one printer, publisher, or company appears in the imprint, usually only the first is listed. A printer is so designated; otherwise, it is to be assumed that the name immediately following the place of publication is that of the publisher.

Dates The undated books were most troublesome, especially those that contained copyright dates prior to 1851. Whenever possible, the printers and publishers of those particular books were checked against directories, and, if found at the addresses given in the books before 1851, were included, even though the printers or publishers continued at the same place of business after 1851. For example, Theophilus B. Peterson was listed in contemporary Philadelphia directories as follows: 1845-53 [located] at No. 98 Chestnut Street, 1854-57 [located] at No. 102 Chestnut Street, and after 1858 at No. 306 Chestnut Street. On the basis of this information, undated T. B. Peterson books published only at No. 98 Chestnut Street were included, providing that the copyright dates were prior to 1851 and that other internal evidence—advertisements or inscriptions—of copies examined did not establish a date later than 1850. The copyright dates were used for many of the undated books. The date is preceded by the abbreviation "cop." and both are placed in square brackets. Roman numerals have been transliterated into arabic.

Pagination Formal pagination is not given; usually the last numbered page of text is noted to afford an idea of the length of the contents. Imperfections of located copies are seldom recorded.

Illustrations The abbreviation "illus." is used to designate all types of illustrations within the book: plates, portraits, frontispieces, textual illustrations, etc. Vignettes are not indicated nor included in the abbreviation.

Format The format has been determined from the gatherings in a copy, when the copy examined was not too tightly bound. The qualifying "Sm." or "La." has not been used.

Notes The notes are for the most part self-explanatory. Books containing two or more stories have one of the three following types of notes: "Contents," which lists all the stories in the book; "Also contains," which lists all stories following the first (the first being used as the title of the book); or "Contains," which lists only those stories that fall within the scope of this work.

The notes "LC has a title page" and "LC has a cover title" refer to the valuable collection of approximately 40,000 title pages and cover titles, ranging in date from 1787 to 1870, in the Library of Congress. The title pages and cover titles, deposited for copyright purposes, have the date of entering written on them by the copyright clerk. In some cases, the author's name is also penned in, even though the publisher obtained the copyright and the book appeared anonymously.

Annotations A note suggesting the locale and date of a separately published story is occasionally added. This is done when the title furnishes no clue, and a cursory examination of the book supplies it. When the place mentioned is apparently fictitious, it is given within quotation marks.

Cross References Cross references, with the exception of titles, appear in the main body of the bibliography.

When two or more stories by different authors occur in one publication, provided the author's name is given, each one is analyzed. No attempt has been made to identify the anonymous stories.

A later edition of a work, published under a different title, is arranged chronologically under the first-entered edition, with the later title indicated in a note.

INDEXES

The first or earliest listed edition of each title entered in the bibliography is noted in the Chronological Index. The Title Index lists the titles of all entries in the main body of the work.

ACKNOWLEDGMENTS

To the individuals and institutions who were so cooperative and helpful in compiling earlier editions of this bibliography, I wish to express again my sincere thanks. It is now my pleasure also to acknowledge those who have been instrumental in preparing this revised edition.

I am indebted, first of all, to the Trustees of the Huntington Library, the Director, James Thorpe, and the Librarian, Robert O. Dougan, for making it possible for me to visit many of the libraries listed in the census in order to search out and examine new material. Mrs. Kathleen Beyloos of the Publications Department deserves special mention for her assistance and editorial ability in the final phases of the work. Miss Mary Isabel Fry, Head of Reader Services, has been unfailing in her continued interest and cooperation.

To the following institutions and librarians, I am most grateful for their very generous help, without which this revision could not have been accomplished:

Marcus A. McCorison and Mary Brown, of the American Antiquarian Society.

Elizabeth C. Wescott, Mrs. Christine D. Hathaway, and Mrs. Mary Russo, of Brown University Library.

Mrs. Joan Spunt, of the Boston Athenaeum, and Margaret Hackett, formerly of that library.

John Alden, of the Boston Public Library.

Roger E. Stoddard, Richard A. Wasso, and Joseph P. McCarthy, of the Houghton Library, Harvard University.

Mrs. Dorothy Whittemore, of the Howard-Tilton Memorial Library, Tulane University.

David A. Randall, of the Lilly Library, Indiana University.

Thomas Adams, of the John Carter Brown Library.

Frederick R. Goff, of the Library of Congress.

Edwin Wolf, 2nd, of the Library Company of Philadelphia.

Also, I wish to thank Richard Colles Johnson, Lois Turbitt, and Arthur Miller, of the Newberry Library.

James Gregory and Margaret Cushing, of the New York Historical Society.

Lewis M. Stark, James Tobin, and Mrs. Maud D. Cole, of the New York Public Library.

Sylvia C. Hilton, of the New York Society Library.

Robert Rosenthal and Robert A. Tibbetts, of the University of Chicago Library.

Norma Hovden, of the Walter Library, University of Minnesota.

Mrs. Neda M. Westlake, Mrs. Riley, and Mrs. Baker, of the Charles Patterson Van Pelt Library, University of Pennsylvania.

Ruth Salisbury, of the Darlington Memorial Library, University of Pittsburgh.

William H. Runge, of the Alderman Library, University of Virginia.

Donald Gallup and Donald G. Wing, of the Yale University Library.

And to the following, who have contributed in one way or another to this work, I extend my sincere thanks:

Jacob Blanck	George T. Goodspeed
Carey S. Bliss	William F. Kelleher
Roger Butterfield	John S. Van E. Kohn
C. E. Frazer Clark, Jr.	Howard S. Mott
Earle E. Coleman	William S. Powell
	Nolan E. Smith

Information supplied by other libraries and individuals is acknowledged in the text.

To my wife Marjorie, who worked with me in locating new material in eastern libraries and who contributed so much to the entire visit, I am deeply grateful.

L. H. W.

KEY TO AUTHORS AND TITLES
OF BOOKS REFERRED TO IN THE NOTES

ALLIBONE
Allibone, S. A. *A Critical Dictionary of English Literature and British and American Authors.* Philadelphia, 1897-98.

APPLETON
Appleton's Cyclopaedia of American Biography. New York, 1887-89.

BAL
Blanck, Jacob N. *Bibliography of American Literature.* Vols. I-IV. New Haven, 1955-63.

BROWNE
Browne, N. E. *A Bibliography of Nathaniel Hawthorne.* Boston, 1905.

CATHCART
Cathcart, W. H. *Bibliography of the Works of Nathaniel Hawthorne.* Cleveland, O., 1905.

CURRIER
Currier, T. F. *A Bibliography of John Greenleaf Whittier.* Cambridge, Mass., 1937.

CUSHING
Cushing, W. *Initials and Pseudonyms.* New York, 1885.

FOLEY
Foley, P. K. *American Authors, 1795-1895.* Boston, 1897.

HEARTMAN & CANNY
Heartman, C. F., and J. R. Canny. *A Bibliography of First Printings of the Writings of Edgar Allan Poe.* Hattiesburg, Miss., 1943.

HEROLD
Herold, A. L. *James Kirke Paulding.* New York, 1926.

JOHNSON
Johnson, J. G. *Southern Fiction Prior to 1860.* Charlottesville, Va., 1909.

LANGFELD & BLACKBURN
Langfeld, W. R., and P. C. Blackburn. *Washington Irving: A Bibliography.* New York, 1933.

LIVINGSTON
Livingston, L. S. *A Bibliography of . . . Henry Wadsworth Longfellow*. New York, 1908.

MINNIGERODE
Minnigerode, M. *Some Personal Letters of Herman Melville, and a Bibliography*. New York, 1922.

ROBERTSON
Robertson, J. W. *Bibliography of the Writings of Edgar A. Poe*. San Francisco, 1934.

ROORBACH
Roorbach, O. A. *Bibliotheca Americana*. New York, 1852.

SABIN
Sabin, J. *Bibliotheca Americana*. New York, 1868-1936.

SHAW
Shaw, Ralph R., and Richard H. Shoemaker. *American Bibliography: A Preliminary Checklist, 1801-1819*. New York, 1958-66.

SPILLER & BLACKBURN
Spiller, R. E., and P. C. Blackburn. *A Descriptive Bibliography of the Writings of James Fenimore Cooper*. New York, 1934.

VAIL
Vail, R. W. G. "Susanna Haswell Rowson . . . a Bibliographical Study," American Antiquarian Society, *Proceedings*, N.S., XLII, Pt. I (1932).

VAN WINKLE
Van Winkle, W. M. *Henry William Herbert*. Portland, Me., 1936.

WAGNER-CAMP
Wagner, H. R. *The Plains and the Rockies . . . Rev. by C. L. Camp*. Columbus, O., 1953.

WEGELIN
Wegelin, O. *Early American Fiction, 1774-1830*. New York, 1929.

WEGELIN's *Paulding*
Wegelin, O. *A Bibliography . . . of James Kirke Paulding*. Chicago, 1918.

WILLIAMS & EDGE
Williams, S. T., and M. A. Edge. *A Bibliography of the Writings of Washington Irving*. New York, 1936.

ABBREVIATIONS USED FOR LIBRARIES APPEARING IN THE CENSUS

AAS
American Antiquarian Society, Worcester, Massachusetts

B
Brown University Library, Providence, Rhode Island

BA
Boston Athenaeum, Boston, Massachusetts

BP
Boston Public Library, Boston, Massachusetts

CLS
Charleston Library Society, Charleston, South Carolina

H
Harvard University Library, Cambridge, Massachusetts

HEH
Henry E. Huntington Library and Art Gallery, San Marino, California

HM
Howard-Tilton Memorial Library, Tulane University, New Orleans, Louisiana

IN
Lilly Library, Indiana University, Bloomington, Indiana

JCB
John Carter Brown Library, Providence, Rhode Island

LC
Library of Congress, Washington, D.C.

LCP
Library Company of Philadelphia, Philadelphia, Pennsylvania

N
Newberry Library, Chicago, Illinois

NYH
New York Historical Society Library, New York, N.Y.

NYP
New York Public Library, New York, N.Y.

NYS
New York Society Library, New York, N.Y.

UC
University of Chicago Library, Chicago, Illinois

BIBLIOGRAPHY

American Fiction
1774-1850

—1 ABEEL, DAVID. The Missionary Convention at Jerusalem; or, An
Exhibition of the Claims of the World to the Gospel ... New
York: John S. Taylor, 1838. 244 p. 12mo   H, HEH, Y
A fictional convention of representatives from every nation and of different
creeds.

1 AN ACCOUNT OF THE MARVELOUS DOINGS of Prince Alcohol, as
Seen by One of His Enemies, in Dreams. [N.p.], 1847. 72 p.
12mo   NYP, Y

2 ADAMS, JOHN STOWELL. Sam Squab, the Boston Boy ... Founded on Fact. Boston: Printed by Justin Jones, 1844. 48 p.
8vo   AAS, B, BP, LC, Y

3 ADELIO, *pseud.* A Journey to Philadelphia; or, Memoirs of
Charles Coleman Saunders. An Original Tale. By Adelio
[pseud.]. Hartford: Printed by Lincoln & Gleason, 1804. 72
p. 12mo   AAS

4 ADSONVILLE; or, Marrying Out. A Narrative Tale ... Albany:
S. Shaw, 1824. 285 p. 12mo   AAS, B, BA, BP, IN, LC, UV, Y
Possibly by an unidentified Edward Hull.
New York State; contemporary.

5 ADVENTURES IN A CASTLE. An Original Story, Written by a Citizen
of Philadelphia. Harrisburg: Printed by J. Elder, 1806. 71 p.
12mo   AAS

6 ADVENTURES OF A BACHELOR; or, Stolen Vigils ... Philadelphia:
Grigg & Elliot, 1837. 163 p. 12mo   B, HM, IN, UM, Y
LC has a title page, deposited Nov. 11, 1837.

7 AESOP, *pseud.* The Hypocrite; or, Sketches of American Society
from a Residence of Forty Years. By Aesop [pseud.] ... New
York: Thomas Fox & Co., 1844. 117 p., illus. 8vo   BP, NYP

3

7a AN AFFECTING HISTORY of the Captivity & Sufferings of Mrs. Mary Velnet, an Italian Lady, Who Was Seven Years a Slave in Tripoli ... Written by Herself. The First American Edition. Boston: William Crary [1804?]. 96 p., illus. 12mo

H, HEH, LC, NYP

See No. 1208a for a similar story.

7b ———— 2d ed. Sag-Harbour, New York: Printed by Alden Spooner, 1806. 71 p.

Shaw 11753 locates a copy in East Hampton Free Library.

7c AN AFFECTING NARRATIVE of the Captivity and Sufferings of Thomas Nicholson <a Native of New-Jersey>. Who Has Been Six Years a Prisoner among the Algerines, and from Whom He Fortunately Made His Escape a Few Months Previous to Commodore Decature's Late Expedition ... Boston: Printed for G. Walker [181-?]. 24 p., illus. 8vo   AAS, BP, LC

Based on Royal Tyler's *The Algerine Captive* (No. 2628).

7d ———— Boston: Printed for N. Coverly, Jr., 1816. 24 p., illus. 8vo

HEH, LC

7e ———— Boston: Printed by H. Trumbull, 1816. 24 p., illus. 8vo

AAS

7f ———— Boston: Printed for N. Coverly, 1818. 24 p., illus. 8vo

AAS, HEH, NYP

7g AFLOAT AND ASHORE; or, A Sailor's Life. Boston: F. Gleason, 1848. 100 p., illus. 8vo   HEH

Also contains: Jeemes Simmuns' Fox Hunt.
LC has a title page, deposited Dec. 31, 1847.
Not to be confused with Cooper's *Afloat and Ashore* (No. 579).
Printed in double cols.

AGAPIDA, *Fray* ANTONIO, *pseud.* *See* Irving, Washington

8 ALDEN, JOSEPH. Alice Gordon; or, The Uses of Orphanage ... New York: Harper & Brothers [cop. 1847]. 198 p., illus. 12mo   AAS, LC, NYP, Y

9 —————— Elizabeth Benton; or, Religion in Connection with Fashionable Life [anon.]. New York: Harper & Brothers, 1846. 187 p. 12mo   AAS, B, LC, NYP, UV, Y
New York City.

10 —————— The Lawyer's Daughter . . . New York: Harper & Brothers [cop. 1847]. 186 p., illus. 12mo AAS, HEH, LC, UV, Y

11 —————— The Old Revolutionary Soldier ... New York: Gates & Stedman, 1848. 152 p., illus. 12mo   LC, UP, UV, Y

11a ——————— ————— New York: Gates & Stedman, 1849. 152 p., illus. 12mo   AAS

12 ——————— ————— [New York: Gates and Stedman, cop. 1847.] 152 p., illus. 12mo   HEH, NYP, Y
Title reads: *The Old Revolutioner.*

13 —————— The Young Schoolmistress . . . New York: Harper & Brothers, 1848. 197 p., illus. 12mo   AAS, LC
"Archford."

14 ALLEN, ELIZABETH. Sketches of Green Mountain Life. With an Autobiography of the Author . . . Lowell: Nathaniel L. Dayton, 1846. 160 p. 12mo
                AAS, B, BP, H, HEH, IN, LC, N, NYP, UC, UM, UP, UV, Y
Contents: The Maid of the Mountain; or, The Lone Little Cot—Effects of Indulgence—The Mourner of the Lake—The Mysterious Passenger—Anna Rowland; or, Folly and Its Effects—The Transformation—Love and Disappointment—A Travelling Adventure—The Victim to an Error—The Deluded—De Olon.

15 ALLEN, HANNAH (BOWEN). Farmer Housten and the Speculator: A New England Tale [anon.]. Portland [Me.]: O. L. Sanborn & Co., 1839. 69 p. 12mo AAS, BP, H, LC, NYH, UM, Y
New Hampshire; 1835-36.

16 ALLEN, SAMUEL ADAMS. My Own Home and Fireside: Being Illustrative of the Speculations of Martin Chuzzlewit and Co., among the "Wenom of the Walley of Eden." By Syr [pseud.]. Philadelphia: John W. Moore, 1846. 384 p. 12mo
                                                          BA, LC, UV, Y

17 ALLSTON, WASHINGTON. Monaldi: A Tale ... [anon.]. Boston:
Charles C. Little and James Brown, 1841. 253 p. 8vo
> AAS, B, BA, BP, CLS, H, HEH, IN, LC, N, NYP, UC, UM, UP, UV, Y
> Italy; 17- -.

18 THE ALMIGHTY DOLLAR; or, The Brilliant Exploits of a Killer. A
Thrilling Romance of Quakerdelphia . . . Philadelphia: J.
Shipley Jones, printer, 1847.
> LC has a title page, deposited Mar. 26, 1847.

19 AMBROSE AND ELEANOR; or, The Disinherited Pair. A Tale of the
Revolution, by an Officer ... New York: Joseph A. Clussman,
1834. 2 vols. in 1. 24mo
> AAS, BP, H, HEH, LC, N, NYP, UC, UM, UP, UV, Y

20 ——— New York: Nafis & Cornish, No. 278 Pearl Street [cop.
1834]. 2 vols. in 1, illus. 24mo   B, NYP, UV, Y

21 ——— New York: Richard Marsh, No. 374 Pearl Street [n.d.].
2 vols. in 1. 16mo   AAS, HEH, IN, Y
> One copy examined in original binding contained *Alonzo and Melissa, by
> Daniel Jackson* [i.e., I. Mitchell]; see No. 1909.

22 AMELIA; or, The Faithless Briton. An Original American Novel,
Founded upon Recent Facts. To Which Is Added: Amelia; or,
Malevolence Defeated; and Miss Seward's Monody on Major
Andre. Boston: Printed for and sold by W. Spotswood, and
C. P. Wayne, 1798. 61, 22 p., illus. 12mo
> AAS, B, BP, H, HEH, IN, LC, LCP, N, NYP, UC, UM, UP, UV, Y
> Also published with *The New Pygmalion* (1798), and J. P. C. de Florian,
> *Galatea* (1798).
> HEH has an ed. printed in German and published at Baltimore in 1809.

23 AMELIA SHERWOOD; or, Bloody Scenes at the California Gold
Mines. With a Narrative of the Tragic Incidents on a Voyage
to San Francisco. New York: C. W. & G. E. Kenworthy, 1849.
32 p., illus. 8vo   AAS, NYP
> Attributed to the Rev. Walter Graham.

24 ——— Richmond: Barclay & Co., 1850. 32 p., illus. 8vo
> AAS, BA, LC

AMEREL, *pseud.* [Pseudonymous author of the stories listed in note below.] *In* The Fountain and the Bottle (1850), No. 996.

The Emigrant's Wife—George Sandford—Locked Out—Ned Summers, the Cabin-Boy—The Pledge by Moon-light—The Temperance Grocer—The Temperance Lecture.

25 THE AMERICAN BEE: A Collection of Entertaining Histories, Selected from Different Authors . . . The First Edition. Leominster, Mass.: Printed by and for Charles Prentiss, 1797. 249 p. 12mo   AAS, B, BP, H, HEH, IN, LC, LCP, N, NYP, UV, Y

Contents: The Adventures of Socivizca: A Notorious Robber and Assassin of the Race of the Morlachians—The Refined Lovers: A Spanish Tale—Story of Aristoclea from Plutarch—Omar; or, The Folly of Envy: An Eastern Tale—Edwin and Adela: A Tragic Story—Mirzim and Selima: A Turkish Tale—The Weasles and the Ferrets: An Occasional Fable—Story of Florimore and Leontine—Justice and Generosity; or, The Remarkable History of Sir Wilbraham Wentworth—The Fatal Effects of Gaming—The Unhappy Lovers—The Happy Deliverance—Hamet; or, The Insufficiency of Luxury to the Attainment of Happiness: A Oriental Tale—Lindor to Caroline, Containing the Story of Philander and Honoria—The Stage-coach: A Moral Tale—The Paradise of Schedad: An Eastern Tale—Two Letters from Mr. Everard, F. S. M., Containing an Adventure, of Which He Was an Eye Witness, at the Quick-silver Mine of Idra—Caroline to Lindor. Including The Nymph of the Grove: A Sentimental Historiette—Kintair and Seaton; or, The Unfortunate Sisters—The Fatal Effects of Misplaced Confidence—A Turkish Story—The History of Leonora; or, The Unfortunate Jilt—The Story of the Two Sisters—Alcander and Rosilla—Matrimonial Infidelity Detected—History of Miss Hortensia Melmoth.

26 AMERICAN TALES, by Mark Bancroft, and Others. Philadelphia: Samuel C. Atkinson, 1837. 316 p. 12mo

Title supplied by Mr. Oscar Wegelin.

AMES, NATHAN. The Student's Story. *In* M. M. Ballou, The Naval Officer (1845), No. 245.

27 AMES, NATHANIEL. An Old Sailor's Yarns . . . New York: George Dearborn, 1835. 388 p. 12mo
AAS, B, BP, IN, NYH, NYP, UP, UV, Y

Contents: Mary Bowline—Old Cuff—The Rivals—Morton—The Pirate of Masafuero.

28 AMORY, JOHN H. Alnomuc; or, The Golden Rule. A Tale of the Sea . . . [anon.]. Salem: D. B. Brooks and Brother, 1837. 144 p., illus. 12mo   LC

28a ——— ——— Boston: Weeks, Jordan & Co., 1837. 144 p.,
illus. AAS, HEH

29 ——— ——— 2d ed. Boston: Weeks, Jordan & Company,
1838. 144 p., illus. 12mo Y

30 ——— ——— Boston: James B. Dow, 1840. 144 p., illus.
12mo AAS, B, UP, UV, Y

31 ——— ——— Boston: James B. Dow, 1841. 144 p., illus.
12mo AAS, H, Y

32 ——— ——— Boston: James B. Dow, 1842. 144 p., illus.
12mo Y

33 ——— Old Ironside. First Number. The Story of a Shipwreck [anon.]. Boston: B. B. Mussey, 1837. 144 p., illus.
12mo BP, H, UV, Y
South Seas.

33a ——— ——— Boston: James B. Dow, 1839. 144 p., illus.
12mo AAS

34 ——— ——— Boston: James B. Dow, 1840. 144 p., illus.
12mo AAS, BP, H, N, NYH, Y

35 ——— ——— Boston: B. B. Mussey, 1841. 144 p., illus. 12mo
Y

ANDERSON, JOTHAM, *pseud. See* Ware, Henry

36 ANNA ARCHDALE; or, The Lowell Factory Girl . . . Boston: F.
Gleason [185-?]. 100 p. 8vo HEH, LC
Also contains: The Innkeeper's Wife: A Tale of the Revolution—A Wash-
ing Day Experience—Annie Sinclair; or, The Fourth of July Sail—Lilias
Atherton; or, The Rescue—The Fairy Fountain—A Picnic of Olden Time—
The Bachelor at Home—The Prima Donna—The Scientific Angler—The
Widow's Lesson—The Generous Lovers—The Volunteer's Return—The
Lady Blanche—The Captive Maiden.
Cover title: "The Lowell Factory Girl."
Printed in double cols.

37   APPLETON, EMILY.   Alice Mannering; or, The Nobleman's Son. A Tale of London . . .   Boston: Gleason's Publishing Hall, 1845. 54 p., illus.   8vo   AAS, HEH, LC, UP, UV, Y

38   ————   The Miser's Daughter; or, The Coined Heart . . .   Boston: Gleason's Publishing Hall, 1846.   50 p.   8vo
            AAS, B, HEH, N, NYP, UC, UM, UP, UV, Y

Large eastern city; contemporary.

APPLETON, MRS. JANE SOPHIA.   Sequel to the "Vision of Bangor in the Twentieth Century."   *In* [the following entry].

39   ———— *ed.*   Voices from the Kenduskeag . . . [anon.].   Bangor [Me.]: David Bugbee, 1848.   286 p.   12mo
            AAS, B, BP, HEH, IN, LC, N, NYP, UC, UP, UV, Y

Contains: The Speculator: A Story of the Fourth Decade [by John E. Godfrey]—Love and Romance [by Mrs. Henrietta C. Ingersoll]—A Vision of Bangor in the Twentieth Century [by Edward Kent]—Asa Glover, Esquire [by Mrs. Cornelia C. Barrett]—The Field of the Incurables [by Edward Kent]—The Festival at the Casa de Campo—First Impressions—A Simple Sketch of Simple Things [by Miss Mary Moulton]—The Resolve [by Mrs. Cornelia C. Barrett]—Sequel to the "Vision of Bangor in the Twentieth Century" [by Mrs. Jane S. Appleton].

Mrs. Cornelia Crosby Barrett, jt. ed.

For complete contents see Joseph Williamson, *A Bibliography of the State of Maine* (1896), I, 41-42.

40   ARDEN, the Unfortunate Stranger, Who Was Tried for the Murder of Miss Harriet Finch; but Was Acquitted through the Interposition of a Young Lady Whom He Afterwards Married.   A True Story.   New York: J. Broderick, 1822.   28 p.   12mo
            B, H, Y

New York City; 1760.

41   ————   New York: S. King, 1822.   28 p., illus.   12mo
            AAS, H, Y

42   ————   New York: W. Borradaile, 1824.   28 p., illus.   12mo
            AAS, Y

43   ————   To Which Is Added: Glenwar, the Scottish Bandit. A Tale of Former Times . . .   Philadelphia: Freeman Scott, 1827. 72 p.   12mo   AAS, B, UV, Y

44 ——— New York: S. King [1830?]. 28 p., illus. 12mo

               UP, UV, Y

45 ARGUS, *pseud.* A Tale of Lowell. Norton; or, The Lights and Shades of a Factory Village: Wherein Are Developed Some of the Secret Incidents in the History of Lowell. By "Argus" [pseud.]. Lowell: "Vox Populi Office," 1849. 80 p. 8vo

              AAS, HEH, N, Y

Printed in double cols.

184-.

46 ARMSTRONG, ARTHUR. The Mariner of the Mines; or, The Maid of the Monastery. A Tale of the Mexican War . . . Boston: F. Gleason [n.d.]. 100 p. 8vo   AAS, H, UV, Y

Also contains: Annie Sinclair; or, The Fourth of July Sail—Lilias Atherton; or, The Rescue—The Fairy Fountain.

Printed in double cols.

47 ARRINGTON, ALFRED W. The Desperadoes of the South-west: Containing an Account of the Cane-Hill Murders, Together with the Lives of Several of the Most Notorious Regulators and Moderators of That Region. By Charles Summerfield [pseud.]. New York: William H. Graham, 1847. 48 p., illus. 8vo LC, Y

No printer's name on verso of title page; 44 lines on p. 48.

Arkansas; 1840.

48 ——— ——— New York: William H. Graham, 1847. 48 p., illus. 8vo   HEH

"John R. M'Gow, printer, 106 Fulton Street," on verso of title page; 44 lines on p. 48.

49 ——— ——— New York: William H. Graham, 1847. 48 p., illus. 8vo   LC, NYP, UV, Y

"John R. M'Gow, printer, 106 Fulton Street," on verso of title page; 42 lines on p. 48.

50 ——— Duelists and Duelling in the South-west. With Sketches of Southern Life. Being the Second and Concluding Part of "The Desperadoes of the South-west." By Charles Summerfield [pseud.], of Texas. New York: William H. Graham, 1847. 54 p. 8vo   Y

"John R. M'Gow, printer, 106 Fulton Street," on verso of title page.

51 —— Illustrated Lives and Adventures of the Desperadoes of the New World: Containing an Account of the Different Modes of Lynching; the Cane Hill Murders; the Victims; the Execution... As Well as the Lives of the Principal Duellists, and Their Duelling . . . By Charles Summerfield [pseud.], of Texas. Philadelphia: T. B. Peterson, No. 98 Chesnut St. [1849?]. 117 p., illus. 8vo   HEH, UV
Preface dated June 1849.

52 —— The Lives and Adventures of the Desperadoes of the South-west: Containing an Account of the Duelists and Dueling; Together with the Lives of Several of the Most Notorious Regulators and Moderators of That Region. By Charles Summerfield [pseud.], of Texas. New York: William H. Graham, 1849. 98 p., illus. 12mo   LC, NYH, Y
First 48 p. of text from the same plates as No. 47.

53 ARTHUR, TIMOTHY SHAY. Agnes; or, The Possessed. A Revelation of Mesmerism . . . Philadelphia: T. B. Peterson, No. 98 Chesnut Street [cop. 1848]. 116 p. 8vo AAS, B, LC, UM, UV, Y
LC has a title page, deposited Sept. 23, 1848.

53a —— Alice; or, The Victim of One Indiscretion [anon.]. New York: John Allen, 1844. 37, [3]-32 p. 8vo   Y
Cover title adds: ". . . And the Runaway Match," which is separately paged. The caption title of the latter reads: "Mary Ellis; or, The Runaway Match." This was first published in 1841 (No. 184a) and reprinted in 1850 (No. 125).
Printed in double cols.

—— Alice Mellville; or, The Indiscretion . . . Philadelphia: Henry F. Anners, No. 48 North Fourth Street [cop. 1850]. 90 p.
Issued with his *Mary Ellis* [cop. 1850], No. 125.

54 —— All for the Best; or, The Old Peppermint Man. A Moral Tale . . . Boston: Crosby and Nichols, 1850. 130 p., illus. 12mo   AAS, HEH, N, UV, Y
LC has a title page, deposited Sept. 20, 1850.

55 —— Anna Milnor, the Young Lady Who Was Not Punctual, and Other Tales . . . New York: E. Ferrett & Co., 1845. 92 p. 8vo   AAS, HEH, UV, Y

Also contains: Governor Tenderheart–False Friends and True–Fun with the Doctor–Non-Resistance–The Good Match–It's None of My Business –The Code of Honor–What Will the World Say?–Ups and Downs.

56 ——— The Beautiful Widow . . . Philadelphia: Carey and Hart, 1847. 103 p. 8vo LC, UP, UV, Y
In the West.

57 ——— Bell Martin; or, The Heiress: An American Story of Real Life . . . Philadelphia: Burgess & Zieber, 1843. 32 p. Fol.
AAS, B, HEH, LC, N, NYH, UM, UP, Y
Printed in double cols.
Philadelphia.

58 ——— ——— 2d ed. Philadelphia: R. G. Berford, 1843. 47 p. 8vo AAS, HEH, UP, UV
Printed in double cols.

58a ——— ——— Philadelphia: Henry F. Anners, 1849. 166 p. 12mo AAS, HEH, Y
Title reads: *Bell Martin: An American Story of Real Life.* Arthur rewrote the end of the story.

58b ——— ——— Philadelphia: Henry F. Anners [cop. 1843]. 162 p. 12mo AAS

59 ——— ——— Philadelphia: Henry F. Anners [cop. 1847]. 162 p. 12mo Y

60 ——— ——— Philadelphia: Henry F. Anners [cop. 1848]. 162 p. 12mo AAS, B, Y

60a ——— ——— Philadelphia: Henry F. Anners [cop. 1850]. 162 p. 12mo HEH

——— Brother and Sister. *In* The Fountain and the Bottle (1850), No. 996.

61 ——— Cecilia Howard; or, The Young Lady Who Had Finished Her Education . . . New York: John Allen, 1844. 92 p. 8vo AAS, B, BP, H, HEH, LC, UV, Y

62 ——— A Christmas Box for the Sons and Daughters of Temperance . . . Philadelphia: William Sloanaker, 1847. 133 p. 12mo

BA, BP, LC, NYP

63 ——— The Club Room and Other Temperance Tales . . . Philadelphia: E. Ferrett & Co., 1845. 160 p. 12mo

AAS, HEH, LC, UP, UV, Y

Also contains: What Shall I Do? — The Temperance Tract—A Daughter's Love—Jack Ketch.

64 ——— Debtor and Creditor: A Tale of the Times . . . New York: Baker & Scribner, 1848. 180 p. 12mo

AAS, B, BA, HEH, IN, N, NYP, UP, UV, Y

Baltimore.

65 ——— ——— New York: Baker & Scribner, 1849. 180 p. 12mo

AAS, H, IN, UV, Y

66 ——— ——— New York: Baker & Scribner, 1850. 180 p. 12mo

AAS, HEH, UV, Y

67 ——— ——— New York: Collins & Brother, 84 Leonard St. [cop. 1847]. 180 p. 12mo

AAS, Y

68 ——— The Debtor's Daughter; or, Life and Its Changes . . . Philadelphia: T. B. Peterson, No. 98 Chestnut Street [cop. 1850]. 100 p. 8vo

AAS, B, BA, H, HEH, LCP, N, UP, Y

69 ——— The Divorced Wife . . . Philadelphia: T. B. Peterson, No. 98 Chestnut Street [cop. 1850]. 96 p. 8vo

AAS, H, HEH, N, UP, Y

69a ——— Family Pride; or, The Palace and the Poor House. A Romance of Real Life [anon.]. Philadelphia: R. G. Berford, 1844. 71 p. 12mo

HEH

Later eds. are frequently found bound with Arthur's *Pride or Principle.* "B—"; contemporary.

70 ——— ——— Philadelphia: Lindsay and Blakiston, 1844. 71 p. 12mo

AAS, HEH, N, Y

71 ——— ——— Boston: S. Colman, 1846. 71 p. 12mo

BA

72 ———— ———— Philadelphia: Henry F. Anners, 1849. 71 p.
    12mo
                          AAS, UV

72a ———— ———— Philadelphia: Henry F. Anners [cop. 1843].
    71 p. 12mo
                          UP

73 ———— ———— Philadelphia: Henry F. Anners [cop. 1845]. 71
    p. 12mo
                          AAS, UM

74 ———— ———— Philadelphia: Henry F. Anners [cop. 1848].
    71 p. 12mo
                          AAS, BP, UP, Y

75 ———— ———— Philadelphia: Henry F. Anners [1850?]. 71 p.
    12mo
                          HEH, UV

75a ——— Fanny Dale; or, The First Year after Marriage ... Philadelphia: R. G. Berford, 1843. 30 p. 8vo   AAS, HEH
Printed in double cols.

76 ———— ———— Philadelphia: Burgess & Zieber, 1843. 32 p.
    Fol.
                          B, UP, Y
Also contains: The Widow's Children.
Printed in double cols.

77 ———— ———— Philadelphia: Henry F. Anners, 1847. 130 p.
    12mo
                          BP
Title reads in this and the following eds.: *Fanny Dale; or, A Year after Mar-riage.*

77a ———— ———— Philadelphia: Henry F. Anners, 1848. 130 p.
    12mo
                          HEH

78 ———— ———— Philadelphia: Henry F. Anners, 1849. 130 p.
    12mo
                          AAS, UV, Y

79 ———— ———— Philadelphia: J. & J. L. Gihon, 1850. 130 p.
    12mo
                          AAS, B, Y

——— Gentility. *In* E. Leslie, Mr. and Mrs. Woodbridge
(1841), No. 1653.

80 ——— Golden Grains from Life's Harvest Field . . . Philadelphia: J. W. Bradley, 1850. 240 p., illus. 12mo

AAS, B, HEH, IN, LC, N, UC, UP, UV, Y

Contains: The Night and the Morning—A Merry Christmas—Sowing Tears and Reaping in Joy—The Mother—A Domestic Sketch: How to Correct a Husband's Faults—All for the Best—Good for Evil—I Said So—Bread in the Winter Night—A Domestic Scene—Going to Heaven—The Poor Man—Too Busy: A Mother's Confession.

81 ——— The Heiress: A Novel . . . Philadelphia: E. Ferrett & Co., 1845. 96 p. 8vo   AAS, B, N, UM, UV, Y
Philadelphia.

82 ——— ——— New York: E. Ferrett & Co., 1845. 141 p.
12mo   AAS, HEH, Y

83 ——— ——— Boston: S. Colman, 30 Cornhill [1846]. 141 p.
12mo   AAS, UP
Colman at this address in 1846 only.

83a ——— ——— Philadelphia: Henry F. Anners, 1849. 141 p.
12mo   AAS

84 ——— ——— Philadelphia: Henry F. Anners [cop. 1842]. 141
p. 12mo   AAS

84a ——— ——— Philadelphia: Henry F. Anners [cop. 1843]. 141
p. 12mo   AAS

85 ——— Hints and Helps for the Home Circle; or, The Mother's Friend. By Mary Elmwood [pseud.] . . . New York: John Allen, 1844. 88 p. 12mo   B, Y

86 ——— Hiram Elwood, the Banker; or, Like Father Like Son . . . [anon.]. New York: John Allen, 1844. 93 p. 8vo
AAS, B, HEH, Y
New York; contemporary.

——— I Knew How It Would Be. *In* M. M. Ballou, Albert Simmons (1849), No. 229.

87 —————— Illustrated Temperance Tales . . . Philadelphia: J. W. Bradley, 1850. 320 p., illus. 8vo   AAS, HEH, LC, N, UP, UV, Y

Contents: The Factory Girl—Two Pictures—Brandy as a Preventive—The Temperance Pledge—Time, Faith, Energy—Flushed with Wine—Swearing Off—The Failing Hope—Taking Toll—"Thou Art the Man"—The Touching Reproof—The Temperance Song—The Distiller's Dream—The Ruined Family—The Rum-Seller's Dream—How to Cure a Toper—The Broken Pledge—The Wanderer's Return: A Thanksgiving Story—Jim Braddock's Pledge—The Fair Tempter; or, Wine on the Wedding-Night.

88 —————— Insubordination: An American Story of Real Life . . . [anon.]. Baltimore: Knight & Colburn, 1841. 207 p. 12mo

AAS, B, UM, UV

Baltimore.

88a ——— ——— New York: Samuel Colman, 1841. 207 p. 12mo   Y

89 ——— ——— Philadelphia: R. G. Berford, 1844. 77 p. 8vo

AAS, H, HEH, UC, Y

Title reads: *Insubordination; or, The Shoemaker's Daughters.*
Printed in double cols.

90 ——— ——— Philadelphia: T. B. Peterson, No. 98 Chesnut Street [cop. 1848]. 104 p. 8vo   UP

Title same as of the 1844 ed.
Printed in double cols.

91 —————— Keeping Up Appearances; or, A Tale for the Rich and Poor . . . New York: Baker & Scribner, 1847. 194 p. 12mo

AAS, BA, HEH, LC, N, UV, Y

92 ——— ——— 2d ed. New York: Baker & Scribner, 1847. 194 p. 12mo   AAS, HEH, NYP, Y

93 ——— ——— 3d ed. New York: Baker & Scribner, 1848. 194 p. 12mo   AAS, Y

94 ——— ——— 4th ed. New York: Baker & Scribner, 1848. 194 p. 12mo   AAS, UP, Y

94a ——— ——— Sixth Thousand. New York: Baker & Scribner, 1849. 194 p. 12mo   HEH, Y

94b ———— ———— Seventh Thousand.   New York: Baker & Scribner, 1849.   194 p.   12mo   AAS

95 ——— The Ladies' Fair.   Contents: The Ladies Fair; How to Be a Gentleman; Taking Boarders; As Good as Anybody; The Two Beauties; The Soft Answer.   Philadelphia: Godey & McMichael, 1843.   30 p.   8vo   HEH
LC has a title page, deposited May 27, 1843.
HEH lacks title page.
Printed in double cols.

96 ——— The Lady at Home; or, Leaves from the Every-day Book of an American Woman.   By Mrs. Mary Elmwood [pseud.].   New York: John Allen, 1844.   96 p.   12mo
AAS, B, LC

97 ———— ———— Philadelphia: W. A. Leary and Company, 1850.   178 p.   12mo   Y

97a ———— ———— Philadelphia: W. A. Leary & Co., No. 138 North Second Street [cop. 1847].   178 p., illus.   12mo   AAS

98 ———— ———— Philadelphia: Henry F. Anners [cop. 1847].   178 p.   12mo   AAS, B, BP, HEH, NYP, UP

99 ——— The Little Pilgrims: A Sequel to The Tailor's Apprentice . . . [anon.].   Philadelphia: Godey & McMichael, 1843.   Cover title, 72 p.   8vo   LC
New York City and B———.

100 ——— The Lost Children: A Temperance Tale . . .   New York: Oliver & Brother, 1848.   32 p., illus.   8vo   AAS, BP, H, HEH, UP
On cover: "New York Organ Temperance Tales, No. 3."
Printed in double cols.

100a ———— ———— New York: Brognard & Co., 1850.   32 p., illus.   8vo   AAS
Cover title same as 1st ed., except this is "Third Edition."

101 ——— Love in a Cottage . . . Philadelphia: T. B. Peterson, No. 98 Chestnut Street [cop. 1848].   104 p.   12mo
AAS, N, UP, Y
LC has a title page, deposited April 10, 1848.

102 —————— Love in High Life: A Story of the "Upper Ten." . . .
Philadelphia: T. B. Peterson, No. 98 Chesnut Street [cop. 1849].
100 p., illus. 8vo   B, N, UM, UP, UV, Y
New York City.

103 —————— Lovers and Husbands: A Story of Married Life . . .
New York: Harper & Brothers, 1845.   155 p.   12mo
                                         AAS, HEH, LCP, UM, Y
New Jersey; contemporary.

104 ———— ———— Boston: S. Colman, 1846.   155 p.   12mo   LCP

105 ———— ———— Philadelphia: Henry F. Anners, 1847.   155 p.
12mo   AAS, NYP, UP, UV

106 ———— ———— Philadelphia: Henry F. Anners, 1848.   155 p.
12mo   AAS, N, UV, Y

106a ———— ———— Philadelphia: Henry F. Anners [cop. 1843].   155
p.   12mo   UP

107 ———— ———— Philadelphia: Henry F. Anners [cop. 1845].   155
p.   12mo   AAS, B, UC, Y

108 ———— ———— Philadelphia: Henry F. Anners [cop. 1846].   155
p.   12mo   AAS, Y

108a —————— Lucy Sanford: A Story of the Heart.   A Temperance
Tale . . .   Philadelphia: T. B. Peterson, 98 Chesnut Street [cop.
1848].   131 p.   8vo   UP

108b —————— Madeline; or, A Daughter's Love and Other Tales . . .
Philadelphia: Henry F. Anners [cop. 1843].   158 p.   12mo
                                                   AAS, HEH
Also contains: The Temperance Tract—What Shall I Do?—Jack Ketch—
The Club Room.
Copyrighted by T. S. Arthur.

109 ———— ———— Philadelphia: Henry F. Anners [cop. 1845].   158
p.   12mo   AAS, NYP, UP, Y
Copyrighted by E. Ferrett & Co.

18

110 ——— The Maiden: A Story for My Young Countrywomen
... Philadelphia: E. Ferrett & Co., 1845. 162 p. 12mo
AAS, B, HEH, LC, N, UP, UM, UV, Y
Philadelphia.

111 ——— ——— Boston: S. Colman, 1846. 162 p. 12mo
AAS, HEH, N, Y

111a ——— ——— Philadelphia: Henry F. Anners, 1847. 162 p.
12mo AAS, Y

112 ——— ——— Philadelphia: Henry F. Anners, 1848. 162 p.
12mo AAS, NYP, UC

113 ——— Making a Sensation, and Other Tales . . . Contents:
Going into Mourning; The Kind Providence; Let. of Recom-
mendation; Making a Sensation; The Prodigal's Return; Retir-
ing from Business. Philadelphia: Godey & McMichael, 1843.
Cover title, 72 p. 12mo Y
LC has a title page, deposited Oct. 2, 1843.

114 ——— Making Haste to Be Rich; or, The Temptation and Fall
... New York: Baker & Scribner, 1848. 170 p. 12mo
AAS, HEH, LC, LCP, N, UV, Y

114a ——— ——— 6th ed. New York: Baker & Scribner, 1849.
149 p. 12mo UP

115 ——— ——— 7th ed. New York: Baker & Scribner, 1850.
170 p. 12mo UV, Y

116 ——— Married and Single; or, Marriage and Celibacy Contrasted, in a Series of Domestic Pictures... New York: Harper
& Brothers, 1845. 157 p. 12mo AAS, H, HEH, NYP, UP, UV, Y

117 ——— ——— Boston: S. Colman, 1846. 157 p. 12mo
AAS, LCP

118 ——— ——— New York: Burgess, Stringer & Co., 1846. 157 p.
12mo AAS

119 ——— ——— Philadelphia: Henry F. Anners, 1847. 157 p.
12mo Y

120 ——— ——— Philadelphia: Henry F. Anners, 1848. 157 p.
12mo   HEH, LCP

121 ——— ——— Philadelphia: Henry F. Anners [cop. 1843]. 157
p. 12mo   AAS, B, UP, Y

121a ——— ——— Philadelphia: Henry F. Anners [cop. 1845]. 157
p. 12mo   AAS

122 ——— The Martyr Wife: A Domestic Romance. By the
Author of "Hiram Elwood, the Banker; or, Like Father, Like
Son" [anon.]. New York: John Allen, 1844. 96 p. 8vo
                                                           B, LC, Y

Also contains: Dick Lawson; or, The Young Mocking Bird—Nancy Newell
and the Fortune Teller.
Later eds. are frequently found bound with Arthur's *Ruined Gamester.*
Philadelphia; contemporary.

123 ——— ——— Philadelphia: Henry F. Anners, 1850. 70 p.
12mo   B, LC

124 ——— ——— Philadelphia: Henry F. Anners [cop. 1849]. 70
p. 12mo   HEH, UC, UP

125 ——— Mary Ellis; or, The Runaway Match . . . Philadelphia:
Henry F. Anners, No. 48 North Fourth Street [cop. 1850]. 72
p. 12mo   AAS, HEH, N, UP

With this was issued his *Alice Mellville; or, The Indiscretion* . . . Philadelphia: Henry F. Anners, No. 48 North Fourth Street [cop. 1850]. 90 p.

126 ——— Mary Moreton; or, The Broken Promise. A True Story
of American Life . . . Philadelphia: T. B. Peterson, 98 Chesnut
Street [cop. 1849]. 100 p. 8vo   AAS, HEH, NYP, UV

127 ——— The Mother . . . Philadelphia: E. Ferrett & Co., 1846.
141 p. 12mo   LC, N, UV, Y
Philadelphia; contemporary.

128 ——— ——— Boston: S. Colman, 1846. 141 p. 12mo
                                                 AAS, HEH, UM, UP, Y

129 ——— ——— Philadelphia: Henry F. Anners, 1847. 141 p.
12mo   AAS, HEH, Y

130 ———— ———— Philadelphia: Henry F. Anners, 1848. 141 p.
   12mo   NYP

131 ———— ———— Philadelphia: Henry F. Anners [cop. 1845]. 141
   p. 12mo   AAS, B

132 ———— ———— Philadelphia: Henry F. Anners [cop. 1846]. 141
   p. 12mo   AAS, N, UV, Y

———— Not at Home. *In* J. Jones, The Belle of Boston (1849),
No. 1483.

133 ———— The Orphan Children: A Tale of Cruelty and Oppression . . . Philadelphia: T. B. Peterson, No. 98 Chesnut Street
   [cop. 1850]. 128 p. 8vo   B, UM, UP, UV, Y
   "One of the Atlantic Cities."

133a ———— Our Children: How Shall We Save Them? . . . Also,
   Keeping It Up, and The Problem, by James Nack . . . New
   York: Oliver & Brother, printers and publishers, 1849. 32 p.,
   illus. 8vo   HEH
   At head of title: "Prize Tale."
   Printed in double cols.

134 ———— ———— New York: Brognard & Co., 1850. 32 p., illus.
   8vo   HEH
   At head of title: "Prize Tale."
   Printed in double cols.

135 ———— Pride and Prudence; or, The Married Sisters . . . Philadelphia: T. B. Peterson, No. 98 Chesnut Street [cop. 1850].
   100 p. 8vo   AAS, NYP, UM, UP, UV, Y

136 ———— Pride or Principle—Which Makes the Lady? [anon.].
   Philadelphia: R. G. Berford, 1844. 71 p. 12mo   N, Y
   Later eds. are frequently found bound with Arthur's *Family Pride*.

137 ———— ———— Philadelphia: Lindsay & Blakiston, 1844. 71 p.
   12mo   AAS, Y

138 ———— ———— Boston: S. Colman, 1846. 71 p. 12mo   BA

139 —— —— Philadelphia: Henry F. Anners, 1849. 71 p.
12mo   LCP, Y

140 —— —— Philadelphia: Henry F. Anners, 1850. 71 p.
12mo   HEH, UP

141 —— —— Philadelphia: Henry F. Anners [cop. 1843]. 71
p. 12mo   BP, UP

142 —— —— Philadelphia: Henry F. Anners [cop. 1848]. 71
p. 12mo   AAS, UM, UP, Y

143 —— Prose Fictions. Written for the Illustrations of True
Principles, in Their Bearing upon Every-day Life ... Philadelphia: G. B. Zieber & Co., 1844. 2 vols. 12mo
                                            B, LC, UV (v. 1), Y
Issued, according to the advertisement, "in a regular series of numbers," apparently of 80 p. each, four numbers to the volume.

144 —— Random Recollections of an Old Doctor ... Baltimore:
William Taylor and Company, 1846. 132 p. 8vo
                                            AAS, NYH, UV, Y
Cover title: "Life Pictures; or, The Random Recollections of an Old Doc-
tor. Edited by T. S. Arthur."

145 —— Retiring from Business; or, The Rich Man's Error . . .
New York: Baker & Scribner, 1848. 166 p. 12mo
                              AAS, HEH, LC, LCP, N, NYP, UM, UP, UV, Y

146 —— —— New York: Baker & Scribner, 1849. 166 p.
12mo   AAS, BP, H, Y

147 —— —— New York: Baker & Scribner, 1850. 166 p.
12mo   UV

148 —— Riches Have Wings; or, A Tale for the Rich and Poor
. . . New York: Baker & Scribner, 1847. 192 p. 12mo
                                   AAS, HEH, LC, N, NYP, UP, UV, Y

148a —— —— New York: Baker & Scribner, 1848. 192 p.
12mo   AAS, HEH, IN, Y

149 —— —— 5th thousand. New York: Baker & Scribner, 1849. 192 p. 12mo   AAS, B, HEH, Y

149a —— —— New York: Baker & Scribner, 1850. 192 p. 12mo   HEH

150 —— Rising in the World; or, A Tale for the Rich and Poor . . . New York: Baker & Scribner, 1848. 198 p. 12mo
AAS, BA, HEH, LC, N, UP, UV, Y
Philadelphia; contemporary.

150a —— —— New York: Baker & Scribner, 1849. 198 p. 12mo   HEH

150b —— —— New York: Baker & Scribner, 1850. 198 p. 12mo   Y

151 —— The Ruined Family and Other Tales . . . In Two Parts . . . Philadelphia: Godey & M'Michael, 1843. 196, 195 p.
12mo   AAS, UP
Title page of Pt. II: *Swearing Off and Other Tales* . . . Philadelphia: Godey & M'Michael, 1843.
Contents: Pt. I. The Ruined Family—Jim Braddock's Pledge—The Cold Water Wedding—The Rum-Seller's Dream—The Hasty Marriage—The Fair Tempter; or, Wine on the Wedding-Night—The Temperance Pledge—The Sisters. Pt. II. Swearing Off—The Failing Hope—Flushed with Wine—The Fiery Trial—The Temperate Drinker—The Touching Reproof—The Broken Pledge—Thou Art the Man—Julia Forrester.
This work is the first issue of Arthur's *Temperance Tales* (No. 172).

151a —— The Ruined Gamester; or, Two Eras in My Life . . . [anon.]. Philadelphia: Lindsay & Blakiston, 1844. 64 p. 12mo
AAS, UV, Y
Later eds. are frequently found bound with Arthur's *Martyr Wife*.

152 —— —— Philadelphia: Henry F. Anners [cop. 1842]. 64 p. 12mo   AAS, B, HEH, LC, UC, Y

153 —— The Seamstress: A Tale of the Times . . . [anon.]. Philadelphia: R. G. Berford, 1843. 48 p. 8vo   AAS, UP, Y
Printed in double cols.
Boston.

154 ———— Six Nights with the Washingtonians. A Series of Original Temperance Tales . . . Philadelphia: L. A. Godey & Morton M'Michael, 1842. 6 pts., as issued. 8vo
AAS, B (pt. 4), BP (pt. 1), H (pts. 3-6), HEH (pts. 1-2), NYP (pt. 1), UV, Y (pt. 3)

Contents: Night the First: The Broken Merchant—Night the Second: The Experience Meeting—Night the Third: The Tavern-Keeper—Night the Fourth: The Drunkard's Wife—Night the Fifth: The Widow's Son—Night the Sixth: The Moderate Drinker.

155 ———— ———— Philadelphia: Godey & M'Michael, 1843. 192 p., illus. 8vo
H, HEH, Y

156 ———— ———— Philadelphia: R. G. Berford, 1843. 96 p., illus. 8vo
AAS, N, Y

Printed in double cols.

157 ———— ———— Philadelphia: Henry F. Anners, 1849. 2 vols. 12mo
Y

Title reads: *Temperance Tales; or, Six Nights with the Washingtonians.*

158 ———— ———— Philadelphia: W. A. Leary & Co., 1849. 2 vols. 12mo
AAS

Title reads: *Temperance Tales; or, Six Nights with the Washingtonians.*

159 ———— ———— Philadelphia: W. A. Leary & Co., 1850. 2 vols. in 1. 12mo
BP, HEH, UV, Y

Title reads: *Temperance Tales; or, Six Nights with the Washingtonians.*

160 ———— ———— New York: E. Ferrett and Co. [cop. 1842]. 2 vols. 12mo
Y

161 ———— ———— Philadelphia: W. A. Leary & Co., 138 North Second Street [cop. 1848]. 2 vols. in 1, illus. 12mo
AAS, N, NYP, UP, UV, Y

Title reads: *Temperance Tales; or, Six Nights with the Washingtonians.*

161a ———— Sketches of Life and Character . . . Philadelphia: J. W. Bradley, 1849. 417 p., illus. 8vo
AAS, UV

Contents: The Methodist Preacher; or, Lights and Shadows in the Life of an Itinerant—Conquering a Peace—A Rise in the Butter Market—Deacon Smith and His Violin—The Knight, the Hermit, and the Man—Happy on a Little—The Village Horse-Block—The Ideal and the Real—The Belle of the Ball Room—The Daguerreotypist—Seed Time and Harvest—The History of a Day and a Life: A Sketch for Husbands—Never Too Late—The Sleigh Ride—Charity Begins at Home—Dyed in the Wool—The Pic-nic; or, The Young Lady Who Was Not Punctual—We Only Know What We Have Lived—The Child Stealer—Love Tests of Halloween—Living It Down—The Chowder Party—A Dream of City Life—Can't Get Along—A Stage-coach Adventure—Half Lengths in Outline—The Quilting Party—If You Will Do No Good, Do No Harm—Speak Gently—Is It Economy? An Experience of Mr. John Jones—The Donation Visit—Treasure on Earth, and Treasure in Heaven—The Engraver's Daughter—Washing Day: Another Experience of Mr. Jones.

162 —————— ——— Philadelphia: J. W. Bradley, 1850. 416 p., illus.
8vo   AAS, B, BP, HEH, IN, LC, N, UM, UP, Y

——— The Soft Answer. *In* E. Leslie, Mr. and Mrs. Wood-bridge (1841), No. 1653.

163 ——— The Stolen Wife: An American Romance . . . [anon.]. Philadelphia: R. G. Berford, 1843. 32 p. 8vo   AAS, HEH
Printed in double cols.

164 ——— Sweethearts and Wives; or, Before and after Marriage . . . New York: Harper & Brothers, 1843. 163 p. 12mo
          AAS, H, HEH, N, UP, Y
Westbrook; contemporary.

164a —————— ——— New York: Harper & Brothers, 1844. 163 p.
12mo   AAS, UV

165 —————— ——— New York: Burgess, Stringer & Co., 1846.
LC has a title page, deposited April 15, 1846.

166 —————— ——— Boston: S. Colman, 1846. 163 p. 12mo
          AAS, HEH, Y

166a —————— ——— Philadelphia: Henry F. Anners, 1847. 163 p.
12mo   Y

167 —————— ——— Philadelphia: Henry F. Anners, 1848. 163 p.
12mo   AAS, UP

168 —————— ——— Philadelphia: Henry F. Anners, 1849. 163 p.
12mo   AAS, Y

169 ———— ———— Philadelphia: Henry F. Anners, 1850.   163 p.
12mo   AAS, N

170 ———— ———— Philadelphia: Henry F. Anners [cop. 1846].   163
p.   12mo   AAS, Y

171 ———— The Tailor's Apprentice: A Story of Cruelty and Oppression [anon.].   Philadelphia: Godey & McMichael, 1843.
LC has a title page, deposited May 31, 1843.

171a ———— Tales of Married Life . . .   Philadelphia: Henry F. Anners, 1850.   157, 163, 155 p.   12mo   AAS, Y
This is made up of Nos. 116, 164, and 103.

172 ———— Temperance Tales . . .   Philadelphia: Godey & M'Mi-
chael, 1843.   2 vols. in 1.   12mo   B
Contents: Vol. I. The Ruined Family—Jim Braddock's Pledge—The Cold-
Water Wedding—The Rum-Seller's Dream—The Hasty Marriage—The
Fair Tempter; or, Wine on the Wedding-Night—The Temperance Pledge—
The Sisters. Vol. II. Swearing Off—The Failing Hope—Flushed with Wine
—The Fiery Trial—The Temperate Drinker—The Touching Reproof—The
Broken Pledge—"Thou Art the Man"—Julia Forrester.
For the first issue of this work see No. 151.

173 ———— ———— Philadelphia: E. Ferrett & Co., 1844.   2 vols.,
illus.   12mo   B, IN, LC

———— Temperance Tales; or, Six Nights with the Washingtonians. *See* Six Nights with the Washingtonians.

173a ———— Temptations: A Story for the Reformed . . . With Other
Tales.   New York: Oliver & Brother, printers and publishers,
1848.   32 p., illus.   8vo   HEH
Also contains: The Freedom Party—The Tempter Punished—The Mother
and Her Sailor Boy.
Printed in double cols.

174 ———— The Three Eras in a Woman's Life . . .   Philadelphia:
Henry F. Anners, 1848.   3 pts. in 1 vol.   12mo   AAS, HEH, IN
Contents: The Maiden: A Story for My Young Countrywomen—The
Wife: A Story for My Young Countrywomen—The Mother.
This is made up of Nos. 110, 185, and 127, with half titles only.

174a ——— ——— Philadelphia: Henry F. Anners [cop. 1845]. 3
pts. in 1 vol. 12mo   AAS, UV

175 ——— Tired of Housekeeping . . . New York: D. Appleton
and Company [cop. 1842]. 167 p., illus. 12mo
                                                                                                AAS, B, LC, LCP, Y
LC copy was deposited for copyright purposes Oct. 22, 1842.

176 ——— ——— New York: D. Appleton and Company, 1843.
167 p., illus. 12mo   AAS, N, UP, UV, Y

177 ——— ——— New York: D. Appleton and Company, 1846.
167 p., illus. 12mo   AAS, HEH, UV

177a ——— ——— New York: D. Appleton & Co., 1847. 167 p.,
illus. 12mo   AAS

178 ——— ——— New York: D. Appleton & Co., 1849. 167 p.,
illus. 12mo   AAS

179 DELETE. This is a reprint of Wright II, 138a.

180 ——— The Two Brides . . . Philadelphia: T. B. Peterson, No.
98 Chesnut Street [cop. 1850]. 90 p. 8vo   UP, Y

181 ——— The Two Husbands and Other Tales . . . Philadelphia:
E. Ferrett & Co., 1845. Cover title, [81]-160 p. 12mo   Y
Also contains: A Word to the Wise—The Two Systems—The Temperance
Tract—Match Making—A Peevish Day and Its Consequences—The Merchant's Dream.

182 ——— The Two Merchants; or, Solvent and Insolvent . . . Philadelphia: Burgess & Zieber, 1843. 32 p. Fol.   B, UC, Y
Printed in double cols.
New York City.

182a ——— ——— Philadelphia: R. G. Berford, 1844. 47 p. 8vo
Printed in double cols.
Swann auction catalog 290:158.

183 ——— The Two Sisters; or, Life's Changes . . . [anon.]. Philadelphia: G. B. Zieber & Co., 1844. 94 p. 12mo   B, LC, Y

184 —— The Village Doctors and Other Tales . . . Philadelphia: Godey & McMichael, 1843. 72 p. 12mo   AAS, H, LC, NYP

Also contains: Doing as Other People—The Bargains—The Portrait—If That Were My Child—The Temptation.

184a —— The Widow Morrison: A Leaf from the Book of Human Life. By the Author of "Insubordination." Baltimore: Knight & Colburn. New York: James P. Giffing, 1841. 110 p. 16mo

AAS

This was later included in No. 53a under title *Mary Ellis* and published under that title, No. 125.

185 —— The Wife: A Story for My Young Countrywomen . . . Philadelphia: H. F. Anners, 1845. 161 p. 12mo

B, HEH, LC, UC, UV

186 —— —— Philadelphia: E. Ferrett & Co., 1845. 161 p. 12mo   AAS, HEH, LC, N, UM, UP, Y

Verso of title page of some copies reads: "Printed by T. K. & P. G. Collins"; other copies read: "Stereotyped by B. M. Dusenberg. Printed by Barrett & Jones." Census of copies does not distinguish between the two.

187 —— —— Boston: S. Colman, 1846. 161 p. 12mo

AAS, HEH, N, UP, Y

187a —— —— Philadelphia: Henry F. Anners, 1847. 161 p. 12mo   AAS, HEH, Y

187b —— —— Philadelphia: Henry F. Anners [cop. 1845]. 161 p. 12mo   AAS, UP

188 —— The Young Artist; or, The Dream of Italy . . . New York: M. W. Dodd, 1850. 108 p. 12mo

AAS, LC, LCP, N, UM, UP, UV, Y

189 —— The Young Music Teacher and Other Tales . . . Philadelphia: Henry F. Anners, 1847. 182 p. 12mo

AAS, BA, HEH, LC, N, UV, Y

Also contains: The Unhappy Wife—Life's First, Best Lesson—Ups and Downs—The Gift of Beauty—A Leaf from the Book of Human Life—The Father's Dream—I'll See about It—The Sum of Trifles; or, A Penny Saved Is a Penny Gained.

190 —————— Philadelphia: J. & J. L. Gihon, 1850. 182 p.
12mo   AAS, UV, Y

191 ASHBY, *Professor*.   Helen Howard; or, The Bankrupt and Broker.
A Mysterious Tale of Boston . . .   Boston: F. Gleason, 1845. 64
p. 8vo   AAS, BP, NYP, UP, Y
LC has a title page which reads: "Helen Howard; or, the Bankrupt and
Broker. A Tale of New England."

192 —————— Viola: The Redeemed.   A Domestic Tale . . .   Boston:
Gleason's Publishing Hall, 1845. 66 p., illus. 8vo   AAS, B, Y
Washington; contemporary.

192a ASHLAND, ARIA.   Dark Sybil; or, The Fortunes of the Cather-
woods . . .   Boston: F. Gleason, 1848.   100 p., illus. 8vo
                                                                     AAS, UP, UV, Y
Printed in double cols.

193 —————— Muscoma; or, Faith Campbell.   A Romance of the Revolution . . .   Boston: Hotchkiss & Co., 1848.   100 p., illus. 8vo
                                                                      AAS, LC, UV, Y
Printed in double cols.

193a ASMODEUS, *pseud*.   The Jenny Lind Mania in Boston; or, A Sequel to Barnum's Parnassus.   By Asmodeus [pseud.] . . .   Boston, 1850. 40 p., illus. 12mo   H
Cushing attributes to "Thaddeus W. Meighan?."

194 —————— Sharps and Flats; or, The Perils of City Life.   Being the
Adventures of One Who Lived by His Wits.   By Asmodeus
[pseud.].   Boston: William Berry & Co., 27 Devonshire Street
[cop. 1850].   100 p. 8vo   HEH, Y
Printed in double cols.

ATALL, PETER, *Esq., pseud*.   *See* Waln, Robert, Jr.

195 THE ATLANTIC CLUB-BOOK: Being Sketches in Prose and Verse by
Various Authors . . .   New York: Harper and Brothers, 1834.
2 vols. 12mo
                     AAS, B, BA, BP, H, HEH, LC, N, NYH, NYP, NYS, UM, UP, Y
Contains: Jonathan's Visit to the Celestial Empire, by J. K. Paulding—
Steam, by William Cox—The Main Truck; or, A Leap for Life, by William
Leggett—Snorers, by T. S. Fay—The Uneducated Wife, by Mrs. L. Larned

—The Little Hard-faced Old Gentleman, by T. S. Fay—Uncle Zim and Deacon Pettibone, by W. L. Stone—Sketches from the Springs, by G. P. Morris—An Outline Sketch, by T. S. Fay—Benefactors, by J. H. Payne—Knickerbocker Hall; or, The Origin of the Baker's Dozen, by J. K. Paulding—The Mysterious Countess, by C. Stuart—Two Yards of Jaconet; or, A Husband, by J. G. Bennett—A Sea Piece, by W. G. Simms—The Legend of Brick-House Creek, by W. P. Hawes—Charles Maitland; or, The Mess-Chest, by William Leggett—The Author, by T. S. Fay—Biography of Jacob Hays, by William Cox—The Will and the Law-suit, by W. C. Baldwin—A Night on the Banks of the Tennessee, by Charles Sealsfield—Fire and Water; or, The Pirate's Night Cruise, by William Leggett—The Rivals: A Tale of Love and Marriage, by William Cox—A Charcoal Sketch of Pot Pie Palmer, by Edward Sanford.

196 ———— 3d ed. New York: Harper & Brothers, 1847. 2 vols. 12mo   BP(V.1), N, NYP

ATTERLEY, JOSEPH, *pseud. See* Tucker, George

197 AUSTIN, CHARLES. Frank Marston; or, The Queen of May . . . Boston: Gleason's Publishing Hall, 1847. 50 p. 8vo   Y
Printed in double cols.

AUSTIN, WILLIAM. Peter Rugg the Missing Man. *In* H. St. Clair, *comp.*, Tales of Terror (1833), Nos. 2266-68.

198 AUTOBIOGRAPHY of a Reformed Drunkard; or, Letters and Recollections, by an Inmate of the Alms-house. Philadelphia: Griffith and Simon, 1845. 159 p., illus. 16mo AAS, NYP, UP, UV, Y

AVERILL, CHARLES E. The Boarding-School Miss; or, The Young Back-Woodsman's Bride. *In* E. Z. C. Judson, Love's Desperation (1848), No. 1524.

199 ———— The Cholera-Fiend; or, The Plague Spreaders of New York. A Mysterious Tale of the Pestilence in 1849 . . . Boston: G. H. Williams, 1850. 100 p. 8vo   UM

200 ———— The Corsair King; or, The Blue Water Rovers. A Romance of the Piratical Empire . . . Boston: F. Gleason, 1847. 100 p., illus. 8vo   AAS, UC, UM, UV
Printed in double cols.
LC has a title page, deposited Aug. 26, 1847.

201 —————— The Female Fishers; or, The Beautiful Girl of Marble-
head. A Thrilling Story of the Sea Coast! . . . Boston: T.
Wiley, Jr., 1848.
Printed in double cols.
LC has a title page, deposited Dec. 30, 1847.
For information about the issues see *Midland Notes*, No. 17: 15.

—————— The Italian Lazzaroni; or, The Miser-Prince of Palermo.
In E. Z. C. Judson, The Red Revenger (1848), No. 1532.

202 —————— Kit Carson, the Prince of the Gold Hunters; or, The Ad-
venturers of the Sacramento. A Tale of the New El Dorado,
Founded on Actual Facts . . . Boston: Printed and published
by George H. Williams, 1849. 124 p., illus. 8vo   LC, N, Y

203 —————— Life in California; or, The Treasure Seekers' Expedition.
A Sequel to Kit Carson . . . Boston: Printed and published by
George H. Williams, 1849. 108 p., illus. 8vo   HEH, LC, UV
Printed in double cols.

204 —————— —————— Boston: Printed and published by George H.
Williams, 1850. 100 p., illus. 8vo   HEH, LC
At head of cover title: "Second edition."
Printed in double cols.

205 —————— —————— Boston: Printed and published by George H.
Williams [n.d.]. 100 p., illus. 8vo   LC, Y
Cover imprint: "New York: Published by Samuel French, 151 Nassau
Street."
Copyright notice on p. 100 dated 1849.
Printed in double cols.

206 —————— The Mexican Ranchero; or, The Maid of the Chapparal.
A Romance of the Mexican War . . . Boston: F. Gleason, 1847.
100 p., illus. 8vo   AAS, HEH, UV, Y
Printed in double cols.
LC has a title page, deposited Oct. 20, 1847.

207 —————— —————— Boston: F. Gleason, 1849. 100 p., illus. 8vo
UV, Y
Printed in double cols.

208 ———— The Pirates of Cape Ann; or, The Freebooter's Foe. A Tale of Land and Water ... Boston: F. Gleason [1848?]. 100 p. 8vo AAS, HEH, LC, UM, UV, Y
Printed in double cols.

209 ———— The Secret Service Ship; or, The Fall of San Juan D'Ulloa. A Thrilling Tale of the Mexican War ... Boston: F. Gleason, 1848. 100 p., illus. 8vo AAS, HEH, NYP, UV, Y
At head of title: "100 Dollar Prize Tale."
Printed in double cols.

210 ———— ———— Boston: F. Gleason, 1849. 100 p., illus. 8vo Y
Printed in double cols.

211 ———— The Secrets of the High Seas; or, The Mysterious Wreck in the Gulf Stream. A Tale of the Ocean's Exciting Incidents ... Boston: Williams, 1849. 132 p., illus. 8vo
The Union Catalogue at LC locates a copy in the University of Iowa Library.

212 ———— The Secrets of the Twin Cities; or, The Great Metropolis Unmasked. A Startling Story of City Scenes in Boston and New York ... Boston: Printed and published by George H. Williams, 1849. 124 p. 8vo NYP, Y
Printed in double cols.

213 ———— The Wanderers; or, The Haunted Nobleman. A Story of Sea and Land Adventure ... Boston: F. Gleason [cop. 1848]. 100 p. 8vo AAS, B, Y
Printed in double cols.
LC has a title page, deposited Sept. 15, 1848.

214 ———— The Wreckers; or, The Ship-Plunderers of Barnegat. A Startling Story of the Mysteries of the Sea-Shore ... Boston: F. Gleason, 1848. 100 p. 8vo B, UV, Y
Printed in double cols.
LC has a title page, deposited April 7, 1848.

214a AYER, I. W. The Hungarian Refugee; or, The Bold Magyar. A Tale of the Hungarian Revolution ... Boston: Star Spangled Banner Office [1850]. 99 p. 8vo AAS, BP, Y
Also contains: A Borer Outbored, by the Author of The Lawyer and His Clerk.

At head of title: "A Novel of Extraordinary Interest."
Cover imprint: "Boston: Jones's Publishing House, 1850."
Printed in double cols.
Author may be I. Winslow Ayer.

215 AZTEC REVELATIONS; or, Leaves from the Life of the Fate-Doomed. An Auto-Biography of an Early Adventurer in Mexico. Translated by an Officer of the Army. Oquawka, Ill.: J. B. & E. H. N. Patterson, 1849. 96 p. 8vo   LC, Y
Written by Edward Howard Norton Patterson.

B., B. A Tale of St. Domingo. *In* The Romantic Historian (1834), No. 2154.

216 B., J. A. Mary Bean, the Factory Girl: A Domestic Story, Illustrative of the Trials and Temptations of Factory Life. Founded on Recent Events ... By Miss J. A. B. of Manchester. Boston: Hotchkiss & Co., 1850. 42 p. 8vo   AAS, UV, Y
On cover: "4th Edition—Immense Success! Mary Bean; or, The Mysterious Murder. With the Sequel."
Printed in double cols.
Canada.

B., M. A. The Victims of Revenge. *In* The Romantic Historian (1834), No. 2154.

217 BACHE, MRS. ANNA. The Fire Screen; or, Domestic Sketches ... Philadelphia: W. J. & J. K. Simon, 1841. 191 p. 12mo
                         AAS, BP, H, HEH, LC, N, NYP, UC, UP, UV, Y
Allibone lists an 1843 ed.

218 BACON, DELIA SALTER. The Bride of Fort Edward, Founded on an Incident of the Revolution [anon.]. New York: S. Colman, 1839. 174 p. 8vo
         AAS, B, BA, BP, H, HEH, IN, LC, N, NYH, NYP, UC, UM, UP, UV, Y
Written in a series of dialogues.

———— Love's Martyr. Prize Tale. *In* Mrs. H. Wilkinson, *ed.*, The Treasure (1838), No. 2716.

219 ———— Tales of the Puritans. The Regicides—The Fair Pilgrim —Castine [anon.]. New Haven: A. H. Maltby, 1831. 300 p.
8vo AAS, B, BA, BP, H, HEH, IN, LC, N, NYH, NYP, UC, UM, UP, UV, Y

220 BAILEY, CHARLES. The Drop of Blood; or, The Maiden's Rescue ... Springfield: William B. Brockett, 1845. 40 p. 8vo

B, UV, Y

221 ———— The Jilted Doctor; or, "Circumstances Make the Man." ... Springfield: Ben. F. Brown, 1844. 40 p. 8vo UM, Y
New York and Boston.

222 ———— The Reclaimed Student: A Tale of College Life ... Springfield: Ben. F. Brown, 1844. 60 p. 8vo AAS, H, NYP, UV

223 BAKER, HARRIETTE NEWELL (Woods). The Twin Brothers ... [anon.]. New York: Harper & Brothers, 1843. 243 p. 12mo

AAS, BA, HEH, LC, UV, Y

224 ———— ———— New York: Harper & Brothers [cop. 1843]. 243 p. 12mo Y

225 BAKER, T. M. The Slave Lover; or, Pride Humbled ... Boston: The Author, 1848. 36 p. 12mo AAS, B, N, UM

BALDWIN, WILLIAM C. The Will and the Law-suit. *In* The Atlantic Club-Book (1834), Nos. 195-196.

226 BALLOU, MATURIN MURRAY. The Adventurer; or, The Wreck on the Indian Ocean. A Land and Sea Tale. By Lieutenant Murray [pseud.] ... Boston: F. Gleason, 1848. 100 p., illus. 8vo

AAS, LC, UM, UV, Y
At head of title: "A Prize Tale."
Printed in double cols.

227 ———— Albert Simmons; or, The Midshipman's Revenge. A Tale of Land and Sea. By Frank Forester [pseud.], Author of "The Smuggler's Child," "The Phantom Rock," "Tale of Manhattan," "The Highwayman," "The Two Purses" ... Boston: F. Gleason, 1845. 47 p. 8vo AAS, B, HEH, LC, UC, UM, UV, Y
Boston; 18--.

228 ———— ———— 2d ed. Revised by the Author. Boston: F. Gleason, 1845. 48 p., illus. 8vo BP, HEH, Y

229 —————— —————— By Lieutenant Murray [pseud.]. Boston: F. Gleason, 1849. 100 p., illus. 8vo   AAS, UP, UV, Y

Also contains: The Deformed, by Calvin Porter—More Scared Than Hurt: A Bear Story, by Henrietta Luzee—The Spirit of the Ford. An Irish Ghost Story, by A. J. H. Duganne—I Knew How It Would Be, by T. S. Arthur—The Wanderer's Return, by Horace Judson—The Diamond Star; or, The Englishman's Adventure. A Story of Valencia, by F. A. Durivage—Grace Morland; or, The Weight of Trifles, by E. C. Embury—Smoking 'Em Out; or, The Yankee Schoolmaster Out West, by the Green Mountain Bard—The Adopted Son; or, The Reward of Charity, by Paul Creyton [i.e., John T. Trowbridge].

Printed in double cols.

230 —————— The Belle of Madrid; or, The Unknown Mask. A Tale of Spain and the Spanish. By Lieutenant Murray [pseud.] ... Boston: F. Gleason, 1849. 100 p., illus. 8vo   AAS, Y

Printed in double cols.

231 —————— Ben Bobstay, the Boatswain's Mate, and Rosetta of Boston. By the Author of the "Smuggler's Child," "The Two Purses," and Other Popular Tales [anon.]. Boston: John B. Hall, 1845.

LC has a title page, deposited Nov. 24, 1845.

232 —————— The Cabin Boy; or, Life on the Wing. A Story of Fortune's Freaks and Fancies. By Lieutenant Murray [pseud.] ... Boston: F. Gleason [cop. 1848]. 100 p., illus. 8vo

AAS, HEH, N, UV, Y

Printed in double cols.

233 —————— The Child of the Sea; or, The Smuggler of Colonial Times. And The Love Test. By Lieutenant Murray [pseud.] ... Boston: United States Publishing Company, 1846. 100 p., illus. 8vo   B, HEH, NYP, UP, UV, Y

Also contains: The Rescue: A Story of the Gaming House—The Love Test: A Tale of the Heart—The Gipsey Girl.

Printed in double cols.

234 —————— Fanny Campbell, the Female Pirate Captain. A Tale of the Revolution, by Lieutenant Murray [pseud.]. Boston: F. Gleason, 1845. 100 p., illus. 8vo   AAS, B, H, LC, Y

Printed in double cols.

235 ———— ———— Boston: United States Publishing Company, 1846. 100 p., illus. 8vo   B, LC
Printed in double cols.

236 ———— ———— Boston: Gleason's Publishing Hall, 1847. 100 p., illus. 8vo   AAS, HEH
Printed in double cols.

237 ———— ———— Boston: F. Gleason, 1849. 100 p., illus. 8vo
AAS, UP
Printed in double cols.

238 ———— ———— New York: Samuel French, 151 Nassau [cop. 1844]. 100 p. 8vo   AAS, H, NYP, UM, UV, Y
Also contains: The Tattler; or, The Friends' Misunderstanding, by Sylvanus Cobb, Jr.

239 ———— The Gipsey; or, The Robbers of Naples. A Story of Love and Pride. By Lieutenant Murray [pseud.] . . . Boston: F. Gleason, 1847. 100 p., illus. 8vo   H, UP, UV, Y
At head of title: "100 Dollar Prize Tale."
Printed in double cols.

240 ———— The Magician of Naples; or, Love and Necromancy. A Story of Italy and the East. By Lieutenant Murray [pseud.]. New York: Samuel French, 151 Nassau [1850?]. 100 p., illus. 8vo   AAS, H, HEH, LC, NYP, UV
Printed in double cols.

241 ———— The Naval Officer; or, The Pirates Cave! A Tale of the Last War. By Lieutenant Murray [pseud.] . . . Boston: F. Gleason, 1845. 100 p., illus. 8vo   HEH, N, UP, UV, Y
Printed in double cols.

242 ———— ———— Boston: United States Publishing Company. F. Gleason, 1845. 98 p., illus. 8vo   B
Printed in double cols.

243 ———— ———— Boston: F. Gleason, 1847. 100 p., illus. 8vo
AAS, Y
Printed in double cols.

244 ——— ——— Boston: F. Gleason, 1849. 100 p., illus. 8vo

AAS, Y

Printed in double cols.

245 ——— ——— New York: Samuel French, 151 Nassau [cop.
1845]. 100 p., illus. 8vo   LC, UM, Y
Also contains: The Student's Story, by Nathan Ames.
Printed in double cols.

246 ——— The Protege of the Grand Duke: A Tale of Italy.   By
Frank Forester [pseud.], Author of "Albert Simmons," "The
Smuggler's Child" . . .   Boston: F. Gleason, 1845.   50 p.   8vo

AAS, B, BP, HEH, N, UC, UM, UV, Y

247 ——— Red Rupert, the American Bucanier.   A Tale of the
Spanish Indies, by Lieutenant Murray [pseud.].   Boston: Gleason's Publishing Hall, 1845.   54 p.   8vo

AAS, HEH, LC, UC, UV, Y

248 ——— ——— Boston: F. Gleason, 1848.   100 p., illus.   8vo

AAS, BP, LC, UM, UP, UV, Y

Also contains: The Disguised Maiden: A Tale of the Colombian Rebellion,
by Harry Longcliffe—The Spectre of the Woods; or, The Hermit's Re-
venge, by Harry Halyard—Henry Wilber; or, A Short Chapter from the
Book of Life, by G. H. Manning—Heloise; or, The Heroine of Paris: A
Tale of the Late French Revolution, by Benjamin Barker.
Printed in double cols.

249 ——— Roderick the Rover; or, The Spirit of the Wave.   By
Lieutenant Murray [pseud.] . . .   Boston: Gleason's Publishing
Hall, 1847.   100 p., illus.   8vo   AAS, B, HEH, LC, Y
At head of title: "$100 Prize Tale."
Printed in double cols.

250 ——— ——— Boston: F. Gleason, 1848.   100 p., illus.   8vo

UM, Y

At head of title: "100 Dollar Prize Tale."
Printed in double cols.

251 ——— ——— Boston: F. Gleason, 1849.   100 p., illus.   8vo

AAS, UP

Printed in double cols.

252 ——— Rosalette; or, The Flower Girl of Paris. A Romance of France. By Lieutenant Murray [pseud.] ... Boston: F. Gleason, 1848. 100 p., illus. 8vo AAS, HEH, UV
Printed in double cols.
Late 18th cent.

253 ——— ——— New York: Samuel French, 151 Nassau [cop. 1848]. 100 p., illus. 8vo B, H, NYP, Y
Printed in double cols.

254 ——— The Spanish Musketeer. A Tale of Military Life, by Lieutenant Murray [pseud.] ... Boston: Gleason's Publishing Hall, 1847. 100 p., illus. 8vo AAS, H, LC, N, UV, Y
At head of title: "100 Dollar Prize Tale."
Printed in double cols.
Havana, Cuba.

255 ——— ——— Boston: F. Gleason, 1849. 100 p., illus. 8vo
AAS, HEH, UP, Y
Printed in double cols.

256 ——— The Turkish Slave; or, The Mahometan and His Harem. A Story of the East, by Lieutenant Murray [pseud.] ... Boston: F. Gleason, 1850. 100 p. 8vo AAS, HEH, UV, Y
Printed in double cols.

257 BANG, THEODORE, *pseud.* The Mysteries of Papermill Village, by Theodore Bang [pseud.]. Papermill Village, N. H.: Walter Tufts, Jr., 1845. 31 p. 8vo AAS, UV, Y

258 BAR, M. Ro., *pseud.* Mary the Maniac; or, The Mother Her Own Victim! In Eight Letters to a Young Lady at the South. By M. Ro. Bar,—(Lev.) [pseud.]. New York: Nafis & Cornish, 1843. 118 p., illus. 12mo LC

259 ——— ——— New York: Nafis & Cornish, 1844. 120 p., illus. 12mo AAS, BA, LCP, UM, UV, Y

260 BARKER, BENJAMIN. Blackbeard; or, The Pirate of the Roanoke. A Tale of the Atlantic ... Boston: F. Gleason, 1847. 50 p. 8vo AAS, H, LC, Y

261 ———— Cecilia; or, The White Nun of the Wilderness. A Romance of Love and Intrigue ... Boston: Gleason's Publishing Hall, 1845. 56 p., illus. 8vo   AAS, BP, UC, UM, UP, UV, Y
French and Indian War.

262 ———— Clarilda; or, The Female Pickpocket. A Romance of New York City ... Boston: F. Gleason, 1846. 50 p., illus. 8vo   AAS, BP, HEH, NYP, UP, UV, Y

263 ———— Coriilia; or, The Indian Enchantress. A Romance of the Pacific and Its Islands ... Boston: Flag of Our Union office, 1847. 50 p. 8vo   AAS, HEH

264 ———— The Dwarf of the Channel; or, The Commodore's Daughter. A Nautical Romance of the Revolution ... Boston: Gleason's Publishing Hall, 1846. 100 p., illus. 8vo
AAS, NYP, UV, Y
Printed in double cols.

265 ———— Ellen Grafton, the Lily of Lexington; or, The Bride of Liberty. A Romance of the Revolution ... Boston: F. Gleason, 1845. 100 p., illus. 8vo   AAS, B, Y
Printed in double cols.

266 ———— ———— Boston: Gleason's Publishing Hall, 1846. 100 p., illus. 8vo   AAS, B, BP, LC, N, NYH, Y
Printed in double cols.

267 ———— Emily Elwood; or, The Hermit of the Crags. A Romance of the Last War ... Boston: F. Gleason, 1845. Cover title, 58 p., illus. 8vo   AAS, BP, N, UC, UM, UP, UV, Y

268 ———— The Female Spy; or, The Child of the Brigade. A Romance of the Revolution ... Boston: Gleason's Publishing Hall, 1846. 100 p. 8vo   Y
Also contains: The Happiness of Wealth.
Printed in double cols.

269 ———— Francisco; or, The Pirate of the Pacific. A Tale of Land and Sea. .. Boston: Gleason's Publishing Hall, 1845. 58 p. 8vo   AAS, BP, HEH, LC, N, NYH, UC, UV, Y

270 ——— The Gold Hunters; or, The Spectre of the Sea King. A Romance of the Sea . . . Boston: Gleason's Publishing Hall, 1846. 50 p. 8vo AAS, UV

LC has a title page, deposited May 6, 1846.

——— Heloise; or, The Heroine of Paris. A Tale of the Late French Revolution. *In* M. M. Ballou, Red Rupert (1848), No. 248.

271 ——— The Indian Bucanier; or, The Trapper's Daughter. A Romance of Oregon . . . Boston: F. Gleason, 1847. 50 p. 8vo

AAS, HEH, N, UM, UV, Y

Columbia River settlement.

272 ——— The Land Pirate; or, The Wild Girl of the Beach. A Tale of New Jersey Shore . . . Boston: F. Gleason, 1847. 50 p., illus. 8vo LC

273 ——— Mary Moreland; or, The Fortunes and Misfortunes of an Orphan . . . Boston: Gleason's Publishing Hall, 1845. 46 p. 8vo AAS, B, BP, H, HEH, LC, N, UP, UV, Y

Boston; contemporary.

274 ——— Mornilva; or, The Outlaw of the Forest. A Romance of "Lake" Wenham . . . Boston: Gleason's Publishing Hall, 1846. 58 p., illus. 8vo AAS, B, BP, HEH, UM, UV, Y

17—.

275 ——— The Nymph of the Ocean; or, The Pirate's Betrothal. A Tale of the Sea . . . Boston: United States Publishing Company, 1846. 50 p., illus. 8vo AAS, BP, HEH, Y

1796.

276 ——— ——— Boston: United States Publishing Company, 1847. 50 p., illus. 8vo

Ed. supplied by Mr. Oscar Wegelin.

277 ——— The Pirate Queen; or, The Magician of the Sea. A Tale of the Piratical Era . . . Boston: F. Gleason, 1848. 99 p. 8vo

Also contains: Heloise; or, The Heroine of Paris—The Maiden; or, The Man-at-Arms—Ever Constant—Luweze, the Little Dutch Cook—The Disguised Maiden.

Copy listed in Tuttle catalog No. 125:26.

40

278 —————— The Sea Serpent; or, The Queen of the Coral Cave. A
Romance of the Ocean . . . Boston: F. Gleason, 1847. 100 p.
8vo   LC, Y
Printed in double cols.

279 —————— The Suicide Restored; or, Mystery Unravelled . . . Boston: Gleason's Publishing Hall, 1846. 46 p. 8vo
                                                AAS, UC, UV, Y

280 —————— The Widow's Bridal; or, The Signal Light of the Sands.
A Legend of the Gay Head Indians . . . Boston: Gleason's Pub-
lishing Hall, 1846. 50 p., illus. 8vo   Y
LC has a title page, deposited Aug. 27, 1846.

281 —————— Zoraida; or, The Witch of Naumkeag! A Tale of the
Olden Time. By Egbert Augustus Cowslip, Esq. [pseud.] . . .
Boston: Gleason's Publishing Hall, 1845. 48 p. 8vo
                        AAS, BP, H, HEH, N, NYP, UC, UP, UV, Y
Salem; late 17th cent.

BARNACLE, *Capt., pseud.* *See* Newell, Charles Martin

281a BARNES, CHARLOTTE MARY SANFORD. Plays, Prose, and Poetry . . .
Philadelphia: E. H. Butler & Co., 1848. 489 p., 1 l. 8vo
                                          B, BP, H, HEH, LC, NYP, Y
Contains: The Maiden Aunt: A Tale of Texas—The Sisters: A Tale of the
Mississippi—The Marriage Vow: A Tale of Florida.
The author married Edmon S. Conner in 1847.

BARRETT, MRS. CORNELIA CROSBY. [Author of the stories listed in
note below, and jt. ed. of "Voices."] *In* J. S. Appleton, *ed.*,
Voices from the Kenduskeag (1848), No. 39.
Asa Glover, Esquire—The Resolve.

BARRINGTON, F. CLINTON, *pseud.* *See* Piper, A. G.

281b BASTINADO: A POLITICAL ROMANCE, in Four Chapters . . . Charleston (S.C.): The author, 1834. 72 p. 8vo   IN, NYH

282 BATCHELDER, EUGENE. A Romance of the Sea-Serpent; or, The
Ichthyosaurus . . . [anon.]. Cambridge: John Bartlett, 1849.
172 p., illus. 8vo AAS, B, BA, BP, H, HEH, LC, NYP, UM, UP, UV, Y
Sabin 3906 lists "[2d Ed. *ibid.*]."

283 ——— ——— 4th ed. Cambridge: J. Bartlett, 1850. 172 p.
8vo   AAS, B, NYP, UC, UV, Y

284 BATES, MARY. Recollections of Jamie ... [anon.]. Charleston:
John Russell, 1850. 62 p. 12mo   BP, UV

285 THE BEACON! Rhode-Island Temperance Tale. By a Gentleman
of Providence. Founded on Fact. Providence, R.I.: B. T.
Albro, printer, 1839. 35 p. 16mo   LC, NYP
At head of title: "Number Two."

286 BEARDSLEY, CHARLES E.   The Victims of Tyranny ... Buffalo:
D. June, 1847. 2 vols. 16mo   BP
LC has a title page, deposited Nov. 14, 1846.
Niagara frontier; 1812.

286a THE BEAUTIFUL FRENCH GIRL; or, The Daughter of Monsieur
Fontanbleu. A Story of Thrilling Interest Founded on Facts
in Real life . . . Philadelphia: T. B. Peterson, 1848. 109 p.
8vo   N, NYP

287 THE BEAUTY OF BALTIMORE; or, The Fate of the Coquette. Boston: Henry L. Williams, 1845. Cover title, 48 p. 8vo
                                                       BP, UV, Y
LC has a cover title.

288 BEECHER, CHARLES. The Incarnation; or, Pictures of the Virgin
and Her Son ... New York: Harper & Brothers, 1849. 227 p.
12mo   B, BP, LC, LCP, NYP, Y

289 BELKNAP, JEREMY. The Foresters, an American Tale: Being a
Sequel to the History of John Bull the Clothier. In a Series of
Letters to a Friend [anon.]. Printed at Boston, by I. Thomas
and E. T. Andrews, 1792. 216 p., illus. 12mo
        AAS, BP, H, HEH, IN, JCB, LC, N, NYP, UC, UM, UP, UPI, UV, Y

290 ——— ——— 2d ed. Printed at Boston, by I. Thomas and E.
T. Andrews, Nov., 1796. 240 p. 8vo   AAS, B, BA,
     BP, H, HEH, HM, IN, JCB, LC, LCP, N, NYP, NYS, UC, UM, UP, UV, Y

291 ——— ——— Exeter: Benj. H. Meder, 1831. 156, 26 p., illus.
24mo   AAS, BP, H, IN, LC, NYP, UC, UM, Y
With this is bound and was issued: *Boston Two Hundred Years Ago; or,
The Romantic Story of Miss Ann Carter* (1831).

292 ——— ——— Exeter: S. Hardy, 1831. 156, 26 p., illus. 24mo
AAS, B, BP, HEH, IN, N, NYP, UV, Y
With this is bound and was issued: *Boston Two Hundred Years Ago* (1831).

293 ——— ——— Exeter: Ulman & Jefferds, 1834. 156, 26 p.
24mo
AAS, IN, NYP, UV, Y
With this is bound and was issued: *Boston Two Hundred Years Ago* (1831).

294 BELL, MRS. MARTIN. Julia Howard: A Romance... New York:
Harper & Brothers, 1850. 113 p. 8vo
BP, NYP
Printed in double cols.

Mr. A. Algar, of Essex, England, has informed me that this is "a reprint of
Mrs. Mary Letitia Martin's *Julia Howard*, London, 1850. 3 vols." I have not
compared the two stories.

294a THE BELLE OF PARIS; or, The Triumph of Liberty. A Tale of the
French Revolution. Boston: Star Spangled Banner Office,
1849. 84 p. 8vo
HEH, Y
Also contains: Jack Trysail.

Not to be confused with Fred Hunter's *The Bell of Paris* (1851), Wright II,
1306a.
Printed in double cols.

295 BENNETT, EMERSON. The Bandits of the Osage: A Western Ro-
mance... Cincinnati: Robinson & Jones, 1847. 121 p. 8vo
LC, UC, UV, Y
Printed in double cols.

296 ——— ——— Cincinnati: L. Stratton, 1850. 130 p. 8vo LC
LC copy withdrawn from circulation.

297 ——— The Forest Rose: A Tale of the Frontier . . . Cincin-
nati: J. A. & U. P. James, 1850. 111 p. 8vo
AAS, LC, Y
Printed in double cols.

298 ——— Kate Clarendon; or, Necromancy in the Wilderness. A
Tale of the Little Miami . . . Cincinnati: Stratton & Barnard,
1848. 135 p. 8vo
AAS, HEH, LC, N, NYP, UC, UP, UV, Y
Printed in double cols.

299 ——— The League of the Miami . . . Louisville: C. Hagan &
Co., 507 Main Street [n.d.]. 116 p. 8vo
NYP, UV, Y
Preface dated Dec. 1850.
Printed in double cols.

300 ———— Leni-Leoti; or, Adventures in the Far West . . . Cincinnati: Stratton & Barnard, 1849. 117 p. 8vo   HEH, LC, N, Y
Printed in double cols.

301 ———— ———— Cincinnati: J. A. & U. P. James, 1850. 110 p. 8vo   NYP
Printed in double cols.

302 ———— Mike Fink: A Legend of the Ohio . . . Cincinnati: Robinson & Jones, 1848. 102 p. 8vo   LC, N, Y
Printed in double cols.

303 ———— Oliver Goldfinch; or, The Hypocrite . . . Cincinnati: Stratton & Barnard, 1850. 133 p. 8vo   AAS, HEH, LC, UV, Y
Printed in double cols.
New York City; 18--.

304 ———— The Prairie Flower; or, Adventures in the Far West . . . Cincinnati: Stratton & Barnard, 1849. 128 p. 8vo
        HEH, LC, N, Y
Printed in double cols.
See Wagner-Camp, No. 162, for discussion of authorship.

304a ———— ———— Cincinnati: J. A. & U. P. James. Stereotyped by A. C. James, 1850. 120 p. 8vo   Y
Printed in double cols.

305 ———— The Renegade: A Historical Romance of Border Life . . . Cincinnati: Robinson & Jones, 1848. 138 p. 8vo   LC, UV, Y
At head of cover title: "Library of Western Romance."
Kentucky.

306 ———— The Traitor; or, The Fate of Ambition . . . Cincinnati: Stratton and Barnard, 1850. 2 pts. 8vo   AAS, H, LC, Y
Pt. II pub. by Lorenzo Stratton.
Printed in double cols.
American Revolution.

306a ———— The Trapper's Bride; or, Spirit of Adventure . . . [anon.]. Cincinnati: Stratton & Barnard, 1848. 154 p., illus. 8vo
        HEH, LC, N, UV
Printed in double cols.
See BAL 1053 for discussion of authorship.

306b ——— ——— Cincinnati: Stratton and Barnard, 1849.   154 p.,
     illus.   8vo   y
     Printed in double cols.

BENNETT, JAMES GORDON.   Two Yards of Jaconet; or, A Husband.
In The Atlantic Club-Book (1834), Nos. 195-196.

307 BERESFORD, FANNY.   Confessions of a Lady's Waiting Maid: Be-
     ing a True Record of Marvelous Adventures in Both Hemi-
     spheres . . .   New York: The authoress, 1848.   240 p., illus.
     8vo   y
     LC has a title page, deposited Jan. 28, 1848.

BERKELEY, MRS. HELEN, *pseud.*   *See* Ritchie, Anna Cora (Ogden)
Mowatt

308 BESCHKE, WILLIAM.   The Dreadful Sufferings and Thrilling Ad-
     ventures of an Overland Party of Emigrants to California . . .
     Compiled from the Journal of Mr. George Adam, One of the
     Adventurers . . .   St. Louis, Mo.: Barclay & Co., 1850.   60 p.,
     illus.   8vo   AAS, BA, H, HEH, IN, N, NYP, UM

309 ——— ——— St. Louis, Mo.: Barclay & Co., 1850.   71, [1] p.,
     illus.   8vo   HEH, LC, N

BEY, ALI, *pseud.*   *See* Knapp, Samuel Lorenzo

310 BICKLEY, LLOYD WHARTON.   The Aristocrat: An American Tale
     . . . [anon.].   Philadelphia: Key & Biddle, 1833.   2 vols.   12mo
                              AAS, B, BP, H, IN, LC, NYP, UC, UP, UV, Y
     Variant copies noted: (1) verso of title pages of both vols. contains the
     copyright notice; (2) verso of title page of Vol. I contains copyright notice
     and printer's slug, verso of title page of Vol. II blank. Census of copies does
     not distinguish between the variants.

311 ——— Zoe; or, The Sicilian Sayda . . . [anon.].   Philadelphia:
     Key & Biddle, 1833.   2 vols.   12mo   H, HEH, UV, Y
     LC has a title page.

312 BIGELOW, JACOB.   The Wars of the Gulls: An Historical Romance
     . . . [anon.].   New York: Published at the Dramatic Reposi-
     tory, Shakespeare Gallery, 1812.   36 p.   12mo
                       AAS, B, BA, BP, H, HEH, IN, LC, N, NYH, NYP, UM, UP, UV, Y
     Nathan Hale, jt. au.

45

BIGLY, CANTELL A., *pseud.* *See* Peck, George Washington

313 THE BIOGRAPHY of a Bottle. By a Friend of Temperance. Boston: Perkins, Marvin & Co., 1835. 100 p. 12mo   LC

314 BIRD, ROBERT MONTGOMERY. The Adventures of Robin Day ... [anon.]. Philadelphia: Lea & Blanchard, 1839. 2 vols. 12mo
AAS, B, BP, H, HEH, IN, LC, LCP, N, NYP, UM, UP, UV, Y
Philadelphia and Florida.

315 —— Calavar; or, The Knight of the Conquest. A Romance of Mexico ... [anon.]. Philadelphia: Carey, Lea & Blanchard, 1834. 2 vols. 12mo
AAS, B, H, HEH, IN, LC, LCP, N, NYP, NYS, UC, UM, UP, UV, Y
An ed. in German was printed at St. Louis in 1848.
1520-40.

316 —— —— Philadelphia: Carey, Lea & Blanchard, 1835. 2 vols. 12mo   BP, N, Y

317 —— —— 3d ed. Philadelphia: Carey, Lea & Blanchard, 1837. 2 vols. 12mo   AAS, BA, IN, NYH, Y

318 —— —— Philadelphia: Lea and Blanchard, 1847. 2 vols. 12mo   LC, NYP, UP, UV, Y

319 —— The Hawks of Hawk-Hollow. A Tradition of Pennsylvania ... [anon.]. Philadelphia: Carey, Lea & Blanchard, 1835. 2 vols. 12mo   AAS, B, BA, H, HEH, HM, IN, LC, LCP, N, NYH, NYP, NYS, UC, UM, UP, UPI, Y
1782.

320 —— The Infidel; or, The Fall of Mexico ... [anon.]. Philadelphia: Carey, Lea & Blanchard, 1835. 2 vols. 12mo
AAS, BA, BP, H, HEH, IN, LC, LCP, N, NYP, NYS, UC, UP, UV, Y
1520-40.

321 —— ——2d ed. Philadelphia: Carey, Lea & Blanchard, 1835. 2 vols. 12mo   B, BP, HEH(V. 1), LCP, Y

322 —— Nick of the Woods; or, The Jibbenainosay. A Tale of Kentucky ... [anon.]. Philadelphia: Carey, Lea & Blanchard, 1837. 2 vols. 12mo
AAS, B, BA, BP, H, HEH, IN, LC, LCP, N, NYP, UC, UP, UV, Y
1780's.

323 ———— Peter Pilgrim; or, A Rambler's Recollections ... [anon.]. Philadelphia: Lea & Blanchard, 1838. 2 vols. 12mo

AAS, B, BP, H, HEH, HM, IN, LC, LCP, NYH, NYP, UC, UP, UV, Y

Contents: Merry the Miner—A Tale of a Snag—My Friends in the Madhouse—The Extra Lodger—Arkansas Emigrants—The Fascinating Power of Reptiles—A Night on the Terrapin Rocks—The Mammoth Cave—The Bloody Broad-Horn.

324 ———— Sheppard Lee ... [anon.]. New York: Harper & Brothers, 1836. 2 vols. 12mo

AAS, B, BA, BP, H, HEH, IN, LC, N, NYP, UC, UM, UP, UV, Y

Eastern states; contemporary.

325 BLACKBEARD. A Page from the Colonial History of Philadelphia ... New York: Harper & Brothers, 1835. 2 vols. 12mo

AAS, H, HEH, IN, LC, LCP, N, NYP, UC, UM, UP, UV, Y

326 BLEECKER, ANN ELIZA (SCHUYLER). The History of Maria Kittle ... In a Letter to Miss Ten Eyck. Hartford: Printed by Elisha Babcock, 1797. 70 p. 12mo

AAS, B, HEH, IN, JCB, LC, N, NYH, UV, Y

New York; French and Indian War.

327 ———— ———— Hartford: Printed by John Babcock, 1802. 72 p. 12mo
H

328 ———— The Posthumous Works ... New York: Printed by T. and J. Swords, 1793. 375 p., illus. 12mo

AAS, B, BP, H, HEH, LC, LCP, N, NYH, NYP, NYS, UC, UM, UP, UV, Y

Contains: The History of Maria Kittle—The Story of Henry and Anne: Founded on Fact.

329 BLOODGOOD, SIMEON DE WITT. A Sketch of the Olden Time; or, General Lee's Farewell Dinner, at New-York. Founded on Fact. Being the First of a Series of Revolutionary Tales, by an Antiquary [anon.]. New York: G. & C. Carvill, 1829. 44 p. 8vo
AAS, H, HEH, LC, NYH, NYP, NYS, UP, UV, Y

330 BLOOMFIELD, OBADIAH BENJAMIN FRANKLIN, *M.D., pseud.* The Life and Adventures of Obadiah Benjamin Franklin Bloomfield, M.D. [pseud.]. A Native of the United States of America,

Now on a Tour of Europe . . . Written by Himself . . . Philadelphia: Published for the Proprietor, 1818. 210 p. 12mo

AAS, B, H, HEH, LC, LCP, N, NYH, NYP, UC, UM, UP, UV, Y

Copyrighted by Edward Franklin, who may have been the author.

331 A BLOSSOM IN THE DESERT: A Tale of the West. Founded on Fact . . . New York: Scofield & Voorhies, 1838. 32 p., illus. 16mo NYH, UV

332 BOKUM, HERMANN. Never Despair: A Tale of the Emigrants. Founded on Fact [anon.]. New York: Scofield & Voorhies, 1837. 104 p. 12mo AAS, H, LC, N, UP, Y

333 BOLOKITTEN, OLIVER, *Esq.*, *pseud.* A Sojourn in the City of Amalgamation in the Year of Our Lord 19--. By Oliver Bolokitten, Esq. [pseud.]. New York: The author, 1835. 190 p. 12mo BP, N, NYH, NYP, Y

334 BONN, ALEXANDER KERR. An Original, Laughable, and Comical Tale of Hughie Morrison, the Scottish Emigrant . . . By Bramble Brae [pseud.]. Baltimore: Printed by Sherwood & Co., 1846. 35 p. 12mo LC

335 BONNEY, EDWARD. The Banditti of the Prairies; or, The Murderer's Doom! A Tale of the Mississippi Valley . . . Chicago: Edward Bonney, 1850. 196 p., illus. 8vo H, LC, NYH, UV

336 BORGIA, EXPERIENCE, *pseud.* The Confessions of a Magdalen; or, Some Passages in the Life of Experience Borgia [pseud.], in Letters to Forgiveness Mandeville, Esq. . . . New York: Printed for the publisher, 1831. 31 p. 12mo BP, IN, LC, NYP, UV, Y

337 BOSTON TWO HUNDRED YEARS AGO; or, The Romantic Story of Miss Ann Carter, (Daughter of One of the First Settlers,) and the Celebrated Indian Chief, Thundersquall; with Many Humorous Reminiscences and Events of Olden Time. Boston, 1830. 16 p., illus. 4to AAS, B, H, HEH, IN, LC, NYP, UC, UV, Y

Also in J. Belknap, *The Foresters* (1831 and 1834), Nos. 291-293.

337a BOTSFORD, EDMUND. The Spiritual Voyage, Performed in the Ship Convert, under the Command of Capt. Godly-Fear, from the Port of Repentance-unto-Life, to the Haven of Felicity on the Continent of Glory. An Allegory . . . Charleston, S. C.: Printed for the author by J. Hoff, 1814. 26 p. 12mo AAS

337b ——— ——— [N.p.], 1818. 84 p. 12mo   B

338 ——— ——— Philadelphia: Anderson and Meehan, 1819. 32 p. 12mo   AAS, LCP
Title reads: *The Spiritual Voyage, Performed in the Ship Convert, under the Command of Captain Godly-Fear, to the Haven of Felicity . . .*

338a ——— ——— Charleston, S. C.: Printed and published by W. Riley, 1826. 99 p., front. 12mo   HEH, UV, Y
Title reads the same as No. 337a and adds: *To Which Is Prefixed a Sketch of the Life of the Author.*

338b ——— ——— Charleston: W. Riley, 1828. 120 p. 12mo
      JCB, N, UV

339 ——— ——— Harrisburg: Reprinted for D. Barnes, 1828. 126 p. 16mo   LC
Title reads: *The Spiritual Voyage, Performed in the Ship Convert, under the Command of Captain Godly-Fear, from the Port of Repentance-unto-Life . . .*

340 BOTSFORD, MRS. MARGARET. Adelaide: A New and Original Novel. By a Lady of Philadelphia . . . [anon.]. Philadelphia: Printed by Dennis Heartt, 1816. 2 vols. 12mo   BP, UV, Y

341 ——— The Reign of Reform; or, Yankee Doodle Court. By a Lady [anon.]. Baltimore: Printed for the authoress, 1830. 146 p. 12mo   AAS, B, BA, BP, H, HEH, LC, LCP, N, NYP, UC, UP, UV, Y

341a BOUGHTON, JOSEPH. The Conspiracy; or, Triumph of Innocence . . . Rochester: D. M. Dewey; W. H. Beach, 1845. 23 p. 8vo
Copy located in the Rochester Historical Society.

341b ——— Solon Grind; or, The Thunderstruck Hypocrite . . . New York: Burgess, Stringer and Company, 1845. 120 p. 12mo   AAS, H

342 BOURNE, GEORGE. Lorette. The History of Louise, Daughter of a Canadian Nun: Exhibiting the Interior of Female Convents . . . [anon.]. New York: W. A. Mercein, 1833. 244 p., illus. 8vo
      AAS, H, NYP, UM, UV, Y
17- -.

343 —— —— 2d ed. New York: Charles Small, 1834. 208 p.,
illus. 12mo   AAS, H, HEH, LC

344 —— —— 3d ed. New York: Charles Small, 1834. 208 p.,
illus. 12mo   AAS, Y

345 —— —— 4th ed. New York: Charles Small, 1834. 208 p.,
illus. 12mo   N, NYH, Y

346 —— —— 6th ed. New York: Charles Small, 1834. 208 p.,
illus. 12mo   AAS, B, H, UC, Y

346a BOWERS, BENJAMIN. The Bachelor's Escape from the Snare of
the Fowler . . . Swanton [Vt.]: Published by the author, 1845.
35 p. 8vo   AAS

347 BOYCE, JOHN. Shandy McGuire; or, Tricks upon Travellers. Being a Story of the North of Ireland. By Paul Peppergrass, Esq.
[pseud.]. New York: Edward Dunigan & Brothers, 1848.
354 p., illus. 8vo   AAS, LCP, NYP, UM, UP, UV, Y
AAS copy in 2 pts. with original printed wrappers.

348 —— —— New York: Edward Dunigan & Brothers, 1850.
354 p. 8vo   Y

349 BOYNTON, B. H., JR. The White Dart; or, The Cruiser of the
Gulf of Mexico. A True Tale of Piracy and War . . . Boston:
Star Spangled Banner office, 1848. 46 p., illus. 8vo   AAS, Y
At head of title: "An Original Tale of the Sea."
Cover imprint: "Boston: Jones Publishing House, 1848."
Printed in double cols.

349a BOYNTON, CHARLES. Isabel Wilton; or, The Oswegatchie's Captive. A Tale of the Old French War . . . Canton, N. Y.: Published at the Northern Cabinet Office, 1843. Cover title, 25 p.
8vo   N, NYP, Y
At head of title: "New Original Novel."
Printed in double cols.

350 Boz, Jr., *pseud*. The Moral City! Or, Glances at Social Life in Boston; Comprising the History of Thomas Tippleton, Esq., the Libertine, and Many Other Wonderful Matters. By Boz, Junior [pseud.]. Boston: John A. French & Co., 1849.
LC has a title page.

351 BRACE, JOHN PIERCE. Tales of the Devils . . . Hartford: S. Andrus and Son, 1846. 277 p. 8vo   UV, Y

352 ——— ——— Hartford: S. Andrus and Son, 1847. 277 p. 8vo
B, HEH, LC, Y

353 ——— ——— Hartford: S. Andrus and Son, 1850. 277 p. 8vo
AAS, H, NYP, Y

BRACEBLOCK, *pseud*. The Capture: A Spanish Tale. *In* J. Jones, The Belle of Boston (1849), No. 1483.

354 BRACKENRIDGE, HUGH HENRY. Modern Chivalry: Containing the Adventures of Captain John Farrago, and Teague O'Regan, His Servant . . . Philadelphia: Printed and sold by John M'Culloch, 1792-97. 4 vols. 12mo
AAS(V.1), HEH, IN, JCB, LC, LCP, NYP, UP(V.1-3), UPI, UV, Y
Vol. III imprint: "Pittsburgh: Printed and sold by John Scull, M.DCC.XIII" [i.e., 1793].
For complete bibliographical information see BAL 1300.

355 ——— Modern Chivalry: Containing the Adventures of a Captain, &c. Part II . . . Carlisle: Printed by Archibald Loudon, 1804-5. 2 vols. 12mo   AAS, HEH, IN, NYP, UM(V.2), UV

356 ——— Modern Chivalry: Containing the Adventures of a Captain and Teague O'Regan, His Servant . . . Volume I. Philadelphia: J. Conrad & Co. . . . S. H. M'Fetrich, printer, 1804. 210 p. 12mo   AAS, BA, H, HEH, LCP, N, NYP, UC, UPI, UV, Y
Contains text of Vols. I-II, No. 354.

357 ——— ——— Volume II. Philadelphia: Jacob Johnson . . . Alexander & Phillips, printers, Carlisle, 1807. 175 p. 12mo
AAS, BA, H, HEH, LC, LCP, N, NYP, UC, UPI, Y
Contains text of Vols. III-IV, No. 354.

358 ———— ———— Part II. Philadelphia: Jacob Johnson... Alexander & Phillips, printers, Carlisle, 1807. 2 vols. 12mo

AAS, H, HEH, LCP, NYP, UC, UPI, Y

Contains text of No. 355.

359 ———— ———— Volume I. Philadelphia: Jacob Johnson, 1808. 210 p. 12mo   AAS, LC, LCP, NYP, Y

At bottom of p. 210: "S. H. M'Fetrich, printer."

Y has a second copy variant; at bottom of p. 210: "Alexander & Phillips, printers."

Contains text of Vols. I-II, No. 354, revised.

360 ———— ———— Philadelphia: Johnson & Warner, 1815. 4 vols. 12mo   AAS, B, BA, IN, LC, NYP, UM, UP(V.2,4), UV, Y

Contains in Vols. I-III text of Nos. 354-355, revised; Vol. IV contains added material.

361 ———— ———— Wilmington: Printed for and sold by George Metz, 1815. 2 vols. in 1 (276 p.). 12mo

AAS, BP, LCP, NYP, UV, Y

Contains text of No. 354, revised.

362 ———— ———— With the Last Corrections and Additions of the Author. Pittsburgh: R. Patterson & Lambdin. Butler & Lambdin, printers, 1819. 2 vols. 12mo

AAS, BA, BP, H, LC, LCP, NYP, UC, UM, UPI, UV, Y

Contains text of Nos. 354-355, with omissions, and part of Vol. IV, No. 360.

363 ———— ———— Wilmington, (Del.): Printed for and sold by S. Kollock & G. W. Metz, 1825. 252 p. 12mo

AAS, H, IN, LC, NYH, NYP, UM, UP, UV, Y

Contains text of No. 354.

364 ———— ———— 2d ed. since the Author's Death . . . Philadelphia: Carey and Hart, 1846. 2 vols., illus. 12mo

AAS, H, LC, LCP, NYH, NYP, UM, Y

Contains text of Vol. I only, No. 362.

365 BRADBURY, OSGOOD. Agnes Belmont; or, The Broker's Marriage . . . [anon.]. Boston: H. L. Williams, 1846.

LC has a title page, deposited Mar. 21, 1846.

366 ———— Alice Marvin; or, The Fisherman's Daughter . . .[anon.]. Boston: H. L. Williams, 1845. Cover title, 50 p. 8vo   Y
LC has a cover title, deposited Oct. 10, 1845.

367 ———— The Belle of the Bowery . . . [anon.]. Boston: H. L. Williams, 1846. 95 p., illus. 8vo   AAS, BP, H

368 ———— ———— New York: W. F. Burgess, 1849. 95 p., illus. 8vo
AAS

369 ———— The Distiller's Daughter; or, The Power of Woman . . . [anon.]. [N.p., ca. 1844.] Caption title, 48 p. 8vo   UC, UP
Printed in double cols.

370 ———— The Eastern Belle; or, The Betrayed One! A Tale of Boston and Bangor . . . [anon.]. Boston: H. L. Williams, 1845. Cover title, 56 p. 8vo   BP, UV
LC has a cover title, deposited May 21, 1845.

371 ———— Elizabeth Howard; or, The Disguised Peddler . . . Boston: F. Gleason [cop. 1848].
LC has a title page, deposited Dec. 7, 1848.

372 ———— Ellen Templeton; or, The Spectral Cloud . . . [anon.]. Boston: For sale at all bookstores, 1846. 82 p., illus. 8vo
AAS, BP
Printed in double cols.
LC has a title page, deposited Feb. 11, 1846.

373 ———— Emily Mansfield; or, The Gambler's Fate! Lost But Not Won [anon.]. Boston: "Yankee" office, 1845. Cover title, 64 p., illus. 8vo   BP, HEH, LC, UV, Y
Boston.

374 ———— Empress of Beauty . . . [anon.]. Boston: J. N. Bradley & Co., 1844. Cover title, 64 p. 8vo   AAS, B

375 ———— Frances Carleton; or, The Boston Blacksmith . . . [anon.]. Boston: H. L. Williams, 1846. 79 p., illus. 8vo   BP
Printed in double cols.
LC has a title page, deposited Jan. 29, 1846.

376 ——— Francis Abbott; or, The Hermit of Niagara. A Tale of the Old and New World . . . [anon.]. Boston: Gleason's Publishing Hall, 1846. 100 p., illus. 8vo

AAS, BP, H, LC, NYP, UM, UV, Y

Printed in double cols.

377 ——— Helen Clarence. [Boston: H. L. Williams, n.d.] Caption title, 66 p., illus. 8vo   BP, UV
Printed in double cols.
Boston.

378 ——— Henriette; or, The Maiden and Priest . . . [anon.]. Boston: H. L. Williams, 1845. Cover title, 48 p., illus. 8vo

BP, H, UM

LC has a cover title, deposited July 25, 1845.

379 ——— Hutoka; or, The Maid of the Forest. A Tale of the Indian Wars . . . [anon.]. Boston: Gleason's Publishing Hall, 1846. 66 p., illus. 8vo   AAS, BP, H, HEH, LC, NYP, UV, Y

380 ——— Isabelle; or, The Emigrant's Daughter. A Tale of Boston and the West . . . Boston: F. Gleason, 1848. 100 p., illus. 8vo   LC, Y
Also contains: The Rescued Maiden, by S. Nelson.
Printed in double cols.

381 ——— Julia Bicknell; or, Love and Murder! Founded on a Recent Terrible Domestic Tragedy . . . [anon.]. Boston: Henry L. Williams, 1845. 72 p., illus. 8vo   B, BP, UV
Printed in double cols.
LC has a title page, deposited Dec. 9, 1845.

382 ——— Larooka: The Belle of the Penobscots . . . [anon.]. Bangor: David Bugbee, 1846. 45 p. 8vo   H, HEH, Y
Caption title: "Larooka: The Belle of the Penobscots; or, The Wood Nymphs of the East."
Printed in double cols.

383 ——— Little Emma . . . [anon.]. [Boston: H. L. Williams, cop. 1845.] Caption title, 48 p. 8vo   BP, UV
Boston; early 19th cent.

384 ——— Louise Kempton; or, Vice and Virtue Contrasted . . . [anon.]. Boston: F. Gleason, 1844. Cover title, 66 p., illus. 8vo　　　　　　　　　　　　　　　　　AAS, UC, UV
New York City; contemporary.

385 ——— ——— Boston: F. Gleason. Printed by J. N. Bradley & Co., 14 & 16 State Street [184-?]. Cover title, 48 p., illus. 8vo
　　　　　　　　　　　　　　　　　AAS, HEH, UP, Y
Printed in double cols.

386 ——— Lucelle; or, The Young Iroquois! A Tale of the Indian Wars . . . [anon.]. Boston: Henry L. Williams, 1845. 75 p., illus. 8vo　　　　　　　　　　　　　AAS, BP, UV, Y
Printed in double cols.
LC has a title page, deposited Dec. 16, 1845.

——— Maniac Beauty (1844). See No. 1797 for title entry which is now identified as by Bradbury.

387 ——— Manita of the Pictured Rocks; or, The Copper Speculation. A Tale of Lake Superior . . . Boston: F. Gleason, 1848. 100 p., illus. 8vo　　　　　　　　　　　　　　　　B
Printed in double cols.

388 ——— Metallak: The Lone Indian of the Megalloway . . . [anon.]. Boston: F. Gleason; C. W. Child, Portland; David Bugbee, Bangor, 1844. 31 p., illus. 4to　　　　　　N, Y
Printed in double cols.
LC has a title page, deposited April 18, 1844.

389 ——— ——— Boston: United States Publishing Co., 1845. Cover title, 66 p., illus. 8vo　　　AAS, BP, HEH, NYP, UP, Y

390 ——— ——— Boston: F. Gleason, 1849. 84 p., illus. 8vo
　　　　　　　　　　　　　　　　　AAS, UM
Printed in double cols.

391 ——— Monira; or, The Wandering Heiress . . . [anon.]. Boston: H. L. Williams, 1845. 48 p. 8vo　　BP, HEH, UP, UV, Y
Printed in double cols.
LC has a title page, deposited Sept. 5, 1845.

392 —— The Mysteries of Boston; or, Woman's Temptation. By a Member of the Suffolk Bar . . . [anon.]. Boston: J. N. Bradley & Co., 1844. Cover title, 40 p. 8vo   AAS, B, Y

Printed in double cols.

LC has a cover title.

393 —— Mysteries of Lowell . . . [anon.]. Boston: Edward P. Williams, 1844. 40 p. 8vo   AAS, B, UP, Y

Printed in double cols.

LC has a cover title.

394 —— The Mysterious Mother; or, Theory of Second Love . . . [anon.]. Boston: F. Gleason, 1844. Cover title, 48 p. 8vo   Y

Printed in double cols.

395 —— Pierpold, the Avenger; or, The Lost Child. A Tale of the Forest . . . Boston: F. Gleason, 1848. 100 p., illus. 8vo   B, BP, Y

Printed in double cols.

Maine.

396 —— Pontiac; or, The Last Battle of the Ottawa Chief. A Tale of the West . . . Boston: F. Gleason, 1848. 100 p., illus. 8vo   BA, NYP

Printed in double cols.

397 —— The Spanish Pirate; or, The Terror of the Ocean . . . [anon.]. Boston: H. L. Williams, 1845. 74 p., illus. 8vo   BP, Y

Printed in double cols.

LC has a title page, deposited Dec. 22, 1845.

398 —— Walton; or, The Banditt's Daughter . . . [anon.]. Boston: H. L. Williams, 1845. Cover title, 48 p. 8vo   AAS, BP, UM, UV, Y

Printed in double cols.

LC has a cover title, deposited June 10, 1845.

399 BRADFORD, EBENEZER. The Art of Courting, Displayed in Eight Different Scenes . . . [anon.]. Newburyport: Printed by William Barrett, 1795. 225 p. 12mo   AAS, B, BA, BP, H, IN, N, NYH, NYS, UV, Y

Written in a series of letters.

BRAE, BRAMBLE, *pseud.* *See* Bonn, Alexander Kerr

BRAINARD, JOHN GARDINER CALKINS. Fort Braddock Letters. *See* Letters Found in the Ruins of Fort Braddock.

400 ———— Letters Found in the Ruins of Fort Braddock, Including an Interesting American Tale . . . [anon.]. New York: O. Wilder and J. M. Campbell, 1824. 78 p. 12mo AAS, UC, UV

401 ———— ———— Worcester: Dorr & Howland, 1827. 98 p., illus. 12mo AAS, HEH, IN, LC, N, NYP, UP, UPI, Y
Title reads: *Fort Braddock Letters; or, A Tale of the French and Indian Wars in America.*

402 ———— ———— Washington, D.C.: Printed and published by Charles Galpin, 1830. 97 p. 18mo LC, NYP, Y
At head of title: "Fugitive Tales, No. 1."
Title reads: *Fort Braddock Letters.*

403 ———— ———— Peekskill: Huestis & Brewer, printers, 1832. 128 p., illus. 16mo AAS, LC, NYH, NYP, Y
Title reads: *The Fort Braddock Letters.*

404 BRICE, JAMES F. Castle Crosier. A Romance, by an American [anon.]. Annapolis: Printed by W. M. M'Neir, 1827. 79 p. 8vo LC, UM

405 ———— ———— Annapolis: W. M. M'Neir, printer, 1839. 119 p. 8vo NYP

406 THE BRIGANTINE; or, Admiral Lowe. A Tale of the 17th Century, by an American. New York: Crowen & Decker, 1839. 201 p. 12mo AAS, B, H, IN, LC, N, NYH, NYP, UC, UP, UV, Y

407 BRIGGS, CHARLES FREDERICK. The Adventures of Harry Franco [pseud.]: A Tale of the Great Panic . . . New York: F. Saunder, 1839. 2 vols. 12mo
AAS, B, BA, H, HEH, IN, LC, N, NYP, UC, UM, UV, Y
New York City.

408 ———— Bankrupt Stories, Edited by Harry Franco [pseud.]. New York: John Allen, 1843. 381 p., illus. 8vo
AAS, BP, HEH, NYP, UV, Y
Contains: The Haunted Merchant.

409 ———— ———— 2d ed. New York: John Allen, 1844. 381 p.,
illus. 8vo   AAS, N, UP, Y

410 ———— The Trippings of Tom Pepper; or, The Results of Ro-
mancing. An Autobiography by Harry Franco [pseud.].
New York: Burgess, Stringer & Co., 1847-50. 2 vols. 12mo
                                   BA(V.1), H, IN, NYH, NYP, Y
At head of title, Vol. I: "Mirror Library, New Series"; Vol. II: "Mirror Li-
brary, No. II, New Series."
Imprint of Vol. II: "New York: Mirror Office, Wm. H. Graham; Dewitt &
Davenport; Long & Brother, George Dexter, 1850."

411 ———— Working a Passage; or, Life in a Liner . . . By B. C. F.
New York: John Allen, 1844. 108 p. 18mo
                                             AAS, BP, NYP, UP, Y

412 ———— ———— New York: Homan & Ellis, 1846. 81 p., illus.
12mo   NYP

413 BRIGGS, EMILY EDSON. Ellen Parry; or, Trials of the Heart. By
Olivia [pseud.] . . . New York: D. Appleton & Co., 1850. 186
p. 12mo   AAS, BA, BP, HEH, LC, N, UC, UP, UV, Y
England.

414 BRISBANE, ABBOTT HALL. Ralphton; or, The Young Carolinian of
1776. A Romance on the Philosophy of Politics . . . Charleston: Burges and James, printers, 1848. 242 p. 12mo
                              BP, CLS, H, HM, IN, LC, NYH, NYP, UV

415 BRISBANE, WILLIAM HENRY. Amanda: A Tale for the Times . . .
Philadelphia: Merrihew & Thompson, printers, 1848. 51 p.
12mo   BP, LC
Eastern cities.

416 ———— ———— New York: Anti-Slavery Society, 1849. 52 p.
12mo
Ed. from Sabin 8006.

416a BROCKWAY, THOMAS. The European Traveller in America, Contained in Three Letters to His Friend in London . . . [anon.].
Hartford: Printed by Hudson & Goodwin, 1785. 40 p. 4to
                              AAS, BA, BP, HEH, JCB, LC, NYH, NYP

417   BROOKS, MARIA (GOWEN).   Idomen; or, the Vale of Yumuri.   By
       Maria del Occidente [pseud.] . . .   New York: Samuel Colman,
       1843.   236 p.   12mo   AAS, B, BA, BP, H, IN, LC, N, NYP, UV, Y

417a   BROUGHAM, JOHN.   The Incendiary!   A Tale of Love and Re-
       venge . . .   Boston: H. L. Williams, 1845.   40 p., illus.   8vo
                                                          AAS, BP, Y

418   BROWN, CHARLES BROCKDEN.   Arthur Mervyn; or, Memoirs of the
       Year 1793 . . . [anon.].   Philadelphia: Printed and published by
       H. Maxwell, 1799-1800.   2 pts.   12mo
            AAS (pt.1), BA, BP(pt.1), H, HEH, IN, JCB, LC, LCP, N, NYP, UC
                                              (pt.1), UM, UP, UV, Y
       Imprint of second part: "New York: Printed and sold by George F. Hop-
       kins, 1800."
       Philadelphia.

419   ———   Clara Howard: In a Series of Letters . . . [anon.].   Phila-
       delphia: Asbury Dickins, 1801.   268 p.   12mo
                                            AAS, IN, LCP, NYP, NYS, UV
       New York and Philadelphia; contemporary.

420   ———   Edgar Huntley; or, Memoirs of a Sleep-walker . . .
       [anon.].   Philadelphia: Printed by H. Maxwell, 1799.   3 vols.
       12mo   AAS, HEH, IN, LC, LCP, N, NYP, NYS, UP, UV, Y
       For differences between the dated 1799 and 1800 Vol. III, see BAL 1499-
       1500.

421   ——— ———   2d ed.   Philadelphia: Printed by H. Maxwell,
       1801.   3 vols.   12mo   AAS, BA, BP, LCP, NYP(V.3), UV, Y(V.2-3)

422   ———   Jane Talbot . . . [anon.].   Philadelphia: John Conrad &
       Co., 1801.   346 p., illus.   12mo
                                  AAS, BP, HEH, IN, LC, LCP, NYS, UP, UV, Y
       Written in a series of letters to and from Philadelphia.

423   ———   The Novels . . .   Boston: S. G. Goodrich, 1827.   7 vols.
       12mo
       General title page in Vol. I only.
       Wieland. AAS, BA, BP, H, IN, LC, LCP, NYP, NYS, UM, UP, Y
       Arthur Mervyn. AAS, BA, BP, H, IN, LC, LCP, NYP, NYS, UM, UP, Y
       Clara Howard. AAS, BA, BP, IN, LC, LCP, NYP, NYS, UC, UM, UP, Y
       Edgar Huntley. AAS, BA, BP, H, IN, LC, LCP, NYP, NYS, UC, UM, UP, Y
       Jane Talbot. AAS, BA, BP, H, IN, LC, LCP, NYP, NYS, UC, UM, UP, Y
       Ormond. AAS, BA, BP, HEH, IN, LC, LCP, NYP, NYS, UM, UP, Y

424 ———— Ormond; or, The Secret Witness . . . [anon.]. New York: Printed by G. Forman, 1799. 338 p. 12mo

AAS, BP, HEH, IN, LC, LCP, NYP, NYS, UC, UP, UV, Y

Philadelphia; 1793.

425 ——— ——— New York: William Taylor & Co., 1846. 144 p. 8vo AAS, LC, UV, Y
On cover: "No. II Library of Standard Romance."

426 ——— Wieland; or, The Transformation . . . [anon.]. New York: Printed by T. & J. Swords, 1798. 298 p. 12mo

AAS, H, HEH, IN, JCB, LC, LCP, N, NYP, NYS, UP, UV, Y

Schuylkill River; 1760's.

427 ——— ——— New York: William Taylor & Co., 1846. 124 p. 8vo AAS, HEH, LC, UV, Y
On cover: "No. I Library of Standard Romance."

428 BROWN, JOHN WALKER. Julia of Baiae; or, The Days of Nero. A Story of the Martyrs . . . [anon.]. New York: Saxton & Miles, 1843. 260 p. 12mo AAS, H, N, UC, UP, UV, Y

429 ——— ——— 2d ed. New York: Saxton & Miles, 1843. 260 p. 12mo AAS, HEH, IN, NYP, Y

——— See Nos. 574-576, 2642 for title entries which are now identified as by Brown.

430 BROWN, PHOEBE (HINSDALE). The Tree and Its Fruits; or, Narratives from Real Life . . . New York: Ezra Collier, 1836. 142 p., illus. 12mo AAS, HEH, LC, NYP, Y
Contents: The Reading Club: A Tale of Real Life—The Victim—The Infidel—The Aged Cottager.

431 ——— ——— 2d ed. New York: Ezra Collier & Co., 1838. 142 p., illus. 12mo BP, Y

432 BROWN, WILLIAM HILL. Ira and Isabella; or, The Natural Children . . . Boston: Belcher and Armstrong, 1807. 118 p. 8vo
AAS, BA, H, IN, LC, UV, Y

433 ——— The Power of Sympathy; or, The Triumph of Nature
... [anon.]. Printed at Boston, by Isaiah Thomas and Company, 1789. 2 vols., illus. 12mo

AAS, BA, BP, H, HEH, IN, JCB, LC, N, NYP, UC, UP, UV, Y

Formerly attributed to Sarah Wentworth Morton.
Written in a series of letters.
Boston; contemporary.

434 BROWNE, JOHN ROSS. Confessions of a Quack; or, The Autobiography of a Modern Aesculapian ... Louisville, Ky.: Printed
by James B. Marshall, April, 1841. 32 p. 8vo LC, UC
Printed in double cols.

435 BROWNLEE, WILLIAM CRAIG. The Whigs of Scotland; or, The
Last of the Stuarts. An Historical Romance of the Scottish
Persecution ... [anon.]. New York: Printed and published by
J. & H. Harper, 1833. 2 vols. 12mo

AAS, B, BA, HEH, LC, UP, UV, Y

436 BROWNSON, ORESTES AUGUSTUS. Charles Elwood; or, The Infidel
Converted . . . Boston: Charles C. Little and James Brown,
1840. 262 p. 8vo

AAS, B, BA, BP, H, HEH, IN, LC, N, NYP, NYS, UC, UM, UP, UV, Y

437 BRYANT, JOHN DELAVAN. Pauline Seward: A Tale of Real Life ...
Baltimore: Printed and published by John Murphy, 1847. 2
vols. 12mo AAS, B, IN, UM, UP, UV, Y

437a ——— ——— 3d ed. Baltimore: Printed and published by
John Murphy, 1847. 2 vols. 12mo UP

438 ——— ——— 4th ed. Baltimore: Printed and published by
John Murphy, 1848. 2 vols. in 1. 12mo HEH

439 BRYANT, WILLIAM CULLEN, ed. Tales of Glauber-Spa. By Several American Authors ... New York: Printed and published
by J. & J. Harper, 1832. 2 vols. 12mo BA, HEH, IN, UM, UV, Y
Contents: Le Bossu, by C. M. Sedgwick–Childe Roeliff's Pilgrimage: A
Travelling Legend, by J. K. Paulding–The Skeleton's Cave, by W. C. Bryant–Medfield, by W. C. Bryant–The Block-house: A Western Story, by
W. Leggett–Mr. Green, by R. C. Sands–Selim, the Benefactor of Mankind,
by J. K. Paulding–Boyuca, by R. C. Sands.
Copyright notice in Vol. II is dated 1831.

440 ——— ——— New York: Printed and published by J. & J. Harper, 1832. 2 vols. 12mo
AAS, B, BP(V.1), H, HEH, HM, IN, LC, N, NYP, NYS, UC, UP, UV, Y
Copyright notice in Vol. II, reset and dated 1832.
Norman Kane informed me in 1957 that he had a set in which the copyright notice in Vol. II had been dropped.

441 ——— ——— New York: Harper & Brothers, 1844. 2 vols.
12mo   AAS, LCP, NYH, NYP, Y

442 BRYNE, FRANK. The Spanish Beauty; or, The Cruise of the Gentile. A Nautical Tale ... Boston: "Star Spangled Banner" office [1848]. 92 p., illus. 8vo   UP, UV, Y
Also contains: Bellamira; or, The Last Days of Calloa, by Ned Buntline [i.e., E. Z. C. Judson].
At head of title: "A Splendid Tale of the Sea."
Cover title reads: "The Spanish Beauty and Bellamira ... Boston: Jones's Publishing House, 1848."
Printed in double cols.

442a ——— ——— Boston: "Star Spangled Banner" office, 1849. 92 p., illus. 8vo   Y
Also contains: Bellamira; or, The Last Days of Calloa, by Ned Buntline [i.e., E. Z. C. Judson].
At head of title: "A Splendid Tale of the Sea."
Printed in double cols.

443 BUCHANAN, HARRISON GRAY. Asmodeus; or, Legends of New York. Being a Complete Exposé of the Mysteries, Vices and Doings, as Exhibited by the Fashionable Circles of New York ... Facts without Fiction. New York: John D. Munson & Co., 1848. 96 p. 8vo   H, LC, UC, UV, Y
LC has a title page which reads: "Asmodeus; or, The Iniquities of New York. Being a Complete Exposé of the Crimes, Doings and Vices as Exhibited in the Haunts of Gamblers and Houses of Prostitution, Both in High and Low Life ... New York: Published for the proprietors, by C. G. Graham & Co., 1849." Deposited Aug. 12, 1848.

443a ——— ——— New York: W. F. Burgess, 1850. 85 p., illus. 8vo   AAS
Title reads the same as the deposit title page noted under No. 443.

BUCKINGHAM, EDWIN, *jt. au. See* P's and Q's, Nos. 2083-84

BUCKINGHAM, JOSEPH H., *jt. au.* *See* P's and Q's, Nos. 2083-84

BULL-US, HECTOR, *pseud.* *See* Paulding, James Kirke

444 BULLARD, ANNE TUTTLE (JONES). Louisa Ralston; or, What Can I Do for the Heathen . . . [anon.]. Boston, 1846.
Title from Cushing I, 395, giving author's name as Anna Tuthill (Jenkins) Bullard.

445 ———— The Reformation: A True Tale of the Sixteenth Century . . . [anon.]. Boston, 1841.
Title from Cushing II, 552.

446 ———— The Wife for a Missionary . . . [anon.]. Cincinnati: Truman, Smith and Co., 1834. 158 p. 12mo   AAS, N, UP, Y

447 ———— ———— 2d ed. Cincinnati: Truman and Smith, 1835. 158 p. 12mo   AAS, HEH, Y

448 ———— ———— 3d ed. Cincinnati: Truman and Smith, 1835. 158 p. 12mo   H

BUNTLINE, NED, *pseud.* *See* Judson, Edward Zane Carroll

449 BURDETT, CHARLES. Arthur Martin; or, The Mother's Trials . . . New York: Harper & Brothers [cop. 1847]. 225 p., illus. 12mo   AAS, HEH, LC, N, NYP, UV, Y
New York City; 183-.

450 ———— Chances and Changes; or, Life as It Is. Illustrated in the History of a Straw Hat . . . New York: D. Appleton & Co., 1846. 158 p. 12mo   AAS, HEH, LC, N, NYP, UV, Y
New York City.

450a ———— ———— New York: D. Appleton & Co., 1847. 158 p. 12mo   HEH

450b ———— ———— New York: D. Appleton & Co., 1849. 158 p. 12mo   AAS, UP

451 ———— The Convict's Child . . . New York: Baker and Scribner, 1846. 288 p. 12mo   LC, UP, UV
New York City.

452 ———— The Elliott Family; or, The Trials of New York Seam-
stresses . . . New York: E. Winchester, 1845. 162 p. 12mo
HEH, UV
At head of title: "The Wrongs of American Women—Part One."

453 ———— ———— Second Thousand. New York: E. Winchester,
1845. 162 p. 12mo Y
At head of title: "The Wrongs of American Women—Part One."

454 ———— ———— New York: Baker & Scribner, 1850. 162 p., illus.
12mo AAS, B, BP, HEH, N, NYH, NYP, Y

454a ———— Emma; or, The Lost Found; or, Reliance on God Rewarded . . . [anon.]. New York: Dayton & Newman, 1842.
193 p. 12mo HEH

455 ———— The Gambler; or, The Policeman's Story . . . New
York: Baker and Scribner, 1848. 179 p. 12mo
AAS, HEH, LC, N, NYP, UV, Y

456 ———— Lilla Hart: A Tale of New York . . . New York: Baker
and Scribner, 1846. 197 p. 12mo
AAS, B, HEH, LC, N, NYH, NYP, UV, Y
183-.

457 ———— Mary Grover; or, The Trusting Wife. A Domestic
Temperance Tale . . . New York: Harper and Brothers, 1848.
165 p. 8vo AAS, HEH, UV, Y

458 ———— Never Too Late . . . New York: D. Appleton & Co.,
1845. 180 p. 12mo AAS, HEH, NYH, NYP, UP, UV, Y
New York City; 18--.

458a ———— ———— New York: D. Appleton & Co., 1846. 180 p.
12mo N, Y
Eds. also published in 1847 and 1848 not seen.

458b THE BURGLAR'S COMPANION; or, Fatal Elopement of Sarah Williamson, the Misguided Victim of Artful Depravity. A Melancholy Tale of Truth . . . New York: Printed for George Watson, E. E. Barclay, and others, 1841. 24 p., illus. 8vo
H, HEH, N, NYP
Signed at end: "S—— W——."

459 BURLEIGH, GEORGE SHEPARD. Mason Hodges: A Tale of Our Village. By S. C. Merrick [pseud.]. Philadelphia: Merrihew & Thompson, printers, 1848. 36 p. 12mo   AAS, B, Y

BURLINGHAM, MARIA-ANN, *pseud. See* Spafford, Horatio Gates

BURNHAM, A. A.   *See* Stanwood, Avis A. (Burnham)

460 BURNHAM, GEORGE PICKERING. The Banker's Clerk; or, Lost and Found. A Story of Old England. By the "Young 'Un" [pseud.] . . . Boston: Hotchkiss & Co., 1850. 84 p. 8vo
AAS, NYP

461 ———— Gleanings from the Portfolio of the "Young 'Un" [pseud.]. A Series of Humorous Sketches . . . Boston: R. B. Fitts & Co., 1849. 142 p., illus. 12mo   AAS, BP, H, N, NYH, UV

461a ——— ——— 2d ed. Boston: R. B. Fitts & Co., 1849. 142 p., illus. 12mo   AAS

462 ——— ——— 3d ed. Boston: R. B. Fitts & Co., 1849. 142 p., illus. 12mo   AAS, B, BP, HM, IN, LC, UM

——— The Poisoned Chalice: A Story of Naples. *In* M. A. Clough, Paolina (1849), No. 552.

——— The Steamboat Captain Who Was Averse to Racing. *In* W. T. Porter, *ed.*, A Quarter Race in Kentucky (1847), Nos. 2063-64.

——— *jt. au. See* Durivage, Francis A. Stray Subjects . . . Being the Fugitive Offspring of the "Old 'Un" [pseud.] and the "Young 'Un" [pseud.] . . . Philadelphia, 1848, Nos. 886-887.

463 BURTON, WARREN. The District School as It Was. By One Who Went to It [anon.]. Boston: Carter, Hendee, and Co., 1833. 156 p. 12mo   AAS, BP, H, HEH, IN, LC, N, NYP, UP, UV, Y
Wilton, N. H.

464 ——— ——— New York: J. Orville Taylor, 1838. 156 p. 12mo   AAS, B, H, HEH, NYH, NYP, UV

465 ——— ——— Boston: Phillips, Sampson and Company, 1850.
206 p., illus. 12mo

AAS, B, BA, BP, H, HEH, IN, LC, N, NYH, NYP, UM, UV, Y

465a BURTON, WILLIAM EVANS. The Baronet's Daughter. And The
Secret Cell ... Boston: Henry L. Williams, 1845. 49 p. 8vo

HEH, NYP

466 ——— Waggeries and Vagaries. A Series of Sketches, Humorous and Descriptive . . . Philadelphia: Carey & Hart, 1848.
192 p., illus. 12mo   AAS, H, LC, NYP, UM, UV

467 BURTS, ROBERT. The Scourge of the Ocean: A Story of the Atlantic, by an Officer of the U. S. Navy ... [anon.]. Philadelphia: E. L. Carey & A. Hart, 1837. 2 vols. 12mo

AAS(V.2), HEH, N, UP, UV, Y

LC has a title page for Vol. II, deposited May 12, 1837.
American Revolution.

468 ——— ——— Philadelphia: Carey and Hart, 1847. 109 p.
8vo   AAS, HEH, LC, Y
Printed in double cols.

BUTLER, MRS. CAROLINE H. Emma Alton. *In* The Fountain and
the Bottle (1850), No. 996.

469 BUTLER, JAMES. Fortune's Foot-ball; or, The Adventures of
Mercutio. Founded on Matters of Fact . . . Harrisburgh,
Pennsylvania: Printed by John Wyeth, 1797-98. 2 vols. in 1.
12mo   AAS, H, HEH, IN, LC, N, NYP, NYS, UC, UP, UPI, UV, Y
Various countries; contemporary.

470 THE BUTTONWOODS; or, The Refugees of the Revolution. A Historical Sketch . . . By the Author of "Legends of the Revolution," "The Forest Inn"... Philadelphia: Martin E. Harmstead,
1849. 95 p. 8vo   BP, LC, UV
On cover: "Legends of the Revolution, No. I."
Printed in double cols.

470a CALHOUN, JOHN S. Life and Confession of Mary Jane Gordon,
Who Was ... Hung, on the 24th Day of February, 1847. For
the Murder of Jane Anderson, a Native of Vassalboro, Maine ...
Augusta [Me.]: Published for the author, 1847. 32 p., illus.
8vo   LC, NYH

470b ——— Life and Confession of Mary Jane Gordon, Who Was
. . . Hung, on the 24th Day of May, 1848 . . . Augusta: Pub-
lished for the author, 1848.   32 p., illus.   8vo
Not located.

470c ——— Life and Confession of Mary Jane Gordon, Who Was
. . . Hung, on the Twenty-Fourth Day of February, 1849, for
the Murder of Jane Anderson, a Native of Covington, Kentucky . . . Covington: Published by the author, 1849.   32 p.,
illus.   8vo   H, HEH, NYH

471 CALVERT, GEORGE HENRY.   A Volume from the Life of Herbert
Barclay [anon.].   Baltimore: William & Joseph Neal, 1833.
190 p.   12mo   AAS, H, HEH, IN, LC, NYP, UP, UV, Y

472 CAMBRIDGE, WILLIAM G.   Moral Tales and Sketches from Real
Life . . . Lowell: Printed and published for the author, 1842.
32 p.   8vo   Y
Contents: The Orphan—George and Caroline—Ellen Rose—The Lost Is
Found—Life, Death, Home: An Allegory.

473 CAMP CHARLOTTE: A Tale of 1774.   By a Member of the Bar.
Philadelphia: G. B. Zieber & Co., 1844. 39 p. 8vo   HEH, UV, Y
Printed in double cols.
Ohio Valley.

473a CAMPBELL, MRS. JANE C.   Catharine Clayton: A Tale of New
York . . . Boston: Gleason's Publishing Hall, 1846.   66 p.
8vo   UP
——— Steps to Ruin.   In The Fountain and the Bottle (1850),
No. 996.

474 CANNON, CHARLES JAMES.   Facts, Feelings, and Fancies . . .   New
York: Bliss, Wadsworth & Co., 1835.   191, [1] p.   12mo
                                             AAS, B, NYH, NYP, UV, Y
Contents: Remorse—Estelle—The Fratricide—The Real Fire—Amy Dayton
—Cousin Sue.

475 ——— Father Felix: A Tale . . . [anon.].   New York: Edward
Dunigan, 1845. 219 p.   12mo   UV, Y
Cushing refers to a New York, 1850 ed.

476 —— Harry Layden: A Tale . . . New York: John A. Boyle, 1842. 118 p. 8vo   Y
New York City.

477 —— Mora Carmody; or, Woman's Influence . . . [anon.]. New York: Edward Dunigan, 1844. 140 p. 12mo   LC

—— Oran, the Outcast (1833). *See* No. 1981 which is now identified as by Cannon.

478 —— Scenes and Characters from the Comedy of Life . . . [anon.]. New York: Edward Dunigan, 1847. 216 p. 12mo
B, LC
New York City.

479 CAPRICORN, CORNELIUS, *pseud.* Speculations on the Comet, by Cornelius Capricorn [pseud.] . . . New York: Printed by James Kelly, 1832. 43 p. 12mo   UP, UV, Y

480 CAREY, CHARLEY, *pseud.* The Lady of the Green and Blue; or, The Magic Figure Head. By Charley Carey [pseud.] of the United States Navy. Boston: George H. Williams, 1847. 103 p., illus. 8vo   H, LC
Printed in double cols.
American Revolution.

CARLTON, ROBERT, *Esq., pseud.* *See* Hall, Baynard Rush

481 CAROLINE HARGRAVE, the Merchant's Daughter: Being the First Series of the Mysteries of Salem! or, Modern Witchcraft. Salem: Varney, Parsons & Co., 1845. 36 p. 12mo   AAS, UV

482 DELETE.

483 CAROLINE TRACY, the Spring Street Milliner's Apprentice; or, Life in New York in 1847-8. Being the Narrative of Actual Occurrences Which Came to the Knowledge of a Young Physician of New York City. New York: Stearns & Co., 1849. 91 p., illus. 8vo   AAS, HEH, UV, Y
Also contains: The Sister-in-Law: A Tale of Real Life.
Printed in double cols.

483a ——— New York: W. F. Burgess. Cincinnati, Ohio: Burgess & Wood, 1849. 91 p., illus. 8vo   HEH

Also contains: The Sister-in-Law: A Tale of Real Life.

Printed in double cols.

HEH has second copy with imprint, New York: W. F. Burgess, 22 Ann-street [n.d.].

484 CARPENTER, WILLIAM HENRY. Claiborne the Rebel: A Romance of Maryland, under the Proprietary . . . New York: E. Ferrett & Co., 1845. 104 p. 8vo   HEH, LC, LCP, UV, Y

HEH front wrapper dated 1846.

Printed in double cols.

485 ——— Ruth Emsley, the Betrothed Maiden: A Tale of the Virginia Massacre . . . Philadelphia: A. Hart, 1850. 130 p. 12mo
LC, UV

486 THE CARPENTER AND HIS FAMILY. Also Pride Subdued . . . Boston: Light and Horton, 1835. 120 p. 12mo
AAS, BP, HEH, NYP, UP, Y

487 CARR, MARY. The Last Resource; or, Female Fortitude. A Novel, Founded on Recent Facts in the Western Parts of Pennsylvania. By a Lady of Philadelphia [anon.]. Philadelphia, 1809.

LC has a title page, deposited Oct. 13, 1809.

488 CARRA, EMMA, *pseud.* Estelle; or, The Castle of M'Anvah. A Tale of Domestic Life. By Emma Carra [pseud.] . . . Boston: F. Gleason [cop. 1848]. 100 p. 8vo   AAS

Printed in double cols.

LC has a title page, deposited Dec. 7, 1848.

489 ——— The Hermit of the Hudson; or, The Farmer's Daughter. A Tale of the Seventeenth Century. By Emma Carra [pseud.]. Boston: F. Gleason, 1848. 100 p. 8vo   NYP, Y

Also contains: The Seahawk; or, The Marshal's Daughter of the Baltic, by M. T. Gibbons—The Returned Prodigal; or, The Reward of Merit, by Lewis Gridley.

Printed in double cols.

490 —— A Tale of the West; or, Life with a Sister. By Emma
Carra [pseud.]. Providence: H. H. Brown, printer, 1846. 72
p. 8vo   AAS, UV, Y

491 —— Viroqua; or, The Flower of the Ottawas. A Tale of the
West. By Emma Carra [pseud.] ... Boston: F. Gleason [cop.
1848]. 100 p., illus. 8vo   AAS, H, HEH, Y
Printed in double cols.

492 CARTER, ST. LEGER LANDON. Nugae, by Nugator [pseud.]; or,
Pieces in Prose and Verse ... Baltimore: Printed by Woods
and Crane, 1844. 215 p. 12mo
                    AAS, B, BP, H, HEH, LC, N, NYH, NYP, UC, UP, UV, Y
Contains: March Court—The Sale—The Mechanician and Uncle Simon—
Sally Singleton—The Dyspeptic Man—Pinkney's Eloquence—Modern
Travelling—Great Rascally Dinner—The Oldfield School.

493 CARUTHERS, WILLIAM ALEXANDER. The Cavaliers of Virginia; or,
The Recluse of Jamestown. An Historical Romance of the
Old Dominion ... [anon.]. New York: Harper & Brothers,
1834-35. 2 vols. 12mo
                    AAS, BP, HEH, HM, IN, N, NYP, NYS(V.1), UC, UP, UV, Y

494 —— The Kentuckian in New York; or, The Adventures of
Three Southerns. By a Virginian ... [anon.]. New York:
Harper & Brothers, 1834. 2 vols. 12mo
                    AAS, BP, H, HEH, IN, LC, N, NYH, NYP, UC, UP, UV, Y
Related principally by letters.
18--.

495 —— The Knights of the Horseshoe: A Traditionary Tale of
the Cocked Hat Gentry in the Old Dominion ... [anon.]. We-
tumpka, Alabama: Printed and published by Charles Yancey,
1845. 248 p. 8vo   HEH, IN, N, NYP, UP, UV, Y

CARVER, JOHN, pseud. See Dodge, Nathaniel Shatswell

CASENDER, DON PEDRO, pseud. See Smith, Michael

496 CASSIMER SARAL: A Tale ... Charleston: W. Riley, 1835. 264 p.
12mo   HEH
Attributed to Bernard H. Reynolds by T. Hunt, Le Roman Américain,
1830-1850 (1937), p. 200.
War of 1812.

496a THE CASTLE OF ALTENHEIM; or, The Mysterious Monk. A Tale
... Philadelphia: A. I. Dickinson, 1836. 173 p. 12mo LCP
Time of the Holy Roman Empire.

496b —— Philadelphia: J. Van Court, printer; New York: Burgess,
Stringer & Co., 1845. 112 p. 8vo AAS, Y
Title reads: *The Mysterious Monk; or, The Castle of Altenheim.*

497 THE CATASTROPHE: A Tale of the Nineteenth Century. Lowell:
Rand & Southmayd, 1833. 18 p. 12mo AAS, H, LC, NYP

498 CATE, ELIZA JANE. A Year with the Franklins; or, To Suffer and
Be Strong ... New York: Harper & Brothers, 1846. 276 p.
12mo AAS, H, HEH, LC, N, UP, UV, Y
Newburyport; contemporary.

499 CAUDLE, JOB, *pseud.* Job Caudle's Dinner-Table Harangues. Re-
vealed in Self-Defence, by the Ghost of Mrs. Caudle. New
York: E. Winchester, 1845. 32 p. 8vo
AAS, B, BA, NYP, UC, UV, Y

CAULDWELL, T. H. History of Lorenzo and Virginia; or, Virtue
Rewarded (1834). *See* No. 1206.
This is a plagiarism of *The History of Constantius & Pulchera; or, Con-
stancy Rewarded,* first published in 1795.

500 CELADON, *pseud.* The Golden Age; or, Future Glory of North
America Discovered by an Angel to Celadon, in Several Entertaining Visions ... By Celadon [pseud.]. [N.p.]: Printed in
the year 1785. 16 p. 8vo LC

501 THE CHAMELEON; or, The Mysterious Cruiser! By an Old Salt,
Author of "The Meteor." New York: Smith, Adams & Smith,
1848. 96 p. 8vo LC, Y
Also contains: Arnold; or, The British Spy, by J. H. Ingraham.
Printed in double cols.

502 CHANGING SCENES, Containing a Description of Men and Manners
of the Present Day, with Humourous Details of the Knickerbockers ... By a Lady of New York ... New York: Printed
for the author, 1825. 2 vols. 12mo
B(v.2), HEH, LC, N, NYH(v.1), UV

503 CHAPIN, WILLIAM. Village Sketches; or, Tales of Somerville . . . [anon.]. Norristown, Pa.: Printed by David Sower, Jr., 1825. 154 p. 12mo   AAS, H, HEH, LC, LCP, N, NYP, UC, UP, UPI, UV, Y
Contents: Somerville—The Marriage—Childhood—The Mother—Friends Meeting—The Village Grave-yard—The Love Adventures of Tom Lumpkin—The Storm—Letter Writing—Mary Irvine—The Prisoner—The Poor Debtor—The Evening Visit.

504 CHEEVER, GEORGE BARRELL. The Dream; or, The True History of Deacon Giles's Distillery, and Deacon Jones's Brewery . . . [anon.]. New York and Boston: Printed for the publishers [184-?]. 32 p., illus. 8vo   AAS, NYP, UP, UV

505 ———— ———— New York, 1844. 48 p., illus. 8vo
B, H, LC, NYP, UM
Title reads: *The True History of Deacon Giles' Distillery.*

506 ———— ———— New York: Printed for the publishers, 1846. 24 p., illus. 8vo   AAS, B, BP, HEH, NYP, Y

507 ———— ————' New York: Printed for the publishers, 1848. 31 p., illus. 8vo   AAS, B, N, UM, Y

508 ———— The Hill Difficulty, and Some Experiences of Life in the Plains of Ease, With Other Miscellanies . . . New York: John Wiley, 1849. 383 p., illus. 8vo
AAS, B, H, HEH, LC, LCP, N, NYH, NYP, UM, UP, UV, Y

———— The True History of Deacon Giles' Distillery. *See* No. 505.

509 CHEEVER, HENRY P. The Rival Brothers; or, The Corsair and Privateer. A Tale of the Last War . . . Boston: Gleason's Publishing Hall, 1845. 66 p., illus. 8vo   AAS, BP, H, HEH, UV, Y

509a ———— ———— Boston: H. L. Williams, 1845. 57 p., illus. 8vo
Y
Printed in double cols.

510 ———— The Witch of the Wave; or, The Corsair's Captive . . . Boston: F. Gleason, 1847. 100 p., illus. 8vo   H, NYP, Y
At head of title: "100 Dollar Prize Tale."
Printed in double cols.

511 CHENEY, HARRIET VAUGHAN (FOSTER). Confessions of an Early Martyr... Boston: Benjamin H. Greene, 1846. 141 p. 12mo
BP, UM

512 ——— A Peep at the Pilgrims in Sixteen Hundred Thirty-Six: A Tale of Olden Times . . . [anon.]. Boston: Wells and Lilly, 1824. 2 vols. 12mo   AAS, B, H, LC, NYS, UM, UP, UV, Y

513 ——— ——— 2d ed. Boston: Wells and Lilly, 1826. 2 vols. 12mo   B, BP, NYP, UM, UP, Y

514 ——— ——— Boston: Phillips, Sampson and Company, 1850. 463 p. 12mo   AAS, BA, BP, H, HEH, IN, LCP, NYP, UC, UM, Y

515 ——— The Rivals of Acadia: An Old Story of the New World . . . [anon.]. Boston: Wells and Lilly, 1827. 271 p. 12mo
AAS, B, BA, BP, H, HEH, LC, N, UC, UM, UV, Y

CHILD, LYDIA MARIA (FRANCIS). The Church in the Wilderness. *In* N. P. Willis, *ed.*, The Legendary (1828), No. 2739.

516 ——— The Coronal: A Collection of Miscellaneous Pieces . . . Boston: Carter and Hendee, 1832. 285 p., illus. 18mo
AAS, BA, BP, H, HEH, IN, LC, N, NYH, NYP, UC, UM, UP, UV, Y
Contains: The Lone Indian—The Sagacious Papa: A Hint for Those in Similar Circumstances—The Rival Brothers: A Tale of the Revolution—La Rosiere; or, The Triumph of Goodness—The Recluse of the Lake—Harriet Bruce—The Bold and Beautiful Convict—The Indian Wife—Stand from Under—The Adventures of a Rain Drop—The Young West-Indian—Chocorua's Curse.

517 ——— Fact and Fiction: A Collection of Stories . . . New York: C. S. Francis & Co., 1846. 282 p. 12mo
AAS, BA, H, HEH, IN, LC, LCP, N, NYH, NYS, UC, UP, UV, Y
Contents: The Children of Mount Ida—The Youthful Emigrant: A True Story of the Early Settlement of New Jersey—The Quadroons—The Irish Heart: A True Story—A Legend of the Apostle John—The Beloved Tune—Elizabeth Wilson—The Neighbour-in-Law—She Waits in the Spirit Land: A Romance Founded on an Indian Tradition—A Poet's Dream of the Soul—The Black Saxons—Hilda Silfverling: A Fantasy—Rosenglory—A Legend of the Falls of St. Anthony: Founded on Indian Tradition—The Brothers.

518 ——— ——— New York: C. S. Francis & Co., 1847. 282 p. 12mo   AAS, B, BP, H, IN, LC, NYP, UM, UV, Y

519 ———— ———— New York: C. S. Francis & Co., 1849. 282 p.
12mo   AAS, BP, NYP, UP, Y

520 ———— Hobomok: A Tale of Early Times. By an American ...
[anon.]. Boston: Cummings, Hilliard & Co., 1824. 188 p.
12mo   AAS, BA, BP, H, HEH, IN, LC, N, NYP, UC, UM, UP, UV, Y
Massachusetts; 1630.

———— The Indian Wife. *In* N. P. Willis, *ed.*, The Legendary
(1828), No. 2739.

521 ———— Letters from New-York . . . New York: Charles S.
Francis and Company, 1843. 276 p. 12mo
       AAS, B, BA, BP, H, HEH, IN, LC, N, NYH, NYP, NYS, UC, UP, UV, Y
Tales, essays, etc.

522 ———— ———— 2d ed. New York: C. S. Francis and Company,
1844. 288 p. 12mo   AAS, B, BP, H, HEH, IN, NYH

523 ———— ———— 3d ed. New York: C. S. Francis & Co., 1845.
288 p. 12mo   AAS, H, LC, NYP, UC, UP, UV, Y

524 ———— ———— 3d ed. New York: C. S. Francis & Co., 1846.
288 p. 12mo   AAS, UC, Y

525 ———— ———— 3d ed. New York: C. S. Francis & Co., 1847.
288 p. 12mo   AAS

526 ———— ———— 9th ed. New York: C. S. Francis & Co., 1848.
288 p. 12mo   H, HEH, LC, UP

527 ———— ———— 10th ed. New York: C. S. Francis & Co., 1849.
288 p. 12mo   AAS, H

528 ———— ———— 11th ed. New York: C. S. Francis & Co., 1850.
288 p. 12mo   AAS, NYH, NYP, UP, Y

529 ———— ———— Second Series. New York: C. S. Francis & Co.,
1845. 287 p. 12mo
       AAS, B, BA, BP, H, HEH, LC, N, NYH, NYP, NYS, UC, UM, UP, UV, Y

530 ———— ———— Second Series. New York: C. S. Francis & Co., 1846. 287 p. 12mo AAS, IN, NYP, UC, Y

530a ———— ———— Second Series. New York: C. S. Francis & Co., 1847. 287 p. 12mo AAS

531 ———— ———— Second Series. 5th ed. New York: C. S. Francis & Co., 1848. 287 p. 12mo HEH, Y

532 ———— ———— Second Series. 10th ed. New York: C. S. Francis & Co., 1849. 287 p. 12mo H, Y

533 ———— ———— Second Series. 11th ed. New York: C. S. Francis & Co., 1850. 287 p. 12mo AAS, IN, NYH, UP, Y

534 ———— Philothea: A Romance . . . Boston: Otis, Broaders & Co., 1836. 284 p. 12mo
AAS, BA, BP, H, HEH, IN, N, NYH, NYP, UP, UV, Y
Grecian classical times.

535 ———— ———— 2d ed. Boston: Otis, Broaders & Company, 1839. 284 p. 12mo AAS, BP, H, LC, UM

536 ———— ———— New ed. New York: C. S. Francis & Co., 1845. 290 p. 12mo AAS, B, BP, H, HEH, IN, NYS, UC, UM, UP, UV, Y

537 ———— ———— New ed. New York: C. S. Francis & Co., 1848. 290 p. 12mo B, H, Y

538 ———— The Rebels; or, Boston before the Revolution . . . [anon.]. Boston: Cummings, Hilliard and Company, 1825. 304 p. 12mo
AAS, B, BA, BP, H, HEH, IN, LC, N, NYP, UC, UM, UP, UV, Y

539 ———— ———— Boston: Phillips, Sampson & Company, 1850. 287 p. 12mo
AAS, BA, BP, H, HEH, IN, LC, N, NYH, NYP, NYS, UC, UP, Y

540 CHILDE, EDWARD VERNON. Edward Vernon: My Cousin's Story . . . New York: Harper & Brothers, 1848. 194 p. 12mo
AAS, B, LC, NYP, Y

541 CHINTZ, CHARLEY, *pseud.* The Gem of the Mines; or, The Conjuror of Iron Cave. By Charley Chintz [pseud.]. Springfield: William B. Brockett, 1845. 64 p. 8vo   AAS, B, N, UM, Y
Vermont.

CHIPMAN, H. G. An Appeal to Heaven. *In* J. H. Robinson, Kosato (1850), No. 2136.

542 CHIPMAN, J. L. George Pembleton; or, Love and Hate . . . Boston: F. Gleason, 1848. 50 p. 8vo   AAS, H, UV, Y
"Axel"; 184-.

543 THE CHRISTIAN INDIAN; or, Times of the First Settlers . . . New York: Collins and Hannay, 1825. 251 p. 12mo
AAS, B, BA, BP, H, HEH, IN, LC, LCP, N, NYH, NYP, UC, UM, UP, Y

544 A CHRONICLE OF LOUISIANA: Being an Account of One of the Wars of Don Diego Rosa, Called He, of the Iron Arm, the Last Catholic Governor of That Province. Paraphrased from the Spanish of the Learned Doctor Frai Pedro Prado. New York: Linen & Fennell, 1838. 87 p., illus. 8vo   AAS, BA, LC, UV

CHUBBUCK, EMILY. *See* Judson, Emily (Chubbuck)

544a CHUMASERO, JOHN C. The Landlord and Tenant: A Tale of the Present Day, Founded on Facts . . . [anon.]. Rochester: D. M. Dewey; W. H. Beach, 1845. 39 p. 8vo   UV

544b ——— Laura, the Sicilian Girl: A Tale of Sicily . . . [anon.]. Rochester, William H. Beach, 1845. 40 p. 8vo
Copy located in the Rochester Historical Society.

544c ——— Life in Rochester; or, Sketches from Life. Being Scenes of Misery, Vice, Shame, and Oppression in the City of the Genesee. By a Resident Citizen . . . [anon.]. Rochester, New York: D. M. Dewey, 1848. 100 p., illus. 8vo N, NYH, NYP, UV

544d ——— The Mysteries of Rochester . . . Rochester: William H. Beach, 1845. 6 pts. (192 p.) 8vo   UV, Y
Printed in double cols.

544e ———— ———— 2d ed.   Rochester: William H. Beach, 1845.   6 pts. (192 p.)   8vo

Copy located in the Rochester Historical Society.

545 CLARK, LEWIS GAYLORD, *ed.*   The Knickerbocker Sketch-book: A Library of Select Literature . . .   New York: Burgess, Stringer and Company, 1845.   243 p.   12mo

AAS, BA, BP, HEH, N, NYH, NYP, NYS, UC, UM, UP, UV, Y

Contains: The First Locomotive—The First Locomotive Again, by Irving—The Early Experiences of Ralph Ringwood, by Irving—Peter Cram; or, The Row at Tinnecum: A Sketch of Long Island, by Frederick W. Shelton—Guests from Gibbett-Island: A Legend of Communipaw, by W. Irving—The Iron Foot-step—Mountjoy; or, Some Passages Out of the Life of a Castle-Builder, by W. Irving—The Married Man's Eye.

CLARK, WILLIS GAYLORD.   Everard Graham.   *In* W. Fields, Jr., *comp.*, The Literary and Miscellaneous Scrap Book (1833), Nos. 956-957.

546 ———— The Literary Remains of the Late Willis Gaylord Clark, Including the Ollapodiana Papers, The Spirit of Life, and a Selection from His Various Prose and Poetical Writings.   Edited by Lewis Gaylord Clark.   New York: Burgess, Stringer & Co., 1844.   480 p.   8vo

AAS, B, BP, H, HEH, IN, LC, LCP, N, NYH, NYP, UC, UM, UP, UV, Y

Issued originally in 5 pts. with the title page in Pt. I only. See BAL 3282.

547 ———— ———— New York: Burgess, Stringer & Co., 1847.   480 p.   8vo   AAS, B, Y

548 CLARKE, HENRY A.   The War Scout of Eighteen Hundred Twelve . . .   Chicago, Ill.: W. W. Danenhower, 1850.   92 p.   8vo

Title from D. C. McMurtrie, "Books and Pamphlets Printed in Chicago, 1835-1850," *Bull. of the Chicago Historical Society*, 2nd Ser., I (1935), 121.

CLAVERS, MRS. MARY, *pseud.*   *See* Kirkland, Caroline Matilda (Stansbury)

548a CLEVELAND, ALICE.   Grace Loveland; or, The Blind Man's Dream. A Tale of Love . . .   Boston: Gleason's Publishing Hall, 1846. 100 p.   8vo   Y

Also contains: The Black Valley—Going into the Country Cures Baldness—Wooing, Wedding & Repenting.

Printed in double cols.

549 —— Lucy Morley; or, The Young Officer. A Tale of the Texan Revolution... Boston: Gleason's Publishing Hall, 1846. 100 p. 8vo   B, H
Also contains: The Haunted Castle, pp. [42]-100.
Printed in double cols.

550 CLEWLINE, FRANK, *pseud*. The Nautilus; or, The American Privateer. A Tale of Land and Sea during the Last War. By Frank Clewline [pseud.]. Boston: F. Gleason, 1847. 50 p. 8vo   LC

551 CLOPPER, JONAS. Fragments of the History of Bawlfredonia: Containing an Account of the Discovery and Settlement of That Great Southern Continent: And of the Formation and Progress of the Bawlfredonian Commonwealth. By Herman Thwackius [pseud.] ... [Baltimore?]: Printed for the American booksellers, 1819. 164 p., illus. 8vo
AAS, B, BA, BP, H, HEH, IN, LC, LCP, N, NYH, NYP, UM, UP, UV, Y

551a CLOUGH, MARTHA ANN. Annie Merrivale; or, The Test of Love ... Boston: Published at the Yankee Nation Office, 138½ Washington Street [1850]. 48 p. 8vo   UV
Also contains: Cecelia; or, Woman's Love, by J. H. Robinson—The Old Man's Bequest: A Story of Gold.
Cover imprint: "Boston: Published by Isaac Crooker," etc., n.d.
Printed in double cols.
Advertised as "Just published" on the back cover of No. 3126.

552 —— Paolina; or, The Sybil of the Arno. A Tale of the Time of Cosmo III ... Boston: F. Gleason's Publishing Hall, 1849. 280 p., illus. 8vo   B, HEH, IN, Y
At head of title: "Gleason's Series of Prize Tales, No. 2."
Also contains: Rosalie de Clairville: A Legend of the Olden Days of France, by Francis A. Durivage—The Poisoned Chalice: A Story of Naples, by Geo. P. Burnham—The Secret Panel; or, The Spirit of Hartz Mountains, by Sylvanus Cobb, Jr.—The Blue Velvet Bonnet: A Parisian Tale, by Fred Hunter —A Sailor's Love; or, The Dangers of the Sea, by Capt. Robert Barnacle [pseud.].
Cancel slip, pasted on imprint in B copy, reads: "Dimond & Connolly's Cheap Book & Stationery Store. No. 1 Ann Street, opp. Herald office. New York."

553 —— Zuleika; or, The Castilian Captive. A Romance of the Time of Ferdinand and Isabella ... Boston: F. Gleason, 1849. 100 p. 8vo   AAS, HEH, UP, UV, Y
Printed in double cols.

553a COBB, ENOS. Fame and Fancy; or, Voltaire Improved. Containing the Story of Candide—Revised . . . By Lord Hail-Fair [pseud.] . . . Boston, 1826. 2 vols., illus. 12mo

AAS, B, BP, H, HEH, LC, N, NYP, UC, UP, UV, Y

554 COBB, JOSEPH BECKHAM. The Creole; or, Siege of New Orleans. An Historical Romance, Founded on the Events of 1814-15 . . . Philadelphia: A. Hart, 1850. 131 p. 8vo

AAS, H, HM, LC, NYS, UV

———— "Glorious." In W. T. Porter, ed., A Quarter Race in Kentucky (1847), Nos. 2063-64.

———— Uncle Billy Brown. In W. T. Porter, ed., A Quarter Race in Kentucky (1847), Nos. 2063-64.

555 COBB, SYLVANUS, JR. Drosendorf; or, The Wild Mountain Chieftain. A Moravian Tale of Bygone Times . . . New York: Samuel French, 151 Nassau [1850?]. 100 p. 8vo   UM, UV

556 ———— The Golden Eagle; or, The Privateer of '76. A Tale of the Revolution . . . Boston: F. Gleason, 1850. 100 p. 8vo

LC, UV, Y

Also contains: The Peasant Countess; or, The Wolf of Montauban. Printed in double cols.

557 ———— ———— New York: Samuel French, 151 Nassau [cop. 1850]. 100 p. 8vo

Y

Also contains: Ida Gould; or, A Sunbeam in a Dark Place, by Miss Harriet N. Hathaway. Printed in double cols.

558 ———— The Prophet of the Bohmer Wald; or, The Venetian Buccaneer. A Tale of the Times of Joseph II, Emperor of Germany . . . Boston: F. Gleason, 1850. 100 p., illus. 8vo

AAS, B, UP, UV, Y

Also contains: The French Guardsman, by Francis A. Durivage. Printed in double cols.

———— The Secret Panel; or, The Spirit of Hartz Mountains. *In* M. A. Clough, Paolina (1849), No. 552.

———— The Tattler; or, The Friends' Misunderstanding. *In* M. M. Ballou, Fanny Campbell [cop. 1844], No. 238.

559 CODMAN, JOHN. Sailors' Life and Sailors' Yarns. By Captain Ringbolt [pseud.]. New York: C. S. Francis & Co., 1847. 252 p. 12mo   AAS, BP, H, HEH, IN, LC, N, NYH, NYP, UP, UV, Y

Contents: A Sailor's Life—Nathan Smith; or, The Man That Was Laughed At—Captain Dodge—The Pretty Missionary—Tom Brown; or, Superstition —Harry Spanker's Love Story—Charley Brail's True Story—David Williams, the Steward—A Bargain's a Bargain—The Old Sailor—Vessels in Distress— Sailors' Rights and Sailors' Wrongs.

560 COLE, EMMA, *pseud.* The Life and Sufferings of Miss Emma Cole, Being a Faithful Narrative of Her Life. Written by Herself. Boston: M. Aurelius, 1844. 36 p., illus. 12mo

AAS, HEH, N, NYH, NYP, UV, Y

Two printings noted: (1) verso of title page, "A. J. Wright, printer, Boston."; (2) "Mead and Beal, printers, Boston." Census does not distinguish between them.

Bangor, Boston, etc.; late 18th cent.

561 —————— 2d ed. Boston: M. Aurelius, 1844. 36 p., illus. 12mo   AAS, BA, IN, LC, UC, UP, Y

561a —————— 3d ed. Boston: M. Aurelius, 1844. 36 p., illus. 12mo   HEH

562 —————— 5th ed. Boston: M. Aurelius, 1844. 36 p., illus. 12mo   AAS, H, Y

563 A COLLECTION OF MORAL AND ENTERTAINING STORIES, Calculated for the Instruction and Entertainment of Youth. Containing: I, Story of Frank Leeson; II, Florio, an Affecting Story; III, Story of Edward and Maria; IV, The Generosity of an Injured Daughter; V, Fraternal Affection; VI, The Remarkable Duel. Printed at Northampton, 1798. 80+ p. 16mo   AAS

With this is bound and was issued: *The New Pygmalion, a Novel. To Which Is Added: Amelia; or, The Faithless Briton . . .* Northampton: Printed by Andrew Wright, 1798.

564 COMFIELD, AMELIA (STRATTON). Alida; or, Miscellaneous Sketches of Occurrences during the Late American War. Founded on Fact . . . [anon.]. New York: Printed for the author, 1841. 222 p., illus. 12mo   AAS, B, BA, LC, UP

565 —————— 2d ed. New York: Printed for the author, 1841. 222 p., illus. 12mo   AAS, BA, Y

566 —————— ————— 3d ed. New York: Printed for the author, 1841. 244 p., illus. 12mo   AAS, B, HEH, NYH, NYP, UV, Y
Beginning with this ed., "Occurrences" in title changed to "Incidents."

567 —————— ————— 4th ed. New York: Printed for the author by Angell & Engel, 1849. 240 p., illus. 12mo
AAS, B, BP, H, IN, LC, NYH, NYP, NYS, UM, Y

568 COMSTOCK, WILLIAM. The Life of Samuel Comstock, the Terrible Whaleman. Containing an Account of the Mutiny, and Massacre of the Officers of the Ship Globe, of Nantucket; with His Subsequent Adventures, and His Being Shot at the Mulgrave Islands . . . Boston: James Fisher, 1840. 115 p., illus. 12mo   BP, LC, UV

568a CONARD, JESSE. The Secrets of Mount Echo; or, Mother's Mysteries. An American Romance. By Jesse Conard, Esq., Author of "Stephen Morland." Cincinnati: Robinson & Jones, 1848. 121 p. 8vo   UV
Printed in double cols.

————— Stephen Moreland (1834). See No. 2494 which is now identified as by Conard.

569 THE CONFESSION OF A RUM-SELLER. By the Author of "Passing Thoughts." Boston: Printed by Lothrop and Bense, 1845. 24 p. 12mo   BP

569a CONFESSIONS OF A FEMALE INEBRIATE; or, Intemperance in High Life. By a Lady. Founded on Fact . . . Boston: William Henshaw, 1842. 36 p. 12mo   AAS, UP

570 THE CONFESSIONS OF A MAGNETISER. Being an Expose of Animal Magnetism. Boston: Gleason's Publishing Hall, 1845. 50 p. 8vo   AAS, HEH, N, UP, Y

571 CONFESSIONS OF A REFORMED INEBRIATE... New York: American Temperance Union, 1844. 180 p. 16mo   HEH, NYP, UV

572 ————— New York: American Temperance Union, 1848. 180 p. 16mo   NYP

573 CONKEY, MRS. M. The Perennial Flower; or, Virtue's Conquest:
An Authentic Narrative . . . New York: A. S. Gould, 1841.
320 p. 12mo NYP, UM, UV

574 CONSTANCE; or, The Merchant's Daughter. A Tale of Our Times
. . . New York: Gould, Newman and Saxton, 1841. 160 p.
12mo AAS, HEH, N, UP, UV, Y
Written by John Walker Brown.
New York City.

575 ———— 2d ed. New York: Dayton and Saxton, 1841. 162 p.
12mo AAS, N, NYP, UP, Y

576 ———— New York: Mark H. Newman, 1843. 160 p. 12mo
AAS

577 THE CONSUL'S DAUGHTER, and Other Interesting Stories . . . New
York: Nafis and Cornish, 278 Pearl Street [cop. 1841]. 191 p.,
illus. 12mo AAS, HEH, NYP, Y
S. G. Goodrich denied authorship in his *Recollections of a Lifetime* (1857),
II, 550.

578 CONWAY, WILLIAM B. The Cottage on the Cliff: A Tale of the
Revolution . . . Ebensburg, Pa.: Printed by James Morgan,
1838. 144 p. 16mo BP, HEH, LC, UC, UPI
Delaware.

579 COOPER, JAMES FENIMORE. Afloat and Ashore; or, The Adventures of Miles Wallingford . . . [anon.]. Philadelphia: Published by the author, 1844. 4 vols. in 2. 12mo
AAS, BP, H, HEH, LC, LCP, N, NYH, NYP, UC, UM, UP, Y
Two printings noted: (1) verso of title pages of Vols. I-II, "J. Fagan, stereotyper; C. Sherman, printer"; (2) "J. Fagan, stereotyper; T. K. and P. G.
Collins, printers." Census does not distinguish between the printings.
Vols. III-IV also issued with imprint: "New York: Published for the author,
and for sale by Burgess, Stringer & Co., 1844."

579a ———— ———— New York: Stringer & Townsend, 1850. 2 vols.
in 1. 12mo H

580 ———— The Bravo: A Tale . . . [anon.]. Philadelphia: Carey &
Lea, 1831. 2 vols. 12mo
AAS, B, BA, BP, H, HEH, IN, LC, LCP, N, NYH, NYP, UC, UM, UP, UV, Y
Some copies of Vol. II dated 1832.
Venice.

581 ———— ———— Philadelphia: Carey & Lea, 1833.   2 vols.   12mo
AAS, H, Y(V.2)

581a ———— ———— Philadelphia: Carey, Lea & Blanchard, 1835.   2
vols.   12mo
AAS, UV, Y

582 ———— ———— Philadelphia: Carey, Lea & Blanchard, 1836.   2
vols.   12mo
AAS, H, LCP, NYP, UC

583 ———— ———— Philadelphia: Carey, Lea & Blanchard, 1838.   2
vols.   12mo
B, BP, Y

584 ———— ———— Philadelphia: Lea & Blanchard, 1840.   2 vols.
12mo
Y
Spiller & Blackburn list an 1841-42 ed.

585 ———— ———— Philadelphia: Lea & Blanchard, 1843.   2 vols. in
1.   12mo
AAS, NYP

586 ———— ———— New York: Stringer & Townsend, 1849.   2 vols.
in 1.   12mo
HEH, NYP

587 ———— The Chainbearer; or, The Littlepage Manuscripts . . .
[anon.].   New York: Burgess, Stringer & Co., 1845.   2 vols.
12mo   AAS, BP, H, HEH, LC, LCP, N, NYH, NYP, UM, UP, UV, Y
New York; last quarter of 18th cent.

588 ———— The Crater; or, Vulcan's Peak.   A Tale of the Pacific . . .
[anon.].   New York: Burgess, Stringer & Co., 1847.   2 vols.
12mo   AAS, B, H, HEH, IN, LC, LCP, N, NYP, UM, UP, UV, Y

589 ———— The Deerslayer; or, The First Warpath . . . [anon.].
Philadelphia: Lea & Blanchard, 1841.   2 vols.   12mo
AAS, BA, BP, H, HEH, IN, LC, N, NYP, UM, UP, UV, Y
New York; 1740-45.

590 ———— ———— Philadelphia: Lea & Blanchard, 1845.   2 vols.
12mo
AAS, NYP

590a ———— ———— Philadelphia: Lea & Blanchard, 1846.   2 vols.
12mo
AAS(V.1), Y

591 —————— ————— Philadelphia: Lea & Blanchard, 1849. 2 vols. in
1. 12mo   LCP

592 —————— ————— New York: Stringer and Townsend, 1849. 2 vols.
in 1. 12mo   NYP

593 —————— ————— New York: George P. Putnam, 1850. 12mo
Ed. from *Cat. of the Library of the Boston Athenaeum* (1874), I, 669.

594 —————— The Headsman; or, The Abbaye des Vignerons . . .
[anon.]. Philadelphia: Carey, Lea & Blanchard, 1833. 2 vols.
12mo   AAS, BA, BP, H, HEH, HM, IN, LC, N, NYH, NYP, UM, UP, UV, Y
Switzerland; early 18th cent.

594a —————— ————— Philadelphia: Carey, Lea & Blanchard, 1835. 2
vols. 12mo   AAS

595 —————— ————— Philadelphia: Carey, Lea & Blanchard, 1836. 2
vols. 12mo   AAS, H, HEH, LCP, UC, UM, Y

596 —————— ————— Philadelphia: Carey, Lea & Blanchard, 1838. 2
vols. 12mo   NYP, Y

597 —————— ————— Philadelphia: Lea and Blanchard, 1839. 2 vols.
12mo   AAS, BP, UV, Y

597a —————— ————— Philadelphia: Lea and Blanchard, 1841. 2 vols.
12mo   N

598 —————— ————— Philadelphia: Lea and Blanchard, 1843. 2 vols.
12mo   AAS, B, H, Y

599 —————— ————— Philadelphia: Lea and Blanchard, 1848-49. 2
vols. in 1. 12mo   HEH, NYH, NYP
Vol. II imprint: "New York: Stringer & Townsend, 1849."

600 —————— ————— New York: George P. Putnam, 1850.
Information from an old LCP card.

601 —————— The Heidenmauer; or, The Benedictines. A Legend of
the Rhine . . . [anon.]. Philadelphia: Carey & Lea, 1832. 2
vols. 12mo
              AAS, B, BA, BP, H, HEH, IN, LC, LCP, N, NYP, UM, UP, UV, Y
16th cent.

602 —————— ——— Philadelphia: Carey, Lea & Blanchard, 1834. 2 vols. 12mo NYP(V.1)

602a —————— ——— Philadelphia: Carey, Lea & Blanchard, 1835. 2 vols. 12mo AAS

603 —————— ——— Philadelphia: Carey, Lea & Blanchard, 1836. 2 vols. in 1. 12mo AAS, H, LCP, NYP, UC, UP, Y

604 —————— ——— Philadelphia: Carey, Lea & Blanchard, 1838. 2 vols. 12mo Y

605 —————— ——— Philadelphia: Lea & Blanchard, 1839. 2 vols. 12mo AAS

606 —————— ——— Philadelphia: Lea & Blanchard, 1840. 2 vols. 12mo AAS, Y

607 —————— ——— Philadelphia: Lea & Blanchard, 1841. 2 vols. in 1. 12mo AAS, H, N, NYP, Y

608 —————— ——— Philadelphia: Lea & Blanchard, 1848. 2 vols. 12mo NYH

609 —————— ——— New York: Stringer & Townsend, 1849. 2 vols. in 1. 12mo HEH, NYP

610 —————— Home as Found . . . [anon.]. Philadelphia: Lea & Blanchard, 1838. 2 vols. 12mo
AAS, B, BA, BP, H, HEH, IN, LC, LCP, N, NYH, NYP, NYS, UC, UM, UP, UV, Y
New York City; contemporary.

610a —————— ——— Philadelphia: Lea & Blanchard, 1848. 2 vols. 12mo AAS

611 —————— ——— New York: Stringer and Townsend, 1849. 2 vols. in 1. 12mo AAS, H, N, NYP

612 —————— Homeward Bound; or, The Chase. A Tale of the Sea . . . [anon.]. Philadelphia: Carey, Lea & Blanchard, 1838. 2 vols. 12mo
AAS, BP, H, HEH, HM, IN, LC, LCP, N, NYP, UC, UM, UP, UPI, UV, Y

85

613 —— —— A New Ed. Philadelphia: Carey, Lea & Blanchard, 1838. 2 vols. 12mo   AAS, H, LCP, NYP, UP, UV

614 —— —— Philadelphia: Lea & Blanchard, 1841. 2 vols.
12mo   AAS

615 —— —— Philadelphia: Lea & Blanchard, 1842. 2 vols.
12mo   AAS, HEH, N, NYP, UP, Y
HEH and NYP cover titles dated 1843.

615a —— —— New York: Burgess, Stringer & Co., 1845. 2 vols.
12mo   AAS, Y

615b —— —— New York: Stringer & Townsend, 1849. 2 vols.
in 1. 12mo   AAS, H, Y

616 —— —— New York: Stringer and Townsend, 1850. 2
vols. in 1. 12mo   N, Y

617 —— Jack Tier; or, The Florida Reef ... [anon.]. New York:
Burgess, Stringer & Co., 1848. 2 vols. 12mo
        AAS, BP, HEH, LC, LCP, N, NYH, NYP, UM, UP, Y
1840's.

618 —— —— New York: Stringer and Townsend, 1850. 2
vols. in 1. 12mo   AAS, NYP

619 —— The Last of the Mohicans: A Narrative of 1757 . . .
[anon.]. Philadelphia: H. C. Carey & I. Lea, 1826. 2 vols.
12mo
AAS(V.1), BA, BP, H, HEH, IN(V.1), LC, N, NYH, NYP, UM, UP, UV, Y
New York.

620 —— —— 2d ed. Philadelphia: H. C. Carey & I. Lea, 1826.
2 vols. 12mo   AAS, IN, Y

621 —— —— 3d ed. Philadelphia: H. C. Carey & I. Lea, 1827-
28. 2 vols. 12mo   AAS, Y

622 —— —— 4th ed. Philadelphia: H. C. Carey & I. Lea, 1829.
2 vols. 12mo   HM

622a ———— ———— 4th ed. Philadelphia: H. C. Carey & I. Lea, 1832.
2 vols. 12mo   H

622b ———— ———— 4th ed. Philadelphia: H. C. Carey & I. Lea, 1834.
2 vols. 12mo   AAS

623 ———— ———— Philadelphia: Carey, Lea & Blanchard, 1835. 2
vols. 12mo   BA(V.2), BP, HEH

623a ———— ———— Philadelphia: Carey, Lea & Blanchard, 1836. 2
vols. 12mo   AAS, LCP, UV

624 ———— ———— Philadelphia: Carey, Lea & Blanchard, 1838. 2
vols. 12mo   AAS, B, BP, NYP, Y
Spiller & Blackburn also list an 1839 ed.

625 ———— ———— Philadelphia: Lea & Blanchard, 1840. 2 vols.
12mo   AAS, Y

626 ———— ———— Philadelphia: Lea & Blanchard, 1841. 2 vols.
12mo   N

626a ———— ———— Philadelphia: Lea & Blanchard, 1843. 2 vols.
12mo   AAS, Y

627 ———— ———— Philadelphia: Lea & Blanchard, 1846. 2 vols.
in 1. 12mo   LCP, Y

627a ———— ———— Philadelphia: Lea & Blanchard, 1847. 2 vols.
12mo   HEH(V.1)

627b ———— ———— Philadelphia: Lea & Blanchard, 1848. 2 vols.
12mo   AAS

627c ———— ———— Philadelphia: Lea & Blanchard, 1849. 2 vols.
12mo   Y

628 ———— ———— New York: Stringer and Townsend, 1849. 2
vols. in 1. 12mo   AAS

629 ———— ———— New York: George P. Putnam, 1850. 443 p.
12mo   H, NYP, Y

630 ——— ——— New York: Stringer and Townsend, 1850. 2 vols. in 1. 12mo   AAS, Y

631 ——— Lionel Lincoln; or, The Leaguer of Boston . . . [anon.]. New York: Charles Wiley, 1825-24. 2 vols. 12mo
AAS, B, BA, BP, H, HEH, IN, LC, N, NYP, UC, UM, UP, UV, Y
American Revolution.

631a ——— ——— 2d ed. Philadelphia: Carey & Lea, 1827. 2 vols. 12mo   AAS

632 ——— ——— 4th ed. Philadelphia: Carey, Lea & Carey, 1829. 2 vols. 12mo   AAS

633 ——— ——— 5th ed. Philadelphia: Carey & Lea, 1831. 2 vols. 12mo   AAS, LC(V.2), Y

634 ——— ——— 5th ed. Philadelphia: Carey & Lea, 1832. 2 vols. 12mo   AAS, H, LC, UC(V.1), Y

635 ——— ——— New York: Justin Carpenter, 1834. 2 vols. 12mo   NYP

636 ——— ——— Philadelphia: Carey, Lea & Blanchard, 1836. 2 vols. 12mo   AAS, HEH, LCP, UP, UV, Y

637 ——— ——— Philadelphia: Carey, Lea & Blanchard, 1838. 2 vols. 12mo   AAS, Y

638 ——— ——— Philadelphia: Lea & Blanchard, 1840-39. 2 vols. 12mo   Y

638a ——— ——— Philadelphia: Lea & Blanchard, 1840. 2 vols. 12mo   H

639 ——— ——— Philadelphia: Lea & Blanchard, 1841. 2 vols. 12mo   AAS

640 ——— ——— Philadelphia: Lea & Blanchard, 1842. 2 vols. 12mo   N, Y

641 —— —— Philadelphia: Lea & Blanchard, 1843. 2 vols. 12mo
B, LC(V.2)

642 —— —— Philadelphia: Lea & Blanchard, 1847. 2 vols. 12mo
AAS, LC(V.1), LCP

643 —— —— New York: Stringer & Townsend, 1849. 2 vols. in 1. 12mo
H, HEH, NYP

644 —— Mercedes of Castile; or, The Voyage to Cathay . . . [anon.]. Philadelphia: Lea and Blanchard, 1840. 2 vols. 12mo   AAS, BP, H, HEH, HM, IN, LC, N, NYP, NYS, UM, UP, UV, Y
Late 15th cent.

645 —— —— New York: Burgess, Stringer & Co., 1845. 2 vols. in 1. 12mo
BP, H, Y

646 —— —— New York: Stringer and Townsend, 1849. 2 vols. in 1. 12mo
NYP

647 —— The Monikins . . . [anon.].   Philadelphia: Carey, Lea & Blanchard, 1835. 2 vols. 12mo
AAS, B, BA, BP, H, HEH, LC, N, NYP, UC, UM, UP, UV, Y

648 —— —— Philadelphia: Lea & Blanchard, 1841. 2 vols. 12mo
AAS, N, NYP, UP

649 —— —— Philadelphia: Lea & Blanchard, 1843. 2 vols. 12mo
NYH

650 —— —— Philadelphia: Lea & Blanchard, 1848. 2 vols. in 1. 12mo
LCP

651 —— —— New York: Stringer and Townsend, 1849. 2 vols. in 1. 12mo
H, NYP

652 —— Ned Myers; or, A Life before the Mast . . . Philadelphia: Lea and Blanchard, 1843. 232 p. 12mo
AAS, HEH, IN, LC, LCP, N, NYP, NYS, UM, UP, UV, Y
Early 19th cent.

652a —— —— Philadelphia: Lea and Blanchard, 1843. 232 p. 12mo
H

652b ——— ——— New York: Burgess, Stringer & Co., 1845. 232
p. 12mo
AAS

652c ——— ——— New York: Stringer & Townsend, 1849. 232 p.
12mo
H

653 ——— ——— New York: Stringer & Townsend, 1850. 232 p.
12mo
NYP

654 ——— The Oak Openings; or, The Bee-Hunter . . . [anon.].
New York: Burgess, Stringer & Co., 1848. 2 vols. 12mo
AAS, BA, H, HEH, HM, LC, N, NYP, UC, UM, UP, UV, Y
Michigan; 1812.

655 ——— ——— New York: Stringer & Townsend, 1849-48. 2
vols. in 1. 12mo
HEH, IN, NYP
Vol. II imprint: "New York: Burgess, Stringer & Co., 1848."

656 ——— The Pathfinder; or, The Inland Sea . . . [anon.]. Phila-
delphia: Lea and Blanchard, 1840. 2 vols. 12mo AAS, BA, BP,
H, HEH, HM, IN, LC, LCP(V.1), N, NYP, NYS, UC, UM, UP, UV, Y
Great Lakes; 1750.

657 ——— ——— Philadelphia: Lea & Blanchard, 1843. 2 vols. in
1. 12mo
AAS, Y

657a ——— ——— Philadelphia: Lea and Blanchard, 1846. 2 vols.
12mo
AAS, Y

658 ——— ——— New York: Stringer & Townsend, 1850-49. 2
vols. in 1. 12mo
AAS, NYP
Spiller & Blackburn list eds. in 1841 and 1845.

659 ——— The Pilot: A Tale of the Sea . . . [anon.]. New York:
Charles Wiley, 1823. 2 vols. 12mo
AAS, B, BA, BP, H, HEH, LC, N, NYH, NYP, UC, UM, UP, UV, Y

660 ——— ——— 2d ed. New York: Charles Wiley, 1824. 2 vols.
12mo
AAS, BA, H, HEH, LCP, NYP, UP, Y

661 ——— ——— 3d ed. Philadelphia: Carey, Lea & Carey, 1827.
2 vols. 12mo
AAS, LC(V.1), LCP
Spiller & Blackburn list the 4th ed. in 1827.

662 —— —— 5th ed. Philadelphia: Carey, Lea & Carey, 1829.
2 vols. 12mo   AAS

663 —— —— 5th ed. Philadelphia: Carey & Lea, 1831. 2
vols. 12mo   LCP

663a —— —— 5th ed. Philadelphia: Carey & Lea, 1832. 2 vols.
12mo   H

664 —— —— 5th ed. Philadelphia: Carey & Lea, 1833. 2
vols. 12mo   LC(v.1)

664a —— —— New York: Justin Carpenter, 1834. 2 vols.
12mo   AAS

664b —— —— Philadelphia: Carey & Lea, 1835. 2 vols. 12mo
                      Y

665 —— —— Philadelphia: Carey, Lea & Blanchard, 1836. 2
vols. 12mo   AAS, HEH, LCP, NYP, UC(v.1), Y

665a —— —— Philadelphia: Carey, Lea & Blanchard, 1838. 2
vols. 12mo   Y

666 —— —— Philadelphia: Lea and Blanchard, 1839. 2 vols.
12mo   AAS, HM(v. 1), Y

667 —— —— Philadelphia: Lea & Blanchard, 1841. 2 vols.
12mo   Y

668 —— —— Philadelphia: Lea & Blanchard, 1842. 2 vols.
12mo   AAS, B, LCP, N, NYP, Y

668a —— —— Boston: Saxton & Peirce, 1842. 2 vols. in 1.
12mo   IN, Y

668b —— —— New York: Burgess, Stringer & Co., 1845. 2
vols. in 1. 12mo   Y

669 —— —— New York: George P. Putnam, 1849. 2 vols. in 1.
12mo   AAS, LCP, NYS, UP, Y

670 —— —— New York: Stringer & Townsend, 1849. 2 vols.
12mo   BA, H, UV

671 —— The Pioneers; or, The Sources of the Susquehanna . . .
[anon.]. New York: Charles Wiley; E. B. Clayton, printer,
1823. 2 vols. 12mo
        AAS, B, BP, H, HEH, IN, LC, N, NYH, NYP, UC, UM, UP, UV, Y
Some copies of Vol. I printed by "J. Seymour."
New York; 1793.

672 —— —— New York: Collins and Hannay, and Charles
Wiley, 1825. 2 vols. 12mo   AAS, H, UP, UV, Y

673 —— —— 4th ed. Philadelphia: Carey, Lea & Carey, 1827.
2 vols. 12mo   AAS, H(V.2), LC(V.2)

674 —— —— 5th ed. Philadelphia: Carey, Lea & Carey, 1828.
2 vols. 12mo   H(V.1), NYP, Y

675 —— —— 6th ed. Philadelphia: Carey, Lea & Carey, 1829.
2 vols. 12mo   AAS, HM(V.1)

676 —— —— Philadelphia: Carey & Lea, 1832. 2 vols. 12mo
                                                    AAS, LC

677 —— —— New York: Justin Carpenter, 1834. 2 vols.
12mo   AAS, NYP

677a —— —— Philadelphia: Carey, Lea & Blanchard, 1835. 2
vols. 12mo   AAS

678 —— —— Philadelphia: Carey, Lea & Blanchard, 1836. 2
vols. 12mo   AAS, HEH, LCP, NYP, UC
Spiller & Blackburn list an 1835 ed.

679 —— —— Philadelphia: Carey, Lea & Blanchard, 1838. 2
vols. 12mo   H, Y

680 —— —— Philadelphia: Lea & Blanchard, 1839. 2 vols.
12mo   B(V.2), Y

681 —— —— Philadelphia: Lea & Blanchard, 1840. 2 vols.
    12mo   AAS, Y

682 —— —— Philadelphia: Lea & Blanchard, 1841. 2 vols.
    12mo   AAS

683 —— —— Philadelphia: Lea & Blanchard, 1843. 2 vols. in
    1.   12mo   AAS, N, NYP, Y

684 —— —— Philadelphia: Lea & Blanchard, 1846. 2 vols. in
    1.   12mo   LCP

685 —— —— Philadelphia: Lea & Blanchard, 1849. 2 vols. in
    1.   12mo   AAS, LCP

686 —— —— New York: Stringer & Townsend, 1849. 2 vols.
    in 1.   12mo
No copy located.

687 —— —— New York: Stringer & Townsend, 1850. 2 vols.
    in 1.   12mo   AAS, NYP(V.1), Y

688 —— The Prairie . . . [anon.]. Philadelphia: Carey, Lea &
Carey, 1827. 2 vols. 12mo
      AAS, B, BA, BP, H, HEH, LC(V.1), N, NYP, UM, UP, UPI, UV, Y

689 —— —— Philadelphia: Carey, Lea & Carey, 1828. 2 vols.
    12mo   AAS, LCP, Y

690 —— —— Philadelphia: Carey, Lea & Carey, 1829. 2 vols.
    12mo   AAS

690a —— —— Philadelphia: Carey & Lea, 1831. 2 vols. 12mo
                                                   UP

690b —— —— Philadelphia: Carey & Lea, 1832-31. 2 vols.
    12mo   AAS, Y

691 —— —— Philadelphia: Carey & Lea, 1833. 2 vols. 12mo
                                            AAS(V.1), LC

692 —— —— Philadelphia: Carey, Lea & Blanchard, 1835.   2 vols. in 1.   12mo   AAS, BP, Y

693 —— —— Philadelphia: Carey, Lea & Blanchard, 1836.   2 vols.   12mo   AAS, HEH, LCP, NYP, UC(V.2), Y

693a —— —— Philadelphia: Carey, Lea & Blanchard, 1838.   2 vols.   12mo   Y

694 —— —— Philadelphia: Lea and Blanchard, 1840.   2 vols. 12mo   AAS, Y

695 —— —— Philadelphia: Lea and Blanchard, 1841.   2 vols. 12mo   AAS

696 —— —— Philadelphia: Lea and Blanchard, 1842.   2 vols. 12mo   N, Y

697 —— —— Philadelphia: Lea and Blanchard, 1843.   2 vols. in 1.   12mo   NYP

698 —— —— Philadelphia: Lea and Blanchard, 1846.   2 vols. in 1.   12mo   LCP

698a —— —— Philadelphia: Lea and Blanchard, 1849.   2 vols. in 1.   12mo   AAS

699 —— —— New York: Stringer & Townsend, 1849.   2 vols. in 1.   12mo   NYP

700 —— —— New York: Stringer & Townsend, 1850.   2 vols. in 1.   12mo   AAS, Y

701 —— Precaution . . . [anon.].   New York: A. T. Goodrich & Co., 1820.   2 vols.   12mo
                    AAS, BA, H, HEH, IN, LC, N, NYP, UC, UP, UV, Y

702 —— —— Philadelphia: Lea & Blanchard, 1839.   2 vols. 12mo   AAS, BP, IN, LC, LCP, N, UM, UP, UV, Y
Spiller & Blackburn list an 1849 ed.

703 ———— The Red Rover... [anon.]. Philadelphia: Carey, Lea
& Carey, 1828-27. 2 vols. 12mo
AAS, B, BA, BP, H, HEH, LC, LCP(V.1), N, NYP, UC, UM, UP, UV, Y

704 ———— ———— 2d ed. Philadelphia: Carey, Lea and Carey,
1829-28. 2 vols. 12mo AAS, Y

704a ———— ———— 2d ed. Philadelphia: Carey, Lea & Carey, 1831.
2 vols. 12mo AAS

705 ———— ———— Philadelphia: Carey, Lea and Carey, 1832. 2
vols. 12mo AAS, UV, Y

705a ———— ———— Philadelphia: Carey, Lea and Carey, 1833. 2
vols. 12mo Y

706 ———— ———— Philadelphia: Carey, Lea & Blanchard, 1836. 2
vols. 12mo AAS, H, LCP, UP

707 ———— ———— Philadelphia: Carey, Lea & Blanchard, 1838. 2
vols. 12mo LCP, Y

708 ———— ———— Philadelphia: Lea & Blanchard, 1840. 2 vols.
12mo Y

709 ———— ———— Philadelphia: Lea & Blanchard, 1841. 2 vols.
12mo AAS

710 ———— ———— Philadelphia: Lea & Blanchard, 1843. 2 vols.
12mo N, NYP, Y

711 ———— ———— New York: Burgess, Stringer & Co., 1845. 2
vols. 12mo B
Spiller & Blackburn list an 1849 ed.

712 ———— ———— New York: George P. Putnam, 1850. 522 p.
12mo BA, Y

713 ———— The Redskins; or, Indian and Injin: Being the Conclu-
sion of the Littlepage Manuscripts . . . [anon.]. New York:
Burgess & Stringer, 1846. 2 vols. 12mo
AAS, BP, H, HEH, LC, N, NYP, NYS, UC, UM, UP, UV, Y
New York; contemporary.

95

714 ———— ———— New York: Stringer & Townsend, 1849. 2 vols.
in 1. 12mo
AAS, NYP

715 ——— Satanstoe; or, The Littlepage Manuscripts. A Tale of
the Colony . . . [anon.]. New York: Burgess, Stringer & Co.,
1845. 2 vols. 12mo
AAS, H, HEH, LC, LCP, N, NYH, NYP, UM, UP, UV, Y
New York; 1750.

716 ——— The Sea Lions; or, The Lost Sealers . . . [anon.]. New
York: Stringer & Townsend, 1849. 2 vols. 12mo
AAS, H, HEH, LC, LCP, N, NYH, NYP, UC, UM, UP, UPI, UV, Y
Antarctic; 1820.

717 ——— The Spy: A Tale of the Neutral Ground . . . [anon.].
New York: Wiley & Halsted, 1821. 2 vols. 12mo
AAS, B, HEH, IN, N, NYP, UP, Y
New York; American Revolution.

718 ———— ———— 2d ed. New York: Wiley and Halsted, 1822. 2
vols. 12mo
AAS, H, IN, N, NYH, NYP, UP, Y

719 ———— ———— 3d ed. New York: Wiley and Halsted, 1822. 2
vols. 12mo
BA, NYH, NYP, NYS, UV, Y

720 ———— ———— 4th ed. New York: Charles Wiley, 1824. 2
vols. 12mo
AAS, H, UM, UP, Y

721 ———— ———— 5th ed. Philadelphia: Carey, Lea & Carey, 1827.
2 vols. 12mo
AAS, NYP, Y

722 ———— ———— 6th ed. Philadelphia: Carey, Lea & Carey, 1829.
2 vols. 12mo
AAS

722a ———— ———— 7th ed. Philadelphia: Carey, Lea & Carey, 1829.
2 vols. 12mo
AAS

722b ———— ———— New York: J. & J. Harper, 1832. 2 vols. 12mo
Y
"Seventh Edition" on title page of Vol. I and "Sixth Edition" on title page of
Vol. II.

722c ——— ——— Philadelphia: Carey & Lea, 1833. 2 vols. 12mo
AAS, Y
"Seventh Edition" on title page of Vol. I and "Sixth Edition" on title page
of Vol. II.

722d ——— ——— New York: Justin Carpenter, 1834. 2 vols. in 1.
12mo   AAS

722e ——— ——— Philadelphia: Carey, Lea & Blanchard, 1835. 2
vols. 12mo   AAS, Y

723 ——— ——— Philadelphia: Carey, Lea & Blanchard, 1836. 2
vols. 12mo   AAS, H, LC, LCP(V.2), NYP, UP, Y
Spiller & Blackburn list eds. in 1831 and 1835.

724 ——— ——— Philadelphia: Carey, Lea & Blanchard, 1838. 2
vols. 12mo   AAS, UV, Y

725 ——— ——— Philadelphia: Lea & Blanchard, 1840. 2 vols.
12mo   AAS, Y

726 ——— ——— Philadelphia: Lea & Blanchard, 1841. 2 vols.
12mo   NYP

727 ——— ——— Philadelphia: Lea & Blanchard, 1843. 2 vols.
in 1. 12mo   AAS, LCP, N, UC

728 ——— ——— New York: Burgess, Stringer & Co., 1845. 2
vols. 12mo   LC, Y

729 ——— ——— New York: George P. Putnam, 1849. 463 p.
12mo   UM, UP

729a ——— ——— New York: Stringer & Townsend, 1850. 2 vols.
12mo   AAS, Y

730 ——— Tales for Fifteen; or, Imagination and Heart. By Jane
Morgan [pseud.]. New York: C. Wiley, 1823. 223 p. 12mo
AAS, IN, NYS, Y

731 ——— The Two Admirals ... [anon.]. Philadelphia: Lea and
Blanchard, 1842. 2 vols. 12mo   AAS, B, BA, BP, CLS, H, HEH,
HM(V.1), IN, LC, LCP, N, NYP, NYS, UC, UM, UP, UV, Y

732 —————— —————— Philadelphia: Lea & Blanchard, 1843. 2 vols. in 1.
        12mo   NYP

732a —————— —————— New York: Burgess & Stringer, 1845. 2 vols.
        12mo   Y

733 —————— —————— New York: Stringer & Townsend, 1849. 2 vols.
     in 1.   12mo   AAS, HEH, NYP

734 —————— The Water-Witch; or, The Skimmer of the Seas . . .
     [anon.]. Philadelphia: Carey & Lea, 1831. 2 vols. 12mo
     AAS, B, BA, BP, H, HEH, HM(V.1), IN, LC, LCP, N, NYP, UC, UM, UP,
                                                            UV, Y
     New York harbor; early 18th cent.

735 —————— —————— Philadelphia: Carey & Lea, 1834-33. 2 vols.
        12mo   Y

736 —————— —————— Philadelphia: Carey & Lea, 1834. 2 vols. 12mo
                                                            Y

737 —————— —————— Philadelphia: Carey, Lea & Blanchard, 1835. 2
     vols. in 1.   12mo   AAS, LCP

738 —————— —————— Philadelphia: Carey, Lea & Blanchard, 1836. 2
     vols.   12mo   AAS, HEH, LC, LCP

739 —————— —————— Philadelphia: Carey, Lea & Blanchard, 1838. 2
     vols.   12mo   AAS, BP, UV, Y

740 —————— —————— Philadelphia: Lea & Blanchard, 1840. 2 vols.
        12mo   AAS, Y

741 —————— —————— Philadelphia: Lea & Blanchard, 1841. 2 vols.
        12mo   AAS

742 —————— —————— Philadelphia: Lea & Blanchard, 1843. 2 vols.
        12mo   H, NYP

742a —————— —————— New York: Burgess, Stringer & Co., 1845. 2
     vols.   12mo   AAS, Y

743 ——— ——— New York: Stringer & Townsend, 1849. 2 vols.
in 1. 12mo   AAS, HEH, NYP

744 ——— The Ways of the Hour ... [anon.]. New York: George
P. Putnam, 1850. 512 p. 12mo
       AAS, B, BA, BP, H, HEH, IN, LC, LCP, NYP, NYS, UP, UV, Y

745 ——— The Wept of Wish Ton-Wish ... [anon.]. Philadelphia:
Carey, Lea & Carey, 1829. 2 vols. 12mo
       AAS, B, BA, BP, H, HEH, LC, LCP, N, NYP, UC, UM, UP, UV, Y
Connecticut; late 17th cent.

746 ——— ——— Philadelphia: Carey, Lea & Carey, 1831. 2 vols.
12mo   LCP, NYP(V.1)

747 ——— ——— Philadelphia: Carey, Lea & Carey, 1832. 2 vols.
12mo   AAS, H, UP, Y

748 ——— ——— Philadelphia: Carey, Lea & Carey, 1833. 2 vols.
12mo   AAS, Y
Spiller & Blackburn list an 1834 ed.

748a ——— ——— Philadelphia: Carey, Lea & Blanchard, 1835. 2
vols. 12mo   AAS, Y

749 ——— ——— Philadelphia: Carey, Lea & Blanchard, 1836. 2
vols. 12mo   AAS, H, LCP, NYP, UC(V.1), UP(V.2)

749a ——— ——— Philadelphia: Carey, Lea & Blanchard, 1838. 2
vols. 12mo   Y(V.1)

750 ——— ——— Philadelphia: Lea and Blanchard, 1839. 2 vols.
12mo   AAS, Y

751 ——— ——— Philadelphia: Lea & Blanchard, 1841. 2 vols.
12mo   N, UV

752 ——— ——— Philadelphia: Lea and Blanchard, 1843. 2 vols.
in 1. 12mo   Y

752a ——— ——— Philadelphia: Lea and Blanchard, 1845. 2 vols.
12mo   HEH(V.1)
Cover date 1843.

99

752b ——— ——— Philadelphia: Lea and Blanchard, 1848. 2 vols.
12mo   AAS, Y(V.1)

753 ——— ——— New York: Stringer & Townsend, 1849. 2 vols.
in 1.   12mo   H, NYP

754 ——— The Wing-and-Wing; or, Le Feu-Follett . . . [anon.].
Philadelphia: Lea and Blanchard, 1842. 2 vols. 12mo
AAS, BP, H, HEH, LC, LCP, N, NYP, UC, UM, UP, UV, Y
Mediterranean; 1798-99.

755 ——— ——— New York: Stringer & Townsend, 1849. 2 vols.
in 1.   12mo   AAS, HEH, NYP

756 ——— Wyandotté; or, The Hutted Knoll . . . [anon.].   Phila-
delphia: Lea and Blanchard, 1843. 2 vols. 12mo
AAS, B, BA, BP, H, HEH, IN, LC, LCP, N, NYP, UM, UP, UV, Y
New York; 1770's.

757 ——— ——— New York: Stringer & Townsend, 1849. 2 vols.
in 1.   12mo   H, HEH, NYP

758 DELETE.

759 COOPER, SUSAN FENIMORE.   Elinor Wyllys; or, The Young Folk
at Longbridge.   A Tale, by Amabel Penfeather [pseud.] . . .
Edited by J. Fenimore Cooper.   Philadelphia: Carey and Hart,
1846.   2 vols.   12mo   AAS, BP, LC, LCP, N, NYP, UP, UV, Y

760 COOPER, THOMAS.   Memoirs of a Nullifier, Written by Himself.
By a Native of the South [anon.].   Columbia, S.C.: Printed and
published at the Telescope Office, 1832.   110 p.   12mo
BA, BP, H, HEH, LC, NYP, NYS, Y
It has been determined that Algerson Sidney Johnson was the author of the
Memoirs of a Nullifier, not Cooper.

761 THE COOPER'S SON; or, The Prize of Virtue.   A Tale of the Revolution . . .   Boston: James French; New York: Saxton & Huntington, 1846.   139 p., illus.   12mo   AAS, BA, BP, H, HEH, LC, Y

761a ——— Boston: James French, 1847.   144 p., illus.   12mo
AAS, HEH, LC, Y
Pages 133-144 adverts.

762 ——— 2d ed. Boston: James French, 1847. 144 p., illus.
12mo   AAS, N, UV

763 ——— 3d ed. Boston: James French, 1847. 144 p., illus.
12mo   B, IN, UC, UM, UV, Y

764 CORA; or, The Genius of America. Philadelphia: E. Littell, 1828.
260 p. 12mo   AAS, UC
Also contains: Gaietana—The Mother—Victorine.
Contemporary inscription on the title page of the AAS copy: "By Jannette
M. Hart, Saybrook, Connecticut."

764a CORBIN, AUSTIN. The Eagle; or, The Rover of the Mediterranean . . . Boston: F. Gleason, 1847. 50 p. 8vo   B, UV

765 ——— Mneomi; or, The Indian of the Connecticut . . . Boston:
Gleason's Publishing Hall, 1847. 50 p. 8vo   AAS, LC, UP, Y
Also contains: The Batson Cottage, by Miss Leslie.

766 CORCORAN, D. Pickings from the Portfolio of the Reporter of the
New Orleans "Picayune" . . . [anon.]. Philadelphia: Carey &
Hart, 1846. 216 p., illus. 12mo
                        AAS, H, HEH, HM, LC, LCP, UC, UM, UP, UV

767 ——— ——— Philadelphia: Carey and Hart, 1847. 216 p., illus.
12mo   AAS, BP

768 COULTERSHOGGLE, MUNGO, *Esq., pseud.* Goslington Shadow: A
Romance of the Nineteenth Century . . . By Mungo Coulter-
shoggle, Esq. [pseud.] . . . New York: Printed by and for J. &
J. Harper, 1825. 2 vols. 12mo H(V.2), HEH, IN, LC, N, NYP, Y
England.

769 ——— Leslie Linkfield: A Novel by the Author of Goslington
Shadow . . . [anon.]. Rochester: Printed by Edwin Scrantom,
1826. 2 vols. 12mo   AAS(V.1), H, HEH, LC, UC, UV, Y
Scotland and America.

770 COWEN, J. The First and Last Days of Alcohol the Great . . .
By J. Cowen, N. I. M. . . . Providence: B. T. Albro, printer,
1848. 224 p., illus. 8vo   B, H, NYP, UM, UP, UV, Y

COWSLIP, EGBERT AUGUSTUS, *Esq., pseud.* *See* Barker, Benjamin

COX, WILLIAM. Biography of Jacob Hays. *In* The Atlantic Club-Book (1834), Nos. 195-196.

771 ———— Crayon Sketches. By an Amateur. Edited by Theodore S. Fay . . . New York: Conner and Cooke, 1833. 2 vols. 12mo
AAS, B, BP, HEH, HM, IN, LC, N, NYH, NYP, NYS, UC, UM, UP, UV, Y
Contains: Passages in the Life of an Unfortunate—The Man of the Fly Market Ferry—The Epicurean: A Gastronomic Tale.

———— The Rivals: A Tale of Love and Marriage. *In* The Atlantic Club-Book (1834), Nos. 195-196.

———— Steam. *In* The Atlantic Club-Book (1834), Nos. 195-196.

772 THE CRANBERRY MEADOW: A Temperance Tale, Founded on Fact. By the Author of "The Poor Man's House Repaired" . . . Boston: John Ford, Nov. 1835. 12 p. 12mo   BA, H, HEH, UV
At head of title: "First Series, No. 8."

773 ———— Boston: Printed by Cassady and March, 1837. 12 p. 12mo   AAS, H, HEH, NYH
AAS, HEH, and NYH copies bound with *Joe Anderson and Old Jim Bayley* (1837) with cover title: "Cranberry Meadow, Joe Anderson and Old Jim Bayley."

774 ———— Boston: Printed by Cassady and March, 1838. 12 p. 12mo   H

CRAYON, GEOFFREY, *Gent., pseud.* *See* Irving, Washington

774a CRAZY LUCE; or, A Correct History of the Life and Adventures of the Wandering Woman. Printed for the Pedlars. Cortland Village [N. Y.], 1836. Cover title, 16 p. 12mo   HEH
Cazenovia, N. Y.

775 CREAMER, HANNAH GARDNER. Eleanor; or, Life without Love . . . Boston: James French, 1850. 202 p. 12mo
AAS, B, BP, HEH, LC, N, UP, UV, Y

CREYTON, PAUL, *pseud.* *See* Trowbridge, John Townsend

776 CROOME, W. The Golden Sands of Mexico. A Moral and Religious Tale: To Which Is Added: True Riches; or, The Reward of Self Sacrifice ... Philadelphia: Lindsay and Blakiston, 1850. 211 p., illus. 12mo   AAS, B, BP, H, HEH, LC, LCP, NYH, NYP, UP, Y
Croome was the illustrator only.

777 THE CRUISER; or, 'Tis Thirty Years Ago. [N.p., 1845?]   40 p., illus. 8vo   BP, N
Written by Josiah A. Fraetas.
War of 1812.

778 CUMMINGS, ARIEL IVERS. The Factory Girl; or, Gardez la Coeur ... Lowell: J. E. Short & Co., 1847. 167 p., illus. 8vo
       AAS, B, H, HEH, IN, LC, NYH, NYP, UM, UP, UV, Y
New Hampshire; 18--.

779 CUMMINGS, J. S. Eolah, the White Flower of the Prairie! Or, The Trapper's Bride. A Story of Life in the Far West ... Boston: F. Gleason [cop. 1848]. 100 p. 8vo   UV, Y
Also contains: The Generous Lovers.
Printed in double cols.
LC has a title page, deposited Dec. 7, 1848.

780 CURTIS, HARRIOT F. Jessie's Flirtations. By the Author of "Kate in Search of a Husband" ... [anon.]. New York: Harper & Brothers, 1846. 114 p. 8vo   B, HEH, LC, N, UP, UV, Y
On cover: "Library of Select Novels, No. 76."
Printed in double cols.

781 ———— ———— New York: Harper & Brothers [1846?]. 114 p. 8vo   AAS, NYP
Printed in double cols.

782 ——— The Smuggler and Other Tales. By the Author of "Kate in Search of a Husband" [anon.]. [N.p., cop. 1843.]
LC has a title page, deposited Dec. 28, 1843, by the author Harriot F. Curtis.

783 ——— Two Strings to the Beau; or, Two Beaux to the String ... [anon.]. [N.p.], 1843.
LC has a title page, deposited Dec. 28, 1843.

784 CURTIS, NEWTON MALLORY. The Black-Plumed Riflemen: A
Tale of the Revolution... New York: Burgess, Stringer & Co.,
1846. 125 p. 8vo   AAS, H, HEH, HM, N, NYH, UC, UP, UV, Y
Printed in double cols.

785 ———— ———— Troy, N. Y.: L. Willard, 245 River Street [1849].
192 p. 8vo   AAS, BP, HEH, IN, NYP, UM, UV, Y
Printed in double cols.

786 ———— ———— Troy, N.Y.: L. Willard, 230 River Street [1849].
144 p. 8vo   AAS, HEH
Printed in double cols.

786a ———— ———— Troy, N.Y.: L. Willard, 230 River Street, 1850.
144 p. 8vo   AAS
Printed in double cols.

787 ———— The Bride of the Northern Wilds ... New York: Bur-
gess & Stringer. Boston: Redding and Co. Albany: Geo. Jones.
Philadelphia: G. B. Zeiber. Baltimore: Wm. Taylor, 1843. 64
p. 8vo   AAS, NYP, UV, Y
Caption title: "The Bride of the Northern Wilds."
Printed in double cols.
French and Indian War.

788 ———— ———— New York: Burgess & Stringer, 1843. 71 p. 8vo
AAS, LCP, Y
Caption title: "The Bride of the Northern Wilds. A Tale."
Printed in double cols.

789 ———— ———— Albany: George Jones, 1843. 71 p. 8vo   H, Y
Printed in double cols.

790 ———— ———— New York: Burgess, Stringer & Co. [cop. 1843].
120 p. 8vo   AAS, B, LC, UV
Printed in double cols.

790a ———— ———— Troy, N. Y.: L. Willard, 245 River Street [cop.
1843]. 120 p. 8vo
A copy is in the private collection of William S. Kable, University of South
Carolina.

791 —————————— Troy, N. Y.: L. Willard, 245 River Street [cop. 1843]. 192 p. 8vo   AAS, BP, HEH, N, NYH, NYP, UM, UP, UV, Y
Printed in double cols.

792 DELETE.

793 ————— The Doom of the Tory's Guard ... New York: Burgess and Stringer, and M. Y. Beach, 1843. 48 p. 8vo
AAS, B, HEH, N, UC, UP, Y
Cover title of HEH copy dated 1844.
Printed in double cols.
Mohawk Valley; 1775.

794 DELETE.

795 —————————— Troy, N. Y.: L. Willard, 245 River Street [cop. 1843]. 95, [1] p. 8vo   AAS, BP, H, LC, UM, UV, Y

796 ————— The Foundling of the Mohawk: A Tale of the Revolution ... New York: Williams Brothers, 1848. 89, 7 p. 8vo
AAS, H, LC, UV, Y
Also contains: The Adventures of a Night, 7 p. at end.
Printed in double cols.

797 ————— The Hunted Chief; or, The Female Ranchero. A Tale of the Mexican War ... New York: Williams Brothers, 1847. 86 p. 8vo   HEH, LC, Y
Printed in double cols.

798 ————— The Maid of the Saranac: A Tale of the War of 1812 ... New York: Williams Brothers, 1848. 79 p. 8vo   AAS, Y
Printed in double cols.

799 DELETE.

800 ————— The Marksmen of Monmouth: A Tale of the Revolution ... Troy: L. Willard, 230 River Street [cop. 1848]. 127 p. 8vo   AAS, B, HEH, LC, NYP, UM, UV, Y
Printed in double cols.
LC has a title page, deposited Nov. 13, 1848.

801 —— The Matricide's Daughter: A Tale of Life in the Great Metropolis . . . New York: Williams Brothers, 1847. 102 p. 8vo   HEH, Y

Printed in double cols.

802 —— —— New York: W. F. Burgess, 1850. 94 p. 8vo

AAS, HEH

Printed in double cols.

803 —— The Patrol of the Mountain: A Tale of the Revolution . . . New York: Williams Brothers, 1847. 112 p. 8vo

H, LC, NYP

Printed in double cols.

803a —— —— New York: W. F. Burgess, 1849. 112 p. 8vo

UP, Y

Printed in double cols.

803b —— —— New York: W. F. Burgess, 22 Ann Street [1850]. 112 p. 8vo   HEH

Printed in double cols.

Original paper covers of HEH copy have previous owner's name and date 1850.

804 —— The Prairie Guide; or, The Rose of the Rio Grande. A Tale of the Mexican War . . . New York: W. F. Burgess, 1849. 91 p. 8vo   HEH, UV

HEH cover title dated 1850.

Printed in double cols.

805 —— —— New York: Williams Brothers, Morning Star Office, No. 102 Nassau Street [cop. 1847]. 112 p. 8vo

N, NYII, Y

Also contains: The Texan Ranger; or, The Maid of Matamoras: A Tale of the Mexican War, by J. H. Ingraham.

Printed in double cols.

806 —— The Ranger of Ravenstream: A Tale of the Revolution . . . New York: Williams Brothers, 1847. 118 p. 8vo

AAS, LC, NYP, UP, UV, Y

Printed in double cols.

807 —————— —————— New York: Williams Brothers, 1849. 92 p. 8vo
AAS, UC, UP, Y
Printed in double cols.

808 —————— The Scout of the Silver Pond: A Tale of the Revolution
... New York: H. L. Williams, 1847. 110 p. 8vo AAS, UV, Y
Vermont.

809 —————— —————— New York: Williams Brothers, 1848. 88 p. 8vo
NYP, UV, Y
Printed in double cols.

810 —————— —————— New York: W. F. Burgess [1849]. 88 p. 8vo
AAS, LC
Cover title dated 1849.
Printed in double cols.

811 —————— The Star of the Fallen ... New York: Williams Broth-
ers [1847]. 103 p. 8vo Y
Cover title dated 1847.
Printed in double cols.

812 —————— —————— New York: Williams Brothers, 1848. 103 p.
8vo Y
Printed in double cols.

812a —————— —————— New York: W. F. Burgess, 1850. 96 p. 8vo
AAS, HEH
Printed in double cols.

813 —————— The Victim's Revenge. A Sequel to "The Matricide's
Daughter," and "The Star of the Fallen". . . New York: Wil-
liams Brothers, 1848. 96 p. 8vo UV, Y
Printed in double cols.

814 —————— —————— New York: W. F. Burgess, 1850. 95 p. 8vo
AAS, HEH
Printed in double cols.

815 —————— The Vidette; or, The Girl of the Robber's Pass. A Tale
of the Mexican War ... New York: Williams Brothers, 1848.
96 p. 8vo HEH, UV
Printed in double cols.
Sabin 18061 lists a Boston (184-?) ed.

816 CUSHING, ELIZA LANESFORD (FOSTER). Saratoga: A Tale of the Revolution . . . [anon.]. Boston: Cummings, Hilliard & Co., 1824. 2 vols. 12mo
AAS, B, BA, BP, H, HEH, IN, LC, NYP, NYS, UC, UM, UP, UV, Y

817 ———— Yorktown: An Historical Romance . . . [anon.]. Boston: Wells and Lilly, 1826. 2 vols. 12mo
AAS, BA, BP, HEH, IN, LC, N, NYP, UC, UP, UV, Y

CYPRESS, J., JR., *pseud.* *See* Hawes, William Post

818 DALLAM, JAMES WILMER. The Deaf Spy: A Tale Founded upon Incidents in the History of Texas . . . [anon.]. Baltimore: Wm. Taylor, 1848. 96 p. 8vo   HEH, LC, N, UM
Printed in double cols.

819 ———— The Lone Star: A Tale of Texas. Founded upon Incidents in the History of Texas . . . New York: E. Ferrett & Co., 1845. 95 p. 8vo   AAS, HEH, UV, Y

819a ———— ———— 2d ed. New York: E. Ferrett & Co., 1845. 96 p. 8vo   Y

820 DAMON, NORWOOD. The Chronicles of Mount Benedict: A Tale of the Ursuline Convent . . . [anon.]. Boston: Printed for the publisher, 1837. 191 p. 12mo   AAS, BP, HEH, LC, N, UV, Y

DANA, MARY S. B. *See* Shindler, Mary Stanley Bunce (Palmer) Dana

821 DANA, RICHARD HENRY. Poems and Prose Writings . . . Boston: Russell, Odiorne, and Co., 1833. 450 p. 8vo
AAS, B, BA, BP, H, HEH, IN, LCP, N, NYH, NYP, NYS, UC, UP, UV, Y
Contains: Tom Thornton—Edward and Mary—Paul Felton—The Son.

822 ———— ———— Philadelphia: Marshall, Clark, and Co.; Boston: Russell, Odiorne, and Co., 1833. 450 p. 8vo
AAS, B, BP, IN, LC, N, UM, UV, Y

823 ———— ———— New York: Baker and Scribner, 1850. 2 vols. 12mo   AAS, B, BA, BP, H, HEH, IN, LC, LCP, N, NYH, NYP, NYS, UC, UM, UP, Y

DANFORTH, HARRY, *pseud.* *See* Peterson, Charles Jacobs

823a DARK AND TERRIBLE DEEDS of George Lathrop, Who, After Passing through the Various Degrees of Crime, Was Finally Convicted and Hung in New Orleans, June 5, 1848, for the Robbery and Murder of His Father, March 8, 1847. New Orleans: Published by Rev. W. Stuart, 1848. 31, [1] p., illus. 8vo
H, HEH, LC

823b ——— for the Robbery and Murder of His Father, June 8, 1847. New Orleans: Published by Rev. W. Stuart, 1848. 31, [1] p., illus. 8vo
HEH, LC

824 DAVIDSON, MARGARET (MILLER). Selections from the Writings of Mrs. Margaret M. Davidson . . . With a Preface by Miss C. M. Sedgwick. Philadelphia: Lea & Blanchard, 1843. 232 p.
12mo
AAS, HEH, N, NYP, UM, UV, Y
Contains: The Events of a Few Eventful Days in 1814.

825 ——— ——— Philadelphia: Lea & Blanchard, 1843. 272 p.
12mo
AAS, BP, H, LC, LCP, NYS, Y

825a DAVIES, EDGAR W., JR. Alphonse; or, The Mystic Riders of the Aga Hassan. A Tale of France and the Nile in 1799 . . . New York: E. W. Davies, Jr., 1849. 100 p. 8vo
UV, Y
Printed in double cols.

825b ——— ——— Boston: F. Gleason, 1849. 100 p. 8vo   AAS
Printed in double cols.

825c ——— The Knight of the Silver Cross; or, Hafed, the Lion of Turkestan: A Tale of the Ottoman Empire . . . Boston: F. Gleason's Publishing Hall, 1849. 280 p., illus. 8vo
AAS, BA, HEH, Y
At head of title: "Gleason's Series of Prize Tales, No. 1."

826 DELETE.

827 DAVIS, CHARLES AUGUSTUS. Letters of J. Downing, Major [pseud.], Downingville Militia, Second Brigade, to His Old Friend, Mr. Dwight, of the New York Daily Advertiser. New York: Harper & Brothers, 1834. 245, [235]-240 p., illus. 12mo
AAS, BP, H, HEH, HM, IN, LCP, N, NYH, NYP, UP, UV, Y
Contains 29 letters; 28 only listed in table of contents.
"Appendix," paged [235]-240, follows p. 245 of text.
See BAL 4494-4501 for bibliographical variations of this and the following eds.

828 ——— ——— New York: Harper & Brothers, 1834. 259, [4] p., illus. 12mo   AAS, BA, BP, CLS, LCP, NYP, UM, UP, UV, Y
Contains 31 letters; binder's label, "Second Edition."

829 ——— ——— New York: Harper & Brothers, 1834. 259, [4] p., illus. 12mo   AAS, B, HEH, LCP, N, NYP, UC, Y
Contains 31 letters; binder's label, "Third Edition."

830 ——— ——— New York: Harper & Brothers, 1834. 270, [6] p., illus. 12mo   AAS, HEH, IN, LC, N, NYP, UM, UP, UV, Y
Contains 32 letters.

831 ——— ——— New York: Harper & Brothers, 1834. 306, [4] p., illus. 12mo   AAS, BP, NYP, UC, UV, Y
Contains 35 letters.

832 ——— ——— New York: Harper & Brothers, 1834. 318, [4] p., illus. 12mo   AAS, H, HEH, Y
Contains 36 letters.

833 ——— ——— New York: Harper & Brothers, 1834. 336 p., illus. 12mo   AAS, H, UP, Y
Contains 38 letters.

834 ——— ——— New York: Harper & Brothers, 1834. 367 p., illus. 12mo   AAS, B, HEH, NYP, UC, UP, Y
Contains 41 letters.

835 ——— ——— New York: Harper & Brothers, 1834. 400 p., illus. 12mo   AAS, HEH, UP, UV, Y
Contains 45 letters; binder's label, "Ninth Edition."

836 ——— ——— New York: Harper & Brothers, 1835. 400 p., illus. 12mo   AAS, H, NYH, Y
Contains 45 letters; binder's label, "Ninth Edition."

837 ——— ——— New York: Harper & Brothers, 1836. 400 p., illus. 12mo   HEH, HM, NYH, Y
Contains 45 letters; binder's label, "Eighth Edition."

838 DAVIS, EDGAR W., JR. *See* Davies, Edgar W., Jr.

839 DAVIS, MARY ELIZABETH (MORAGNE). The British Partizan: A Tale of the Times of Old ... Augusta, Ga.: Printed and published by William T. Thompson, 1839. 150 p. 12mo

CLS, HEH

Georgia; American Revolution.

840 DAWES, RUFUS. Nix's Mate: An Historical Romance of America ... [anon.]. New York: Samuel Colman, 1839. 2 vols. 12mo

AAS, B, BA, BP, H, HEH, IN, LC, N, NYP, UM, UP, UV, Y

Massachusetts; late 17th cent.

841 THE DEAD CHILD: A Story of My Childhood. By a Lady. Boston: Kidder & Wright, 1842. 24 p. 12mo

BA

Cold Water Army Tales, No. 1.

842 THE DEBTOR'S PRISON: A Tale of a Revolutionary Soldier ... New York: A. Greene, 1834. 164 p. 12mo

AAS, B, N

Appleton and Roorbach attribute to Asa Greene.

843 —— New York: Bliss, Wadsworth & Co., 1835. 174 p., illus. 12mo

H, HEH, LC, Y

844 DECORIS, AMICUS, *pseud*. Mayor Jones; or, My Cigar. By Amicus Decoris [pseud.]. New York: M. W. Dodd, 1846. 71 p. 12mo

AAS, HEH

845 —— —— New York: M. W. Dodd, 1850.

Ed. from Roorbach.

DEL LORRAINE, ADELA, *pseud*. *See* Hart, *Miss*

845a DEMING, EBENEZER, *supposed au*. Western Emigration. Narrative of a Tour to, & One Year's Residence in "Edensburgh" (Illinois), by Major Walter Wilkey [pseud.], an Honest Yeoman of Mooseboro, State of Maine. A More Humorsome and Interesting "Traveller's Guide to the West" Was Never Before Published... New York: G. C. Clairborne and Others, 1839. 24 p., illus. 8vo

BP, LC, N

845b —— Western Emigration. Narrative of a Tour to, and One Year's Residence in "Edensburgh," ... New York: Sackett & Sargent, printers, 1839. 24 p., illus. 8vo

Y

846 DENISON, CHARLES WHEELER. Old Ironsides and Old Adams. Stray Leaves from the Log Book of a Man-of-War's Man . . . Boston: W. W. Page, 1846. 48 p., illus. 8vo

AAS, BP, H, UP, UV, Y

At head of title: "Stories of the Sea. No. 3."
LC has a title page, deposited Aug. 24, 1846.
War of 1812.

847 ——— Old Slade; or, Fifteen Years Adventures of a Sailor . . . Boston: John Putnam, 81 Cornhill [cop. 1844]. 108 p., illus. 12mo   LC

At head of title: "Stories of the Sea. No. 1."

848 ——— The Yankee Cruiser: A Story of the War of 1812 . . . Boston: J. E. Farwell & Co., 1848. 50 p., illus. 8vo   LC

At head of title: "American Popular Tales. No. 2."
Printed in double cols.

849 DENISON, MARY (ANDREWS). Edna Etheril, the Boston Seamstress: A Narative [sic] of Facts. And, Crime and Consequence: A Tale of the South, by a Southerner . . . New York: Burgess, Stringer & Co., 1847. 69 p. 8vo   BP, UV

849a ——— Gertrude Russel; or, Parental Example, by Mrs. C. W. Denison . . . Also The Twins; The Patriarch and the Vine; and The Apples of Sodom, by Mrs. L. H. Sigourney . . . New York: Oliver & Brother, printers and publishers, 1849. 64 p., illus. 8vo   AAS, HEH, NYP, UV, Y

At head of title: "Prize Tale."
On front cover of NYP copy: "Fourth Edition."

850 ——— Raphael Inglesse; or, The Jew of Milan! A Thrilling Tale of the Victories of Virtue and the Punishments of Vice . . . Boston: J. E. Farwell & Co., 1848. 112 p., illus. 8vo   LC, UV

On cover: "American Popular Tales. No. 1."
Printed in double cols.

851 DESULTORIA: The Recovered Mss. of an Eccentric. New York: Baker and Scribner, 1850. 220 p. 12mo

AAS, BA, BP, H, HEH, LC, LCP, N, NYP, UC, UP, Y

DE WITT, SUSAN (LINN). Justina; or, The Will (1823). *See* No. 1560 for title entry which is now identified as by De Witt.

852 THE DIARY OF A PAWNBROKER; or, The Three Golden Balls. New
York: H. Long & Brother, 43 Ann Street [cop. 1849]. 134 p.,
illus. 8vo   AAS, HEH, LC, NYP, UP, UV, Y
Philadelphia.

DIDIMUS, HENRY, *pseud.* *See* Durell, Edward Henry

852a DIX, WILLIAM GILES. An Imaginary Conversation between
William Shakespeare and His Friend Henry Wriothesly, Earl of
Southampton. Also, an Imaginary Conversation between the
Same Mr. Shakespeare and Mr. Richard Quyner . . . [anon.].
Boston: Jordan and Company, 1844. 40 p. 12mo
                                                    BP, H, LC, NYP, Y

852b DODGE, NATHANIEL SHATSWELL. Sketches of New England; or,
Memories of the Country. By John Carver, Esquire [pseud.]
. . . New York: E. French, 1842. 286 p. 12mo
                            B, BP, H, LC, N, NYH, NYP, UC, Y
Sketches and short stories.

853 DONALDSON, JOHN. Jack Datchett, the Clerk: An Old Man's Tale
. . . [anon.]. Baltimore: H. Colburn, 1846. 101 p. 12mo
                            AAS, BA, BP, H, LC, NYH, UC, UV, Y

854 DORR, BENJAMIN. The History of a Pocket Prayer Book. Written by Itself . . . [anon.]. Philadelphia: George W. Donohue,
1839. 192 p. 12mo   AAS, BP, LC, NYP, UP, Y
First published by the General Protestant Episcopal Sunday School Union
at New York in 1830.

855 ——— ——— Philadelphia: R. S. H. George, 1844. 184 p.
12mo   HEH, Y

856 DORSEY, ANNA HANSON (MCKENNEY). The Oriental Pearl; or,
The Catholic Emigrants . . . Baltimore: John Murphy Company [cop. 1848]. 163 p. 16mo   HEH, NYP, Y

857 ——— The Sister of Charity . . . New York: Edward Dunigan,
1846. 2 vols., illus. 12mo   LC
North Carolina.

858 ———— The Student of Blenheim Forest; or, The Trials of a Convert ... Baltimore: J. Murphy, 1846. 544 p., illus. 16mo
Information from LC card, now withdrawn.
A copy of this ed. has not been located; BP and HEH have "Second revised edition." Baltimore: J. Murphy & Co., 1867.

859 ———— Tears on the Diadem; or, The Crown and the Cloister. A Tale of the White and Red Roses ... New York: Edward Dunigan, 1846. 223 p., illus. 12mo   AAS, HEH, UP, UV, Y
England; late 15th cent.

DOUGLASS, ADAM, *attrib. au. See* The Irish Emigrant (1817), No. 1367.

860 DOWNER, MRS. SARAH A. The Contrast; or, Which Is the Christian? A Tale ... Hudson: Printed by Ashbel Stoddard, 1837. 24 p. 16mo   AAS, H, LC, Y
At head of title: "Prize Tale."

861 ———— The Triumph of Truth. A Tale ... Hudson: Printed by Ashbel Stoddard, 1837. 24 p. 16mo   AAS, H, LC, Y

DOWNING, *Major* J., *pseud. See* Davis, Charles Augustus

DOWNING, *Major* JACK, *pseud. See* Smith, Seba

862 DRAKE, BENJAMIN. Tales and Sketches from the Queen City ... Cincinnati: Printed and published by E. Morgan and Co., 1838.
180 p. 12mo   AAS, BP, H, IN, LC, N, NYP, UM, UP, UPI, UV, Y
Contents: The Queen City—The Novice of Cahokia—Putting a Blackleg on Shore—The Baptism—The Yankee Colporteur—The Grave of Rosalie—A Burial by Moon-light—A Kentucky Election—A Visit to the Blue Licks—The Buried Canoe—Trying On a Shoe—The Battle of Brindle and the Buckeyes—The Flag Bearer.

863 THE DREAM FULFILLED; or, The Trials and Triumphs of the Moreland Family. Boston: James French, 1846. 191 p. 12mo
AAS, B, LC, N, NYP, UM, UP, UV, Y
Massachusetts; contemporary.

864 ———— 2d ed. Boston: James French, 1848. 151 p. 12mo   Y

864a ———— 3d ed. Boston: James French, 1848. 151 p. 12mo   Y

864b ——— 4th ed. Boston: James French, 1848. 151 p. 12mo
AAS

865 THE DRUNKARD; or, The Fallen Saved. By the Author of the
Moral Drama of the Same Name, Which Has Been Performed
Nearly One Hundred Times at the Boston Museum, to Over-
flowing Houses. Boston: E. P. Williams [1844]. 38 p. 8vo
AAS, H, HEH, N, UV

Cover title dated 1844.
Printed in double cols.
Sabin 84781 discusses authorship and notes that it has been ascribed to Rev.
John Pierpont.

866 THE DRUNKARD'S ORPHAN SON: His Life in London, His Astonish-
ing Adventures, and Circumstances That Accompanied His
Connection with a Female, a South Sea Islander. Boston: Published for the author, 1842. 36 p., illus. 12mo H, UV

DUCKWORTH, Dr. DODIMUS, A.N.Q., pseud. See Greene, Asa

867 DUER, JOHN K. The Matricide. By John K. Duer, U.S.N. . . .
New York: W. H. Graham, 1846. 143 p. 12mo AAS
Late 18th cent.

868 ——— The Nautilus: A Collection of Select Nautical Tales and
Sea Sketches, with a Full Narrative of the Mutiny of the Somers
. . . New York: J. Winchester, 1843. 48 p. 4to
Title from Sabin 21109.
The only copies found to date were in the omitted *New World, Extra
Series.*

869 DUGANNE, AUGUSTINE JOSEPH HICKEY. The Bravo's Daughter;
or, The Tory of Carolina. A Romance of the American Revolution . . . New York: E. Winchester, 1850. 92 p. 8vo
AAS, H, LC

Printed in double cols.

870 ——— The Daguerreotype Miniature; or, Life in the Empire
City . . . [anon.]. Philadelphia: G. B. Zieber & Co., 1846. 52
p. 8vo N, NYH, NYP

870a ——— Emily Harper; or, The Coquette's Destiny. A Tale of
the Strange Things of Real Existence . . . Worcester: Published
by Thomas Drew, Jr. Philadelphia: Colon and Adriance
[1846?]. 21 p. 8vo AAS

870b ——— Eustace Barcourt; or, The Illegitimate. A Story of Conflict between Good and Evil ... [anon.]. Philadelphia: G. B. Zieber & Co., 1848. 127 p. 8vo   Y

871 ——— The Knights of the Seal; or, The Mysteries of the Three Cities. A Romance of Men's Hearts and Habits ... [anon.]. Philadelphia: Colon and Adriance, 1845. 204 p. 8vo   B, LC

871a ——— ——— 4th ed. Philadelphia: Colon and Adriance, 1846. 204 p. 8vo   NYP
Author's name appears on the title page.

872 ——— ——— 4th ed. Philadelphia: G. B. Zieber & Co., 1848. 204 p. 8vo   BP, Y

873 ——— Secret Guilt; or, The Counterfeiters. An American Tale ... Boston: Brainard & Co., 1844. 47 p. 8vo   AAS, B
Printed in double cols.

——— The Spirit of the Ford: An Irish Ghost Story. *In* M. M. Ballou, Albert Simmons (1849), No. 229.

874 ——— The Two Clerks; or, The Orphan's Gratitude: Being the Adventures of Henry Fowler and Richard Martin ... Boston: Brainard & Co., 1843. 47 p. 8vo   UP, UV, Y
Printed in double cols.

DUMONT, JULIA LOUISA (CAREY). The Soldier's Son. *In* J. T. Parker, *comp.*, The American Legendary (1830), No. 1991.

——— Theodore Harland. *In* J. T. Parker, *comp.*, The American Legendary (1830), No. 1991.

DUNLAP, WILLIAM. Memoirs of a Water Drinker. *See* Thirty Years Ago; or, The Memoirs of a Water Drinker, No. 876.

875 ——— Thirty Years Ago; or, The Memoirs of a Water Drinker ... [anon.]. New York: Bancroft & Holley, 1836. 2 vols. 12mo   AAS, B(V.2), BP, H, HEH, LC, N, NYP, NYS, UP, UV, Y
New York City; contemporary.

876 ——— ——— 2d ed. New York: Saunders and Otley, 1837.
2 vols. in 1. 12mo
AAS, B, BP, H, HEH, IN, LC, N, NYH, NYP, UC, UM, UP, UV, Y
Title reads: *Memoirs of a Water Drinker*.

DUPUY, ELIZA ANN. Celeste: The Pirate's Daughter. *See* The
Pirate's Daughter, No. 879.

877 ——— The Conspirator . . . New York: D. Appleton & Com-
pany, 1850. 299 p. 12mo
AAS, B, HEH, IN, LC, N, NYP, UC, UM, UP, UV, Y
Early 19th cent.

878 ——— The Pirate's Daughter . . . [anon.]. New York: Ely and
Robinson, 1845. 2 vols. 8vo   NYP, UP, UV
LC has a title page of Vol. I, deposited July 2, 1845.

879 ——— ——— Cincinnati: Stratton & Barnard, 1849. 152 p.
8vo   HM, LC
Title reads: *Celeste: The Pirate's Daughter*.
Printed in double cols.

880 DURELL, EDWARD HENRY. New Orleans as I Found It. By H.
Didimus [pseud.] . . . New York: Harper & Brothers, 1845.
125 p. 8vo   AAS, BA, BP, H, HEH, HM, LC, N, NYH, NYS, UP, UV, Y
Printed in double cols.

881 DURIVAGE, FRANCIS ALEXANDER. Angela; or, Love and Guilt. A
Tale of Boston and Its Environs . . . Boston: Charles H. Brain-
ard, 1843. 32 p. 4to   B, BP, UM, UP, UV, Y
Printed in double cols.

——— The Count and the Prima Donna. *In* J. H. Robinson,
The Black Knight (1849), No. 2129.

——— The Diamond Star; or, The Englishman's Adventure.
A Story of Valencia. *In* M. M. Ballou, Albert Simmons (1849),
No. 229.

882 ——— Edith Vernon; or, Crime and Retribution. A Tragic
Story of New England, Founded upon Fact . . . Boston: F.
Gleason, 1845. 52 p. 8vo
AAS, B, BP, H, HEH, LC, N, NYP, UP, UV, Y
Boston; early 19th cent.

———— The Fastest Funeral on Record. *In* W. T. Porter, *ed.*, A Quarter Race in Kentucky (1847), Nos. 2063-64.

———— The French Guardsman. *In* S. Cobb, Jr., The Prophet of the Bohmer Wald (1850), No. 558.

883 ———— Hugh Capet: Count of Paris; or, The Diadem of Charlemagne. A Romance of France at the Close of the 10th Century ... Boston: F. Gleason, 1850. 99, [1] p. 8vo HEH, UP, UV, Y
Verso of p. 99: "The Fatal Receipt."
Printed in double cols.

884 ———— Mike Martin; or, The Last of the Highwaymen. A Romance of Reality ... Boston: Charles H. Brainard, 82 Washington Street, 1845. 48 p., illus. 8vo AAS, H, IN, UV, Y

885 ———— ———— Boston: Charles H. Brainard and Company, 1845. 48 p., illus. 8vo AAS, BP, HEH, UV, Y

———— The Mill of Poissy; or, The Fugitive's Secret. *In* J. Jones, The Belle of Boston (1849), No. 1483.

———— Rosalie de Clairville: A Legend of the Olden Days of France. *In* M. A. Clough, Paolina (1849), No. 552.

886 ———— Stray Subjects, Arrested and Bound Over. Being the Fugitive Offspring of the "Old 'Un" [pseud.] and the "Young 'Un" [pseud.] ... Philadelphia: Carey and Hart, 1848. 199 p., illus. 12mo AAS, B, BP, LC, LCP, NYP, UV, Y
George P. Burnham, jt. au.

887 ———— ———— Philadelphia: Carey and Hart, 1849. 199 p., illus. 12mo AAS, LCP, UM

888 DUTY VERSUS WILL; or, Decision Makes the Man. A Tale for Old and Young. New York: M. W. Dodd, 1849. 251 p. 12mo UV, Y
New Haven, New York; contemporary.

889 ———— New York: Leavitt, Trow & Company, 1849. 251 p. 12mo HEH, NYP, UV
NYP copy has written notation on title page: "Richd M. Strong. By William H. Rossiter. New York City."

889a EARLY IMPRESSIONS . . . Boston: Bowles and Dearborn, 1828.
137 p., illus. 8vo   AAS, Y

889b ——— 2d ed. Boston: Allen and Ticknor, 1833. 143 p.
12mo   BP

890 EASTMAN, MARY (HENDERSON). Dahcotah; or, Life and Legends
of the Sioux around Fort Snelling . . . With Preface by Mrs.
C. M. Kirkland . . . New York: John Wiley, 1849. 268 p.,
illus. 12mo
AAS, B, BA, BP, H, HEH, IN, LC, LCP, N, NYP, UC, UM, UP, UV, Y
Contents: Mock-Pe-En-Dag-A-Win; or, Checkered Cloud, the Medicine
Woman—Red Earth; or, Mocka-Doota-Win—Wenona; or, The Virgin's
Feast—The Dahcotah Convert—Wabasha—The Dahcotah Bride—Shah-Co-
Pee, the Orator of the Sioux—Oye-Kar-Mani-Vim, the Track-Maker—Eta
Keazah; or, Sullen Face—Tonwa-Yah-Pe-Kin, the Spies—The Maiden's
Rock; or, Wenona's Leap—The Indian in a Trance—Oeche-Monesah, the
Wanderer—Tah-We-Chu-Kin, the Wife—Wah-Zee-Yah, Another of the
Giant Gods of the Dahcotahs—Storms in Life and Nature; or, Unktahe and
the Thunder Bird—Haokah Ozape, the Dance to the Giant—U-Mi-Ne-
Wah-Chippe; or, To Dance Around.

891 EASY NAT; or, Boston Bars and Boston Boys. A Tale of Home
Trials, by One Who Knows Them . . . Boston: Redding and
Company, 1844. 48 p. 8vo   AAS, BA, H, UV, Y

892 ——— 3d ed. Boston: Redding and Company, 1844. 48 p.
8vo   AAS, BP

893 EDMUND AND MARGARET; or, Sobriety and Faithfulness Rewarded
. . . Cambridge: Printed by Hilliard and Metcalf, March, 1822.
60 p. 12mo   AAS, B, BA, BP, H, HEH, N, NYH, NYP, UC, UP, UV, Y

894 EDWARD CLAVERING; or, The Fatal Marriage. A Romance of Real
Life. Boston: H. L. Williams, 1846. 50 p. 8vo   Y

895 EDWARDS, CHARLES. Feathers from My Own Wings . . . New
York: William Stodart, 1832. 200 p., illus. 12mo
AAS, B, H, HEH, LC, N, NYH, NYP, UC, UP, UV, Y
Contains: The Cavalier—The Widow and Her Son—A Stray Chapter of
Don Quixotte—The Boy with the Golden Locks—The Baron of Arc—Rose
Raimonde—The Blind Stripling—The Indians.

896 ELLEN MERTON, the Belle of Lowell; or, The Confessions of the "G. F. K." Club. Boston: Brainard & Co., 1844. 32 p. 8vo
HEH, NYP

Printed in double cols.

896a ELLEN STUART; or, The Rescued Heiress ... [N.p., 1850?]. Caption title, 40 p. 8vo
AAS
Printed in double cols.
Boston.

897 ELLEN WOODVILLE; or, Life in the West ... New York: Henry G. Langley, 1844. 160 p. 8vo   AAS, BP, NYH, NYP, Y
Printed in double cols.

898 ELLET, ELIZABETH FRIES (LUMMIS). Evenings at Woodlawn ... New York: Baker and Scribner, 1849. 348 p. 12mo
AAS, BP, HEH, LC, LCP, NYH, NYP, UM, UV, Y
Tales and legends of Europe.

899 ———— Rambles about the Country ... Boston: Marsh, Capen, Lyon, and Webb, 1840. 257 p. 12mo
AAS, BP, H, HEH, LC, N, NYH, UP, UV, Y
Contains essays, poems, and fiction.

900 ———— ———— Boston: Thomas H. Webb & Co. [cop. 1840]. 257 p. 12mo   AAS, UM, UV
This firm is listed in the Boston Directories for the years 1842-45.

901 ———— ———— New York: Harper & Brothers, 1847. 257 p. 12mo   AAS, HEH, NYP, Y

902 ———— Scenes in the Life of Joanna of Sicily ... Boston: Marsh, Capen, Lyon, and Webb, 1840. 256 p. 12mo
AAS, B, BA, BP, H, HEH, LC, N, NYP, UC, UP, UV, Y

903 ELLIOT, SAMUEL HAYES. Rolling Ridge; or, The Book of Four and Twenty Chapters ... [anon.]. Boston: Crocker and Brewster, 1838. 266 p. 12mo   AAS, B, HEH, LC, N, NYP, UP, UV, Y
New England; contemporary.

904 ———— The Sequel to Rolling Ridge. By the Author of the Latter, Assisted by the Worthy Mr. Fory ... [anon.]. Boston: Crocker and Brewster, 1844. 248 p. 12mo
AAS, LC, N, UP, UV, Y

ELMWOOD, ELNATHAN, *Esq., pseud.* *See* Greene, Asa

ELMWOOD, MRS. MARY, *pseud.* *See* Arthur, Timothy Shay

EMBURY, EMMA CATHERINE (MANLEY). The Blind Girl. *See* No. 905.

905 ———— Constance Latimer; or, The Blind Girl. With Other Tales
... New York: Harper & Brothers, 1838. 169 p. 12mo
AAS, BA, LC, N, NYP, UP, UV, Y
Also contains: The Son and Heir—The Village Tragedy.

906 ———— ———— New York: Harper & Brothers, 1845. 222 p.
12mo AAS, UV, Y
Title reads: *The Blind Girl. With Other Tales.*
Contents: Constance Latimer; or, The Blind Girl—The Son and Heir—The
Village Tragedy—Newton Ainslie—Frank Morrison.

907 ———— Glimpses of Home Life; or, Causes and Consequences
... New York: J. C. Riker, 1848. 324 p. 12mo
AAS, BP, HEH, NYP, UP, UV, Y
Contents: Marriage—Flora Lester; or, Scenes in the Life of a Belle—The
One Fault—The Lady's Lesson; or, How to Lose a Lover—Fortune-Hunt-
ing; or, The Heiress—Faith Templeton—The Mistaken Choice; or, Three
Years of Married Life—Love at First Sight—Wilfulness; or, The Wife's Tale
—Money-making; or, Success Not Always Happiness—The Mother and
Daughter—The Village Bride—Manoeuvring; or, The Doctor's Visit—The
First and Second Wife; or, The Confessions of a Discontented Man.

908 ———— ———— New York: J. C. Riker, 129 Fulton Street [n.d.].
324 p., illus. 12mo AAS, B, HEH, N, UM, Y
Preface dated 1848.
Title reads: *The Home Offering; or, Causes and Consequences.*

———— Grace Moreland; or, The Weight of Trifles. *In* M. M.
Ballou, Albert Simmons (1849), No. 229.

———— The Home Offering. *See* Glimpses of Home Life, No.
908.

———— Our Jessie; or, The Exclusives. *In* Stories from Real
Life (1848), No. 2512.

909 EMMA SOMERVILLE; or, The Violated Sanctuary. An Interesting
Tale. By an American Lady. Lowell: Nathl. L. Dayton, 1845.
127 p. 8vo   AAS, B, HEH, Y
Massachusetts; early 19th cent.

910 ENGLISH, THOMAS DUNN. 1844; or, The Power of the "S.F." A
Tale, Developing the Secret Action of Parties during the Pres-
idential Campaign of 1844 ... New York: Burgess, Stringer &
Co., 1847. 300 p. 12mo   BP, LC, N, Y
At head of title: "Mirror Library—New Series."

911 ——— Walter Woolfe; or, The Doom of the Drinker ... New
York: William B. Smith & Co., 1847. 89 p., illus. 8vo   NYP

912 ENGLISH, WILLIAM B. Gertrude Howard, the Maid of Humble
Life; or, Temptations Resisted . . . Boston: Redding & Co.,
1843. Cover title, 32 p., illus. 8vo   AAS, B, BP, NYP, UP, Y
On p. 32: "Williams & Burkhead, Franklin Press, 22 Congress St."
Printed in double cols.
Boston; contemporary.

913 ——— ——— 2d ed. Boston: Redding & Co., 1843. 32 p.,
illus. 8vo   UC, UV
Printed in double cols.

914 ——— Hazards of the Heart; or, Woman's Wrongs and Woman's Revenge ... [Boston: Bradley & Co., 184-?] 40 p. 8vo
     AAS, BP, UM, Y
Caption title.

915 ——— Morton; or, Smiles and Tears. A Story of the Past and
Present ... Boston: Redding & Co., 1845. Cover title, 46 p.
8vo   HEH, Y
Printed in double cols.

916 ——— ——— Boston: Published at 66 Cornhill, (upstairs),
1847. Cover title, 46 p. 8vo   B
Title reads: *Smiles and Tears; or, The Lost and Won. A Thrilling Story of
the Past and Present* [anon.].
Caption title and headlines: "Morton; or, The Lost and Won."
Printed in double cols.

917 ⸻ Rosina Meadows, the Village Maid; or, Temptations Unveiled. A Story of City Scenes and Every Day Life ... Boston: Redding & Co., 1843. Cover title, 32 p., illus. Fol.

AAS, B, HEH, IN, LC, N, NYP, UP, UV, Y

Printed in double cols.

918 ⸻ ⸻ Boston: Redding & Co., 1843. 78 p., illus. 12mo

H

919 ⸻ ⸻ Boston: Redding & Co., 1846. 72 p., illus. 8vo

HEH, Y

⸻ Smiles and Tears. *See* Morton; or, Smiles and Tears, No. 916.

920 ENGOLLS, WILLIAM. The Countess; or, The Inquisitor's Punishments. A Tale of Spain . . . Boston: Gleason's Publishing Hall, 1847. 100 p., illus. 8vo AAS, B, UV, Y

Printed in double cols.

LC has a title page, deposited Nov. 16, 1846.

920a EQUALITY; or, A History of Lithconia. Philadelphia: Published by the Liberal Union, 1837. 119 p. 16mo HEH

The 1947 reprint suggests Dr. James Reynolds, of Philadelphia, as the author.

Utopian novel.

921 ERNEST HARCOURT; or, The Loyalist's Son. A Romance of the Revolution, by the Author of "Marion's Men," "The Southern Whig," ... Philadelphia: A. J. Rockafellar, 1843. 59 p. 8vo

AAS, H, LC, N, UC, UP, UV, Y

Printed in double cols.

922 EUGENIUS AND SELIMA; or, The Fatal Effects of Parental Tyranny. A Moral Story. West Springfield [Mass.]: Sold at the printing office, 1798. 12 p. 12mo LC

923 EVANS, SARAH ANN, *afterwards* MRS. LEMONOSKEY. Resignation: An American Novel, by a Lady . . . [anon.]. Boston: Printed for the author by John B. Russell, 1825. 2 vols. 12mo

AAS, BA, BP, H, IN, LC, N, UC, UM, UV, Y

American Revolution.

924 EVELINE NEVILLE; or, "A Spirit, Yet a Woman Too." By a Lady
of the South . . . New York: Burgess, Stringer & Co., 1845.
108 p. 8vo   AAS, HEH, LC, NYP, UV, Y
Printed in double cols.
England.
Johnson attributes an *Eveline Neville* to Mrs. Martha Featon Hunter, of
Essex County, Va.

925 EVELINE TREVOR: A Romance of the Revolution, by the Author
of "Marion's Men," "Ernest Harcourt". . . Philadelphia: A. J.
Rockafellar, 1843. 56 p. 8vo   AAS, HEH, N, UC, UP, UV, Y
Printed in double cols.

EVERPOINT, *pseud. See* Field, Joseph M.

F., B. C. Working a Passage; or, Life in a Liner. *See* Briggs,
Charles Frederick, Nos. 411-412.

F., J. The Battle of Lexington. *In* The Romantic Historian
(1834), No. 2154.

FAIRFIELD, SUMNER LINCOLN. The Forest Citadel. *In* J. Hall,
Winter Evenings (1829), No. 1104, and The Soldier's Bride
(1829), No. 1105.

926 —— The Last Night of Pompeii. A Poem . . . New York:
Printed by Elliott and Palmer, 1832. 309 p. 12mo
AAS, B, BP, H, HEH, IN, LC, LCP, N, NYH, NYP, UC, UM, UP, UV, Y
Contains: Walter Colebrook.—A Tale, pp. 239-300.

927 FAIRY TALES; or, Interesting Tales . . . New York: Nafis & Cor-
nish, 278 Pearl Street [cop. 1840]. 192 p., illus. 12mo
AAS, BA, UV, Y
Contents: The Storm Lights of Anzaska—Monos and Daimonos—The Iron
Shroud—The Rock of the Candle—The Sisters—Der Frieschutz—The
Comet—A Night in a Church—The Dummburg—The Legend of Bethel
Rock—The Oratory.
S. G. Goodrich denied authorship in his *Recollections of a Lifetime* (1857).

928 THE FAMILY OF THE SEISERS: A Satirical Tale of the City of New
York . . . New York: Printed for the author, by J. M. Elliott,
1844. 2 pts. 8vo   H, HEH, LC, NYH, UP, UV, Y
Copyrighted by George S. Marshalk, but I have been unable to prove that
he was the author.
Printed in double cols.

929 THE FANATIC; or, The Perils of Peter Pliant, the Poor Pedagogue, by the Author of Winona. Philadelphia: Printed and published at the office of the American Citizen, 1846. 73 p. 8vo
BP, LC, UV, Y

Copyrighted by Wm. H. Brisbane, but I have been unable to prove that he was the author.
Printed in double cols.
Maryland.

930 FANNY FORRESTER. Philadelphia: Thomas Latimer, 1837. 36 p. 12mo
BP, LC, UV
At head of title: "Agrarian Stories. Number One."
A. W. Thayer, attrib. au.

930a FARR, JONATHAN. The Sunday School Teacher's Funeral. With Some Account of Rachel Benson, and the Rev. Mr. Loraine [anon.]. Boston: B. H. Green, 1835. 51 p. 12mo H, HEH

931 FATE OF THE STEAM-SHIP PRESIDENT, Which Sailed from New York, March 11th, 1841, Bound for Liverpool. Boston: For sale at the periodical depots, 1845. 34 p. 8vo AAS, BP, H, UV

932 FATHER OSWALD: A Genuine Catholic Story ... New York: Casserly & Sons, 1843. 304 p. 12mo
AAS, HEH, IN, LC, NYP, NYS, UP, UV, Y
England.

933 ——— Baltimore, 1847. 299 p. 12mo
At head of title: "Murphy's Improved Stereotype Edition."
The Union Catalogue at LC locates a copy in the University of Illinois Library.

FAY, THEODORE SEDGWICK. The Author. In The Atlantic Club-Book (1843), Nos. 195-196.

934 ——— The Countess Ida: A Tale of Berlin ... [anon.]. New York: Harper & Brothers, 1840. 2 vols. 12mo
AAS, B, BA, BP, HEH, IN, LC, N, NYP, UC, UP, UV, Y

935 ——— Hoboken: A Romance of New York ... New York: Harper & Brothers, 1843. 2 vols. 12mo
AAS, B, BP, H, HEH, IN, LC, N, NYH, NYP, UC, UP, UV, Y

———— The Little Hard-faced Old Gentleman. *In* The Atlantic Club-Book (1834), Nos. 195-196.

936 ———— Norman Leslie: A Tale of the Present Times... [anon.]. New York: Harper & Brothers, 1835. 2 vols. 12mo AAS, B, BA, BP, H(V.2), HEH, IN, LC, N, NYH, NYS, UC(V.2), UM, UP, UV, Y New York City and Italy.

937 ———— ———— 2d ed. New York: Harper & Brothers, 1835. 2 vols. 12mo AAS, NYP, UV, Y

938 ———— ———— 2d ed. New York: Harper & Brothers, 1836. 2 vols. 12mo HM

939 ———— ———— 2d ed. New York: Harper & Brothers, 1841. 2 vols. 12mo AAS, H, Y

———— An Outline Sketch. *In* The Atlantic Club-Book (1834), Nos. 195-196.

940 ———— Robert Rueful; or, A Lesson to Valetudinarians... Philadelphia: Louis A. Godey, 1844. 69 p. 8vo AAS, HEH, Y New York City.

———— Snorers. *In* The Atlantic Club-Book (1834), Nos. 195-196.

941 ———— Sydney Clifton; or, Vicissitudes in Both Hemispheres. A Tale of the Nineteenth Century... [anon.]. New York: Harper & Brothers, 1839. 2 vols. 12mo
AAS, B, BP, H, HEH, IN, LC, N, NYP, NYS, UP, UV, Y

———— *ed.*, Crayon Sketches. *See* Cox, William, No. 771.

941a THE FEMALE LAND PIRATE; or, Awful, Mysterious, and Horrible Disclosures of Amanda Bannorris, Wife and Accomplice of Richard Bannorris, a Leader of That Terrible Band of Robbers and Murderers, Known Far and Wide as the Murrell Men. Cincinnati: E. E. Barclay, 1847. 28 p., illus. 8vo AAS

941b ———— Cincinnati: E. E. Barclay, 1848. 32 p., illus. 8vo
Listed in the *Annotated Eberstadt Catalogs of Americana*, II, 132:245.

942 FEMALE ROBINSON CRUSOE: A Tale of the American Wilderness
... New York: Printed by Jared W. Bell, 1837. 286 p. 12mo
BP, LC, N, NYP, NYS, UV, Y
Also contains: Indian Legends—Imlac and Clara—The Missed Ship—The
Drunken Wife.

943 THE FEMALE WANDERER: An Interesting Tale Founded on Fact.
Written by Herself. [N.p.]: Printed for the proprietor, 1824.
24 p. 12mo   AAS
New York; contemporary.
A Cordelia Stark may be the author, as suggested by Mrs. Emory C. Skarshaug, in "Bibliographical Notes," *Papers of the Bibliographical Society of
America,* XXXVI (1942), 230-231. Mrs. Skarshaug has since informed me
that the Michigan copy mentioned in her article is not dated 1820 but 1829,
"with the figure 9 altered or worn to the point where it was practically a
zero." The 1820 ed. recorded in *Amer. Fict.,* 1st ed., is in error.
H has an 1854 ed. with author statement on the title page, "By W. P. Thompson," not identified. This claim of authorship has not been otherwise substan-
tiated.

943a ——— Rochester, N. Y.: Printed by Edwin Scrantom, 1826.
47 p. 12mo   AAS
Title reads: *The Female Wanderer: A Tale Founded on Fact.*

944 ——— Wells River, Vt.: White & Reed; E. & W. Eaton, printers,
Danville, Vt., 1826. 60 p. 24mo   AAS, BP, H, HEH, UV, Y
Title reads: *The Female Wanderer: A Very Interesting Tale Founded on
Fact. Written by the Wanderer Herself.*

945 ——— Danville, Vt.: White & Reed; E. & W. Eaton, printers,
1826.
Ed. from a 1939 Tuttle catalog.

946 ——— Bridgeport: Rufus Langdon, 1826. 43 p., illus. 24mo
Y

947 ——— Bridgeport: Rufus Langdon, 1827. 43 p., illus. 24mo
Ed. from sales catalog.

948 ——— Boston, (Mass.): Leonard Deming; Hooton & Teprell,
printers, 1829. 34, [2] p. 12mo   AAS, H, UC, Y

949 ——— Wells River, Vt.: I. White, 1834. 58 p. 24mo AAS, B, Y

949a ——— Brattleboro, Vt.: Wm. E. Ryther, printer, 1838. 43,
[1] p. 24mo   AAS

950 ——— Boston: Published for the author, 1846. 24 p., illus.
12mo   H, UP, UV, Y
Title reads: *The Remarkable Narrative of Cordelia Krats; or, The Female Wanderer. Written by Herself.*

950a ——— Boston: Printed for the public, 1849. 48 p., illus. 12mo
                                                                    AAS, Y
Title reads: *The Remarkable Narrative of Cordelia and Edwin; or, The Female Wanderer.*

FIBBLETON, GEORGE, *Esq., pseud.* *See* Greene, Asa

951 FIDELITY REWARDED; or, The History of Polly Granville. In a
Series of Letters . . . Boston: From the press of Young and
Minns, 1796. 99 p. 12mo   AAS, UV
Philadelphia; contemporary.

952 FIDFADDY, FREDERICK AUGUSTUS, *Esq., pseud.* The Adventures of
Uncle Sam in Search after His Lost Honor. By Frederick
Augustus Fidfaddy, Esq. [pseud.] . . . Middletown [Conn.]:
Printed by Seth Richards, 1816. 142 p. 12mo
                            AAS, B, BA, H, HEH, IN, LC, N, NYP, UC, UP, UV, Y
War of 1812.

953 FIELD, JOSEPH M. The Drama in Pokerville: The Bench and Bar
of Jurytown, and Other Stories . . . Philadelphia: Carey and
Hart, 1847. 200 p., illus. 12mo
                            AAS, B, BP, HEH, LC, LCP, N, UC, UP, UV

954 ——— ——— Philadelphia: A. Hart, 1850. 200 p., illus. 12mo
                                                                    BA, BP, LC

——— French without a Master, by "Straws." *In* W. T. Porter,
ed., A Quarter Race in Kentucky (1847), Nos. 2063-64.

——— Kicking a Yankee. *In* W. T. Porter, *ed.*, A Quarter Race
in Kentucky (1847), Nos. 2063-64.

955 ——— Taos: A Romance of the Massacre, Founded upon the Terrible Events of January and February, 1847, in Taos Valley . . . By Everpoint [pseud.] . . . Saint Louis: Reveille Job Office, 1847. 26 p. 8vo   H
Printed in double cols.

956 FIELDS, WILLIAM, JR., *comp.* The Literary and Miscellaneous Scrap Book, Consisting of Tales and Anecdotes . . . Knoxville, Tenn.: Printed and published by William Fields, Jr., 1833. 600 p. 8vo   HEH, LC
Contains: Lafitte the Baratarian Chief: A Tale Founded on Fact—The Gambler—Henry and Caroline—Everard Graham, by Willis G. Clark—The Hazlewood Family: A Tale of the Revolution—The Friends.

957 ——— ——— Knoxville, Tenn.: Printed and published by William Fields, Jr., 1837. 600 p. 8vo   NYH

FINCH, JOHN, *attrib. au. See* The Soldier's Orphan (1812), No. 2478.

957a FLAGG, EDMUND. Edmond Dantes. With Elegant Illustrations. A Sequel to the Count of Monte-Cristo, by Alexandre Dumas . . . [anon.]. Louisville, Ky.: George W. Noble, 1849. 203 p., illus. 8vo   HEH

957b ——— The Howard Queen: A Romance of History . . . St. Louis, Missouri, 1848. 78 p., illus. 8vo   LC
Printed in double cols.

957c ——— Monte-Cristo's Daughter. Sequel to Alexander Dumas' Great Novel, "The Count of Monte-Cristo," and Conclusion of "Edmond Dantes" . . . [anon.]. New York: Wm. L. Allison Company [1849?]. 372 p. 8vo   NYP

FLETCHER, JULIA A. The Poetry of Poverty. *In* M. Woodruff, *ed.,* A Drop from the Bucket (1847), No. 2759.

958 FLINT, TIMOTHY. Francis Berrian; or, The Mexican Patriot . . . [anon.]. Boston: Cummings, Hilliard and Company, 1826. 2 vols. 12mo
AAS, BA, BP, H, HEH, HM (V.2), IN, N, NYP, UC, UP, UV, Y
Early 19th cent.

959 ———— ———— 2d ed. Philadelphia: Key & Biddle, 1834. 2 vols.
12mo   AAS, LC, NYP(V.2), Y

960 ———— ———— 2d ed. Cincinnati: E. H. Flint, 1834. 2 vols.
12mo   HM

961 ———— George Mason, the Young Backwoodsman; or, 'Don't
Give Up the Ship.' A Story of the Mississippi . . . [anon.]. Boston: Hilliard, Gray, Little, and Wilkins, 1829. 167 p. 12mo
        AAS, B, BA, BP, H, HEH, IN, LC, N, NYH, NYP, UC, UP, UV, Y

962 ———— The Life and Adventures of Arthur Clenning . . . [anon.].
Philadelphia: Towar & Hogan, 1828. 2 vols. 12mo
        AAS, B, BA, BP, H, HEH, IN, LC, UM, UP, UV, Y
South Sea Islands and New York City; early 19th cent.

963 ———— The Shoshonee Valley: A Romance . . . [anon.]. Cincinnati: E. H. Flint, 1830. 2 vols. 12mo
        AAS, B, BA, BP, H, HEH, LC, N, NYH, NYP, UP, UV, Y
Oregon River; contemporary.

963a FLIP, FRANK, *pseud.* The Cockney in America; or, The Adventures of Triptolemus Snooks, Esq. Edited by Frank Flip
[pseud.] . . . New York: William H. Graham, 1848. 72 p.,
illus. 8vo   AAS, NYP

964 FLORENCE DE LACEY; or, The Coquette. A Novel, by the Author
of "Abel Parsons, a Tale of the Great Fire." New York: E. Winchester, 1845. 106 p. 8vo   LC, N, NYP, UP, UV, Y
Printed in double cols.
New York City.

965 FOLEY, FANNY, *pseud.* Romance of the Ocean: A Narrative of
the Voyage of the Wildfire to California. Illustrated with
Stories, Anecdotes, etc. By Fanny Foley [pseud.] . . . Philadelphia: Lindsay and Blakiston, 1850. 218 p. 12mo
        AAS, H, HEH, LC, LCP, NYP, UP, UV, Y

966 FOLLEN, ELIZA LEE (CABOT). The Skeptic . . . [anon.]. Boston:
James Munroe and Company, 1835. 143 p. 12mo
        AAS, BA, BP, HEH, LC, N, UM, UP, UV, Y
Included in *Scenes and Characters Illustrating Christian Truths.* No. II
(1835).
Boston; contemporary.

967 ——— ——— Boston: James Munroe and Company, 1850. 143 p. 12mo   H

968 ——— Sketches of Married Life . . . Boston: Hilliard, Gray and Co., 1838. 304 p. 8vo   AAS, B, BA, BP, H, HEH, N, UP, Y
Boston; contemporary.

969 ——— ——— Boston: Hilliard, Gray and Co., 1839. 291 p. 8vo   AAS, UC, UM, UV, Y

970 ——— ——— Boston, 1841.
The Union Catalogue at LC locates a copy in the Princeton University Library.

971 ——— ——— Boston: William Crosby and H. P. Nichols, 1847. 291 p. 8vo   AAS, NYP, Y

972 FORBES, GERRITT VAN HUSEN.   Green Mountain Annals: A Tale of Truth . . .   New York: Burnett & Smith, 1832.   140 p. 12mo
AAS, B, HEH, LC, UP, UV, Y
Also contains: Death's Doings—The Materialist—A Fragment.

973 FORD, EDWARD.   The Duchess of Baden: A Tale of the French Revolution.   With a History of the Fall of the Marquis Louis de Beauharnais, and the Flight and Perils of His Family in France, Spain, Saint Domingo, and Philadelphia . . .   Philadelphia: Carey & Hart, 1849.   110 p. 8vo   LC, Y
Cover title reads: "Stephanie Beauharnais, the Duches of Baden . . . 1850."

FORESTER, FANNY, *pseud.   See* Judson, Emily (Chubbuck)

FORESTER, FRANK, *pseud.   See* Ballou, Maturin Murray

FORESTER, FRANK, *pseud.   See* Herbert, Henry William

974 FORREST, H. P.   Nancie; or, The Witch of the Ruined Abbey.   A Romance of France . . .   Boston: F. Gleason, 1848.   100 p., illus. 8vo   B, UV, Y
Printed in double cols.
18—.

975 THE FORTUNATE DISCOVERY; or, The History of Henry Villars. By a Young Lady of the State of New York. New York: Printed by R. Wilson, 1798. 180 p. 12mo

AAS, HEH, IN, LC, LCP, NYP, NYS, UC, UP, UV, Y

New York and England; 1770-90.

976 ——— New York printed—Stockbridge: Reprinted by Rosseter & Willard, 1798. 148 p. 12mo NYP, UV

977 DELETE.

977a THE FORTUNES OF A YOUNG WIDOW: A Veritable Revelation of New York Life in the Nineteenth Century. By an Old Inhabitant. New York: Stearns & Company, 1850. 111 p. 8vo UV
Printed in double cols.

FORY, MR., *jt. au.* *See* Elliot, S. H. The Sequel to Rolling Ridge (1844), No. 904.

978 FOSTER, GEORGE G. Celio; or, New York Above-ground and Under-ground ... New York: Dewitt & Davenport, Tribune Buildings, Nassau Street [cop. 1850]. 144 p. 8vo

AAS, H, HEH, LC, N, NYH, UP, UV, Y

979 ——— New York by Gas-Light: With Here and There a Streak of Sunshine ... New York: Dewitt & Davenport, 1850. 127 p. 8vo AAS, BA, H, HEH, N, NYS, UP, UV, Y

980 ——— New York in Slices, by an Experienced Carver. Being the Original Slices Published in the N. Y. Tribune. Revised, Enlarged, and Corrected by the Author ... [anon.]. New York: William H. Graham, 1849. 121 p., illus. 8vo

N, UC, UV, Y

981 ——— ——— New York: William H. Graham, 1849. 128 p., illus. 8vo AAS, BA, BP, H, NYH, UM, UV

982 ——— ——— New York: W. F. Burgess, 1849. 128 p., illus. 8vo AAS, BA, LC, NYP, Y
NYP cover imprint dated 1850.

983 ——— ——— New York: W. F. Burgess, 22 Ann Street [cop. 1848]. 128 p., illus. 8vo HEH, NYS

984 FOSTER, HANNAH (WEBSTER). The Boarding School; or, Lessons of a Preceptress to Her Pupils ... By a Lady of Massachusetts ... [anon.]. Boston: Printed by I. Thomas and E. T. Andrews, 1798. 252 p. 12mo

    AAS, B, BP, H, HEH, IN, JCB, LC, N, NYP, UC, UM, UP, UV, Y

985 —————— Boston: J. P. Peaslee, 1829. 228 p., illus. 16mo

    AAS, B, BA, BP, H, NYH, UC, UM, UP, UV, Y

986 ——— The Coquette; or, The History of Eliza Wharton. A Novel, Founded on Fact. By a Lady of Massachusetts [anon.]. Boston: Printed by Samuel Etheridge, 1797. 261, [1] p. 12mo

    AAS, HEH, LC, NYP, UC, UV, Y

Written in a series of letters.
Massachusetts; late 18th cent.

987 —————— Charlestown [Mass.]: Printed by Samuel Etheridge, 1802. 261, [1] p. 12mo

    AAS, IN, LC, N, NYP, NYS, UC, UV, Y

988 —————— 3d ed. Newburyport: Thomas & Whipple, 1811. 242 p. 12mo

    AAS, B, BP, H, HEH, IN, LC, N, NYP, UC, UP, UV, Y

989 —————— 4th ed. Newburyport: Charles Whipple, 1824. 303 p. 12mo

    AAS, BA, NYP, Y

990 —————— 10th ed. Exeter: Abel Brown, 1828. 264 p. 12mo

    AAS, B, HEH, IN, UP, UPI, UV, Y

991 —————— 11th ed. Exeter: Abel Brown, 1828. 264 p., illus. 12mo

    AAS, IN, NYP, UM, Y

992 —————— 12th ed. New York: J. P. Clushan, 1831. 264 p., illus. 12mo

    AAS, NYP, UC

993 —————— 30th ed. Boston: Printed and published by Charles Gaylord, 1833. 264 p., illus. 12mo

    AAS, B, H, HEH, NYH, NYP, UP, UV, Y

R. L. Shurter, "Mrs. Hannah Webster Foster and the Early American Novel," *American Literature*, IV (1932), 307, says, "actually this was the thirteenth edition of the work."

994 ——— ——— 30th ed. Boston: Printed and published by Charles Gaylord, 1840. 264 p. 12mo   AAS, BP, H, LC, UV, Y

995 FOSTER, HENRI. Ellen Grafton. The Den of Crime: A Romance of Secret Life in the Empire City . . . Boston: Star Spangled Banner office, 1850. 91 p., illus. 8vo   BP
Also contains: The Scout and the Savages; or, Lovers of the Forest.
At head of title: "A Romance of Secret Life in New York."
Printed in double cols.

996 THE FOUNTAIN AND THE BOTTLE; Comprising Thrilling Examples of the Opposite Effects of Temperance and Intemperance. Edited by a Son of Temperance. Hartford: Case, Tiffany & Co., 1850. 448 p., illus. 8vo   LC
Contains: Mike Smiley, by Father Frank—Emma Alton, by Mrs. Caroline H. Butler—The Fear of Ridicule—The Spoiled Child—Doctor Gray and His Daughter, by J. R. Orton—Brother and Sister, by T. S. Arthur—Charley Randolph, by Francis C. Woodworth—A Single Glass of Wine, by Mrs. R. S. Harvey—John Hinchley, by Mrs. C. M. Kirkland—The Last Interview, by D. Strock, Jr.—The Raftman's Oath, by D. Strock, Jr.—It's Only a Drop —Charles Clifford, by D. Strock, Jr.—James Blair; or, Love in the Valley of the Juniata, by Grace Sherwood—Karl and Corinne, by Mrs. Mary B. Horton—The Pledge by Moon-light, by Amerel—Steps to Ruin, by Mrs. Jane C. Campbell—Ned Summers, the Cabin-Boy, by Amerel—The Emigrant's Wife, by Amerel—The Temperance Lecture, by Amerel—The Man Who Enjoyed Himself, by Henry Travers—Twelve o'Clock, by Henry Travers— Paying for Sport, by Henry Travers—Locked Out, by Amerel—The Man Who Made a Beast of Himself, by Henry Travers—The Temperance Grocer, by Amerel—George Sandford, by Amerel.

996a ——— Boston: Horace Wentworth, 1850. 448 p., illus. 8vo
H, HEH, Y

997 FOWLER, GEORGE. A Flight to the Moon; or, The Vision of Randalthus . . . Baltimore: Printed and sold by A. Miltenberger, 1813. 185 p. 12mo   AAS, H, HEH, LC, N, UM, UV, Y

998 ——— The Wandering Philanthropist; or, Lettres from a Chinese. Written during His Residence in the United States . . . Philadelphia: Printed by Bartholomew Graves, 1810. 300 p. 12mo   AAS, BA, H, IN, LC, NYH, NYP, UM, UP, UV, Y

999 FOX, MARY ANNA. George Allen, the Only Son. By a Young Lady of Boston [anon.]. Boston: William Peirce, 1835. 136 p. 12mo   AAS, BP, NYP, UP, UV, Y
Massachusetts; contemporary.

1000 ——— ——— Boston: D. H. Ela and Co., printers, 1846. 132
p. 12mo   AAS, BP, LC, UC, UP, Y

1001 ——— ——— Boston: Charles Fox, 1847. 132 p., illus. 12mo
                                          AAS, H, HEH, IN, N, NYP, UM, UP, UV, Y

1002 ——— ——— Boston: Charles Fox [cop. 1846]. 132 p. 12mo
                                                          AAS, B, IN, Y

1003 Fox, MARY L. The Ruined Deacon: A True Story. By a Lady
[anon.]. Boston: Ford & Damrell, 1834. 31 p. 16mo
                                                          AAS, HEH, LC, UP, Y

1004 ——— ——— Boston: D. H. Ela and Co., printers, 1846. 36 p.
12mo   AAS, H, IN, Y

1005 ——— ——— Boston: Abner Forbes, printer, 1847. 36 p.
12mo   AAS, HEH, Y

1006 ——— ——— Boston: C. C. P. Moody, printer, 1849. 36 p.
12mo   B, HEH, UM

1006a FRAETAS, JOSIAH A. The Fatal Legacy; or, The Doomed Heir.
By J. Melville [pseud.] . . . New York: William H. Graham,
1846. 64 p. 8vo   HEH

1006b ——— Guildford; or, Tried by His Peers. A Novel, by J. A.
Fraetas. New York: William H. Graham, 1849. 114 p. 8vo
                                                          AAS
Printed in double cols.
Preface states that from 1845 to 1847 the author wrote four novels under the
pseudonym J. Melville, which he thereafter relinquished in deference to
Herman Melville.

——— See also Nos. 777, 1872-74, for title entries which are
now identified as by Fraetas.

FRANCO, HARRY, pseud. See Briggs, Charles Frederick

FRANK, Father. Mike Smiley. In The Fountain and the Bottle
(1850), No. 996.

1007 FRANKLIN, AUGUSTUS. Anne Melbourne; or, The Return to Virtue. A Tale of Boston ... Boston: H. L. Williams, 1846. 48 p., illus. 8vo HEH, UV
  LC has a title page, deposited Feb. 20, 1846.

1008 —— Izora; or, The Lost One Found. A Tale of the 18th Century ... Boston: Gleason's Publishing Hall, 1846. 66 p. 8vo
  HEH, NYP, UP, UV, Y

1009 —— The Sea-Gull; or, The Pirates League ... Boston: H. L. Williams, 1846. 88 p., illus. 8vo BP, Y
  Printed in double cols.
  LC has a title page, deposited Jan. 23, 1846.

1010 —— The Widow's Pirate Son; or, Pauline Coustry, the Corsair's Mate. A Tale of the Province of Massachusetts ... Boston: H. L. Williams, 1845. 48 p., illus. 8vo BP, HEH
  LC has a title page, deposited Sept. 19, 1845.

FRANKLIN, EDWARD, *attrib. au.* *See* Bloomfield, Obadiah Benjamin Franklin, *M.D., pseud.*

1011 FRENCH, JAMES STRANGE. Elkswatawa; or, The Prophet of the West. A Tale of the Frontier ... [anon.]. New York: Harper & Brothers, 1836. 2 vols. 12mo
  AAS, B, BA, BP, H, HEH, IN, LC, N, NYP, UC, UM, UP, UV, Y

1012 FRIDAY CHRISTIAN; or, The First-Born on Pitcairn's Island. By a Poor "Member of Christ" ... New York: D. Appleton & Co., 1849. 138 p., illus. 12mo AAS, H, HEH, NYP, UV, Y

1013 FRINK, HENRY CLAY. Alow and Aloft: On Board and on Shore ... Rochester: William Alling, 1842. 179 p. 12mo
  AAS, HEH, N, NYP, UC, UP, UV, Y

FULLER, FRANCES A. *See* Victor, Frances (Fuller) Barrett

1014 FURMAN, GARRIT. Redfield: A Long-Island Tale, of the Seventeenth Century ... [anon.]. New York: O. Wilder, & Jas. M. Campbell, 1825. 214 p. 12mo
  AAS, BP, HEH, IN, LC, LCP, NYH, Y

G., PERCIVAL, *pseud.* *See* Irving, Peter

1014a GALES, WINIFRED (MARSHALL). Matilda Berkely; or, Family Anecdotes . . . [anon.]. Raleigh (N.C.): Printed by J. Gales, printer to the State, 1804. 224 p. 12mo   HEH

1014b GALLAHER, JAMES. The Pilgrimage of Adam and David, with Sketches of Their Heavenly Employment. A Bible Allegory . . . Cincinnati: Derby, Bradley & Co., 1846. 420 p. 12mo
B, BP

1014c —————— ——— 2d ed. Boston: Crocker and Brewster, New York: M. W. Dodd. Philadelphia: William S. Martien, 1849. 420 p. 12mo   AAS, BP

1014d —————— ——— 4th ed. Boston: Crocker and Brewster. New York: M. W. Dodd. Philadelphia: William S. Martien, 1850. 420 p. 12mo   H

1014e —————— ——— 5th ed. Boston: Crocker and Brewster. New York: M. W. Dodd. Philadelphia: William S. Martien, 1850. 420 p. 12mo   H

1015 ——— The Western Sketch-Book . . . Boston: Crocker and Brewster, 1850. 408 p. 12mo
AAS, B, BP, H, HEH, LC, N, NYH, NYP, UC, UP, UV, Y

1016 THE GAMBLER; or, Memoirs of a British Officer, Distinguished in the War of the American Revolution. The Second Edition. Washington City: Printed at the Apollo press, by W. Duane & Son, 1802. 94 p. 12mo
AAS, H, HEH, LC, LCP, N, NYP, NYS, UV, Y

GANILH, ANTHONY. Ambrosio de Letinez; or, The First Texian Novel. *See* No. 1018.

1017 ——— Mexico versus Texas: A Descriptive Novel . . . By a Texian . . . [anon.]. Philadelphia: N. Siegfried, printer, 1838. 348 p. 12mo   HM, LC, N, NYP, UC, UP, Y

1018 —————— ——— New York: Charles Francis & Co., 1842. 2 vols. 12mo   H, HEH, LC, N, NYP, UM, UV, Y
Title reads: *Ambrosio de Letinez; or, The First Texian Novel . . . With Incidents of the War of Independence. By A. T. Myrthe* [pseud.].

137

1019 GARDINER, MRS. MARY L.   A Collection from the Prose and Poetical Writings of Mary L. Gardiner.   New York: Printed and
published for the author by J. Winchester, 1843.   359 p.   12mo
AAS, B, HEH, N, NYH, NYP, UV, Y

Contains: The Force of Education—Filial Piety Rewarded—The Contrast;
or, The Blue Mantilla—The Disappointment: A True Story—The Return—
A Tale of the Revolution—Thoughts on the Past—A Sketch—Contentment—
The Cousins.
"List of Subscribers," pp. 351-359.

GARRETSON, HANS VAN, *pseud., jt. au. See* Schnap, J., *pseud.*
Old Times and New (1846), No. 2320.

1020 GAZER, GILES, *Esq., pseud.*   Frederick de Algeroy, the Hero of
Camden Plains.   A Revolutionary Tale, by Giles Gazer, Esq.
[pseud.] . . .   New York: Collins and Hannay, 1825.   235 p.
12mo   AAS, H, IN, LC

1020a THE GENTLEMAN'S DAUGHTER; or, A Great City's Temptations . . .
New York: Burgess & Stringer, 1843.   54 p.   8vo
AAS, H, NYP, Y
Printed in double cols.

1021 DELETE.

1022 DELETE.

GIBBONS, M. T.   The Seahawk; or, The Marshal's Daughter of
the Baltic.   *In* E. Carra, *pseud.,* The Hermit of the Hudson
(1848), No. 489.

1023 GIBSON, *Capt.* T. WARE.   The Priest of the Black Cross.   A Tale
of the Sea . . .   Cincinnati: "Great West" office, 1848.   118 p.
8vo   LC, Y
Printed in double cols.

1024 GILMAN, CAROLINE (HOWARD).   Love's Progress . . . [anon.].
New York: Harper & Brothers, 1840.   171 p.   12mo
AAS, B, BP, CLS, H, HEH, IN, LC, LCP, N, NYH, NYP, UM, UP, UV, Y
Trenton Falls; contemporary.

1025 ——— Recollections of a Housekeeper.   By Mrs. Clarissa Packard [pseud.].   New York: Harper & Brothers, 1834.   155 p.
12mo   AAS, B, BA, BP, HEH, HM, LC, N, NYP, UC, UP, Y

1026 —————— ————— New York: Harper & Brothers, 1836.   155 p.
12mo   AAS, H, HEH, UP, Y

1027 —————— ————— New York: Harper & Brothers, 1838.   155 p.
12mo   AAS, BP, H, Y

1028 —————— ————— New York: Harper & Brothers, 1842.   155 p.
12mo   BP

1029 —————— Recollections of a Southern Matron . . .   New York:
Harper & Brothers, 1838.   272 p.   12mo
AAS, B, BP, CLS, H, HEH, IN, LC, LCP, N, NYP, NYS, UC, UP, UV, Y

1030 —————— ————— New York: Harper & Brothers, 1839.   272 p.
12mo   AAS, BP, HEH, LC, Y

1031 —————— Tales and Ballads . . .   New York: Samuel Colman, 1839.
190 p.   8vo   AAS, B, CLS, H, NYS, UC, UP, Y
Contains: The Missionaries: A Tale—The Young Conspirators: A Tale—Mr.
Niblo, the Bashful Lecturer—The Lost Mail: A Tale of the Forest—The
Wife—The Student of Valencia: A Tale—Mr. Inklin; or, The Man of
Leisure.

1032 —————— ————— Boston: William Crosby & Company, 1839.   190
p.   8vo   AAS, BP, HEH, IN, LC, N, NYH, NYP, UC, UM, Y

1033 GILMAN, CHANDLER ROBBINS.   Legends of a Log Cabin.   By a
Western Man . . . [anon.].   New York: George Dearborn, 1835.
277 p.   12mo   AAS, B, BP, H, HEH, LC, NYH, NYS, Y
Contents: The Log Cabin—The Hunter's Vow—The Heiress of Brandsby—
The Log Cabin—The Frenchman's Story—George Grey: A Tale of the
English Law—The Sleigh-Ride—The Wyandot's Story—The Minute Men:
A Tale of '75.

1034 —————— Life on the Lakes: Being Tales and Sketches Collected
during a Trip to the Pictured Rocks of Lake Superior . . .
[anon.].   New York: George Dearborn, 1836.   2 vols., illus.
12mo   AAS, BA, H, HEH, IN, LC, N, NYH, NYP, NYS, UP, Y
Written in a series of letters.

1035 GILMAN, SAMUEL.   Memoirs of a New England Village Choir.
With Occasional Reflections, by a Member . . . [anon.].   Bos-
ton: S. Goodrich & Co., 1829.   149 p.   12mo
AAS, B, BA, BP, H, HEH, N, UM, UP, UV, Y

1036 ———— ———— 2d ed. Boston: Benjamin H. Greene, 1834. 152
p. 16mo   AAS, B, BP, HEH, IN, NYH, NYP, UC, Y

1037 ———— ———— 3d ed. Boston: Benjamin H. Greene, 1846. 152
p. 16mo   AAS, BP, LC, Y

1038 GLENN, SAMUEL F. Gravities and Gaities [sic] ... Washing-
ton: R. Farnham, 1839. 116 p. 12mo AAS, B, BP, HEH, LC, N, Y
Contains short stories, essays, and poems.
B, HEH, LC, and Y title pages read "Gaieties."

GODFREY, JOHN EDWARDS. The Speculator: A Story of the
Fourth Decade. *In* J. S. Appleton, *ed.*, Voices from the Kenduskeag (1848), No. 39.

1038a GOODRICH, SAMUEL GRISWOLD, *ed.* The Flower Basket; or, A
Selection of Interesting Stories. By the Author of Peter Parley
[anon.]. New York: Nafis & Cornish, 278 Pearl Street [cop.
1840]. 192 p., illus. 12mo   N, NYP, Y
A new ed. of Vol. II of *Moral Tales* (1840), No. 1040.

1039 ———— A Home in the Sea; or, The Adventures of Philip
Brusque—Designed to the Nature and Necessity of Government ... [anon.]. Philadelphia: Sorin and Ball, 1845. 167 p.,
illus. 12mo   AAS, B, BA, LC, N, UP, Y

1040 ———— *ed.* Moral Tales ... [anon.]. Boston: E. Littlefield,
1840. 2 vols. 12mo   AAS, BP
Contents: The Two Coats—Passages in the Life of an Old Maid—My Friend
Plum—The Broken Miniature—Wealth and Fashion—The Mysterious Cor-
respondent—Katrina Schuyler—The Cobbler of Brusa—He Is So Amiable—
The Blind Boy—The Bank Note—Sketch of a Blue-Stocking—The Wed-
ding Knell [by N. Hawthorne]—David Swan [by N. Hawthorne]—The
Indian Fighter—Curiosity. [Vol. II]: The Tiara—New Year's Day—Night
Sketches beneath an Umbrella [by N. Hawthorne]—The Canterbury Pil-
grims [by N. Hawthorne]—The Legacy-hunter—Parental Hopes—The
World as It Is—The Haunted Mind [by N. Hawthorne]—Reconciliation—
The Dream Fulfilled—Iretta the Fairy—A Love Match—The Man with the
°°°—Sights from a Steeple [by N. Hawthorne]—Something That Actually
Happened—The Diamond—The Tempter—The Discharged Workman.

1041 ———— ———— New York: Nafis & Cornish, 278 Pearl Street
[cop. 1840]. 192 p., illus. 12mo
                                            AAS, BA, HEH, LC, N, NYP, UP, Y
A reissue of Vol. I of preceding ed.

1042 ——— *ed.* The Rose Bud: Being a Selection of Interesting Stories . . . [anon.]. New York: Nafis & Cornish, 278 Pearl Street
[cop. 1841]. 190 p., illus. 12mo   H, Y
A reissue of Vol. II of *Tales of Loves* (1841), No. 1044d.

1043 ——— *ed.* Short Stories; or, A Selection of Interesting Tales . . .
[anon.]. New York: Nafis & Cornish, 278 Pearl Street [cop.
1840]. 191 p., illus. 12mo   AAS, BA, H, IN, NYP, UP, Y
Contents: The Hermitess—The Spate: A Tale of the Clyde—The Night
Alarm—The Rattlesnake Hunter—The Tapestried Chamber; or, The Lady
in the Sacque—The Land's-End of Cornwall—The Necromancer—Bernard,
the Decoré—The Old Hall—Marie; or, The Blue Kerchief—The Regicide—
Adèle—The Piedmontesse Courier—The French Officer—The Last Trial of
Fidelity.

1044 ——— A Tale of Adventure; or, The Siberian Sable Hunter . . .
[anon.]. New York: Wiley & Putnam, 1843. 170 p., illus.
12mo   AAS, BA, H, LC, UC, Y

1044a ——— ——— [anon.]. New York: Wiley & Putnam, 1844.
170 p., illus. 12mo   AAS

1044b ——— A Tale of the Revolution, and Other Sketches. By the
Author of Peter Parley's Tales [anon.]. Philadelphia: Sorin
and Ball, 1845. 160 p., illus. 12mo   N
Also contains: The Lottery Ticket; or, The Danger of Prosperity—Dick
Hieldover; or, Crime Its Own Punishment—The Old Man's Story.

1044c ——— ——— Hartford: H. H. Hawley & Co. Utica: Hawley,
Fuller & Co., 1850. 160 p., illus. 12mo   AAS, Y

1044d ——— *ed.* Tales of Love . . . [anon.]. Boston: E. Littlefield,
1841. 2 vols. 12mo
Contents: The Lily of Liddesdale—The Maid of Malines—Second Thoughts
Best—The Lover's Last Visit—Rachel Morisson—The Consul's Daughter—
Lawrence Bayley's Temptation—The Drowned Fisherman—Bianca. [Vol.
II]: The Dead and the Living Husband—The Peasant Girl's Love—The
Two Kates—Count Rodolph's Heir—The Parting Kiss—The Lowly Lady—
Women Are Fickle—Love in the Olden Time—The Muffled Priest—Isabelle,
Her Sister Kate, &c.—Spanish Duchess and Orphan Boy—Snow-Storm in
Scotland—Bertha Clerville—Love's Recompense—The Young Minister and
the Bride—Tradition of Rolandseck.
Added title pages: "Economical Library Vol. V [VI]. Tales of Love, Vol. I
[II]. E. Littlefield, Boston [N.d.]."
Advertisement on back wrapper of Vol. V, notes that the first two volumes

in the Economical Library "will consist of *Moral Tales* [see Wright, Nos. 1040 and 1041] . . . the second series will consist of *Tales of Humor* [see Wright, Nos. 1242 and 2533]."

Copies examined of these items did not contain the added title pages.

A copy of *Tales of Love* is in the collection of Mr. C. E. Frazer Clark, Jr., Bloomfield Hills, Michigan.

1045 GOULD, EDWARD SHERMAN. The Sleep-Rider; or, The Old Boy in the Omnibus. By the Man in the Claret-Colored Coat [pseud.] . . . New York: J. Winchester, New World Press, 30 Ann Street [cop. 1843]. 115 p. 12mo

AAS, BP, H, HEH, LC, NYH, NYP, UC, UP, Y

New York City; 1834.

1046 GOULD, HANNAH FLAGG. Gathered Leaves; or, Miscellaneous Papers . . . Boston: William J. Reynolds, 1846. 304 p., illus. 12mo AAS, BA, BP, H, HEH, N, NYH, NYP, UC, UP, Y

Contains short stories, essays, and poems.

1047 GOULD, JOHN W. Forecastle Yarns, by the Late John W. Gould. Edited by His Brother, Edward S. Gould. Baltimore: William Taylor & Co., 1845. 64 p. 8vo B, Y

Contents: The Haunted Brig—Off Cape Horn—A Portugue Breakfast— The Capture of the Frigate President—Capture of the Cyane and Levant— The Mutiny—My First and Last Flogging—Cruise of a Guineaman—The Pirate of the South Pacific—The Cruise of the Sparkler.

LC has a title page, deposited Oct. 22, 1845.

1048 ——— ——— New York: J. Winchester, New World Press, 30 Ann Street [n.d.]. 64 p. 8vo AAS, B, Y

1049 ——— ——— New York: F. A. Brady [n.d.]. 64 p. 8vo UM

1050 ——— John W. Gould's Private Journal of a Voyage from New York to Rio de Janeiro. Together with a Brief Sketch of His Life and His Occasional Writings. Edited by His Brothers. Printed for Private Circulation Only. New York, 1838. 207 p. 8vo LC, NYH, UP

Contains the stories which were later issued with title, *Forecastle Yarns*.

1051 ——— ——— New York, 1839. 207 p., map. 8vo

AAS, BA, BP, H, HEH, LC, N, NYH, NYP, Y

1052 GRACE, PIERCE C.   The Unknown: A Prize Tale . . .   St. Louis: Chambers and Knapp, 1849. 168 p. 12mo   LC, N, UC, Y
England.

1053 GRAMMONT, JUSTIN.   The League of the Merrimack Mysteries of Manchester, No. 2. Founded on Facts . . .   Manchester, N.H.: Fisk & Moore, 1848. 36 p. 8vo   NYP, Y
Printed in double cols.

1054 GRANNISS, MRS. M. C.   Emma Clermont; or, Life's Changes. A Tale . . .   Hartford: Steam Press of J. Gaylord Wells, 1850. 94 p. 16mo   AAS, BP, HEH, Y

1055 GRAVES, MRS. A. J.   Girlhood and Womanhood; or, Sketches of My Schoolmates . . .   Boston: T. H. Carter & Co., and Benjamin B. Mussey, 1844. 216 p. 12mo
AAS, B, H, HEH, LC, N, NYP, UP, Y

1056 ———— ————   Boston: T. H. Carter & Co., 1844. 216 p. 12mo
BP
On cover: "Second Edition. Boston: Redding & Co., 1847."

1057 ———— ————   Boston: Phillips and Sampson, 1848. 216 p., illus. 12mo
Y

1058 GRAY, ARTHUR.   The Neglected Wife; or, A Hint to Husbands and Wives, Young Men, and Young Women . . .   Boston: Sold by book agents throughout the United States, 1847. 48 p., illus. 8vo   AAS, NYP, Y

1058a GRAY, M.   Zilpha and Maria, the Rival Female Orphans . . .   Boston [1848]. 32 p., illus. 8vo   AAS, UV, Y
Cover title reads: "Zilpha and Maria: The Rival Orphan Girls; or, Virtue Triumphant . . . by M. Gray. Boston: Printed for the Publisher, . . . 1848."

1059 GRAY, THOMAS.   The Vestal; or, A Tale of Pompeii . . . [anon.].   Boston: Gray and Bowen, 1830. 220 p. 12mo
AAS, B, BA, BP, H, HEH, IN, LC, N, UM, UP, Y

GRAYSON, ELFRED, Esq., pseud. See Hare, Robert

1060 THE GREATEST BLESSING of Life; or, The Adventures of Catherine Sinclair, a Domestic, in Search of a Good Mistress. By a Servant of Servants [anon.]. Pawtucket: Bliss, Potter & Co., 1850. 167 p. 24mo AAS, UP, Y
New England; contemporary.

1061 GREELEY, ROBERT F. Arthur Woodleigh: A Romance of the Battle Field in Mexico . . . New York: William B. Smith & Co., 1847. 94 p., illus. 8vo AAS, B, HEH, LC
Also contains: The Bloody Nuptials; or, A Soldier by Chance: A Tale of the Mexican Campaign—The Female Spy: A Domestic Tale of the Revolution, by Samuel Woodworth.
Printed in double cols.

1062 ———— The Child of the Islands; or, The Shipwrecked Gold Seekers . . . New York: Stringer & Townsend, 1850. 87 p. 8vo HEH, LC

1063 ———— The Crimes of Paris. A Record of Scenes and Events of Daily Occurrence in the French Metropolis . . . New York: Wm. H. Graham, 1849. 75 p. 8vo Y
Printed in double cols.

1064 ———— Old Cro' Nest; or, The Outlaws of the Hudson. A Romance of American Forest Life in the Olden Time . . . New York: Ward and Company, 1846. 110 p. 8vo AAS, H, Y
Printed in double cols.

1065 GREENE, ASA. The Life and Adventures of Dr. Dodimus Duckworth, A.N.Q. [pseud.]. To Which Is Added: The History of a Steam Doctor . . . New York: Peter Hill, 1833. 2 vols. 12mo AAS, B, II, LC, N, NYH, NYP, UC, UM, UP, Y
New England.

1066 ———— The Perils of Pearl Street, Including a Taste of the Dangers of Wall Street . . . [anon.]. New York: Betts & Anstice, and Peter Hill, 1834. 232 p. 12mo
AAS, B, BA, H, HEH, IN, LC, N, NYH, NYP, NYS, UC, UM, UP, UV, Y
New York City.

1067 ——— Travels in America. By George Fibbleton, Esq. [pseud.] . . . New York: William Pearson, 1833. 216 p. 12mo

> AAS, B, BA, BP, H, HEH, HM, IN, LC, N, NYH, NYP, NYS, UC, UM, UP
> New York City and state.

1068 ——— A Yankee among the Nullifiers: An Auto-biography. By Elnathan Elmwood, Esq. [pseud.] . . . New York: Wm. Stodart, 1833. 152 p. 12mo

> AAS, BA, H, HEH, IN, LC, N, NYP, UM, UP, Y
> South Carolina; contemporary.

1069 ———— ——— 2d ed. New York: Printed and published by William Pearson, 1833. 143 p. 12mo

> AAS, B, BP, HEH, LC, NYP, UM, UP, Y

GREENHORN, *pseud.* *See* Thompson, George

GREENWOOD, GRACE, *pseud.* *See* Lippincott, Sara Jane (Clarke)

1070 GREGORY, JAMES. Nag's Head; or, Two Months among "The Bankers." A Story of Sea-shore Life and Manners. By Gregory Seaworthy [pseud.]. Philadelphia: A. Hart, 1850. 180 p. 12mo BP

> It has been determined that George Higby Throop was the author, not James Gregory. See Richard Walser, "The Mysterious Case of George Higby Throop," *North Carolina Historical Review*, XXXIII (1956), 12-44.

GRIDLEY, LEWIS. The Returned Prodigal; or, The Reward of Merit. *In* E. Carra, *pseud.*, The Hermit of the Hudson (1848), No. 489.

GRIEVOUS, PETER, *Esq.*, *pseud.* *See* Hopkinson, Francis

1071 GRIFFITH, MRS. MARY. Camperdown; or, News from Our Neighbourhood: Being Sketches, by the Author of "Our Neighbourhood," &c. [anon.]. Philadelphia: Carey, Lea & Blanchard, 1836. 300 p. 12mo

> AAS, H, HEH, IN, LC, N, NYS, UP, UV, Y
> *Contents:* Three Hundred Years Hence—The Surprise—The Seven Shanties —The Little Couple—The Baker's Dozen—The Thread and Needle Store.

1072 —— Our Neighborhood; or, Letters on Horticulture and Natural Phenomena, Interspersed with Opinions on Domestic and Moral Economy [anon.]. New York: E. Bliss, 1831. 332 p. 12mo $\qquad$ H, HEH, IN, LC, N, UP, Y

1073 —— The Two Defaulters; or, A Picture of the Times . . . New York: D. Appleton and Co., 1842. 172 p., illus. 12mo $\qquad$ AAS, BA, HEH, N, UM, UP, Y

1074 GRUMMETT, FLEXIBLE, *pseud.* Grummett's Log. Leaves from My Log Book. By Flexible Grummett, P. M. [pseud.]. Philadelphia: Carey, Lea & Blanchard, 1835. 206 p. 12mo $\qquad$ AAS, BP, H, LC, LCP, NYP, UP, Y

1075 GUY, W. H. Abby Forbes: A Tale of Unparalleled Sufferings. Founded on Facts . . . Boston: Published by the author, 1846. 36 p., illus. 12mo $\qquad$ AAS, LC, NYP
Maine and Quebec; 1820's.

1076 ———— —— 2d ed. Boston: Published for the author, 1846. 64 p., illus. 16mo $\qquad$ BP, HEH, NYP, UM, Y
Title reads: *Abbe Forbes; or, The Unfortunate Family. A Tale of Sea and Land.*

HAIL-FAIR, *Lord, pseud. See* Cobb, Enos

1077 HALE, EDWARD EVERETT. Margaret Percival in America: A Tale. Edited by a New England Minister . . . [anon.]. Being a Sequel to Margaret Percival: A Tale. Edited by Rev. William Sewell . . . Boston: Phillips, Sampson & Company, 1850. 284 p. 12mo $\qquad$ AAS, BP, H, HEH, IN, LCP, N, NYP, UC, UM, UP, Y

1078 ———— —— 2d ed. Boston: Phillips, Sampson & Company, 1850. 284 p. 12mo $\qquad$ AAS, BP, IN, N, Y

HALE, NATHAN, *jt. au. See* Bigelow, J., The Wars of the Gulls (1812), No. 312.

1079 HALE, SARAH JOSEPHA (BUELL). "Boarding Out": A Tale of Domestic Life . . . [anon.]. New York: Harper & Brothers, 1846. 129 p. 12mo $\qquad$ AAS, N, NYP, UM, UP, Y

—— The Frontier House. *In* N. P. Willis, *ed.,* The Legendary (1828), No. 2739.

1080 ———— Keeping House and Housekeeping: A Story of Domestic Life . . . New York: Harper & Brothers, 1845. 143 p.
12mo   AAS, BP, HEH, LC, NYP, UM, UP, Y

1081 ———— The Lecturess; or, Woman's Sphere . . . [anon.]. Boston: Whipple and Damrell, 1839. 124 p. 12mo
                                              BP, HEH, LC, Y

1082 ———— My Cousin Mary; or, The Inebriate. By a Lady . . . [anon.]. Boston: Whipple and Damrell, 1839. 64 p. 12mo
                                                        LC
Sarah Hale wrote only the preface.

1083 ———— Northwood: A Tale of New England . . . Boston: Bowles & Dearborn, 1827. 2 vols. 12mo
                        AAS, B, BA, BP, H, HEH, IN, LC, N, NYP, UP, Y

1084 ———— Sketches of American Character . . . Boston: Putnam & Hunt, 1829. 287 p. 12mo   AAS, B, BP, HM, N, UP, Y
Contents: Walter Wilson—The Soldier of the Revolution—The Wedding and the Funeral—Ann Ellsworth—The Village Schoolmistress—The Belle and the Bleu—The Poor Scholar—The Springs—Prejudices—The Apparition—William Forbes—A Winter in the Country.

1085 ———— ———— Portland: S. Colman, 1829. 287 p. 12mo
                                              AAS, H, Y

1086 ———— ———— 2d ed. Boston: Putnam & Hunt, 1830. 287 p.
12mo   BP, UP, Y

1087 ———— ———— 3d ed. Boston: Putnam & Hunt, 1830. 287 p.
12mo   B, HEH

1088 ———— ———— 4th ed. Boston: Freeman Hunt, 1831. 287 p.,
illus. 12mo   AAS, B, H, HEH, IN, N, NYH, NYP, UM, Y

1089 ———— ———— 4th ed. Boston: Russell, Odiorne & Co., 1833.
287 p., illus. 12mo   AAS, BP, UP

1090 ———— ———— 6th ed. Philadelphia: Henry Perkins. Boston: Benjamin Bradley, 1838. 287 p., illus. 12mo
                                              AAS, BA, H, LC, NYP, Y

1091 ———— ———— 6th ed. Boston: Benjamin Bradley, 1838. 287
p., illus. 12mo   AAS, IN, NYH, Y

1092 ———— ———— Boston: Benjamin Bradley, 1839. 287 p., illus.
12mo
Ed. from sales catalog.

1092a ———— ———— 8th ed. Philadelphia: Henry Perkins. Boston:
Ives & Dennet, 1840. 287 p., illus. 12mo   AAS, HEH, Y

1093 ———— ———— Philadelphia: Perkins & Purves, 1843. 287 p.
12mo   AAS, HEH, LC, LCP, UC, Y

1094 ———— Traits of American Life . . . Philadelphia: E. L. Carey
& A. Hart, 1835. 298 p. 12mo
              AAS, B, BA, BP, H, IN, LC, LCP, N, NYP, NYS, UM, UP, Y
Contents: The Lloyds—The Catholic Convert—The Silver Mine—Political
Parties—A New-Year's Story—Captain Glover's Daughter—The Fate of a
Favourite—The Romance of Travelling—The Thanksgiving of the Heart—
The Lottery Ticket—An Old Maid—Ladies' Fairs—The Mode—The Mys-
terious Box.

1095 HALL, BAYNARD RUSH. The New Purchase; or, Seven and a
Half Years in the Far West. By Robert Carlton, Esq. [pseud.]
. . . New York: D. Appleton & Co., 1843. 2 vols. 12mo
              AAS, BA, BP, BU, H, HEH, IN, LC, LCP, N, NYP, UP, Y
Indiana.

1096 ———— Something for Every Body: Gleaned in the Old Purchase, from Fields Often Reaped. By Robert Carlton, Esq.
[pseud.] . . . New York: D. Appleton & Company, 1846. 223
p. 12mo   AAS, BP, H, IN, LC, NYH, NYP, NYS, UC, UP, Y
Written in a series of letters.
On cover: "Appleton's Literary Miscellany, No. 16."

1097 HALL, JAMES. The Harpe's Head: A Legend of Kentucky . . .
Philadelphia: Key & Biddle, 1833. 256 p. 12mo   AAS, B,
CLS, H, HEH, HM, IN, LC, LCP, N, NYH, NYP, UC, UM, UP, UV, Y
Late 18th cent.

1098 ———— Legends of the West . . . Philadelphia: Harrison Hall,
1832. 265 p. 12mo
              AAS, BA, BP, HEH, IN, LC, LCP, N, NYP, NYS, UM, UP, UV, Y

148

Contains: The Backwoodsman—The Divining Rod—The Seventh Son—The Missionaries—A Legend of Carondelet; or, Fifty Years Ago—The Intestate; or, Jerry Smith's Widow—Michel de Coucy: A Tale of Fort Chartres—The Emigrants—The Barrack-Master's Daughter: A Legend of Fort Cumberland—The Indian Hater.

1099 ———— ——— 2d ed. Philadelphia: Key & Biddle, 1833. 267 p. 12mo   AAS, HEH, IN, NYP, UC, UM, Y

1100 ——— The Soldier's Bride and Other Tales . . . Philadelphia: Key and Biddle, 1833. 272 p. 12mo
AAS, B, BA, H, HEH, IN, LC, LCP, N, NYP, UP, Y

Also contains: Cousin Lucy and the Village Teacher—Empty Pockets—The Captain's Lady—The Philadelphia Dan—The Bearer of Despatches—The Village Musician—Fashionable Watering Places—The Useful Man—The Dentist—The Bachelor's Elysium—Pete Featherton—The Billiard Table.

Title story included in No. 1104.

1101 ——— Tales of the Border . . . Philadelphia: Harrison Hall, 1835. 276 p. 12mo
AAS, H, HEH, IN, LC, LCP, NYP, UM, UP, UPI, UV, Y

Contains: The Pioneer—The French Village—The Spy: A Tale of the Revolution—The Silver Mine: A Tale of Missouri—The Dark Maid of Illinois—The New Moon: A Tradition of the Omawhaws.

1102 ——— The Wilderness and the War Path . . . New York: Wiley and Putnam, 1846. 174 p. 12mo
AAS, H, HEH, IN, N, NYP, UC, UM, UP, Y

Contains: The Black Steed of the Prairies: A Tale of the Rocky Mountains—The War Belt: A Legend of North Bend—The New Moon: A Tradition of the Omawhaws—The Red Sky of the Morning—The Dark Maid of Illinois—The Indian Hater—Pete Featherton.

1103 ———— ——— New York: John Wiley, 1849. 174 p. 12mo
AAS, LC, NYP, UP

1104 ——— Winter Evenings: A Series of American Tales . . . [anon.]. Philadelphia: Thos. T. Ash, 1829. 264 p. 12mo
HEH

Contents: The Soldier's Bride—A Voyage to Italy—The Forest Citadel—Account of an Attempt to Liberate Lafayette from Prison—Adieu to the Muse.

It has been established that Hall wrote only "The Soldier's Bride." S. L. Fairfield wrote "The Forest Citadel."

1105   ——— ——— Philadelphia: J. P. Ayres and Co., 1829. 264 p.
12mo   LC
Title reads: *The Soldier's Bride, and Other Tales* [anon.].
Title leaf a cancel, otherwise from same setting of type as preceding ed.

1106   HALL, LOUISA JANE (PARK). Alfred. By the Author of Sophia
Morton . . . [anon.]. Boston: James Munroe and Company,
1836. 114 p., 2 l., 24 p. 12mo   AAS, BA, H, HEH, UP, Y
Also contains: The Better Part.
Included in *Scenes & Characters*, No. VI.

1106a   ——— ——— Boston: James Munroe and Company, 1840.
114 p., 2 l., 24 p. 12mo   Y
Also contains: The Better Part.

1107   ——— Joanna of Naples . . . [anon.]. Boston: Hilliard, Gray,
and Company, 1838. 213 p. 12mo
                    AAS, B, BA, BP, H, HEH, IN, LC, LCP, N, UC, UP, Y
14th cent.

1108   ——— Miriam and Joanna of Naples, with Other Pieces in Verse
and Prose . . . Boston: Wm. Crosby and H. P. Nichols, 1850.
403 p. 12mo   AAS, B, BA, BP, H, HEH, LC, LCP, N, NYP, UC, UP, Y

1109   HALL, *Capt.* NEVIL. The Red Wing; or, Belmont, the Buccaneer
of the Bay. A Tale of the Blue Water . . . Boston: H. L. Williams, 1846. 94 p., illus. 8vo   BP, N
LC has a title page, deposited Jan. 14, 1846.

1110   HALYARD, HARRY, *pseud.* The Chieftain of Churubusco; or, The
Spectre of the Cathedral. A Romance of the Mexican War, by
Harry Halyard [pseud.] . . . Boston: F. Gleason, 1848. 100
p., illus. 8vo   AAS, LC, UP
Printed in double cols.

1111   ——— The Doom of the Dolphin; or, The Sorceress of the Sea,
a Tale of Love, Intrigue, and Mystery, by Harry Halyard
[pseud.] . . . Boston: F. Gleason [cop. 1848]. 100 p., illus.
8vo   H
Printed in double cols.
LC has a title page, deposited Dec. 7, 1848.

1112 ——— Geraldine; or, The Gipsey of Germantown. A National and Military Romance, by Harry Halyard [pseud.] ... Boston: F. Gleason, 1848. 100 p. 8vo   LC, UC, Y
Printed in double cols.
American Revolution.

1113 ——— The Haunted Bride; or, The Witch of Gallows Hill. A Romance of the Olden Time, by Harry Halyard [pseud.] ... Boston: F. Gleason [cop. 1848]. 100 p., illus. 8vo   BP
Printed in double cols.
LC has a title page, deposited Dec. 7, 1848.
Salem, 1691.

1114 ——— The Heroine of Paris; or, The Novice of Notre Dame. A Romance of the Last French Revolution, by Harry Halyard [pseud.]. [Boston]: F. Gleason, 1848. 100 p., illus. 8vo
Printed in double cols.
LC has a title page, deposited July 6, 1848.
Ed. from sales catalog.

1115 ——— The Heroine of Tampico; or, Wildfire the Wanderer. A Tale of the Mexican War, by Harry Halyard [pseud.]. Boston: F. Gleason, 1847. 100 p., illus. 8vo   AAS, H, Y
Printed in double cols.

1116 ——— ——— Boston: F. Gleason, 1848. 100 p., illus. 8vo   HEH, LC, Y
Also contains: The Belle of Baltimore.
Printed in double cols.

1117 ——— The Mexican Spy; or, The Bride of Buena Vista. A Tale of the Mexican War, by Harry Halyard [pseud.] ... Boston: F. Gleason, 1848. 100 p., illus. 8vo   LC, Y
Printed in double cols.

1118 ——— The Ocean Monarch; or, The Ranger of the Gulf. A Mexican Romance, by Harry Halyard [pseud.] ... Boston: F. Gleason, 1848. 100 p., illus. 8vo   LC, NYH, Y
Also contains: The Midnight Shipwreck.
Printed in double cols.

1119   ——— The Peruvian Nun; or, The Empress of the Ocean. A Maritime Romance, by Harry Halyard [pseud.] . . . Boston: F. Gleason, 1848. 100 p., illus. 8vo   B, LC, Y
Printed in double cols.

1120   ——— The Rover of the Reef; or, The Nymph of the Nightingale. A Romance of Massachusetts Bay, by Harry Halyard [pseud.] . . . Boston: F. Gleason [cop. 1848]. 100 p., illus. 8vo   AAS, B, BP, LC, UP, Y
Printed in double cols.
LC has a title page, deposited May 22, 1848.

  ——— The Spectre of the Woods; or, The Hermit's Revenge. *In* M. M. Ballou, Red Rupert (1848), No. 248.

1121   ——— The Warrior Queen; or, The Buccaneer of the Brazos! A Romance of Mexico, by Harry Halyard [pseud.] . . . Boston: F. Gleason [cop. 1848]. 100 p., illus. 8vo   Y
Printed in double cols.
LC has a title page, deposited Sept. 15, 1848.

1122   ——— Wharton the Whale-Killer! Or, The Pride of the Pacific. A Tale of the Ocean, by Harry Halyard [pseud.] . . . Boston: F. Gleason [cop. 1848]. 100 p., illus. 8vo   H
Printed in double cols.
LC has a title page, deposited Dec. 7, 1848.

1123   HANDIBOE, EDWARD J. Will Crittenden; or, The Lone Star of Cuba . . . Cincinnati: U. P. James, No. 157 Walnut Street [1850]. 108 p. 8vo   AAS, BP, HEH, UM, Y

1123a   HANNIGAN, DENNIS. The Artisan of Lyons; or, Love's Traces. A Romance . . . New York: W. H. Graham, 1846. 83 p., illus. 8vo   HEH
Printed in double cols.

1123b   ——— The Chain of Destiny; or, The Adventures of a Vagabond . . . [anon.]. New York: Burgess, Stringer, and Company, 1847. 116 p. 8vo   HEH
Printed in double cols.

1124 ——— Leon de Calavar; or, The Age of the Inquisition. An Historical Romance. By Dennis Hannigan, Author of "The Orange Girl of Venice"; "The Artisan of Lyons"; "Bill Simms"; "The Actress and the Scribe"; &c. &c. New York: Wm. H. Graham, 1846. 61 p., illus. 8vo   Y

1125 ——— The Orange Girl of Venice; or, The Downfall of "the Council of Ten!" . . . New York: John Slater, 1845. 59 p., illus. 8vo   AAS, B, H, Y
Printed in double cols.
LC has a title page, deposited Oct. 17, 1845.

1126 ——— The Sicilian Vespers; or, The White Cross of St. Luke's. An Historical Romance . . . New York: William H. Graham, 1846. 62 p. 8vo   UP, Y
Printed in double cols.

1127 THE HAPLESS ORPHAN; or, Innocent Victim of Revenge. A Novel Founded on Incidents in Real Life. In a Series of Letters from Caroline Francis to Maria B——— . . . By an American Lady . . . Boston: Printed at the Apollo Press by Belknap and Hall, 1793. 2 vols. 12mo
      AAS, B, BA, H, HEH, IN, LC, N, NYS, UC, UM, UP, UV, Y
Philadelphia; contemporary.

1127a HARDWICKE, FRANCK. Nezbitt Sinclair: Trenton-up-Delaware . . . Philadelphia: Barrett and Jones, 1844. 28 p. 8vo
Listed in Swann Galleries catalog 479:18.
War of 1812.

1128 HARE, ROBERT. Standish the Puritan: A Tale of the American Revolution. By Eldred Grayson, Esq. [pseud.]. New York: Harper & Brothers, 1850. 320 p. 12mo
      AAS, B, BA, BP, H, HEH, IN, LC, LCP, N, NYP, UM, UP, Y
New York City.

HARRIS, GEORGE WASHINGTON. Dick Harlan's Tennessee Frolic, by "S———l" of Tennessee. In W. T. Porter, ed., A Quarter Race in Kentucky (1847), Nos. 2063-64.

1129 HARRIS, H. A. The Horse Thief; or, The Maiden and Negro. A Tale of the Prairies . . . Boston: Gleason's Publishing Hall, 1845. 66 p., illus. 8vo   AAS, B, BP, HEH, LC, LCP, N, UP, Y

HARRIS, THOMAS LAKE. A Legend of the Inner Life. *In* M. Woodruff, *ed.*, A Drop from the Bucket (1847), No. 2759.

1129a HART, *Miss.* Letters from the Bahama Islands. Written in 1823-4 [anon.]. Philadelphia: H. C. Carey and I. Lea, 1827. 207 p. 8vo   BP, H, HEH, N, NYP
Last letter signed "Adela Del Lorraine."

1130 HART, CYRUS WADSWORTH. Essay on Industry, and Theopholis Radclipp and Emma Jones, a Tale. By a Member of the Bar [anon.]. Steubenville: Printed by James Wilson, 1833. 60 p. 12mo   HEH

1131 ———— Essay on Industry, and Biographical Sketches of Theopholus Radclipp and Emma Jones. By a Member of the Bar [anon.]. Steubenville: Printed by James Wilson, 1835. 60 p. 12mo   AAS, Y

1132 ———— Selections from the Philosophical, Polemical, Amatory, Moral, and Other Works . . . Cincinnati: Printed by S. W. Johns, 1844. 344 p. 12mo   AAS, B, BP, H, HEH, LC, NYH, UP, Y
Contains: The Manchester Beauty: A Tale—Theophilus Radclipp and Emma Jones: A Tale.

HART, JEANETTE M. Nahant; or, "The Floure of Souvenance" (1827). *See* No. 1941 for title entry which is now identified as by Hart.

1133 HART, JOSEPH C. Miriam Coffin; or, The Whale-Fishermen . . . [anon.]. New York: G. & C. & H. Carvill, 1834. 2 vols. 12mo   AAS, BP, H, HEH, IN, LC, N, NYP(V.2), UV, Y
Nantucket; early 19th cent.

1134 ———— ———— 2d ed. New York: Harper & Brothers, 1835. 2 vols. 12mo   AAS, H, HEH, LC, UC, UP, Y

HARVEY, MRS. R. S. A Single Glass of Wine. *In* The Fountain and the Bottle (1850), No. 996.

HASSALL, MARY. *See* Sansay, Mrs. Leonora

HATHAWAY, HARRIET N. Ida Gould; or, A Sunbeam in a Dark Place. *In* S. Cobb, Jr., The Golden Eagle [cop. 1850], No. 557.

1135 THE HAUNTED HOUSE: A Temperance Dream. Rochester, N.Y.: Sold at Dewey's News Room, 1845.

LC has a cover title, deposited Aug. 29, 1845.

1136 HAVEN, ALICE EMILY (BRADLEY) NEAL. The Gossips of Rivertown: With Sketches in Prose and Verse. By Alice B. Neal. Philadelphia: Hazard and Mitchell, 1850. 327 p., illus. 12mo

AAS, BA, HM, LC, LCP, N, NYP, UC, UP, Y

Contains: Sketch the First: The Neighbours—Sketch the Second: More of Mary Butler—Sketch the Third: Death and the Burial—Sketch the Fourth: Mrs. Harden's Quilting—Sketch the Fifth: Male Gossips—Sketch the Sixth: Retaliation—The Portrait; or, The Wife's Jealousy—The New England Factory Girl: A Sketch of Every Day Life—The Story of the Bell—The Sorrow of the Rose—Ideal Husbands; or, School-Girl Fancies—Transplanted Flowers—The Young Bride's Trials.

1137 —————— 2d ed. Philadelphia: Hazard and Mitchell, 1850. 327 p., illus. 12mo AAS, B, HM, LCP, UP, Y

HAWES, WILLIAM POST. A Bear Story. *In* W. T. Porter, *ed.*, A Quarter Race in Kentucky (1847), Nos. 2063-64.

—————— The Legend of Brick-House Creek. *In* The Atlantic Club-Book (1834), Nos. 195-196.

—————— A Shark Story, by "J. Cypress, Jr." [pseud.]. *In* W. T. Porter, *ed.*, A Quarter Race in Kentucky (1847), Nos. 2063-64.

1138 —————— Sporting Scenes and Sundry Sketches: Being the Miscellaneous Writings of J. Cypress, Jr. [pseud.]. Edited by Frank Forester [pseud.] ... New York: Gould, Banks & Co., 1842. 2 vols., illus. 12mo

AAS, B, BP, H, HEH, HM, IN, LC, N, NYH, NYP, NYS, UC, UM, UP, Y

Contains: Fire Island-Ana; or, A Week at the Fire Islands—Legends of Long Island—Classic Rhapsodies.

HAWTHORNE, NATHANIEL. The Canterbury Pilgrims. *In* S. G. Goodrich, *ed.*, Moral Tales (1840), Nos. 1038a, 1040.

1139 —————— The Celestial Rail-road ... Boston: Wilder & Co., 1843. 32 p. 12mo AAS, BA, H, HEH, N, NYP, UP, Y

Also issued with imprint: "Boston: James F. Fish, 1843"—BAL 7596.

1140 ——— ——— Lowell: D. Skinner, 1847. 30, [2] p. 16mo
AAS, BP, H, Y

——— David Swan. *In* S. G. Goodrich, *ed.*, Moral Tales
(1840), Nos. 1040-41.
Also in Nos. 1149-50.

1141 ——— Fanshawe: A Tale . . . [anon.]. Boston: Marsh & Capen,
1828. 141 p. 12mo
BA, BP, H, HEH, IN, LC, N, NYP, UC, UP, Y

1142 ——— The Gentle Boy: A Thrice Told Tale . . . Boston:
Weeks, Jordan & Co., 1839. 20 p., illus. Obl. 4to
AAS, BA, BP, H, HEH, IN, LC, N, NYP, UC, UP, Y
Printed in double cols.

——— The Haunted Mind. *In* S. G. Goodrich, *ed.*, Moral
Tales (1840), Nos. 1038a, 1040.
Also in No. 1150.

——— The Haunted Quack. *In* Tales of Humor (1840), Nos.
1242, 2533.
See BAL 7572 for discussion of authorship.

——— Mr. Higginbotham's Catastrophe. *In* Tales for the
Times [cop. 1840], No. 2530.
Also in Nos. 1149-50.

——— Mrs. Bullfrog. *In* Tales of Humor (1840), Nos. 1242,
2533.
Also in No. 1143.

1143 ——— Mosses from an Old Manse . . . New York: Wiley and
Putnam, 1846. 2 vols. 12mo
AAS, BA, BP, H, HEH, HM, IN, LC, LCP, N, NYP, NYS, UM, UV, Y
For contents see Cathcart.
For bibliographical description see BAL 7598.

1144 ——— ——— New York: John Wiley, 1849. 2 vols. in 1.
12mo
N, NYP, Y

156

1145 ———— ———— New York: George P. Putnam, 1850.   2 vols. in 1.
12mo   BA, UP

———— Night Sketches beneath an Umbrella.   *In* S. G. Goodrich, *ed.*, Moral Tales (1840), Nos. 1038a, 1040.
Also in No. 1140.

———— A Rill from the Town Pump.   *In* Tales for the Times [cop. 1840], No. 2530.
Also in Nos. 1149-50.

1146 ———— The Scarlet Letter: A Romance . . .   Boston: Ticknor, Reed, and Fields, 1850.   322 p.   8vo
AAS, B, BA, BP, H, HEH, IN, LC, LCP, N, NYP, NYS, UM, UP, UV, Y
For bibliographical descriptions of this ed. and the following two entries see BAL 7600-7601.

1147 ———— ———— Boston: Ticknor and Reed, and Fields, 1850.
322 p.   8vo   AAS, BA, BP, H, HEH, IN, LC, NYP, UC, UM, UV, Y

1148 ———— ———— Boston: Ticknor, Reed, and Fields, 1850.   307 p.
8vo   AAS, H, N, NYP, UC, Y

———— Sights from a Steeple.   *In* S. G. Goodrich, *ed.*, Moral Tales (1840), Nos. 1038a, 1040.
Also in Nos. 1149-50.

———— The Threefold Destiny: A Fairy Legend, by Ashley Allen Royce [pseud.].   *In* Tales for You (1841), No. 2531.
Included in his *Twice Told Tales* (1842), No. 1149.

1149 ———— Twice-Told Tales . . .   Boston: American Stationers Co., 1837.   334 p.   12mo
AAS, BA, BP, H, HEH, IN, LC, N, NYP, UM, UP, Y
For contents see either Cathcart or Browne.

1150 ———— ———— Boston: James Munroe and Company, 1842.   2
vols.   8vo   AAS, BA, BP, H, HEH, IN, N, NYP, NYS(v.2), UP, Y
This ed. adds 21 sketches and tales. For contents see either Cathcart or Browne.
For a discussion of the 1845 "false edition" see Bibliographical Society of America, *Papers*, LIX (New York, 1965), 182-189.

———— The Wedding Knell. *In* S. G. Goodrich, *ed.*, Moral Tales (1840), Nos. 1040-41.
Also in Nos. 1149-50.

HAYDN, H.   Monima; or, The Beautiful French Girl.   *See* Reed, Mrs. Martha.   Monima; or, The Beggar Girl, No. 2101.

1151   DELETE.   *See* Wright II, No. 1144.

HAZEL, HARRY, *pseud.*   *See* Jones, Justin

1152   HAZELTON, FRANK.   The Mysteries of Troy: Founded upon Incidents Which Have Taken Place in the City [anon.].   Troy: Troy Publishing Company, 1847.   39 p.   8vo   AAS

HAZZARD, SAMUEL.   Extracts from a Sea Book.   *In* N. P. Willis, *ed.*, The Legendary (1828), No. 2739.

1153   HEATH, JAMES EWELL.   Edge-Hill; or, The Family of the Fitzroyals.   A Novel, by a Virginian . . . [anon.].   Richmond: Printed and published by T. W. White, 1828.   2 vols.   12mo
AAS, BA, H, HEH, LC, UC, UP, UV
Virginia; American Revolution.

HELFENSTEIN, ERNEST, *pseud.*   *See* Smith, Elizabeth Oakes (Prince)

1154   HEMENWAY, S. R.   The Sculptor's Beau-Ideal; or, The Circassian Orphan.   A Romance of the University and the American Studio in Florence . . .   Woodstock, Vt.: Printed at the office of the Spirit of the Age, 1849.   112, [2] p.   8vo   AAS, Y

1155   HENRY RUSSELL; or, The Year of Our Lord Two Thousand . . . New York: William H. Graham, 1846.   115 p.   8vo   NYP, Y
Printed in double cols.
New York State.

1156   HENTZ, CAROLINE LEE (WHITING).   Aunt Patty's Scrap Bag . . . Philadelphia: Carey & Hart, 1846.   168 p., illus.   12mo
AAS, H, HEH, LCP, UP, Y

1157   ———— Linda; or, The Young Pilot of the Belle Creole.   A Tale of Southern Life . . .   Philadelphia: A. Hart, 1850.   276 p.
12mo   AAS, B, BA, HEH, LC, LCP, UM, UV, Y

1158 ———— Lovell's Folly . . . Cincinnati: Hubbard and Edmands, 1833. 333 p. 12mo   BP, HEH, LC
"Cloverdale," New England.

———— Percy; or, The Banished Son. *In* The Prize Articles (1849), No. 2082.

1159 HENTZ, NICHOLAS MARCELLUS. Tadeuskund, the Last King of the Lenape: An Historical Tale [anon.]. Boston: Cummings, Hilliard & Co., 1825. 276 p. 12mo
     AAS, B, BA, BP, H, IN, LC, LCP, NYP, UC, UM, UP, UPI, Y
Pennsylvania; French and Indian War.

1160 HERBERT, HENRY WILLIAM. The Brothers: A Tale of the Fronde . . . [anon.]. New York: Harper & Brothers, 1835. 2 vols. 12mo
     AAS, BA, BP, H, HEH, IN, LC, N, NYP(V.1), NYS, UC, UM, UP, Y
Europe; late 17th cent.

1161 ———— Cromwell: An Historical Novel . . . [anon.]. New York: Harper & Brothers, 1838. 2 vols., illus. 12mo
     AAS, B(V.1), BP, H, HEH, IN, LC, N, NYP, NYS, UC, UM, UP, Y
Van Winkle lists a 2d ed., 1847; also an ed. ca. 1850.

1162 ———— The Deerstalkers; or, Circumstantial Evidence. A Tale of the South-western Counties. By Frank Forester [pseud.] . . . Philadelphia: Carey and Hart, 1849. 198 p., illus. 12mo
     HEH, IN, N, NYH, UP, Y

1163 ———— Dermot O'Brien; or, The Taking of Tredagh. A Tale of 1649 . . . New York: Stringer & Townsend, 1849. 166 p., illus. 8vo   AAS, BA, BP, H, HEH, NYP, NYS, UP, Y

———— Frederick St. Clair; or, The Young Man about Town. *In* J. H. Ingraham, Mark Manly (1848), No. 1318.

1164 ———— Guarica, the Charib Bride. A Legend of Hispaniola . . . Philadelphia: A. J. Rockafellar, 1844. 66 p. 8vo
     AAS, BP, H, HEH, N, UP, Y
Printed in double cols.

1165 ———— Ingleborough Hall, and Lord of the Manor ... New York: Burgess, Stringer & Co., 1847. 96 p. 8vo

AAS, BP, NYP, UC, Y

Printed in double cols.

1166 ———— The Innocent Witch. A Continuation of Ruth Whalley; or, The Fair Puritan. A Romance of the Bay Province ... Boston: Henry L. Williams, 1845. 50 p. 8vo   BP, HEH, Y

1167 ———— Isabel Graham; or, Charity's Reward ... New York: Williams Brothers, 1848. 108 p. 8vo   AAS, LC, UC, UP, Y

Printed in double cols.

1168 ———— The Lord of the Manor; or, Rose Castleton's Temptation. An Old English Story ... Philadelphia: A. J. Rockafellar, 1844. 64 p. 8vo   AAS, Y

Printed in double cols.

1169 ———— Marmaduke Wyvil; or, The Maid's Revenge ... New York: J. Winchester, New World Press, 30 Ann Street [cop. 1843]. 218 p. 12mo   AAS, BP, H, HEH, LC, UC, UP, Y

1170 ——————— 4th ed. New York: Burgess, Stringer & Co. [1846?]. 218 p. 12mo   AAS, BP, NYP, Y

1171 ———— The Miller of Martignè ... New York: Richards & Company, 30 Ann Street [1847]. 124 p. 12mo

AAS, B, H, UC, UP, Y

Cover title dated 1847.
France; 1550.

1172 ———— My Shooting Box. By Frank Forester [pseud.] ... Philadelphia: Carey and Hart, 1846. 179 p., illus. 12mo

AAS, HEH, IN, UC, UP, Y

1173 ———— Pierre, the Partisan: A Tale of the Mexican Marches ... New York: Williams Brothers, 1848. 99 p. 8vo   LC, N, UC, Y

Printed in double cols.

1174 ———— The Revolt of Boston. A Continuation of Ruth Whalley; or, The Fair Puritan. A Romance of the Bay Province ... Boston: Henry L. Williams, 1845. 48 p. 8vo   B, BP, H, Y

1175 —— Ringwood the Rover: A Tale of Florida . . . Philadelphia: William H. Graham, 1843. 55 p. 8vo

AAS, H, HEH, UC, UP, Y

Printed in double cols.

1175a ——— ——— 2d ed. Philadelphia: A. J. Rockafellar, 1843. 55 p. 8vo   AAS

Printed in double cols.

1176 —— The Roman Traitor: A True Tale of the Republic . . . New York: William Taylor & Co., 1846. 2 vols. 12mo

AAS, BP, HEH, N, UC, UP, Y

Van Winkle notes an advertisement of a 3d ed. in 1847.

1177 —— Ruth Whalley; or, The Fair Puritan. A Romance of the Bay Province . . . Boston: Henry L. Williams, 1844. 72 p. 8vo

Title from Van Winkle. Probably a ghost.

1178 ——— ——— Boston: H. L. Williams, 1845. Cover title, 72 p. 8vo

AAS, BP, H, HEH, LC, Y

1178a ——— ——— Three Parts in One. Boston: Henry L. Williams, 1846. Cover title, 72, 50, 48 p. 8vo   HEH

A made up ed. Pt. II is a copy of No. 1166, and Pt. III is a copy of No. 1174.

1179 —— Tales of the Spanish Seas . . . New York: Burgess, Stringer & Co., 1847. 96 p. 8vo   AAS, LC, UP, Y

Contents: Ringwood the Rover—Guarica, the Charib Bride.
Printed in double cols.

1180 —— The Village Inn; or, The Adventures of Bellechassaigne . . . New York: J. Winchester, 1843. 41 p. 8vo   HEH, UV, Y

1181 —— The Warwick Woodlands; or, Things as They Were There Ten Years Ago . . . Philadelphia: G. B. Zieber & Co., 1845. 168 p. 12mo   IN, NYH, NYP, Y

—— *ed. See* Hawes, William Post. Sporting Scenes and Sundry Sketches, No. 1138.

1182 HERBERT WENDALL: A Tale of the Revolution . . . New York: Harper & Brothers, 1835. 2 vols. 12mo

AAS, B, BP, H, HEH, IN, LC, N, UC, UM, UP, Y

An advertisement attributed this title to T. S. Fay.
New Jersey.

1183 HERMA, JOHN. The Spirits of Odin; or, The Father's Curse . . .
[anon.]. New York: Collins and Hannay, 1826. 2 vols.
12mo   AAS, B, HEH, N, NYP, Y(V.2)
Copyrighted in the Southern District of New York by "John Herma of the
said district," who claims the right "as proprietor." He also signs the intro-
duction.
Sweden; late 14th cent.

1184 HERR, ANDREW JACKSON. Fanny Roberteen; or, The Chain of
Destiny: A Romance . . . Boston: Gleason's Publishing Hall,
1847. 100 p., illus. 8vo   AAS, HEH, Y

1185 ——— The Maid of the Valley; or, The Brother's Revenge. A
Tale of the Revolution . . . New York: Wm. H. Graham, 1847.
64 p. 8vo   LC, LCP
Also contains: The Haunted Villa.
Printed in double cols.

1185a HEWSON, JOHN. Christ Rejected; or, The Trial of the Eleven
Disciples of Christ . . . By Captain Onesimus [pseud.] . . .
Philadelphia: Printed for the author by Joseph Rakestraw, 1832.
444, [6] p. 8vo   LC, UV
Two of the 6 p. at end of LC copy are duplicates.

1185b ——— ——— 3d ed. Princeton: Printed for the author by R.
E. Hornor, 1835. 428, [4] p., illus. 12mo   NYP
Four pages at the end for "Family Record."

1185c ——— The Doctrine of the New Birth, Exemplified in the Life
and Religious Experience of Onesimus [pseud.], from the
Eleventh to the Twenty-fifth Year of His Age, or from the Year
1779 to 1793 . . . Philadelphia: Printed by William F. Rackliff,
1839. 164 p., illus. 12mo   AAS, HEH, NYH, NYP

HILBORN, MRS. CHARLOTTE. See Hilbourne, Mrs. Charlotte S.

HILBOURNE, MRS. CHARLOTTE S. The Dreamer: An Original Tale.
In J. N. T. Tucker, The Two Brides (1846), No. 2611b.

1186 HILDRETH, RICHARD. The Slave; or, Memoirs of Archy Moore
. . . [anon.]. Boston: John H. Eastburn, printer, 1836. 2 vols.
12mo   AAS, B, BA, BP, H, HEH, IN, LCP, N, NYH, NYP, UP, UV, Y
Virginia; early 19th cent.

1187 ——— ——— 2d ed. Boston: Munroe & Co., 1839. 2 vols. in
1. 12mo   BP

1188 —— —— 2d ed. Boston: Whipple and Damrell, 1840. 2 vols. in 1. 12mo   BP, H, HEH, NYH, UC, Y

1189 —— —— 3d ed. Boston, Mass.: Anti-slavery Society, 1840. 2 vols. in 1. 12mo   AAS, BA, LC, Y

1189a —— —— 5th ed. Boston: Jordan, Swift & Wiley, 1845. 2 vols. in 1. 12mo   AAS

1190 —— —— 6th ed. Boston: Anti-slavery Office, 1846. 2 vols. in 1. 12mo   AAS, IN, NYP, UP, Y

1191 —— —— 7th ed. Boston: Bela Marsh, 1848. 2 vols. in 1. 12mo   AAS, B, NYP, Y

1192 HINCKLEY, MARY. Sequel to the Seymour Family; or, Domestic Scenes... [anon.]. Boston: Leonard C. Bowles, 1830. 230 p., illus. 12mo   AAS, B, BA, BP, H, UP, Y

1193 —— The Seymour Family; or, Domestic Scenes . . . [anon.]. Boston: Leonard C. Bowles, 1830. 244 p., illus. 12mo   AAS, BA, BP, Y

1194 HINE, E. CURTISS. Orlando Melville; or, The Victims of the Press-gang. A Tale of the Sea . . . Boston: F. Gleason [cop. 1848]. 100 p., illus. 8vo   UP
LC has a title page, deposited Dec. 7, 1848.

1195 —— Roland de Vere; or, The Knight of the Black Plume. A Tale of Italy . . . Boston: F. Gleason, 1848. 100 p., illus. 8vo   UC, UV, Y
Also contains: The Lottery Ticket—Marrying a Tailor.
Printed in double cols.
LC has a title page, deposited Dec. 31, 1847.

1196 —— The Signal; or, The King of Blue Isle. A Sea Tale . . . Boston: F. Gleason, 1848.
LC has a title page, deposited April 7, 1848.

—— Wilson MacFarland. *In* J. H. Robinson, Angela [1850?], No. 2128.

1197 THE HISTORY OF CONSTANTIUS & PULCHERA; or, Constancy Rewarded: An American Novel. Printed at Boston, 1794. 99 p. 4to   IN, UV
Preface dated "January 1, 1794."
American Revolution.

1197a ——— Salem: Printed by T. C. Cushing, 1795. 54 p. 12mo

IN, LC, UV, Y

1198 ——— Norwich: Printed by Thomas Hubbard for Simon Carew, 1796. 45 p. 12mo AAS, BP, JCB, Y

1199 ——— Printed at Leominster (Mass.) by Charles Prentiss for Robert B. Thomas, Sterling, 1797. 102 p. 12mo

AAS, BP, IN, NYH, NYP, Y

1200 ——— Portsmouth, N.H.: Printed by Charles Peirce, 1798. 102 p. 12mo AAS, JCB, UC
At head of title: "A Beautiful Little Novel."

1201 ——— Suffield: Printed by Edward Gray, 1801. 46 p. 12mo

AAS

1202 ——— New York: Printed by and sold by John Tiebout, 1801. 140 p., illus. 8vo AAS, N, NYS, UC, Y

1203 ——— Baltimore: Printed by Robert R. Maxwell, 1802. 147 p. 12mo AAS, B, BP, Y
Also contains: History of Julius and Maria.

1203a ——— Baltimore: Printed by Samuel Sower, 1802. 147 p. 12mo AAS
Also contains: History of Julius and Maria.

1204 ——— Boston: Amos B. Parker, 1821. 106 p. 12mo

AAS, LC, UC, UP, Y

1205 ——— To Which Is Added: Love and Generosity: A Tale Founded on Facts. Exeter: W. C. & S. Hardy, 1831. 118 p. 24mo AAS, HEH, NYP, Y

1206 ——— Concord, N.H.: Eastman & Chadwick, printers, 1834. 59 p. 12mo AAS, B, H, HEH, LC, Y
Title reads: *History of Lorenzo and Virginia; or, Virtue Rewarded ... By T. H. Cauldwell, D.D.*
This is a plagiarism of *The History of Constantius & Pulchera.* Professor Sibley of Cornell directed my attention to this fact, and Mr. Troxell verified it by comparing the two stories at Yale.

1207 THE HISTORY OF THE BOTTLE ... New York: Oliver & Brother, 1848. 32 p., illus. 8vo AAS, HEH, N, NYP, UM, UP, Y
At head of cover title: "New York Organ Temperance Tales, No. I."
Printed in double cols.
New York City; contemporary.

1208 ——— 4th ed. New York: Oliver & Brother, 1848. 32 p., illus. 8vo   AAS, H, Y
Printed in double cols.

1208a HISTORY OF THE CAPTIVITY and Sufferings of Mrs. Maria Martin, Who Was Six Years a Slave in Algiers . . . Written by Herself . . . Boston: Printed for W. Crary, 1807. 72 p., illus. 8vo
                                      AAS, H, HEH, NYP
Many passages are parallel, with slight variations, to *An Affecting History of the Captivity & Sufferings of Mrs. Mary Velnet* [1804?], No. 7a.

1208b ——— Philadelphia: Printed and sold by Joseph Rakestraw, 1809. 107 p., illus. 12mo   AAS, N, NYP

1208c ——— Trenton: Printed by James Oram, 1811. 106 p., illus. 12mo   AAS, HEH

1208d ——— Philadelphia: Jacob Meyer, 1811. 106 p., illus. 12mo
                                      AAS

1208e ——— New Haven: Sidney Press for Increase Cooke & Co., 1812. 107 p. 12mo   AAS, Y

1208f ——— New York: Printed by J. Oram for Evert Duyckinck [1812?].
Shaw, No. 25947.

1208g ——— New York: E. Duyckinck, 1813. 108 p.
Shaw, No. 29055.

1208h ——— St. Clairsville, O.: Printed by John Berry, 1815. 70 p.
Shaw, No. 35189.

1208i ——— Brookfield: Printed by E. Merriam & Co., 1818. 125 p. 12mo   BP

1209 A HISTORY OF THE "STRIPED PIG" . . . Boston: Whipple & Damrell, 1838. 72 p. 16mo   AAS, HEH, LC, N, NYH, NYP, UM, Y
Dedham, Mass.

1210 ——— 2d ed. Boston: Whipple and Damrell, 1838. 72 p. 16mo   AAS, Y

1211 ——— 3d ed. Boston: Whipple and Damrell, 1838. 72 p. 16mo   AAS, BA, Y

1212 ——— 4th thousand. Boston: Whipple and Damrell, 1839. 72 p. 16mo
BP

1213 HITCHCOCK, ENOS. The Farmer's Friend; or, The History of Mr. Charles Worthy ... Printed at Boston, by I. Thomas and E. T. Andrews, 1793. 271 p. 12mo
AAS, B, BA, BP, H, HEH, IN, JCB, LC, N, NYP, NYS, UC, UM, UP, UV, Y
For complete title see Wegelin.
New England.

1214 ——— Memoirs of the Bloomsgrove Family. In a Series of Letters to a Respectable Citizen of Philadelphia ... Printed at Boston, by Thomas and Andrews, 1790. 2 vols. 12mo
AAS, B, BA, BP, H, HEH, IN, JCB, LC, LCP(V.1), N, NYP, NYS, UC, UM, UP, UV, Y
For complete title see Wegelin.

1215 HODGES, M. C. The Mestico; or, The War-path and Its Incidents. A Story of the Creek Indian Disturbances of 1836 ... New York: William H. Graham, 1850. 204 p. 12mo
LC, N
Name printed on cover: "W. C. Hodges."

1216 HOFFMAN, CHARLES FENNO. Greyslaer: A Romance of the Mohawk ... [anon.]. New York: Harper & Brothers, 1840. 2 vols. 12mo
AAS, B, BA, H, HEH, HM, IN, LC, N, NYH, NYP, UC, UM, UP, UV, Y

1217 ——— ——— A New Edition, Corrected by the Author. Philadelbhia [sic]: Lea & Blanchard, 1841. 2 vols. 12mo
AAS, BA, BP, HEH, NYH, NYP, UC

1218 ——— ——— New York: Baker & Scribner, 1842. 2 vols. 12mo
Ed. from Sabin 32385.

1219 ——— ——— 4th ed. New York: Baker & Scribner, 1849. 540 p. 12mo
AAS, B, H, IN, LC, LCP, NYP, NYS, UP, Y

1220 ——— Wild Scenes in the Forest and Prairie: With Sketches of American Life ... New York: William H. Colyer, 1843. 2 vols. 12mo
AAS, BP, H(V.1), HEH, IN, NYP, NYS, UP, Y

1221 HOLBROOK, SILAS PINCKNEY. Sketches by a Traveller ... [anon.]. Boston: Carter and Hendee, 1830. 315 p. 12mo
AAS, BP, H, HEH, LC, N, NYH, NYP, UP, Y

Contents: Letters from a Mariner—Travels of a Tin Pedlar—Letters from a Boston Merchant—Recollections of Japan—Recollections of China—The Schoolmaster (from the Legendary)—The Last of the Blacklegs—Selections. His story "The Last of the Blacklegs" is included in *P's and Q's* (1828), Nos. 2083-84.

1222 HOLMAN, JESSE LYNCH. The Prisoners of Niagara; or, Errors of Education. A New Novel, Founded on Fact ... Frankfort: Printed by William Gerar[d], 1810. 357, [1] p. 12mo HM
American Revolution.

1223 HOLMES, ISAAC EDWARD. Recreations of George Taletell, F.Y.C. [pseud.]. Charleston: Duke & Browne, printers, 1822. 74 p. 8vo   CLS, H, UP, Y
Contents: Recreations—English Country Life—Country Life in Carolina—The Story of Tom—Morning—The Garden—The Piazza—The Village.

1224 HOME; or, An Account of Charles Grafton: A Sailor. Boston: Ford and Damrell, 1834. 36 p. 16mo   AAS, BP, Y
Also contains: The Widow's Son.

HOOPER, JOHNSON JONES. How Simon Suggs "Raised Jack." A Georgia Story, by an Alabamian. *In* W. T. Porter, *ed.,* The Big Bear of Arkansas (1845), Nos. 2061-62.

1224a ———— A Ride with Old Kit Kuncker, and Other Sketches and Scenes of Alabama ... Tuscaloosa, Alabama: M. D. J. Slade, 1849. 120 p.
W. Stanley Hoole, *Alias Simon Suggs* (University, Alabama, 1952), pp. 72, 210, describes his own copy.
Hooper's *The Widow Rugby's Husband* (1851), Wright II, 1259, contains the above stories and four new ones.

1225 ———— Some Adventures of Captain Simon Suggs, Late of the Tallapoosa Volunteers; Together With "Taking the Census," and Other Alabama Sketches. By a Country Editor ... [anon.]. Philadelphia: Carey and Hart, 1845. 201 p., illus. 12mo
                                                      AAS, BA, H, HEH, UPI
Hoole notes (p. 174) that *Some Adventures* "had gone into a second edition before the end of the year, a third by early 1846, a fourth in April, 1848, a fifth and sixth published by A. Hart, successor to Carey & Hart, in 1850."

1226 ———— ———— Philadelphia: Carey and Hart, 1846. 201 p., illus. 12mo   HEH, LC, NYH, UP, Y

———— Taking the Census. *In* W. T. Porter, *ed.*, A Quarter Race in Kentucky (1847), Nos. 2063-64.

1227 HOOPER, LUCY. Scenes from Real Life: An American Tale . . . New York: James P. Griffing, 1840. 83 p. 12mo   AAS, LC, Y

1228 ———— ———— New York: Linen & Fennell, 1841. 152 p. 12mo   AAS, B, BP, NYP, Y
Also contains: The Willow Tree: A Tale Founded on Facts—Choosing a Wife: A New England Tale—Reminiscence of a Clergyman.

1229 HOPKINSON, FRANCIS. The Miscellaneous Essays and Occasional Writings . . . Philadelphia: Printed by T. Dobson, 1792. 3 vols. 8vo   AAS, B, BA, BP, H, HEH, HM(V.2), IN, JCB, LC, LCP, N, NYP, UC, UM, UP, UPI, UV, Y
Contains: A Pretty Story—A Full and True Account of a Terrible Uproar Which Lately Happened in a Very Eminent Family—The New Roof.

1230 ———— A Pretty Story: Written in the Year of Our Lord 2774, by Peter Grievous, Esq., A.B.C.D.E. [pseud.] . . . Philadelphia: Printed and sold by John Dunlap, 1774. 29 p. 8vo
IN, JCB, LCP, UP

1231 ———— ———— 2d ed. Philadelphia: Printed and sold by John Dunlap, 1774. 32 p. 8vo   AAS, BP, HEH, LCP, Y

1232 ———— ———— Williamsburg: Printed by John Pinkney, 1774. 16 p. 8vo   LC

HORTON, MRS. MARY B. Karl and Corinne. *In* The Fountain and the Bottle (1850), No. 996.

1233 HOUSTON, GEORGE, *ed.* National Tales . . . New York: W. B. Gilley, 1825. 264 p. 12mo   AAS, H, N, UP, Y
Contents: The Freebooter—Transmigration—The Thessalian Lovers—Mary Stukeley—The Fair Marseilloise—The Crusaders—The Fortress of Saguntum—Imilda de' Lambertazzi—The Monks of La Trappe—Goodrich Castle: A Tale of the Seventeenth Century—Master and Man.
"Translated and compiled from the writings of different authors, in every country" (Pref.).

1234 ———— National Tales . . . Vol. II. New York: A. P. Houston, 1825. 264 p. 12mo   AAS, H, HEH, N, UC, UP, Y
Contents: Hoosac Mountain—The Fortune Teller—The Falls of St. Anthony—The Statue of Venus: A Grecian Story—The Poet's Dream—Royal Nuptials—Henry Somerset—Cauthleen Kavanagh.

1235   HOWARD, H. R.   The History of Virgil A. Stewart, and His Adventure in Capturing and Exposing the Great "Western Land Pirate" and His Gang...   New York: Harper & Brothers, 1836. 273 p. 12mo

    AAS, B, BA, BP, H, HEH, HM, LC, LCP, N, NYH, NYP, NYS, UC, UP, Y

1235a ———— ———— New York: Harper & Brothers, 1842. 273 p. 12mo   UP

1236 ——— The Life and Adventures of Henry Thomas, the Western Burglar and Murderer, and the Thrilling Narrative of Mrs. Whipple and Jesse Strang ... By the Author of "Lives of Murrell and Hare" [anon.]. Philadelphia: T. B. Peterson, No. 98 Chesnut Street [cop. 1848]. 141 p., illus. 8vo   BA, LC, UM
Printed in double cols.

1237 ——— The Life and Adventures of John A. Murrell, the Great Western Land Pirate . . . [anon.]. New York: H. Long & Brother, 1847. 126 p., illus. 8vo   AAS, UV, Y
Printed in double cols.

1238 ——— ——— New York: H. Long & Brother, 1848. 126 p., illus. 8vo   HEH, Y
Printed in double cols.

1239 ——— The Life and Adventures of Joseph T. Hare, the Bold Robber and Highwayman . . . [anon.]. New York: H. Long and Brother, 1847. 107 p., illus. 8vo   AAS, BA, LC, Y
Printed in double cols.

1240 HOWARD, WALDO. The Mistake of a Life-time; or, The Robber of the Rhine Valley. A Story of the Mysteries of the Shore, and the Vicissitudes of the Sea ... Boston: F. Gleason, 1850. 10 pts. 8vo   AAS, B, H, HEH, HM, IN, N, UM, UP, Y
Paged continuously (319 p.).
Printed in double cols.
LC has a title page, deposited April 17, 1850.

    HUET, M. M. The Seven Brothers of Wyoming [cop. 1850]. *See* No. 2376 for title entry which is now identified as by Huet.

1240a HUGHS, MARY (ROBSON). The Cousins: A Moral Tale ... Philadelphia: R. H. Small, 1826. 260 p. 12mo   AAS
Mrs. Hughs was better known for her juveniles.

1240b ——— Emma Mortimer: A Moral Tale . . . Philadelphia: Thomas T. Ash [cop. 1829]. 249 p. 12mo . . . .

AAS, HEH, LCP, N, Y

1240c ——— Julia Ormond; or, The New Settlement . . . [anon.]. New York: Edward Dunigan, 1846. 220 p., illus. 12mo

HEH, LC, Y

1240d ——— The Two Schools: A Moral Tale . . . Philadelphia: T. T. Ash, 1836. 247 p. 12mo   Y

1240e ——— ——— Baltimore: Fielding Lucas, Jr., No. 170 Market Street [cop. 1835]. 247 p. 12mo   AAS, HEH, LC

1241 HUMANITY IN ALGIERS; or, The Story of Azem. By an American, Late a Slave in Algiers . . . Troy: Printed by R. Moffitt & Co., 1801. 125, [5] p. 12mo   AAS, B, HEH, LC, LCP, N, UP, Y

1242 HUMORIST TALES: Being a Selection of Interesting Stories . . . New York: Nafis & Cornish, 278 Pearl Street [cop. 1840]. 192 p., illus. 12mo   AAS, BA, HEH, Y

This was first issued as Vol. I of *Tales of Humor* (1840). For contents see No. 2533.

S. G. Goodrich denied authorship in his *Recollections of a Lifetime* (1857), II, 550, but he probably edited the collection.

1243 HUNT, THOMAS POAGE. It Will Never Injure Me; or, Those Who Never Drink Often Suffer Most . . . Philadelphia: Griffith & Simon, 1846. 89 p., illus. 16mo   BP, NYP, Y

1244 ——— Jesse Johnston and His Times . . . Philadelphia: Griffith & Simon, 1845. 77 p., illus. 16mo   AAS, BA, HEH, NYP

1245 ——— ——— 2d ed. Philadelphia: Griffith & Simon, 1846. 77 p., illus. 16mo   AAS

1246 ——— The Wedding-Days of Former Times . . . Philadelphia: Griffith & Simon, 1845. 87 p., illus. 12mo

AAS, B, H, HEH, LC, N, NYP, UM, UP, Y

HUNTER, FRED. The Blue Velvet Bonnet: A Parisian Tale. *In* M. A. Clough, Paolina (1849), No. 552.

1247 —————— The Child of the Wreck; or, The Stolen Bracelets. A Romance of the South of England . . . Boston: F. Gleason [cop. 1848]. 100 p., illus. 8vo   AAS, B, UP, Y
Also contains: The Captive Maiden.
Printed in double cols.

—————— The Daguerreotype; or, Love at First Sight. *In* J. Jones, The Belle of Boston (1849), No. 1483.

1248 —————— Hermione; or, The Foundling of St. Antoine. A Romance of the Continent . . . Boston: F. Gleason, 1849.   100 p.
8vo   AAS, UM, Y
Printed in double cols.

1249 —————— The Spaniard; or, The Cruiser of Long Island. A Story of Sunshine and Shadow . . . Boston: F. Gleason, 1849.   100 p.
8vo   B, H, Y
Printed in double cols.
1815.

1250 HUNTINGTON, JEDEDIAH VINCENT. Lady Alice; or, The New Una . . . [anon.].   New York: D. Appleton & Company, 1849.
2 vols.   12mo   AAS, BA, BP, H, HEH, LCP, N, NYP, UC, UM, UP, Y
LC has a title page for "Vol. II," dated 1848, which was deposited May 7, 1849.

1251 —————— —————— New York: D. Appleton & Company. Philadelphia: Geo. S. Appleton, 1849.   152 p.   8vo   AAS, BA, HEH, Y
Printed in double cols.

1252 —————— —————— New York: D. Appleton & Company, 1850.   152 p.   8vo   BA
Printed in double cols.

1253 —————— —————— New York: D. Appleton & Company, 200 Broadway. Philadelphia: Geo. S. Appleton, 164 Chesnut Street [cop. 1849].   152 p.   8vo   NYP, Y
Printed in double cols.

1254 IDA OF TOKENBURG; or, The Force of Jealousy. A Feudal Tale . . . New York: J. D. Myers & W. Smith, printers, 1821.   211 p.
12mo   B, H, NYP, Y

1255 INCIDENTS OF THE REVOLUTION. Tales Illustrating the Events of the American Revolution . . . Bath: R. L. Underhill & Co., 1841. 239 p., illus. 8vo HEH, LC, Y

Contents: Battle of the Cowpens—The White Horseman—Henry Brenton—Attack on the Block House—The Traitor Boy—Captain Morgan—Murder of Miss M'Crea—The Indian Scout—The Heroine of Saratoga—Washington's Escape—Sergeant Jasper—Jacob and Frederick Sammons—The Officer's Visit—His Country's Victim—The First Blood of the Revolution—Honyost Shull—A Tale of Treason.

INGERSOLL, MRS. HENRIETTA C. Love and Romance. *In* J. S. Appleton, *ed.*, Voices from the Kenduskeag (1848), No. 39.

1255a INGRAHAM, JOSEPH HOLT. The Adventures of Will Wizard! Corporal of the Saccarapa Volunteers . . . Boston: H. L. Williams, 1845. 32 p. 8vo AAS, UP

Printed in double cols.

1256 ———— Alice May, and Bruising Bill . . . Boston: Gleason's Publishing Hall, 1845. 50 p. 8vo
AAS, H, HEH, NYP, UC, UM, UP, UV, Y

See BAL 9997 for a postulated title and imprint of a copy at UV.
New Orleans; contemporary.

1257 ———— The American Lounger; or, Tales, Sketches, and Legends, Gathered in Sundry Journeyings . . . [anon.]. Philadelphia: Lea & Blanchard, 1839. 273 p. 12mo
AAS, B, BP, H, HEH, HM, IN, LC, LCP, N, NYH, NYP, UC, UM, UP, Y

Contents: My Lodgings—The Romance of Broadway—Sights from My Window—Yankee Aristocracy—The Kelpie Rock; or, Undercliff—The Mysterious Leaper—The Last of the Whips (pts. 1-2)—The Illegitimate—The Snow Pile—An Essay on Canes—The Black Patch—The Student (pts. 1-5)—Spheeksphobia—The Quadroon of Orleans.

1258 ———— Arnold; or, The British Spy! A Tale of Treason and Treachery . . . Boston: "Yankee" Office, 1844. 39 p. 8vo
AAS, B, BP, LC, NYP, Y

Also contains: The Bold Insurgent: A Tale of the Year 1768.
Printed in double cols.
Title story also in No. 501, and reprinted with a new title, No. 1358.
"The Bold Insurgent" included later in No. 1364.

1259 ———— Arthur Denwood; or, The Maiden of the Inn. A Tale of the War of 1812 . . . Boston: H. L. Williams, 1846. 95 p., illus. 8vo HEH, Y

1260 ——— Beatrice, the Goldsmith's Daughter: A Story of the Reign of the Last Charles . . . New York: Williams Brothers, 1847. 93 p. 8vo   AAS, LC, NYP, Y
Also contains: Duncan Campbell.
Printed in double cols.

——— The Beautiful Cigar Vender, and Its Sequel: Herman de Ruyter (1849). *See* No. 1270.

1260a ——— The Beautiful Unknown; or, Massey Finke . . . Boston: 'Yankee' Office, 1844. 61 p. 8vo   Y

1261 ——— Berkeley; or, The Lost and Redeemed . . . Boston: Henry L. Williams, 1846. 80 p. 8vo   Y
Printed in double cols.

1262 ——— Bertrand; or, The Story of Marie de Heywode. Being a Sequel to Marie, the Fugitive . . . Boston: H. L. Williams, 1845. 40 p., illus. 8vo   AAS, B, NYP, Y
Printed in double cols.

1263 ——— Biddy Woodhull; or, The Pretty Haymaker . . . Boston: E. P. Williams, 1844. 44 p. 8vo   AAS, B, HEH, Y
Printed in double cols.
New York City.

1264 ——— Black Ralph; or, The Helmsman of Hurlgate . . . Boston: Edward P. Williams, 1844. 35 p. 8vo   AAS, H, N, UP, UV, Y
Printed in double cols.
France; 1777.

1265 ——————— Boston: H. L. Williams, 1845. 47 p. 8vo   B, BP, Y

1266 ——— Blanche Talbot; or, The Maiden's Hand. A Romance of the War of 1812 . . . New York: Williams Brothers, 1847. 122 p. 8vo   AAS, LC, UV
Also contains: Henry Temple; or, A Father's Crime.
Printed in double cols.

1267 ——— Bonfield; or, The Outlaw of the Bermudas. A Nautical Novel . . . New York: H. L. Williams, 1846. 98 p. 8vo   B, LC, NYP, UV, Y
Printed in double cols.

1268 ———— La Bonita Cigarera; or, The Beautiful Cigar-Vender! A
Tale of New York ... Boston: "Yankee" Office, 1844. Cover
title, 48 p., illus. 8vo   NYP, UP, UV, Y
Printed in double cols.
For information about variant cover titles see BAL 9970.

1269 ———— ———— New York: H. L. Williams, 1846. Cover title,
48 p., illus. 8vo
Printed in double cols.
Ed. from sales catalog.

1270 ———— ———— And Its Sequel: Herman de Ruyter ... New
York: Williams Brothers, 1849. 96 p. 8vo   UM, Y
Title reads: *The Beautiful Cigar Vender, And Its Sequel: Herman de Ruy-
ter. Tales of City Life, Founded on Facts.*
"Herman de Ruyter," pp. [45]-93, has separate title page.
Also contains: The Suicide.
Printed in double cols.

1271 ———— The Brigantine; or, Guitierro and the Castilian. A Tale,
Both of Boston and Cuba ... New York: Williams Brothers,
1847. 96 p. 8vo   AAS, B, Y
Also contains: The Old Beau; or, The New Valet.
Printed in double cols.

1272 ———— Burton; or, The Sieges ... [anon.]. New York: Harper
& Brothers, 1838. 2 vols. 12mo
     AAS, B, BA, BP, H, HEH, HM, IN, LC, N, NYP, UC, UM, UP, UV, Y
American Revolution.

1272a ———— ———— New York: William H. Colyer, 1847. 2 vols.
12mo
Copy located at University of California at Los Angeles Library.

1273 ———— Captain Kyd; or, The Wizard of the Sea ... [anon.].
New York: Harper & Brothers, 1839. 2 vols. 12mo
     AAS, B, H, HEH, HM, IN, LC, N, NYH, NYP, UM, UP, UV, Y

1273a ———— Caroline Archer; or, The Miliner's [sic] Apprentice. A
Story That Hath More Truth Than Fiction in It ... Boston:
Edward P. Williams [1844]. 38 p. 8vo   AAS, UV, Y
Also contains: The Pretty Feet; or, The Way to Choose a Wife.
Cover imprint dated 1844.
Printed in double cols.

1274 ———— Charles Blackford; or, The Adventures of a Student in Search of a Profession . . . Boston: 'Yankee' Office, 1845. 48 p. 8vo   AAS, B, H, HEH, LC, N, UC, UP, UV, Y
New England.

1275 ———— ———— [Colophon] G. W. Redding, 8 State Street, Boston [n.d.]. Caption title, 32 p. 8vo   H, Y
Printed in double cols.

1276 ———— The Clipper-Yacht; or, Moloch, the Money-lender! A Tale of London and the Thames . . . Boston: H. L. Williams, 1845. 54 p. 8vo   AAS, B, HEH, N, NYP, UP, UV, Y
LC has a cover title, deposited Jan. 22, 1845.

1277 ———— The Corsair of Casco Bay; or, The Pilot's Daughter . . . Gardiner, Maine: G. M. Atwood, 1844. 58 p. 8vo
AAS, BP, H, LC, UP, Y
It has been noted that the publishers differ in various cover imprints.
Printed in double cols.

1278 ———— The Cruiser of the Mist . . . New York: Burgess, Stringer and Company, 1845. 52 p. 8vo
AAS, HEH, NYP, UP, UV, Y
Printed in double cols.
Following War of 1812.

1279 ———— The Dancing Feather; or, The Amateur Freebooters. A Romance of New York . . . Boston: George Roberts, 1842. Cover title, 32 p. 8vo   B, BP, H, HEH, N, UP, Y
Also contains: Detached Thoughts, by Jean Paul Richter.
Printed in double cols.

1280 ———— ———— Boston: 'Yankee' Office, 1844. Cover title, 63 p. 8vo   H, HEH, UC

1280a ———— ———— Boston: H. L. Williams, 1845. Cover title, 63 p. 8vo   Y

1281 ———— ———— Boston: H. L. Williams, 1845. 48 p. 8vo
AAS, Y
Printed in double cols.

1282 ———— ———— And Its Sequel, Morris Graeme; or, The Cruise of the Sea-Slipper . . . New York: Williams Brothers, 1847. Cover title, 92 p., illus. 8vo   LC

Each story has its own title page: the first with imprint, "Boston, 1845"; the second with imprint, "Boston, 1847."
Printed in double cols.
AAS and Y have Pt. II only: "Morris Graeme, Boston, 1847."

1283 —— —— New York: W. F. Burgess, 1849. 48 p. 8vo
NYH
Printed in double cols.

1283a —— —— New York: W. F. Burgess, 1850. 48, [2], [51]-92 p. 8vo
AAS
AAS lacks cover title which may have been similar to No. 1282.
Second pagination is the sequel "Morris Graeme."
Printed in double cols.

1283b —— The Diary of a Hackney Coachman ... Boston: 'Yankee' Office, 1844. Cover title, 42 p. 8vo
UC, UV, Y
Also contains: Donald Fay.

1284 —— Edward Austin; or, The Hunting Flask. A Tale of the Forest and Town ... Boston: F. Gleason, 1842. 66 p. 8vo
AAS, B, H, HEH, HM, LC, N, UC, UP, UV, Y
HEH and HM cover titles dated 1845.
LC has a cover title dated 1845, deposited Dec. 14, 1844.
New York City; contemporary.

1285 —— Edward Manning; or, The Bride and the Maiden ... New York: Williams Brothers, 1847. 120 p. 8vo
AAS, LC, UV, Y
Boston.

1286 —— Eleanor Sherwood, the Beautiful Temptress. A Tale of the Trial of Principle ... Boston: E. P. Williams, 1843. Cover title, 56 p. 8vo
Y
Printed in double cols.

1287 —— Ellen Hart; or, The Forger's Daughter ... Boston: 'Yankee' Office, 1844. Cover title, 46 p. 8vo
AAS
Printed in double cols.
Boston; contemporary.

1288 —— Estelle; or, The Conspirator of the Isle. A Tale of the West Indian Seas ... Boston: 'Yankee' Office, 1844. Cover title, 46 p. 8vo
Y
Printed in double cols.

1289 —— Fanny H——; or, The Hunchback and the Roué . . . Boston: Edward P. Williams, 1843. Cover title, 32 p. Fol.

HEH, NYP, UP, UV, Y

Printed in double cols.
Massachusetts.

1290 —— Fleming Field; or, The Young Artisan. A Tale of the Days of the Stamp Act . . . New York: Burgess, Stringer and Company, 1845. 96 p., illus. 8vo   AAS, LC, UP, UV, Y

Cover imprint dated 1846.
Boston.

1291 —— Forrestal; or, The Light of the Reef. A Romance of the Blue Waers [sic] . . . Boston: H. L. Williams, 1845. 140 p. 8vo   HEH, UP, UV, Y

LC has a title page, deposited Mar. 4, 1845.

1292 —— —— New York: Morning Star office, 1850. 93 p. 8vo   LC

Also contains: Mary Wilbur; or, The Deacon and the Widow's Daughter.
Printed in double cols.

1293 —— Frank Rivers; or, The Dangers of the Town. A Story of Temptation, Trial, and Crime . . . Boston: E. P. Williams, 1843. Cover title, 32 p. 8vo   B, HEH, LC

Printed in double cols.
New York City.

1294 —— —— Boston: Yankee Office, 1845. Cover title, 47 p. 8vo   AAS, HEH, UC

Printed in double cols.
Two printings noted: (1) with copyright notice dated 1844 at head of caption title; (2) without copyright notice at head of caption title.

1295 —— Freemantle; or, The Privateersman! A Nautical Romance of the Last War . . . Boston: George W. Redding & Co. [cop. 1845]. 46 p. 8vo   H, HEH, NYP, UC, UP, UV, Y

LC has a title page, deposited Feb. 15, 1845.

1296 —— The Free-Trader; or, The Cruiser of Narragansett Bay . . . New York: Williams Brothers, 1847. 96 p. 8vo   UV, Y

Printed in double cols.

1297 ——— The Gipsy of the Highlands; or, The Jew and the Heir. Being the Adventures of Duncan Powell and Paul Tatnall ... Boston: Redding & Co., 1843. Cover title, 31 p. 8vo

AAS, B, BA, H, HEH, LC, N, UP, UV, Y

Printed in double cols.
New York.

1298 ——— ——— Boston: Redding & Co., 1845. 68 p. 8vo

AAS, Y

1299 ——— Grace Weldon; or, Frederica, the Bonnet-Girl. A Tale of Boston and Its Bay ... Boston: H. L. Williams, 1845. 108 p. 8vo

AAS, LC, UM, UV, Y

1300 ——— ——— New York: W. F. Burgess, 22 Ann Street [n.d.]. 108 p. 8vo

AAS

1301 ——— Harry Harefoot; or, The Three Temptations. A Story of City Scenes ... Boston: H. L. Williams, 1845. Cover title, 61 p. 8vo

AAS, B, HEH, N, NYP, UC, UP, UV, Y

Printed in double cols.

1302 ——— Henry Howard; or, Two Noes Make One Yes ... Boston: Henry L. Williams, 1845. 32 p. 8vo AAS, LC, NYH, UP, Y
Also contains: Trout Fishing; or, Who Is the Captain?

1303 ——— Herman de Ruyter; or, The Mystery Unveiled. A Sequel to the Beautiful Cigar Vender. A Tale of the Metropolis ... Boston: 'Yankee' Office, 1844. Cover title, 47 p., illus. 8vo

HEH, NYP, UP, Y

Printed in double cols.

1304 ——— ——— Boston: 'Yankee' Office, 1845. Cover title, 48 p., illus. 8vo

UP, Y

Printed in double cols.

1305 ——— Howard; or, The Mysterious Disappearance ... Boston: Edward P. Williams, 1843. Cover title, 31 p. 8vo

B, HEH, UV

Printed in double cols.

1306 ——— Jemmy Daily; or, The Little News Vender. A Tale of Youthful Struggles, and the Triumph of Truth and Virtue over Vice and Falsehood ... Boston: Brainard & Co., 1843. 54 p. 8vo

AAS, B, BA, H, HEH, LC, UC, UP, Y

Printed in double cols.
Boston; contemporary.

1307 ——— Jennette Alison; or, The Young Strawberry Girl. A Tale of the Sea and the Shore . . . Boston: F. Gleason, 1848. 100 p. 8vo　　　　　　　　　　　　UP, Y
Printed in double cols.
LC has a title page, deposited Nov. 8, 1847.

1308 ——— The Knights of Seven Lands . . . Boston: F. Gleason, 1845. 64 p. 8vo　　　AAS, B, BP, HEH, N, UC, Y
Contains seven sketches. For the undated ed. with a new title and one less sketch, see No. 1345.

1309 ——— The Lady of the Gulf: A Romance of the City and the Seas . . . Boston: H. L. Williams, 1846. 95 p. 8vo
　　　　　　　　　　　　　　　　　AAS, B, Y
At head of title: "Price Twenty-Five Cents."
LC has a title page, deposited Mar. 28, 1846.

1310 ——— Lafitte: The Pirate of the Gulf . . . [anon.]. New York: Harper & Brothers, 1836. 2 vols. 12mo
　　　　　　AAS, H, HEH, HM, IN, LC, N, NYP, UC, UP, UV, Y

1311 ——— ——— 2d ed. New York: Harper & Brothers, 1836. 2 vols. 12mo　　　　　AAS, HM, IN, UP, Y

1312 ——— ——— 2d ed. New York: Harper & Brothers, 1842. 2 vols. 12mo　　　　　AAS, BP, Y
An 1847 ed. has been reported; not seen.

1313 ——— ——— New York: De Witt & Davenport, 156 Nassau Street [n.d.]. 200 p. 8vo　　　AAS, B, IN, Y

1314 ——— Leisler; or, The Rebel and King's Man. A Tale of the Rebellion of 1689 . . . Boston: Henry L. Williams, 1846. 90 p., illus. 8vo　　　　　　AAS, B, LC, UV, Y
Printed in double cols.

1315 ——— Marie; or, The Fugitive! A Romance of Mount Benedict . . . Boston: 'Yankee' Office [1845]. 48 p. 8vo
　　　　　　　　　　　　　AAS, B, HEH, UP, UV, Y
Cover imprint dated 1845.
Two printings; see BAL 9980 for variations.

1316 ——— Mark Manly; or, The Skipper's Lad. A Tale of Boston in the Olden Time . . . Boston: E. P. Williams & Co., 1843. Cover title, 31 p. 8vo   B, H, HEH, Y
Printed in double cols.
Advert. at end reads: "Will be published in a few days a sequel to the 'Dancing Feather,'" which was "Morris Graeme."

1317 ——— ——— Boston: E. P. Williams, 1843. Cover title, 45 p. 8vo   AAS, Y
Printed in double cols.
Advert. at end reads: "Lately issued . . . Morris Graeme."

1318 ——— ——— New York: Williams Brothers, 1848. 80 p. 8vo
        LC, Y
Also contains: Frederick St. Clair; or, The Young Man about Town, by Henry William Herbert.
Printed in double cols.

1319 ——— Mary Wilbur; or, The Deacon and the Widow's Daughter . . . Boston: 'Yankee' Office [1845]. 50 p. 8vo   B, UV, Y
Also in No. 1292.

1320 ——— The Mast-Ship; or, The Bombardment of Falmouth . . . Boston: Henry L. Williams, 1845. 50 p. 8vo   B, UP, UV, Y
Printed in double cols.

1321 ——— Mate Burke; or, The Foundlings of the Sea . . . New York: Burgess, Stringer and Company, 1846. 93 p. 8vo
        AAS, B, BA, Y

1322 ——— The Midshipman; or, The Corvette and Brigantine. A Tale of Sea and Land . . . Boston: F. Gleason, 1844. 64 p. 8vo
        AAS, B, HEH, LC, N, UC, UV, Y

1323 ——— ——— 2d ed. Boston: F. Gleason, 1844. 64 p. 8vo
        NYP

1324 ——— ——— Boston: Gleason's Publishing Hall, 1845. 64 p. 8vo   AAS, BP, H, UP, Y

1325 ——— The Miseries of New York; or, The Burglar and Counsellor . . . Boston: 'Yankee' Office, 1844. Cover title, 48 p. 8vo   LC, Y
Printed in double cols.

1326 —— Montezuma, the Serf; or, The Revolt of the Mexitili. A Tale of the Last Days of the Aztec Dynasty . . . [anon.]. Boston: H. L. Williams, 1845. 2 vols. 8vo
AAS, B, HEH, LC, N, UC(V.2), UM, UP, UV, Y

1327 —— Morris Graeme; or, The Cruise of the Sea-Slipper. A Sequel to The Dancing Feather . . . Boston: E. P. Williams, 1843. 32 p. Fol. AAS, B, BP, H, HEH, N, NYH, NYP, UP, UV, Y
Printed in double cols.

1328 —— —— Boston: H. L. Williams, 1845. Cover title, 50 p. 8vo AAS, B, H, HEH, UC, UP, Y

1328a —— —— Boston: Published at the 'Yankee' Office, 22 Congress St.; Hotchkiss & Co., and Haliburton & Dudley, 1845. Cover title, 50 p. 8vo B

1329 —— The Mysterious State-room: A Tale of the Mississippi . . . Boston: Gleason's Publishing Hall, 1846. 50 p., illus. 8vo AAS, LC, Y
Also contains: A Story.

1330 —— Neal Nelson; or, The Seige [sic] of Boston. A Tale of the Revolution . . . Boston: Henry L. Williams, 1845. Cover title, 48 p., illus. 8vo AAS, H, UV, Y
At head of cover title is the copyright notice misdated 1855.
Printed in double cols.

1331 —— —— New York: Williams Brothers, 1847. Cover title, 48 p., illus. 8vo B, LC
Printed in double cols.

1332 —— Norman; or, The Privateersman's Bride. A Sequel to 'Freemantle' . . . Boston: Yankee Office, 1845. Cover title, 48 p. 8vo AAS, H, HEH, LC, UC, UP, UV, Y

1333 —— The Odd Fellow; or, The Secret Association, and Foraging Peter . . . Boston: United States Publishing Company, 1846. 82 p. 8vo AAS, B, HEH, IN, LC, NYP, UM, UV, Y
LC has a cover title which reads: "Lame Davy's Son; With the Birth, Education, and Career of Foraging Peter: A Tale of Boston Aristocracy. The 'Odd Fellow'; or, The Secret Association . . . Boston: George Roberts [n.d.]," deposited Mar. 14, 1843. This title has been found only in the *Boston Notion, Extra Series.*

1334 —— Paul Deverell; or, Two Judgements for One Crime. A Tale of the Present Day . . . Boston: H. L. Williams, 1845. 72 p., illus. 8vo   AAS, B, NYP, UP, Y
Issued in 2 pts. At head of cover title, Pt. II: "In two parts, price 12½ cents each."
Reprinted in a single vol.
Boston.

1335 —— Paul Perril, the Merchant's Son; or, The Adventures of a New-England Boy Launched upon Life . . . Boston: Williams & Brothers [1847]. 2 pts. in 1, illus. 8vo
AAS, B, LC, UP, UV, Y
Cover imprint dated 1847.
South America; 1827.

1335a —— Pierce Fenning; or, The Lugger's Chase. A Romance . . . Boston: Henry L. Williams, 1846. 95 p., illus. 8vo   Y
Printed in double cols.

1336 —— The Quadroone; or, St. Michael's Day . . . [anon.]. New York: Harper & Brothers, 1841. 2 vols. 12mo
AAS, B, BP, H, HEH, IN, LC, N, NYH, NYP, UC, UM, UP, UV, Y
New Orleans; 1769.

1337 ——— ——— New York: William H. Colyer, 1847. 2 vols. in 1. 12mo   NYH, UP

1338 —— Rafael [anon.]. Boston: H. L. Williams, 1845. Cover title, 47 p., illus. 8vo   AAS, H, HEH, LC, N, NYP, UC, UP, UV, Y
Caption title: "Rafael; or, The Twice Condemned. A Tale of Key West."
Some covers erroneously dated 1844.

1339 —— Ramero; or, The Prince and the Prisoner! A Romance of the Moro Castle . . . Boston: Henry L. Williams, 1846. 114 p. 8vo   B
Printed in double cols.
LC has a title page, deposited May 21, 1846.

1339a —— The Ringdove; or, The Privateer and the Cutter . . . Boston: H. L. Williams, 1846. 82 p. 8vo
No copy located.

1340 —— Ringold Griffitt; or, The Raftsman of the Susquehannah. A Tale of Pennsylvania . . . Boston: F. Gleason, 1847. 100 p. 8vo   AAS, LC, UC, Y
Printed in double cols.
182-.

1341 ——— Rodolphe in Boston . . . Boston: E. P. Williams, 1844.
48 p.   8vo   AAS, B, BP, UP, Y
Printed in double cols.
Contemporary.

1342 ——— A Romance of the Sunny South; or, Feathers from a
Traveller's Wing . . . Boston: H. L. Williams, 1845.   35 p.,
illus.   8vo   AAS, HEH, Y
Cover title: "The Southern Belle .."
LC has a title page, deposited Sept. 25, 1845.

1343 ——— Santa Claus; or, The Merry King of Christmas.   A Tale
for the Holidays . . . Boston: H. L. Williams, 1844.   34 p.,
illus.   8vo   AAS, B, NYH, NYP, Y

1344 ——— Scarlet Feather; or, The Young Chief of the Abenaquies.
A Romance of the Wilderness of Maine . . . Boston: F. Gleason,
1845.   66 p., illus.   8vo
                 AAS, B, BA, BP, H, HEH, LC, N, NYP, UC, UM, UP, UV, Y
American Revolution.

1345 ——— The Seven Knights; or, Tales of Many Lands.   Being
Certain Romanceros of Chivalry . . . Boston: H. L. Williams,
22 Congress Street [1845].   43 p.   8vo   AAS, B, NYP, UP, UV, Y
This is the same as No. 1308 but with a new title and one less sketch.

1346 ——— The Silver Bottle; or, The Adventures of "Little Marlboro" in Search of His Father . . . Boston: "Yankee" Office,
1844.   Cover title, 2 pts.   8vo   AAS, B, HEH, Y
Pt. II only has separate title page.
Massachusetts.

1347 ——— The Silver Ship of Mexico: A Tale of the Spanish Main
. . . New York: H. L. Williams, 1846.   98 p.   8vo   LC, Y
Also contains: Arnold Allen: A Romance of the Old Tower at Concord.
LC cover imprint dated 1847.
Printed in double cols.

1348 ——— The Slave King; or, The Triumph of Liberty . . . [Bos-
ton]: H. L. Williams, cop. 1846.   2 vols. in 1, illus.   8vo
                                               AAS, UM, Y
Printed in double cols.

1349 ——— The South-West, by a Yankee . . . [anon.].   New York:
Harper & Brothers, 1835.   2 vols.   12mo   AAS, B, BA, BP, H,
                 HEH, IN, LC, LCP, N, NYH, NYP, NYS, UC, UM, UP, UV, Y

1350 ——— The Spanish Galleon; or, The Pirate of the Mediterranean. A Romance of the Corsair Kidd ... Boston: F. Gleason, 1844. 64 p. 8vo   AAS, B, BA, HEH, N, NYP, UM, UP, UV, Y

1351 ——— ——— Boston: F. Gleason, 1845. 64 p. 8vo
                                                    BP, H, UC, Y

1352 ——— ——— Boston: F. Gleason, 1849. 100 p. 8vo
Also contains: X-ing a Paragrab, by E. A. Poe.
Ed. from Heartman and Canny.

1353 ——— The Spectre Steamer, and Other Tales . . . Boston: United States Publishing Company, 1846. 100 p. 8vo
                                                    AAS, B, H, LC, NYP, UM, UV, Y
Contents: The Spectre Steamer; or, Hugh Northup's Oath: A Tale of the Mississippi—The Frigate's Tender: A Tale of the Last War—The Cascade; or, The Exile's Rock: A Tale of the Valley of the Kennebec—Ildefonse, the Noble Polish Maiden: A Tale of Warsaw—The French Jew; or, "Killing Time" in the Jersies, Taken Down from the Mouth of Tom King—The Lottery Ticket—Annette, the Heiress; or, The Foraging Party: A Tale of the Last War—Dona Inezetta; or, The Duke's Daughter: A Tale of Spain—The Bivouac; or, A Night at the Mouth of the Ohio: A Sketch of Western Voyaging—The Hand of Clay; or, The Sculptor's Task: A Tale of Mysteries—OthoVisconti; or, The Bridal Present: A Tale of Florence—My Uncle the Colonel, with the Story of My Uncle's Friend the Pickpocket.
Printed in double cols.

1354 ——— Steel Belt; or, The Three Masted Goleta. A Tale of Boston Bay . . . Boston: "Yankee" Office, 1844. Cover title, 48 p., illus. 8vo   AAS, H, HEH, NYH, NYP, Y
Printed in double cols.
For variant cover imprints see BAL 9967.

1355 ——— The Surf Skiff; or, The Heroine of the Kennebec . . . New York: Williams Brothers, 1847. 98 p. 8vo
                                                    AAS, H, LC, NYP, Y
Also contains: Captain Velasco and the Young Lieutenant; or, Our Private Buccaneering Adventure.
Printed in double cols.

1356 ——— The Texan Ranger; or, The Maid of Matamoras . . . New York: Williams Brothers, 1847. 96 p. 8vo   AAS, N
Also contains: "Alice Brandon; or, The Sewing Girl."
Printed in double cols.
Title story also in No. 805.

1357 ——— Theodore; or, The "Child of the Sea." Being a Sequel to the Novel of "Lafitte, the Pirate of the Gulf" . . . Boston: Edward P. Williams, 1844. 36 p. 8vo   AAS, HM, Y
Printed in double cols.

1358 ——— The Treason of Arnold: A Tale of West Point during the American Revolution . . . [anon.]. Jonesville (Templeton), Mass.: James M. Barnes, 1847. 46 p. 8vo
                                        AAS, HEH, NYP, UM, UV, Y
A reprint of No. 1258 with a new title.

1359 ——— The Truce; or, On and Off Soundings. A Tale of the Coast of Maine . . . New York: Williams Brothers, 1847. 103 p. 8vo   AAS, LC, Y
Printed in double cols.
Late 18th cent.

1360 ——— Wildash; or, The Cruiser of the Capes . . . New York: Williams Brothers, 1847. 96 p. 8vo   AAS, B, LC, Y
Also contains: The Fire-Screen; or, The Heiress and the Embroidery-Worker—The Embroidery-Worker; or, The Two Cousins. A Sequel to The Fire-Screen.
Printed in double cols.

1361 ——— Will Terril; or, The Adventures of a Young Gentleman Born in a Cellar . . . Boston: 'Yankee' Office, 1845. 48 p. 8vo
                                        AAS, H, HEH

1362 ——— The Wing of the Wind: A Nouelette of the Sea . . . New York: Burgess, Stringer and Company, 1845. 96 p., illus. 8vo   AAS, LC, UM, UP, UV, Y

1363 ——— Winwood; or, The Fugitive of the Seas . . . New York: H. L. Williams, 1846. 93 p. 8vo   LC, Y
Printed in double cols.

1364 ——— The Young Artist and the Bold Insurgent . . . Boston: United States Publishing Co., 1846. 58 p. 8vo
                                        AAS, HEH, UP, UV, Y

1364a ——— The Young Genius; or, Trials and Triumphs . . . Boston: E. P. Williams, 1843. Cover title, 36 p. 8vo   Y
Printed in double cols.

1365   INGRAM, J. K.   Amelia Somers, the Orphan; or, The Buried Alive
     . . . Boston: Wright's steam power press, 1846.   36 p., illus.
     12mo   AAS, H, HEH, LC, N, NYP, UP, Y
     New York City; contemporary.

1366   ——   The Pirate's Revenge; or, A Tale of Don Pedro and Miss
     Lois Maynard . . . Boston: Wright's steam power press, 1845.
     36 p., illus.   12mo   NYP, Y

1367   THE IRISH EMIGRANT.   An Historical Tale Founded on Fact, by
     an Hibernian . . . [anon.].   Winchester, Va.: John T. Shar-
     rocks, 1817.   2 vols.   8vo   BP, H, HEH, LC, NYP(V.2), UP, UV, Y
     Adam Douglass, attrib. au.

1368   IRVING, JOHN TREAT.   The Hawk Chief: A Tale of the Indian
     Country . . . Philadelphia: Carey, Lea & Blanchard, 1837.   2
     vols.   12mo   AAS, B, BP, HM, LCP, N, NYS, UC, UM, UP, UV, Y
     Trans-Mississippi.

1369   ——   The Quod Correspondence; or, The Attorney.   By
     John Quod [pseud.] . . . Boston: Otis, Broaders and Company,
     1842.   2 vols.   12mo
                AAS, BP, H, HEH, IN, N, NYP(V.1), UP(V.1), Y
     New York City.

1370   —— ——   New York: John Allen, 1842.   2 vols.   12mo
                     AAS, BA, NYP, NYS, UM, UP(V.2), Y

1371   —— ——   Boston: Otis, Broaders and Company, 1843.   2
     vols.   12mo   NYP(V.1), UP(V.1), Y

1372   IRVING, PETER.   Giovanni Sbogarro: A Venetian Tale, by Percival
     G—— [pseud.].   New York: Van Winkle, 1820.   2 vols.   8vo
                     AAS, BP, IN, NYH, NYP, NYS, UC, UV

     IRVING, WASHINGTON.   Abbotsford and Newstead Abbey.   *See*
     The Crayon Miscellany, No. 1402.

1373   ——   The Alhambra: A Series of Tales and Sketches of the
     Moors and Spaniards . . . [anon.].   Philadelphia: Carey & Lea,
     1832.   2 vols.   12mo
           AAS, B, BA, H, HEH, IN, LC, LCP, N, NYH, NYP, UM, UP, UV, Y

1374   —— ——   Philadelphia: Carey, Lea and Blanchard, 1836.
     2 vols.   12mo   AAS, BA, H, LCP, NYP, UP, Y

1374a ——— ——— Philadelphia: Carey, Lea and Blanchard, 1837.
2 vols. 12mo   AAS

1374b ——— ——— Philadelphia: Lea and Blanchard, 1839. 2 vols.
12mo   Y

1374c ——— ——— Philadelphia: Carey, Lea and Blanchard, 1840.
2 vols. in 1. 12mo   AAS, Y

1375 ——— ——— Philadelphia: Lea & Blanchard, 1842. 2 vols.
12mo   BP(v.2), NYP(v.2), NYS

1376 ——— The Beauties of Washington Irving . . . Philadelphia:
Carey, Lea & Blanchard, 1835. 270 p. 12mo
                                    AAS, CLS, HEH, LC, NYP, UP, Y

1376a ——— ——— Philadelphia: Carey, Lea & Blanchard, 1837.
270 p. 12mo   AAS, Y

1377 ——— ——— Philadelphia: Carey, Lea & Blanchard, 1838. 307
p. 12mo   AAS, B, H, LC, LCP, UP, Y

1377a ——— ——— Philadelphia: Lea & Blanchard, 1839. 270 p.
12mo   AAS, Y

1377b ——— ——— Philadelphia: Lea & Blanchard, 1841. 270 p.
12mo   AAS, Y

1378 ——— A Book of the Hudson. Collected from the Various
Works of Diedrich Knickerbocker. Edited by Geoffrey Cray-
on [pseud.]. New York: G. P. Putnam, 1849. 215 p. 16mo
                          AAS, BA, HEH, IN, LCP, N, NYP, UC, UM, UP, Y
"R. Craighead, printer and stereotyper, 112 Fulton Street, New York" (verso
of title page).
For contents see Williams & Edge.

1379 ——— ——— New York: G. P. Putnam, 1849. 283 p., illus.
16mo   AAS, B, BP, H, HEH, IN, LCP, NYP, UC, UP, Y
"John F. Trow, printer and stereotyper, 49 Ann Street, N. Y." (verso of title
page).

1380 ——— Bracebridge Hall; or, The Humourists. A Medley, by
Geoffrey Crayon, Gent. [pseud.] . . . New York: Printed by
C. S. Van Winkle, 1822. 2 vols. 12mo (or 8vo)   AAS, B, BA,
            BP, H, HEH, HM(v.2), IN, LC, LCP, N, NYP, UC, UM, UP, UV, Y

1381 ——— ——— 2d ed. New York: Printed by C. S. Van Winkle,
1822. 2 vols. 12mo   AAS, H, HM, Y

1382 ——— ——— 3d ed. New York: Printed by C. S. Van Winkle,
1826. 2 vols. 12mo   B, BP, NYP, UC, Y

1383 ——— ——— 4th ed. Philadelphia: Carey & Lea, 1830. 2
vols. 12mo   HEH(V.I), NYP

1384 ——— ——— 4th ed. Philadelphia: Carey & Lea, 1831. 2
vols. 12mo   AAS, BA, H(V.2), HEH, HM(V.I), LCP, Y

1385 ——— ——— 4th ed. Philadelphia: Carey & Lea, 1835. 2
vols. 12mo   H, NYP, UP, Y

1386 ——— ——— Philadelphia: Carey, Lea & Blanchard, 1835. 2
vols. 12mo   AAS, H, LCP, NYP, NYS

1387 ——— ——— Philadelphia: Carey, Lea & Blanchard, 1836. 2
vols. 12mo   AAS, BA, NYP(V.2), UP, Y

1388 ——— ——— Philadelphia: Carey, Lea & Blanchard, 1838. 2
vols. 12mo   HEH(V.2), NYP, Y

1389 ——— ——— Philadelphia: Lea & Blanchard, 1839. 2 vols.
12mo   AAS, H(V.2), Y

1389a ——— ——— Philadelphia: Lea & Blanchard, 1841. 2 vols. in
I. 12mo   AAS

1390 ——— ——— New York: George P. Putnam, 1849. 487 p.
12mo   H, LC, N, NYP, Y

1391 ——— ——— New York: George P. Putnam, 1850. 487 p.
12mo   BA

1392 ——— A Chronicle of the Conquest of Granada. By Fray
Antonio Agapida [pseud.] . . . Philadelphia: Carey, Lea &
Carey, 1829. 2 vols. 12mo
       AAS, B, BA, BP(V.I), H, HEH, IN, LC, LCP, N, NYP, NYS, UP, UV, Y

1393 ——— ——— Philadelphia: Carey & Lea, 1831. 2 vols. 12mo
                                                           AAS

1394 ——— ——— Philadelphia: Carey & Lea, 1833. 2 vols. 12mo
                                                           LCP, NYP

1395 —— —— Philadelphia: Carey, Lea & Blanchard, 1835. 2 vols. 12mo
LCP, NYP, NYS, Y

1396 —— —— Philadelphia: Carey, Lea & Blanchard, 1836. 2 vols. 12mo
AAS, LCP

1397 —— —— Philadelphia: Carey, Lea & Blanchard, 1837. 2 vols. 12mo
AAS, BA, Y

1398 —— —— Philadelphia: Carey, Lea & Blanchard, 1838. 2 vols. in 1. 12mo
BP, NYP, Y

1399 —— —— Philadelphia: Lea & Blanchard, 1840. 2 vols. 12mo
AAS

1400 —— —— New York: George P. Putnam, 1850. 548 p. 12mo
BA, LC, NYP, UC

1401 —— The Crayon Miscellany . . . No. 1: Containing a Tour on the Prairies [anon.]. Philadelphia: Carey, Lea & Blanchard, 1835. 274 p. 12mo
AAS, B, BA, BP, H, HEH, IN, LC, LCP, N, NYP, NYS, UC, UM, UP, Y

1402 —— —— No. 2: Containing Abbotsford and Newstead Abbey [anon.]. Philadelphia: Carey, Lea and Blanchard, 1835. 230 p. 12mo
AAS, B, BA, BP, H, HEH, HM, IN, LC, LCP, N, NYH, NYP, NYS, UC, UM, UP, UPI, Y

1403 —— —— No. 3: Containing Legends of the Conquest of Spain [anon.]. Philadelphia: Carey, Lea & Blanchard, 1835. 276 p. 12mo
AAS, B, BA, BP, H, HEH, HM, IN, LC, LCP, N, NYP, NYS, UC, UM, UP, UPI, Y

1404 —— —— Complete in One Volume. New York: George P. Putnam, 1849. 379 p. 12mo
BA, H, NYP, Y

1405 —— The Crayon Reading Book: Comprising Selections from the Various Writings of Washington Irving . . . New York: Geo. P. Putnam, 1849. 255 p. 12mo
AAS, BA, BP, LC, NYP

1406 —— —— New York, 1850.
The Union Catalogue at LC locates a copy in Princeton University Library.

1407 —— The Devil and Tom Walker: Together with Deacon Grubb and the Old Nick [anon.]. Woodstock, Vt.: Printed and published by R. & A. Colton, 1830. 32 p. 24mo
AAS, LC, Y

——— The Early Experiences of Ralph Ringwood. *In* L. G. Clark, *ed.*, The Knickerbocker Sketch-Book (1845), No. 545.

——— The First Locomotive Again. *In* L. G. Clark, *ed.*, The Knickerbocker Sketch-Book (1845), No. 545.

——— The Guests from Gibbet-Island: A Legend of Communipaw. *In* L. G. Clark, *ed.*, The Knickerbocker Sketch-Book (1845), No. 545.

1408 ——— A History of New York, from the Beginning of the World to the End of the Dutch Dynasty . . . By Diedrich Knickerbocker [pseud.] . . . New York: Inskeep & Bradford, 1809. 2 vols., illus. 12mo   AAS, BA, BP, CLS, H, HEH, IN, LC, LCP, N, NYH, NYP, NYS(V.2), UM, UP, UV, Y
For complete title see Langfeld & Blackburn.

1409 ——— ——— 2d ed. New York: Inskeep and Bradford, 1812. 2 vols., illus. 12mo   AAS, BP, H, HEH, LCP, NYH, NYP, NYS, UP, Y

1410 ——— ——— 3d ed. Philadelphia: M. Thomas, 1819. 2 vols., illus. 12mo   AAS, BP, H, HEH, LCP, NYH, NYP, Y

1411 ——— ——— 4th ed. New York: Printed by C. S. Van Winkle, 1824. 2 vols. 12mo   AAS, B(V.2), BA, H, IN, LC, NYP, Y

1412 ——— ——— 5th ed. New York: Printed by C. S. Van Winkle, 1826. 2 vols. 12mo   AAS, BP(V.2), H, NYS

1413 ——— ——— 6th ed. Philadelphia: Carey, Lea & Carey, 1829. 2 vols. 12mo   AAS, BA, BP, NYP, Y

1414 ——— ——— 7th ed. Philadelphia: Carey & Lea, 1830. 2 vols. 12mo   HEH(V.2), NYP, UP, Y

1415 ——— ——— 7th ed. Philadelphia: Carey & Lea, 1831. 2 vols. 12mo   LCP, NYP, UP(V.2)

1416 ——— ——— 7th ed. Philadelphia: Carey & Lea, 1832. 2 vols. 12mo   AAS, BA, H, LCP, NYP, Y

1417 ——— ——— 7th ed. Philadelphia: Carey & Lea, 1834. 2 vols. 12mo   BA, HEH(V.2), NYP(V.2)

1418 ——— ——— 7th ed. Philadelphia: Carey & Lea, 1835. 2 vols. 12mo   AAS, NYH, NYP, UP, Y

1419 ——— ——— Philadelphia: Carey, Lea & Blanchard, 1835. 2
vols. 12mo   B(V.1), NYP

1420 ——— ——— Philadelphia: Carey, Lea & Blanchard, 1836. 2
vols. 12mo   AAS, BP, LC, LCP, NYH, NYP, Y

1421 ——— ——— Philadelphia: Carey, Lea & Blanchard, 1837. 2
vols. 12mo   AAS(V.2), BA, LC, LCP, UP, Y

1422 ——— ——— Philadelphia: Carey, Lea & Blanchard, 1838. 2
vols. 12mo   AAS, NYP

1423 ——— ——— Philadelphia: Lea & Blanchard, 1839. 2 vols.
12mo   AAS, BP, NYH, NYP, Y

1424 ——— ——— Philadelphia: Lea & Blanchard, 1840. 2 vols.
12mo   AAS, BP, Y(V.2)

1425 ——— ——— Philadelphia: Lea & Blanchard, 1842. 2 vols.
12mo   LC, NYP(V.2), NYS, Y(V.2)

1426 ——— ——— New York: George P. Putnam, 1848. 452 p.
12mo   AAS, BA, H, N, NYP, Y

1427 ——— ——— New York: George P. Putnam, 1849. 454 p.
12mo   AAS, BP, H, NYP

1428 ——— ——— New York: George P. Putnam, 1850. 454 p.,
illus. 12mo   AAS, BA, LC, NYP, Y

——— Legends of the Conquest of Spain. *See* The Crayon
Miscellany, No. 1403.

1429 ——— Letters of Jonathan Oldstyle, Gent. [pseud.] . . . New
York: William H. Clayton, 1824. 67 p. 8vo
AAS, BA, BP, CLS, H, HEH, IN, LC, LCP, N, NYH, NYP, NYS, UC, UP, Y

——— Mountjoy; or, Some Passages Out of the Life of a Castle-
builder. *In* L. G. Clark, *ed.*, The Knickerbocker Sketch-Book
(1845), No. 545.

1430 ——— The Sketch Book of Geoffrey Crayon, Gent. [pseud.]
. . . New York: Printed by C. S. Van Winkle, 1819-20. 7 pts.
8vo
AAS, B, BA, BP, H, HEH, IN, LCP(5 pts.), N, NYH(5 pts.), NYP, UP, Y
Pts. I-V dated 1819 and paged continuously; Pts. VI-VII dated 1820 and
separately paged.

1431 —————— 2d ed. New York: Printed by C. S. Van Winkle,
1819-20. 7 pts. 8vo   AAS, H, NYH, NYP(pts. 4-7), UC, Y
Pt. I dated 1819, Pts. II-VII dated 1820; Pts. I-II paged continuously, Pts. III-VII separately paged. "Second edition" on covers.

1432 —————— New York: Printed by C. S. Van Winkle, 1822-20.
7 pts. 8vo   AAS, BA, LC, Y(pts. 1-2)
Pts. I-II dated 1822 and paged continuously; Pts. III-VII dated 1820 and separately paged. BA Pt. III dated 1823.
For discussion of textual variations of the first three editions, see Langfeld & Blackburn.

1433 —————— 4th ed. New York: Printed by C. S. Van Winkle, 1824. 2 vols. 12mo   AAS, HM, LCP, NYP(V.1), Y

1434 —————— 5th ed. New York: Printed by C. S. Van Winkle, 1826. 2 vols. 12mo   BP

1435 —————— 6th ed. Philadelphia: Carey, Lea & Carey, 1828.
2 vols. 12mo   H(V.2), HEH(V.2), LCP
Williams & Edge also list a New York, 1828 ed.

1436 —————— 7th ed. Philadelphia: Carey, Lea & Carey, 1829.
2 vols. 12mo   AAS, NYP, UP, Y

1436a —————— Philadelphia: Carey & Lea, 1830. 2 vols. 12mo   AAS

1437 —————— 7th ed. Philadelphia: Carey & Lea, 1831. 2 vols., illus. 12mo   H, NYP

1438 —————— Philadelphia: Carey & Lea, 1832. 2 vols. 12mo   AAS, LCP, NYP(V.2), Y

1439 —————— Philadelphia: Carey & Lea, 1833. 2 vols. 12mo   NYH, NYP(V.1)

1440 —————— Philadelphia: Carey & Lea, 1834. 2 vols. 12mo   H, Y

1441 —————— Philadelphia: Carey & Lea, 1835. 2 vols. 12mo   BP, H, LCP, NYP(V.1), Y

1441a —————— Philadelphia: Carey, Lea & Blanchard, 1835. 2 vols. 12mo   AAS

1442 —————— ————— Philadelphia: Carey, Lea & Blanchard, 1836. 2 vols. 12mo
AAS, B, BA, HEH(V.1), NYP, UM, Y

1443 —————— ————— Philadelphia: Carey, Lea & Blanchard, 1837. 2 vols. 12mo
AAS, BP, HEH(V.2), NYP, UP, Y

1443a —————— ————— Philadelphia: Carey, Lea & Blanchard, 1838. 2 vols. 12mo
LCP

1444 —————— ————— Philadelphia: Lea & Blanchard, 1839. 2 vols. 12mo
AAS, HEH, IN, NYP, Y

1445 —————— ————— Philadelphia: Lea & Blanchard, 1840. 2 vols. 12mo
H

1446 —————— ————— Philadelphia: Lea & Blanchard, 1842. 2 vols. 12mo
AAS(V.2), NYP, NYS

1447 —————— ————— New York: George P. Putnam, 1848. 465 p., illus. 12mo
AAS, BA, BP, H, IN, NYP, UP, Y

1448 —————— ————— New York: George P. Putnam, 1849. 465 p. 12mo
B, BA, H, HM, LC, NYP, Y

1449 —————— Tales of a Traveller . . . By Geoffrey Crayon, Gent. [pseud.] . . . Philadelphia: H. C. Carey & I. Lea, 1824. 4 pts. 8vo
AAS, B, BA, BP, H(pts.1-3), HEH, HM, LC, LCP, N, NYP, UM, UP, UV, Y

See Langfeld & Blackburn for differences in Pt. II.

Contents: Strange Stories, by a Nervous Gentleman (A Hunting Dinner—The Adventure of My Uncle—The Adventure of My Aunt—The Bold Dragoon; or, The Adventure of My Grandfather—The Adventure of the Mysterious Picture—The Adventure of the Mysterious Stranger—The Story of the Young Italian). Buckthorne and His Friends (Literary Life—A Literary Dinner—The Club of Queer Fellows—The Poor Devil Author—Buckthorne; or, The Young Man of Great Expectation—Grave Reflections of a Disappointed Man—The Booby Squire—The Strolling Manager). The Italian Banditti (The Inn at Terracina—The Adventure of the Little Antiquary—The Adventure of the Popkins Family—The Painter's Adventure—The Story of the Bandit Chieftain—The Story of the Young Robber—The Route to Fondi). The Money Diggers (Hell Gate—Kidd the Pirate—The Devil and Tom Walker—Wolfert Webber; or, Golden Dreams—The Adventure of Sam, the Black Fisherman, Commonly Denominated Mud Sam).

1450 —————— ————— 2d ed. New York: Printed by C. S. Van Winkle, 1825. 2 vols. 12mo
AAS, B, BP, H, HEH, LC, NYP, UP, Y

1451 ———— ———— 3d ed. Philadelphia: Carey & Lea, 1832. 2 vols.
12mo   AAS, LCP, NYP(V.2), UC

1452 ———— ———— 3d ed. Philadelphia: Carey, Lea & Blanchard,
1835. 2 vols. 12mo   H(V.2), NYP, Y

1453 ———— ———— Philadelphia: Carey, Lea and Blanchard, 1836. 2
vols. 12mo   AAS, NYP(V.1), Y

1454 ———— ———— Philadelphia: Carey, Lea & Blanchard, 1837. 2
vols. 12mo   AAS, BA, LC, LCP

1455 ———— ———— Philadelphia: Carey, Lea & Blanchard, 1838. 2
vols. 12mo   NYP(V.2)

1456 ———— ———— Philadelphia: Lea & Blanchard, 1841-40. 2 vols.
12mo   AAS, NYP(V.1), NYS

1457 ———— ———— New York: George P. Putnam, 1849. 456 p.
12mo   AAS, BA, CLS, H, Y

1458 ———— ———— New York: George P. Putnam, 1850. 456 p.,
illus. 12mo   B, H, HEH, LC, NYP, Y

———— A Tour on the Prairies. *See* The Crayon Miscellany,
No. 1401.

1459 ———— Works . . . Philadelphia: Lea & Blanchard, 1840. 2
vols., illus. 8vo   HEH(V.1), NYP, UP, Y
Printed in double cols.
For various eds. of the collected works see Williams & Edge.

1460 ISABEL; OR, THE TRIALS OF THE HEART. A Tale for the Young.
In Two Parts . . . New York: Harper & Brothers, 1845. 182 p.
12mo   HEH, UC, UP, Y
Norman Kane has called my attention to the fact that Appleton credits *Isabel* to Margaret Cockburn Conkling (Mrs. Albert Steele) as the author.

1461 ISABELLA; OR, Filial Affection. A Tale, by the Author of "The
Prize," "Self Conquest" . . . Boston: Bowles and Dearborn,
1828. 160 p., illus. 18mo   AAS, UP, Y
Boston; contemporary.

1462 ———— 2d ed. Boston: Leonard C. Bowles, and B. H. Greene,
1832. 119 p., illus. 12mo   HEH, Y

JACKSON, DANIEL, JR. Alonzo and Melissa. *See* Mitchell, Isaac, The Asylum; or, Alonzo and Melissa, No. 1886.

———— A Short Account of the Courtship of Alonzo & Melissa. *See* Mitchell, Isaac, The Asylum; or, Alonzo and Melissa, No. 1887.

1463 JACKSON, FREDERICK. The Effinghams; or, Home as I Found It ... [anon.]. New York: Samuel Colman, 1841. 2 vols. 12mo
AAS, B, BP, H, HEH, IN, LC, N, NYP, UC, UM, UP, UV, Y

1464 ———— Riches and Honor. A New England Story, Founded on Fact ... [anon.]. New York: Josiah Adams, 1847. 160 p., illus. 12mo
AAS, B, HEH, N, UV, Y

1465 ———— The Victim of Chancery; or, A Debtor's Experience ... [anon.]. New York, 1841. 208 p. 12mo
AAS, B, H, HEH, LC, N, NYH, NYP, UP, Y
New York City; contemporary.

1466 ———— A Week in Wall Street. By One Who Knows [anon.]. New York: Published for the booksellers, 1841. 152 p. 12mo
AAS, BA, BP, H, HEH, IN, LC, N, NYH, NYP, NYS, UC, UM, UP, Y

JAHNSENYKES, *Rev.* WILLIAMSON, *pseud.* *See* Jenks, William

JANUARY, PHILLIP B. That Big Dog Fight at Myers's. A Story of Mississippi, by a Mississippian. *In* W. T. Porter, *ed.*, The Big Bear of Arkansas (1845), Nos. 2061-62.

1467 JENKS, WILLIAM. Memoir of the Northern Kingdom, Written A.D. 1872, by the Late Rev. Williamson Jahnsenykes, LL.D. [pseud.] ... In Six Letters to His Son ... Now First Published, Quebeck, A.D., 1901 [Boston, 1808]. 48 p. 8vo
AAS, BA, BP, H, HEH, LC, N, NYH, NYP, UC, UM, UP, Y

1468 JERAULD, CHARLOTTE ANN (FILLEBROWN). Poetry and Prose ... Boston: A. Tompkins, 1850. 440 p., illus. 12mo
AAS, B, H, HEH, IN, N, NYP, UP, Y
Contains: Emma Beaumont—Margaret Leslie—Kate Vincent—Lights and Shadows of Woman's Life—Chronicles and Sketches of Hazlehurst.

1469 JOE ANDERSON and Old Jim Bayley ... Boston: John Ford, 1835. 16 p. 12mo
BA, BP, HEH
At head of title: "First Series. No. 6." of Massachusetts Temperance Society.

1470 —————— Boston: Printed by Cassady and March, 1837. 16 p.
12mo   AAS, H, HEH, NYH

At head of title: "First Series. No. 7." of Massachusetts Temperance Society.
AAS, HEH, and NYH copies bound with *The Cranberry Meadow* (1837), with
cover title that reads: "Cranberry Meadow, Joe Anderson and Old Jim
Bayley."

1471 JOHN ELLIOTT, the Reformed. An Old Sailor's Legacy ... Boston: Usher & Strickland, 1841. 216 p. 18mo
                                        AAS, B, HEH, N, NYP, UM, UP, Y

JOHNSON, ALGERSON SIDNEY. Memoirs of a Nullifier. *See* No.
760 where it is erroneously entered under Thomas Cooper.

JONES, *Major, pseud. See* Thompson, William Tappan

1472 JONES, ALEXANDER. The Privateer; or, The Black Boatswain of
the Atlantic ... Boston: Redding & Co., 1846. 50 p. 8vo
                                                        AAS, HEH, UM
War of 1812.

JONES, EZEKIEL, *Esq., pseud. See* Weld, Horatio Hastings

JONES, HAMILTON CHAMBERLAIN. Cousin Sally Dilliard: A Legal
Sketch in the "Old North State." *In* W. T. Porter, *ed.*, The
Big Bear of Arkansas (1845), Nos. 2061-62.

—————— McAlpin's Trip to Charleston. *In* W. T. Porter, *ed.*, A
Quarter Race in Kentucky (1847), Nos. 2063-64.

1473 JONES, J. ELIZABETH. The Young Abolitionists; or, Conversa-
tions on Slavery ... Boston: Anti-slavery Office, 1848. 131
p. 16mo   AAS, BP, H, LC, N, UM, Y

1474 JONES, JAMES ATHEARN. Haverhill; or, Memoirs of an Officer in
the Army of Wolfe ... New York: J. & J. Harper, 1831. 2
vols. 12mo
                        AAS, B, BP, H, HEH, IN, LC, N, NYP, UC(V.2), UP, UV, Y

1475 —————— The Refugee: A Romance. By Captain Matthew Murgatroyd [pseud.], of the Ninth Continentals in the Revolutionary War ... New York: Wilder & Campbell; D. Fanshaw,
printer, 1825. 2 vols. 12mo
                        AAS, B, BA, BP, H, HEH, IN, LC, N, NYP, UC, UV, Y

1476   JONES, JOHN BEAUCHAMP. The Western Merchant: A Narrative. Containing Useful Instruction for the Western Man of Business . . . By Luke Shortfield [pseud.]. Philadelphia: Grigg, Elliot & Co., 1849. 268 p. 12mo

                         AAS, BP, H, HEH, IN, LC, N, NYH, NYP, UC, UP, Y

1477   ———— Wild Western Scenes: A Narrative of Adventures in the Western Wilderness, Forty Years Ago; Wherein the Conduct of Daniel Boone, the Great American Pioneer, Is Particularly Described . . . New York: Samuel Colman, 1841. 247 p., illus. 8vo

                                    AAS, IN, LC, N

Issued in pts. LC has Pt. I in original green-paper covers, with an advertisement on recto of back cover: "The work will be completed in not less than six nor more than seven numbers." Pt. I contains 44 p.

1478   ———— ———— Philadelphia: E. Ferrett & Co., 1845. 247 p., illus. 8vo

                                    AAS, LC, UP, Y

1479   ———— ———— Philadelphia: Grigg, Elliot and Co., 1849. 270 p., illus. 12mo

                             AAS, H, N, NYH, NYP, Y

1480   JONES, JOSEPH STEVENS. Moll Pitcher, the Fortune-teller of Lynn: A Tale Founded on Events Connected with the Life of That Notorious Woman . . . Boston: Redding and Company, 1843. 46 p. 8vo

                                AAS, H, HEH, Y

1481   JONES, JUSTIN. The Belle of Boston; or, The Rival Students of Cambridge. By Harry Hazel [pseud.] . . . Boston: F. Gleason, 1844. 58 p. 8vo   AAS, B, H, HEH, IN, N, NYP, UC, UP, UV, Y

1482   ———— ———— Boston: Flag of Our Union office, 1847. 58 p. 8vo

                                    BP, UM

1483   ———— ———— Boston: F. Gleason, 1849. 100 p. 8vo   NYP, Y

Also contains: The Mill of Poissy; or, The Fugitive's Secret, by Francis A. Durivage—The Capture: A Spanish Tale, by Braceblock—Not an Invitation to Tea; or, What's Trumps: A Scene in the New York Customhouse, by Uncle Toby—Not at Home, by T. S.Arthur—The Daguerreotype; or, Love at First Sight, by Fred Hunter—The Fair and the Brave: A Sea Tale, by Capt. Robert Barnacle.

Printed in double cols.

1484   ———— Big Dick, the King of the Negroes; or, Virtue and Vice Contrasted. A Romance of High & Low Life in Boston. By Harry Hazel [pseud.] . . . Boston: Star Spangled Banner office, 1846. 100 p., illus. 8vo   AAS, B, UP, Y

Printed in double cols.

1816.

1485 ———— ———— Boston: Jones's Publishing House, 1849. 92 p.
8vo AAS, BP
On cover: "Second Edition."
Printed in double cols.

1486 ———— The Burglars; or, The Mysteries of the League of Honor.
An American Tale, by Harry Hazel [pseud.] . . . Boston:
Hatch and Company, 1844. 63 p. 8vo AAS, HEH, N, UP, Y
LC has a title page, deposited June 24, 1844.
Massachusetts; 183-.

1487 ———— ———— Boston: Gleason's Publishing Hall, 1845. 64 p.,
illus. 8vo AAS, B, UM, Y
AAS cover imprint dated 1846.

1488 ———— The Corsair; or, The Foundling of the Sea. An Ameri-
can Romance. By Harry Hazel [pseud.] . . . Boston: Glea-
son's Publishing Hall, 1846. 100 p., illus. 8vo AAS
Also contains: Florine; or, The Mutineers of the Atlantic—The Broker's
Clerk; or, The Deposited Treasure—The Reconciliation.
Printed in double cols.

1489 ———— Fourpe Tap; or, The Middy of the Macedonian. In
Which Is Contained the Concluding Incidents in the Career of
'Big Dick', the King of the Negroes. By Harry Hazel [pseud.].
Boston: Jones's Publishing House, 1847. Cover title, 100 p.,
illus. 8vo Y
Printed in double cols.

1489a ———— ———— 2d ed. Boston: Jones's Publishing House, 1847.
Cover title, 100 p., illus. 8vo AAS
At head of cover title: "Second Edition." Dated 1848.
Printed in double cols.

1490 ———— Hasserac, the Thief-Taker; or, The Rival Sisters of Tri-
mount . . . By Harry Hazel [pseud.]. Boston: Jones's Publishing House, 1849. 100 p. 8vo NYP, UP, Y

1491 ———— Inez, the Beautiful; or, Love on the Rio Grande. A
Mexican Military Romance, by Harry Hazel [pseud.] . . .
Boston: Published by the author, 1846. 52 p. 8vo B, Y
Printed in double cols.

1492 ———— Jessie Manton; or, The Novice of Sacre-Coeur. A Tale of the Canadian Invasion [anon.]. Boston: "Star Spangled Banner" office, 1848. 42 p., illus. 8vo   AAS
At head of title: "A Splendid Original Tale."
Printed in double cols.
American Revolution.

1493 ———— The King's Cruisers; or, The Rebel and the Rover. By Harry Hazel [pseud.] . . . New York: Evert D. Long, 30 Beekman Street [n.d.]. 91 p. 8vo   UC, UP, UV

1494 ———— The Light Dragoon; or, The Rancheros of the Poisoned Lance. A Tale of the Battle Fields of Mexico. By Harry Hazel [pseud.]. Boston: "Star Spangled Banner" office, 1848. 100 p., illus. 8vo   AAS
At head of title: "A Mexican Military Romance."
Printed in double cols.

1495 ———— Mad Jack and Gentleman Jack; or, The Last Cruise of Old Ironsides around the World! A Tale of Adventures by Sea and Land. By Harry Hazel [pseud.] . . . Boston: Star Spangled Banner office, 1850. 98 p. 8vo   HEH, UP
At head of title: "An Original Nautical Novelette, by Harry Hazel."
Printed in double cols.

1496 ———— The Nun of St. Ursula; or, The Burning of the Convent. A Romance of Mount Benedict. By Harry Hazel [pseud.] . . . Boston: F. Gleason, 1845. 64 p., illus. 8vo
    AAS, BP, HEH, LC, N, NYP, UC, UM, UP, Y

1497 ———— The Pirate's Daughter; or, The Rovers of the Atlantic . . . [anon.]. Boston: "Star Spangled Banner" office, 1847. 100 p. 8vo   LC, N, Y

1498 ———— The Prince and the Queen; or, Scenes in High Life. A Romance of the Court of St. James. By Harry Hazel [pseud.] . . . Boston: U. S. Publishing Company, 1846. 100 p., illus. 8vo   AAS, HEH, N, UP, Y
Printed in double cols.
LC has a cover title, deposited Dec. 31, 1845.

1499 ———— Red King, the Corsair Chieftain. A Romance of the Ocean, by Harry Hazel [pseud.] . . . New York: H. Long & Brother, 43 Ann Street [cop. 1850]. 122 p., illus. 8vo
    HM, LC
Tripolitan War.

1500 —— The Rival Chieftains; or, The Brigands of Mexico. A Tale of Santa Anna and His Times. By Harry Hazel [pseud.] . . . Boston: Gleason's Publishing Hall, 1845. 54 p. 8vo

AAS, B, HEH, N, UC, UP, Y

1501 —— —— Boston: F. Gleason, 1847. 50 p. 8vo LC, Y

1502 —— Sylvia Seabury; or, Yankees in Japan. The Romantic Adventures of a Sailor Boy. By Harry Hazel [pseud.] . . . New York: H. Long & Brother, 43 Ann Street [cop. 1850]. 112 p., illus. 8vo LC

1503 —— Tom, Dick & Harry; or, The Boys and Girls of Boston. A Tale Founded on Metropolitan Adventures by Moonlight! Starlight!! Gaslight!!! Lamplight!!!! Electric Light!!!!! Northern Lights!!!!!! and Total Darkness. By Harry Hazel [pseud.]. Boston: Star Spangled Banner office, 1849. 92 p. 8vo BP, Y
Printed in double cols.

1504 —— The West Point Cadet; or, The Young Officer's Bride. A Romance in Real Life, by Harry Hazel [pseud.] . . . Boston: F. Gleason, 1845. 100 p., illus. 8vo AAS, HEH, N, UP, Y
Printed in double cols.

1505 —— —— Boston: F. Gleason, 1849. 100 p., illus. 8vo

AAS, H, NYH, Y
Printed in double cols.

1506 —— The Young Refugee; or, Love in a Village. A Romance of New England. Founded on Fact. By Harry Hazel [pseud.] . . . Boston: United States Publishing Company, 1846. 99 p., illus. 8vo AAS, HEH, UP, Y
Also contains: Erminia; or, The Belle of Broadway.
Printed in double cols.

1507 JONES, PASCAL. My Uncle Hobson and I; or, Slashes at Life with a Free Broad-axe . . . New York: D. Appleton & Co., 1845. 268 p. 12mo AAS, B, II, IIEII, LC, LCP, N, NYP, UC, UP, Y
Connecticut; contemporary.

1508 JONES, URIAH JAMES. Simon Girty, the Outlaw: An Historical Romance . . . Philadelphia: G. B. Zeiber & Co., 1846. 104 p. 8vo AAS, HEH, LC, UP, Y

JONES, W. J. Somebody in My Bed, by W. J. Jones, Esq., of Harrisburg, Pa. In W. T. Porter, ed., A Quarter Race in Kentucky (1847), Nos. 2063-64.

1509 JUDAH, SAMUEL BENJAMIN HERBERT. The Buccaneers: A Romance of Our Own Count[r]y in Its Ancient Day . . . [by] Yclept Terentius Phlogobombos [pseud.] . . . In Five Books. Boston: Munroe & Francis, 1827. 2 vols. 12mo
BA(V.2), H(V.1), HM, IN, LC, N, NYP, UP, UV, Y
For complete title see Wegelin.

1510 ———— ———— 2d ed. Boston: Munroe & Francis, 1827. 2 vols. 12mo
BA(V.1), BP, H, HEH, HM, LC, NYH, NYP, NYS, UC

1511 ———— ———— The imprint whereof is at New York, A.D. 1827. 2 vols. 12mo
AAS, HEH(V.2), UP

1512 JUDD, SYLVESTER. Margaret: A Tale of the Real and Ideal, Blight and Bloom; Including Sketches of a Place Not Before Described, Called Mons Christi . . . [anon.]. Boston: Jordan and Wiley, 1845. 460 p. 12mo
AAS, B, BA, BP, HEH, IN, LC, LCP, N, NYP, UC, UM, UP, UV, Y
New England; late 18th cent.

1513 ———— Richard Edney and the Governor's Family: A Rus-Urban Tale . . . [anon.]. Boston: Phillips, Sampson & Company, 1850. 468 p. 12mo
AAS, B, BA, BP, H, HEH, IN, LC, LCP, N, NYP, UC, UM, UP, Y
New England; 19th cent.

JUDSON, EDWARD ZANE CARROLL. Bellamira; or, The Last Days of Calloa. By Ned Buntline [pseud.]. In F. Bryne, The Spanish Beauty [1848], Nos. 442-442a.

1514 ———— The B'hoys of New York. A Sequel to the Mysteries & Miseries of New York. By Ned Buntline [pseud.] . . . New York: W. F. Burgess, 1850. 194 p. 8vo HEH
NYP has an ed. with imprint: "New York: Dick and Fitzgerald" [n.d.].

1515 ———— The Black Avenger of the Spanish Main; or, The Fiend of Blood. A Thrilling Story of the Buccaneer Times. By Ned Buntline [pseud.] . . . Boston: F. Gleason, 1847. 100 p., illus. 8vo AAS, H, IN, UP, Y
At head of title: "100 Dollar Prize Tale."
Printed in double cols.

1516 ——— Cruisings, Afloat and Ashore, from the Private Log of Ned Buntline [pseud.] . . . New York: Robert Craighead, printer, 1848. 102 p., illus. 8vo   H, HEH, LC, UP, Y

Imprint in some copies: "New York: Edward Z. C. Judson, 1848."

Contains: The Masquerade; or, A Married Man in a Fix—The Smuggler: A True Yarn of the Mexican Coast—Eating the Captain's Pig; or, The Reefers in a Scrape—The French Captain's Story; or, "Britannia Rule ze Wave!" —The Captured Banner: A Yarn of the Montevidean War—My First Lesson in Spanish; or, A Declaration of Love in Mexico—Uncle Tommy's Ghost Story—A Race on the Bahama Banks—The Way I Caught a Wife—A Chapter on Middies, and the Way We Did One of 'Em—A Storm at Sea—Running a French Blockade; or, The Way They Fooled the Prince De Joinville—One Night in the Gulf of Mexico, Spent in an Open Boat—A Slippery Hope: A Yarn of the Last War.

1517 ——— ——— 2d ed. New York: Robert Craighead, printer, 1848. 102 p., illus. 8vo   B, LC

1518 ——— The Curse! A Tale of Crime and Its Retribution. Founded on Facts of Real Life. By Ned Buntline [pseud.]. Boston: Roberts & Garfield [cop. 1847]. 40 p. 8vo   BP, Y

Printed in double cols.

New York and Boston.

1519 ——— The G'hals of New York: A Novel, by Ned Buntline [pseud.]. New York: Dewitt and Davenport, Tribune Buildings [cop. 1850]. 236 p. 8vo   AAS, B, HEH, Y

——— Harry Halyard's Ruin. A True Tale for the Intemperate to Read, by Ned Buntline [pseud.]. *In* H. P. Mills, Francisco Gerardo (1850), No. 1878.

1520 ——— The Ice-King; or, The Fate of the Lost Steamer. A Fanciful Tale of the Far North, by Ned Buntline [pseud.] . . . Boston: G. H. Williams, 1848. 100 p. 8vo   B, Y

Also contains: Not in Despair, for I've a Friend: A Lesson of a Life.

Printed in double cols.

1521 ——— The King of the Sea. A Tale of the Fearless and Free, by Ned Buntline [pseud.] . . . Boston: Flag of Our Union office, 1847. 100 p., illus. 8vo   AAS, HEH, Y

At head of title: "100 Dollar Tale."

Printed in double cols.

1522 ——— ——— Boston: F. Gleason, 1849. 100 p., illus. 8vo   Y

Printed in double cols.

1523 —— The Last Days of Callao; or, The Doomed City of Sin! A Historical Romance of Peru (Founded on Events of the Great Earthquake in 1746). By Ned Buntline [pseud.]. Boston: Star Spangled Banner office, 1847. 50 p., illus. 8vo   B, Y
Printed in double cols.

1523a —— Love at First Sight; or, The Daguerreotype. A Romantic Story of Real Life. By Ned Buntline [pseud.]. Boston: Lerow and Company, 91 Washington Street [ca. 1847-48]. 15 p. 16mo   AAS
Not to be confused with Fred Hunter's "The Daguerreotype; or, Love at First Sight," in No. 1483.

1523b —— —— Boston: Jones's Publishing House, 82 Washington St. [ca. 1848-50]. 32 p. 16mo   Y

1524 —— Love's Desperation; or, The President's Only Daughter, and Other Tales. By Ned Buntline [pseud.]. Boston: F. Gleason, 1848. 50 p. 8vo   AAS, Y
Also contains: The Tempter and the Tempted: A Tale of a Western Boarding-School—Love and Hate; or, The Emblematic Safety-Guard—Ellen, the Golden-haired Pet—A Letter from a Married Man in the Moon—A Letter from the Married Ladies in the Moon—To the Indomitable Ten—The Boarding-School Miss; or, The Young Backwoodsman's Bride, by Charles E. Averill.

1525 —— Magdalena, the Beautiful Mexican Maid. A Story of Buena Vista. By Ned Buntline [pseud.]. New York: Williams Brothers, 1846. 88 [i.e., 90] p., illus. 8vo   Y
Copyright notice dated 1847, which was probably the year of publication. Contains Whittier's poem, "The Angels of Buena Vista," which first appeared in the *National Era*, Washington, May 20, 1847, according to Currier.

1526 —— Matanzas; or, A Brother's Revenge. A Tale of Florida. By Ned Buntline [pseud.] . . . Boston: Printed and published by George H. Williams, 1848. 100 p. 8vo   AAS, HEH, UM, Y
Also contains: Selling a Green 'Un; or, A Sight at Louis Philippe. Printed in double cols.

1527 —— The Mysteries and Miseries of New York: A Story of Real Life. By Ned Buntline [pseud.] . . . New York: Berford & Co., 1848. 5 pts., illus. 8vo
AAS, B, HEH, IN, LC, N, NYP, UC, Y
NYP and Y also have copies with imprint: "New York: E. Z. C. Judson, 1848."

1528 —————— ————— 2d ed. New York: Berford & Co., 1848. 5 pts.,
illus. 8vo   H(pt.1)
On cover: "Second edition."

1528a —————— ————— 3d ed. New York: Berford & Co., 1848. 5 pts.,
illus. 8vo   AAS(pt.1)

1529 —————— ————— New York: W. F. Burgess, 1849. 584 p., illus.
8vo
Listed in Edward Morrill & Son catalog 3:760.

1530 —————— Norwood; or, Life on the Prairies. By Ned Buntline
[pseud.]. New York: W. F. Burgess, 1850. 75 p. 8vo
                                                        AAS, BP, HEH, Y
Printed in double cols.

1531 —————— The Queen of the Sea; or, Our Lady of the Ocean. A
Tale of Love, Strife, and Chivalry. By Ned Buntline [pseud.]
. . . Boston: F. Gleason, 1848. 100 p. 8vo
                                                  AAS, HEH, NYH, UC, UP, Y
At head of title: "A Prize Tale."
Printed in double cols.

1532 —————— The Red Revenger; or, The Pirate King of the Floridas.
A Tale of the Gulf and Its Islands. By Ned Buntline [pseud.]
. . . Boston: F. Gleason, 1848. 100 p., illus. 8vo
                                                  AAS, BP, HEH, N, UP, Y
At head of title: "100 Dollar Prize Tale."
Also contains: The Italian Lazzaroni; or, The Miser-Prince of Palermo, by
Charles E. Averill.
Printed in double cols.

1533 —————— ————— New York: Samuel French, 151 Nassau [1850?].
100 p. 8vo   AAS
Also contains: The Godfather, by Anne T. Wilbur.
Printed in double cols.

1534 —————— The Romance of Life; or, The Life of Martha E. Miller
(alias Walker). By Ned Buntline [pseud.]. New York: Edward Z. C. Judson, 1849.
LC has a title page, deposited Mar. 9, 1849.

1535 —————— Three Years After: A Sequel to the Mysteries and Mis-
eries of New York. By Ned Buntline [pseud.] . . . New
York: W. F. Burgess, 1849. 175 p. 8vo   Y
Printed in double cols.

1536 —— The Virgin of the Sun: A Historical Romance of the Last Revolution in Peru. By Ned Buntline [pseud.] ... Boston: Hotchkiss & Company, 1847. 100 p. 8vo

AAS, HEH, UC, Y

Printed in double cols.

1537 —— The Volunteer; or, The Maid of Monterey. A Tale of the Mexican War. By Ned Buntline [pseud.] ... Boston: F. Gleason, 1847. 100 p., illus. 8vo   AAS, B, HEH, N, UP, Y

At head of title: "100 Dollar Prize Tale."
Printed in double cols.

1538 —— —— Boston: F. Gleason [cop. 1847]. 100 p., illus. 8vo   AAS

At head of title: "$100 Prize Tale."
Printed in double cols.

1538a —— —— Boston: F. Gleason, 1849. 100 p., illus. 8vo

HEH

Printed in double cols.

1539 JUDSON, EMILY (CHUBBUCK). Alderbrook: A Collection of Fanny Forester's [pseud.] Village Sketches, Poems, etc. By Miss Emily Chubbuck ... Boston: William D. Ticknor and Company, 1847. 2 vols. 12mo

AAS, B, BA, BP, IN, N, UC, UP, UV, Y

Contains: Grace Linden: Four Ages in the Life of an American Woman—Little Molly White—Our May—Save the Erring—My Uncle Stilling—"Nickie Ben"—The Young Dream—The Bank Note—Ally Fisher—Robert Flemming: A Veritable Tale, Showing "What That Boy Did Come to at Last"—The Unuseful—Nora Maylie—Grandfather Bray—Born to Wear a Coronet—Willard Lawson—A Case of Lunacy Not Uncommon—The Great March Holiday—Two Nights in the "Nieuw Nederlandts"—Lucy Dutton—Lilias Fane—Rug Raffles—The French Emigrants—Ida Ravelin: A Fantasy—Dora.

1540 —— —— 2d ed. Boston: William D. Ticknor and Company, 1847. 2 vols., illus. 12mo   AAS, H, LCP, UM(V.2), Y

1541 —— —— 3d ed. Boston: William D. Ticknor and Company, 1847. 2 vols., illus. 12mo

AAS, HEH, IN, LC, NYH, UM(V.1), UP, Y

1542 —— —— 4th ed. Boston: William D. Ticknor and Company, 1847. 2 vols., illus. 12mo   AAS, UP, Y

1543 —— —— 5th ed. Boston: William D. Ticknor and Company, 1848. 2 vols., illus. 12mo   B(V.2), HEH, NYP

1544 —————— —————— 6th ed.   Boston: William D. Ticknor and Company, 1848.   2 vols., illus.   12mo   AAS

1544a —————— —————— 7th ed.   Boston: William D. Ticknor and Company, 1848.   2 vols., illus.   12mo
Copy reported; not seen.

1545 —————— —————— 8th ed.   Boston: William D. Ticknor and Company, 1849.   2 vols. in 1, illus.   12mo   Y

1546 —————— —————— 9th ed.   Boston: Ticknor, Reed and Fields, 1850.
2 vols., illus.   12mo   NYP, Y

1546a —————— —————— Boston: Ticknor, Reed and Fields, 1850.   2 vols.,
illus.   12mo
Vol. I, "Tenth Edition"; Vol. II, "Ninth Edition." Reported by Seven Gables; not seen.

1547 —————— Allen Lucas, the Self-made Man . . . [anon.].   Utica: Bennett, Backus, & Hawley, 1844.   180 p.   16mo   AAS, HEH, Y

1548 —————— —————— New York: L. Colby and Company, 1847.   159 p.   16mo   AAS, N, Y

1549 —————— —————— 3d ed.   New York: L. Colby and Company, 1848.   159 p.   16mo   AAS, B, N, UM, UP, Y

1550 —————— Charles Linn; or, How to Observe the Golden Rule . . . [anon.].   New York: Dayton and Saxton, 1841.   212 p.   12mo
AAS, B, BP, HEH, LC, UC, Y
Also contains: The Selfish Girl—The Mother's Story—A Chapter for Young Ornithologists—Alice Cole.

1550a —————— —————— New York: Mark H. Newman, 1843.   208 p.   12mo
Also contains: The Selfish Girl—The Mother's Story—A Chapter for Young Ornithologists—Alice Cole.
Information supplied by Bruce M. Brown, Librarian, Colgate University Library.

1551 —————— —————— New York: L. Colby and Company, 1847.   173 p.   12mo   Y

1551a —————— —————— 3d ed.   New York: L. Colby and Company, 1848.   173 p.   12mo   Y

1552 —————— 3d ed. New York: L. Colby and Company, 1850. 173 p. 12mo N, Y

1553 ——— The Great Secret; or, How to Be Happy . . . [anon.]. New York: Dayton & Newman, 1842. 311 p. 12mo LC

1553a —————— 2d ed. Utica: Bennett, Backus & Hawley, 1846. 177 p. 12mo AAS
Colgate University Library copy contains 104 p.

1554 —————— Rev. ed. New York: L. Colby and Company, 1847. 256 p. 12mo AAS, HEH, NYP, UP, Y
"The Conclusion," pp. 253-256.

1555 —————— 3d ed. New York: L. Colby and Company, 1848. 256 p. 12mo AAS, LC, N

1556 —————— New York: L. Colby and Company, 1849. 256 p. 12mo Y

1557 ——— Lilias Fane, and Other Stories, by Fanny Forrester [pseud.]. Boston: Gleason's Publishing Hall, 1846. 100 p. 8vo AAS, H, Y
Also contains: How Mr. Abram Esterley Was "Put Down"—Rug Raffles—Little Molly White—The Dissatisfied Spirit—Last Page in a Heart's Book—My Uncle Stilling—Our May—Lucy Dutton—Another Era in the Life of Ida Ravelin—Nancy—Two Nights in the Nieuw Nederlandts.
Printed in double cols.

1558 ——— Trippings in Author-Land, by Fanny Forester [pseud.]. New York: Paine and Burgess, 1846. 281 p. 12mo
AAS, B, BP, H, HEH, LC, N, NYH, NYP, UM, UP, Y
Contents: The Cousins: A Sketch—The Unuseful—Nora Maylie—Cousin 'Bel's Visit—Grace Linden—Reply to a Letter from the Editor of the New York Mirror—Jem Fletcher's Last Flame—Dora—Underhill Cottage—Something about a Man Whom New York Beheaded—Kitty Coleman—Lucy Dutton—Letter to Cousin 'Bel—The Bank Note—The Chief's Daughter.

JUDSON, HORACE. The Wanderer's Return. *In* M. M. Ballou, Albert Simmons (1849), No. 229.

1559 JULIA, THE MANIAC; or, The Mother Her Own Victim. Founded on Fact. New York: Printed for the publisher, 1847. 29 p., illus. 8vo H, HEH

1560 JUSTINA; or, The Will. A Domestic Story . . . New York: Charles Wiley, 1823. 2 vols. 12mo   AAS, B, H, IN, LC, UC, Y
New York City and Philadelphia; contemporary.
Written by Susan (Linn) De Witt.

1560a KARAHMAN: An Owhyheean Tale. Boston: Wells and Lilly, Court Street, 1822. 29 p. 12mo   AAS

1561 KATE, *pseud.* Domestic Sketches: Written for Newspaper Circulation, by Kate [pseud.]. Troy, N.Y.: Press of the Northern Budget, 1847. 50 p. 8vo   H, NYH, Y
Contents: Susette, the Pretty Collar Maker—Jem Dally, the Match Pedler of Dock Square—Clarence Buel, the Gentleman: A Sequel to Jem Dally—The Deserted One—The Emigrants Children—The Aged Widow—Plotting and Planning; or, Unexpected Results—A Sketch from the MSS. of a Student—The Body Snatchers.

KELLY, *Major.* Lanty Oliphant in Court, by Major Kelly of Louisiana. *In* W. T. Porter, *ed.,* A Quarter Race in Kentucky (1847), Nos. 2063-64.

1562 KENDALL, EDMUND HALE. The Twin Sisters: A Narrative of Facts . . . Lawrence City [Mass.], 1848. 32 p., illus. 8vo
AAS, B, H, LC, NYP, Y
New England; late 18th and early 19th cents.

KENDALL, GEORGE WILKINS. Bill Dean, the Texan Ranger. *In* W. T. Porter, *ed.,* A Quarter Race in Kentucky (1847), Nos. 2063-64.

———— Texian Traits. *In* Thrilling Tales (1843), No. 2599a.

1563 KENNEDY, JOHN PENDLETON. Horse Shoe Robinson: A Tale of the Tory Ascendency . . . [anon.]. Philadelphia: Carey, Lea & Blanchard, 1835. 2 vols. 12mo
AAS, BA, H, HEH, IN, LC, N, NYP, NYS, UC, UV, Y

1564 ———— ———— 2d ed. Philadelphia: Carey, Lea and Blanchard, 1835. 2 vols. 12mo   AAS, B, NYP, UC(V.2), Y

1565 ———— ———— 3d ed. Philadelphia: Carey, Lea and Blanchard, 1836. 2 vols. 12mo   AAS, Y

1566 ———— ———— 4th ed. Philadelphia: Carey, Lea & Blanchard, 1836. 2 vols. 12mo   AAS, H, HEH, NYP(V.2), Y

1567 ———— Quodlibet: Containing Some Annals Thereof: With an Authentic Account of the Origin and Growth of the Borough . . . Edited by Solomon Secondthoughts [pseud.] . . . Philadelphia: Lea & Blanchard, 1840. 350 [i.e., 250] p. 12mo

> AAS, B, BP, H, HEH, HM, IN, LC, N, NYH, NYP, UC, UM, UP, Y
> For complete title see Foley.

1568 ———— Rob of the Bowl: A Legend of St. Inigoe's . . . [anon.]. Philadelphia: Lea & Blanchard, 1838. 2 vols. 12mo

> AAS, B, BP, CLS, H, HEH, IN, LC, N, NYP, NYS, UC, UM, UP, UV, Y
> Maryland; late 17th cent.

1569 ———— Swallow Barn; or, A Sojourn in the Old Dominion . . . [anon.]. Philadelphia: Carey & Lea, 1832. 2 vols. 12mo

> AAS, B, BA, BP, CLS, H, HEH, IN, LC, LCP, N, NYH, NYP, UC, UP, UV, Y
> Virginia; early 19th cent.

KENT, EDWARD. The Field of the Incurables. *In* J. S. Appleton, *ed.*, Voices from the Kenduskeag (1848), No. 39.

———— A Vision of Bangor, in the Twentieth Century. *In* J. S. Appleton, *ed.*, Voices from the Kenduskeag (1848), No. 39.

1570 KETTELL, SAMUEL. Daw's Doings; or, The History of the Late War in the Plantations. By Sampson Short-and-Fat [pseud.] . . . Boston: William White & H. P. Lewis, 1842. 68 p., illus. 8vo   AAS, B, BA, BP, H, HEH, LC, N, NYP, UP, Y

1571 ———— Quozziana; or, Letters from Great Goslington, Mass., Giving an Account of the Quoz Dinner, and Other Matters. By Sampson Short-and-Fat [pseud.] . . . Boston: William White & H. P. Lewis, 1842. 68 p. 8vo

> AAS, B, BA, BP, H, HEH, LC, N, NYP, UP, Y

1572 ———— Yankee Notions: A Medley. By Timo. Titterwell, Esq. [pseud.] . . . Boston: Otis, Broaders and Company, 1838. 255, [1] p. 8vo

> AAS, B, BA, BP, H, HEH, LC, N, NYH, NYP, UC, UM, UP, Y
> *Contains:* My First and Last Speech in the General Court, by Tobias Turniptop—Biography of a Broomstick—The Age of Wonders—Our Singing School: A Chapter from the History of the Town of Pigwacket—Benoni Burdock: A Character—Thoughts on Seeing Ghosts—Josh Beanpole's Courtship—Metaphysics—Voyage of Discovery through the Streets of Boston—The Science of Starvation—Decline and Fall of the City of Dogtown—Proceedings of the Society for the Diffusion of Useless Knowledge—Bob Lee: A Tale—The Dead Set—The Two Moschetoes.

1573 —————————— 2d ed. Boston: Otis, Broaders and Company, 1838. 251, [1] p., illus. 8vo AAS, BP, LC, UP

1574 —————————— 3d ed. Boston: Otis, Broaders and Company, 1838. 251, [1] p., illus. 8vo AAS, Y

1575 —————————— 4th ed. Boston: Otis, Broaders and Company, 1847. 251, [1] p., illus. 8vo AAS, H

1576 KILBOURN, DIANA TREAT. The Lone Dove: A Legend of Revolutionary Times. By a Lady [anon.]. Philadelphia: Geo. S. Appleton, 1850. 281 p. 12mo
AAS, B, BA, HEH, LC, LCP, N, UC, UP, Y

1577 KIMBALL, RICHARD BURLEIGH. St. Leger; or, The Threads of Life ... [anon.]. New York: George P. Putnam, 1850. 384 p. 8vo AAS, BP, CLS, H, HEH, LCP, NYP, UC, UP, Y

1578 —————————— 2d ed. New York: George P. Putnam, 1850. 384 p. 8vo AAS, LCP, N

1579 —————————— 3d ed. New York: George P. Putnam, 1850. 384 p. 8vo AAS, LC, Y

1580 KIRKLAND, CAROLINE MATILDA (STANSBURY). Forest Life ... [anon.]. New York: C. S. Francis & Co., 1842. 2 vols. 12mo
AAS, BA, BP, H, HEH, IN, LCP, N, NYP, NYS, UC, UM, UP, Y

1581 —————————— 2d ed. New York: C. S. Francis & Co., 1842. 2 vols. 12mo AAS, B, NYH, UM

1582 —————————— New York: C. S. Francis & Co., 1844. 2 vols. 12mo LC, LCP

————— John Hinchley. *In* The Fountain and the Bottle (1850), No. 996.

1583 ————— A New Home—Who'll Follow? Or, Glimpses of Western Life. By Mrs. Mary Clavers [pseud.] ... New York: C. S. Francis, 1839. 317 p. 12mo
AAS, B, BP, H, HEH, HM, IN, LC, N, NYS, UP, Y
Michigan.

1584 —————————— 2d ed. New York: C. S. Francis, 1840. 337 p. 12mo AAS, B, CLS, HEH, LC, LCP, NYP, UC, Y

1585 ———— ——— 3d ed. New York: Charles S. Francis, 1841. 298 p. 12mo
AAS, H, IN, N, NYP, UM, Y

1586 ———— ——— 4th ed. New York: C. S. Francis & Co., 1850. 298 p., illus. 12mo
AAS, BP, H, HEH, IN, LCP, NYP, UM, Y

1587 ———— Western Clearings ... New York: Wiley and Putnam, 1845. 238 p. 8vo
AAS, B, BA, BP, H, HEH, IN, LC, LCP, N, NYP, NYS, UC, UP, UPI, Y

Contents: The Land-Fever—Ball at Thram's Huddle—A Forest Fête—Love vs. Aristocracy—Harvest Musings—The Bee-Tree—Idle People—Chances and Changes; or, a Clerical Wooing—Ambuscades—Old Thoughts on the New Year—The Schoolmaster's Progress—Half-lengths from Life—An Embroidered Fact—Bitter Fruits from Chance-Sown Seed.

1588 ———— ——— New York: Wiley and Putnam, 1846. 238 p. 8vo
AAS, BP, H, N, NYP, UP, UPI, UM, Y

1589 ———— ——— New York: John Wiley, 1848. 238 p. 8vo AAS

———— *ed. See* Eastman, Mary (Henderson). Dahcotah; or, Life and Legends of the Sioux (1849), No. 890.

1589a KIRKWOOD; or, "The Blue Hen's Chickens." A Romance of the American Revolution. Wilmington: Printed by Harker & Johnson, 1844. 40 p. 4to
UV
Printed in double cols.

1590 KNAPP, SAMUEL LORENZO. The Bachelors, and Other Tales, Founded on American Incidents and Character ... New York: Printed and published by J. and W. Sandford, 1836. 216 p. 12mo
AAS, B, BP, H, HEH, IN, N, NYP, UC, UM, UP, Y

Also contains: The Intemperate—The Infidel Reclaimed—The Corrupted—The Orphan—The Soldier-School-master—The Spectre Beauty—The Hermit—The Philanthropist and the Miser.

1591 ———— Extracts from a Journal of Travels in North America, Consisting of an Account of Boston and Its Vicinity. By Ali Bey [pseud.] ... Boston: Printed by Thomas Badger, Jun., 1818. 124 p. 12mo
AAS, BA, H, HEH, IN, LC, N, NYH, NYP, UM, UP, Y

1592 ———— Extracts from the Journal of Marshal Soult [pseud.], Addressed to a Friend. How Obtained and by Whom Translated Is Not a Subject of Enquiry ... Newburyport: W. B. Allen & Co., 1817. 143 p. 12mo
AAS, BA, BP, H, LC, N, NYP, UP, Y

1592a ——— The Polish Chiefs. An Historical Romance, by Samuel L. Knapp. 3d ed. New York: George H. Evans, 1835. 2 vols. 12mo AAS, Y
For 1st ed. see title entry No. 2058 which is now identified as by Knapp.

1593 ——— Tales of the Garden of Kosciuszko . . . New York: Printed by West & Trow, 1834. 216 p. 12mo
AAS, B, BP, H, HEH, IN, LC, N, NYH, NYP, UC, UM, UP, UV, Y
Contents: The Provost Prison—The Maniac—The Blacksmith; or, The Influence of Letters upon Morals—Acllahua—The Troglodytes—The Tensons—The Lost Child—My Dog—The Exile.

1594 ——— ——— 2d ed. New York: Levison & Brother, 1839. 216p. 12mo HEH, Y

KNICKERBOCKER, DIEDRICH, *pseud.* *See* Irving, Washington

1595 KNIGHT, JAMES. The Life of Dr. Richard Jennings, the Great Victimizer: Giving a History of His Robberies, Poisonings, Seductions, Incests, &c. . . . The Whole Written by Himself. With a Short Account of His Last Days, by James Knight. Louisville: C. Hagan & Co. [cop. 1848]. 111 p. 8vo
Title supplied by Mr. Howard S. Mott.

1596 KRINGLE, KATE, *pseud.* The Beautiful Girl; or, Burning of the Robbers' Den. By Kate Kringle [pseud.], of Kringleston Cottage. A Tale of the Revolution. New York: City Publishing House, 1846. 49, [1] p., illus. 8vo NYH
Mohawk Valley.

L., H. A., *of Philadelphia.* The Martyrs: A Tale of the Revolution. *In* The Romantic Historian (1834), No. 2154.

L., H. C. Cupping on the Sternum, by H. C. L., of Mississippi. *In* W. T. Porter, *ed.*, A Quarter Race in Kentucky (1847), Nos. 2063-64.
Sometimes attributed to Henry Clay Lewis.

1597 LADD, RUSSEL, *comp.* The History of Albert and Eliza. To Which Is Prefixed: The Cruel Father, Founded on Fact . . . Philadelphia: Printed for R. Ladd, 1812. 107 p. 12mo AAS
Also contains: The Cataract of Niagara—The Grotto of Antiparos—The Death of Altamont—An Account of the Earthquake at Calabria.

1598 LAFITTE; or, The Baratarian Chief. A Tale. Fall River: Printed
by Nathan Hall, 1827. 70 p. 8vo
Not to be confused with Ingraham's *Lafitte: The Pirate of the Gulf.*
For 1st ed. see No. 1875a.
B copy withdrawn from circulation.

1599 ——— New York, 1828. 106 p. 16mo   AAS, B, H, NYP, UP, Y

1600 ——— To Which Is Added: The Sea Voyage, by Richard Penn
Smith. Hamilton: Williams, Orton & Co., 1830. 117 p.
18mo   BA, HEH, Y

1601 ——— Wells River, Vt.: Printed and published by Ira White,
1834. 112 p. 16mo   AAS, H, UP

1601a ——— Auburn: Oliphant & Skinner, printers, 1834. 72 p.
12mo   Y

1602 ——— Dansville, N.Y., 1838.   HEH, UP
Issued with *Sophia; or, The Girl of the Pine Woods.*

1603 LAMAS, MARIA. The Glass; or, The Trials of Helen More. A
Thrilling Temperance Tale ... Philadelphia: Martin E. Harm-
stead, 1849. 32 p. 8vo   AAS, BA, BP, H, LC, N, NYP, UM, Y
Printed in double cols.
Philadelphia; contemporary.

1603a ——— ——— 2d ed. Philadelphia, 1850.
Ed. from Todd catalog 104:279.

1604 LARNED, MRS. L. The American Nun; or, The Effects of Ro-
mance ... Boston: Otis, Broaders & Co., 1836. 142 p. 12mo
AAS, UV, Y
Author may be Lucinda (Martin) Larned.

1605 ——— The Sanfords; or, Home Scenes . . . [anon.]. New
York: Elam Bliss, 1830. 2 vols. 12mo   H, LC, UM
South Carolina; contemporary.

——— The Uneducated Wife. *In* The Atlantic Club-Book
(1834), Nos. 195-196.

1606 LAW AND LAZINESS; or, Students at Law of Leisure. New York:
Printed for the author at the Golden Rule office, 1846. 48 p.
12mo   AAS, LC, UC
New York City.

1607 LAWSON, JAMES. Tales and Sketches, by a Cosmopolite . . . [anon.]. New York: Elam Bliss, 1830. 256 p. 12mo
AAS, B, H, HEH, IN, LC, N, NYH, NYP, NYS, UC, UP, Y
Contains: The Clyde–The Tent–Flora MacDonald–The Dapper Gentleman's Story–The Bridal Eve–A Legend of Kent–The Spendthrift.

1608 LEE, ELIZA (BUCKMINSTER). Delusion; or, The Witch of New England . . . [anon.]. Boston: Hilliard, Gray and Company, 1840. 160 p. 8vo   AAS, B, BA, BP, H, HEH, IN, LC, N, UM, UP, Y

1609 ——— Naomi; or, Boston Two Hundred Years Ago . . . Boston: Wm. Crosby & H. P. Nichols, 1848. 448 p. 8vo
AAS, BP, CLS, H, HEH, IN, LC, N, NYP, NYS, UC, UM, UP, UV, Y

1610 ——— ——— 2d ed. Boston: Wm. Crosby and H. P. Nichols, 1848. 324 p. 12mo   B, BA, IN, LC, LCP, UC, Y

1611 ——— Sketches of a New England Village, in the Last Century [anon.]. Boston: James Munroe & Company, 1838. 110 p. 12mo   AAS, BA, BP, H, HEH, IN, LC, N, NYP, UC, UP, Y

1612 LEE, HANNAH FARNHAM (SAWYER). The Backslider . . . [anon.]. Boston: James Munroe and Company, 1835. 144 p. 12mo
AAS, B, BA, BP, H, HEH, LC, N, UC, UM, UP, Y
Included in *Scenes and Characters Illustrating Christian Truths*, No. V.

1613 ——— The Contrast; or, Modes of Education . . . [anon.]. Boston: Whipple and Damrell, 1837. 116 p. 12mo
AAS, B, BA, BP, H, HEH, LC, N, UC, UP, Y
LC has a cover title dated 1838.

1614 ——— Elinor Fulton . . . [anon.]. Boston: Whipple & Damrell, 1837. 144 p. 16mo
AAS, BA, BP, HEH, HM, N, NYP, UC, UP, UV, Y
Cover title: "Sequel to Three Experiments of Living."

1615 ——— ——— 2d ed. Boston: Whipple & Damrell, 1837. 144 p. 16mo   AAS, UM

1616 ——— ——— 7th ed. Boston: Whipple & Damrell, 1837. 144 p. 16mo   Y

1617 ——— ——— 9th ed. Boston: Whipple & Damrell, 1837. 144 p. 16mo   AAS, B, LC, Y
On cover: "Stories from Real Life, No. 2."

1618 ———— ——— 11th ed. Boston: Whipple & Damrell, 1837.
144 p. 16mo   AAS, BP, LC, Y

1619 ——— Grace Seymour . . . [anon.]. New York: Elam Bliss,
1830. 2 vols. 12mo   BA, BP, HEH, UC, UP, Y
Boston, New York; American Revolution.

1620 ——— The Harcourts: Illustrating the Benefit of Retrench-
ment and Reform. By a Lady . . . [anon.]. New York: S.
Colman, 1837. 144 p. 12mo   AAS
Pt. III of Stories from Real Life.
LC has a title page, deposited July 11, 1837.

1621 ———— ——— 2d ed. New York: S. Colman, 1837. 144 p.
12mo   AAS, BP, HEH, Y

1622 ———— ——— 3d ed. New York: S. Colman, 1837. 144 p.
12mo   LC

1623 ———— ——— 4th ed. New York: S. Colman, 1837. 144 p.
12mo   HEH

1623a ———— ——— 5th ed. New York: S. Colman, 1837. 144 p.
12mo   AAS, Y

1624 ——— Historical Sketches of the Old Painters . . . [anon.].
Boston: Hilliard, Gray and Co., 1838. 296 p. 12mo
                   AAS, BA, BP, H, HEH, IN, LC, N, NYP, UP, Y

1625 ———— ——— Boston: Hilliard, Gray and Company, 1841.
350 p. 12mo   AAS, BP, LC, NYP, NYS, UM, Y

1626 ———— ——— Boston: Edward J. Peet, 1845. 350 p. 12mo
                                              AAS, H, NYP, Y

1627 ——— The Log Cabin; or, The World before You . . . [anon.].
Philadelphia: Geo. S. Appleton, 1844. 207 p. 12mo
                        AAS, BA, HEH, LCP, N, NYS, UC, UP, Y

1628 ———— ——— 2d ed. Philadelphia: Geo. S. Appleton, 1844.
207 p. 12mo   AAS, N, Y
Title reads: The World before You; or, The Log Cabin.

1629 ———— ——— 3d ed. Philadelphia: Geo. S. Appleton, 1847.
207 p. 12mo   HM
Title same as of 2d ed.

1630 —— Rich Enough: A Tale of the Times . . . [anon.]. Boston: Whipple & Damrell, 1837. 72 p. 16mo

AAS, B, BA, BP, UC, UP, Y

1631 —— —— 2d ed. Boston: Whipple & Damrell, 1837. 72 p. 16mo

AAS, HEH

1632 —— —— 3d ed. Boston: Whipple & Damrell, 1837. 72 p. 16mo

AAS, HEH, N, NYP

1633 —— Rosanna; or, Scenes in Boston . . . [anon.]. Cambridge: John Owen, 1839. 134 p. 12mo

AAS, B, BA, BP, H, HEH, LC, N, UC, UP, Y

1634 —— Tales . . . [anon.]. Boston: Hilliard, Gray and Company, 1842. 337 p. 8vo   AAS, BP, H, HEH, LC, N, NYP, UC, UP, Y
Contents: The True and the False—Emigration; or, The Township in Maine —Patronage and Friendship—Sketch of Fashionable Life.

1635 —— Three Experiments of Living: Living within the Means; Living Up to the Means; Living beyond the Means . . . [anon.]. Boston: William S. Damrell, 1837. 143 p. 12mo

AAS, BP, H, HEH, LC, UC, UP, Y

1636 —— —— 2d ed. Boston: William S. Damrell, 1837. 143 p. 12mo   AAS, BA, BP, IN, LC, N, NYP, UM, UP, Y
On cover: "Stories from Real Life, No. 1."

1637 —— —— 7th ed. Boston: William S. Damrell, 1837. 143 p. 12mo   AAS, HEH, Y

1638 —— —— 10th ed. Boston: William S. Damrell, 1837. 143 p. 12mo

AAS, NYS

1639 —— —— 15th ed. Boston: William S. Damrell, 1837. 143 p. 12mo

AAS, B, HEH, LC, Y

1640 —— —— 20th ed. Boston: Whipple & Damrell, 1837. 143 p. 12mo

AAS, BP, Y

1640a —— —— 20th ed. Boston: Whippole [sic] & Damrell, 1838. 143 p. 12mo
Copy located at University of California at Los Angeles Library.

1641 —— —— 21st ed. Philadelphia: George S. Appleton, 1846. 143 p. 12mo

AAS, NYP, Y

The publisher also made up a volume with binder's title: "The Three Experiments of Living and Other Tales." Each tale has its own title page dated 1846 and collation. *Three Experiments* is designated the 21st ed.; *Elinor Fulton*, the 12th ed.; and *Rich Enough*, the 4th ed. AAS has a copy.

1642 —————— 19th ed. New York: E. G. Taylor, 1847. 127 p. 24mo   LC

1642a —————— 22d ed. Philadelphia: George S. Appleton, 1848. 127 p. 24mo   AAS

1642b —————— 22d ed. Philadelphia: George S. Appleton, 1849. 127 p. 24mo   AAS, Y

————— The World Before You. *See* The Log Cabin, Nos. 1628-29.

LEGARÉ, JAMES MATHEWES. The New Aria: A Tale of Trial and Trust. *In* The Prize Articles (1849), No. 2082.

The present spelling of the author's middle name is based on information supplied by Mr. A. S. Salley.

1643 A LEGEND OF HELL STREET; or, The Man with Two Heads. A Tale of Lancaster County. [N.p.]: Published for the author, 1849. 95 p. 8vo   AAS, Y
Lancaster, Pa.

1644 LEGENDS OF LAMPIDOSA; or, The Seven Heroines. New York: William H. Graham, 1844. 39 p. 8vo   B, N, NYP

LEGGETT, WILLIAM. The Block-house: A Western Story. *In* W. C. Bryant, *ed.*, Tales of Glauber-Spa (1832), Nos. 439-441.

————— Charles Maitland; or, The Mess-chest. *In* The Atlantic Club-Book (1834), Nos. 195-196.

————— Fire and Water; or, The Pirate's Night-cruise: A Scene on the Seacoast. *In* The Atlantic Club-Book (1834), Nos. 195-196.

————— The Main Truck; or, A Leap for Life. *In* The Atlantic Club-Book (1834), Nos. 195-196.

1645 ————— Naval Stories... New York: G. & C. & H. Carvill, 1834. 179 p. 16mo   AAS, BP, H, HEH, IN, N, NYP, UP, Y
Contents: The Encounter—A Night at Gibraltar—Merry Terry—The Mess-chest—The Main-truck; or, A Leap for Life—Fire and Water—Brought to the Gangway.

1646 ———— ———— 2d ed. New York: G. & C. Carvill & Co., 1835.
201 p. 16mo   HEH, UC, Y
"A Watch in the Main Top" added to this ed.

1646a ——— The Squatter: A Tale of Illinois. By a Country School-
master. [anon.]. Chillicothe, Ohio: S. W. Ely, printer, 1835.
Cover title, 34 p. 8vo
The Thomas W. Streeter copy listed in Parke-Bernet catalog 2605:1454.

1647 ——— Tales and Sketches. By a Country Schoolmaster . . .
[anon.]. New York: Printed by J. & J. Harper, 1829. 248 p.
12mo   AAS, BP, H, HEH, IN, LC, N, NYP, UC, UP, Y
Contents: The Squatter—A Burial at Sea—The Stanton Ghost; or, Mistake
of the Press—The Steel Clasp—The Lie of Benevolence—The Rifle—Near-
sighted—A Watch in the Main-top—White Hands; or, Not Quite in Character—The Mistake.

LEMONOSKEY, SARAH ANN (EVANS). See Evans, Sarah Ann

1648 LESLIE, ELIZA. Althea Vernon; or, The Embroidered Handker-
chief. To Which Is Added: Henrietta Harrison; or, The Blue
Cotton Umbrella . . . Philadelphia: Lea & Blanchard, 1838.
276 p. 12mo   AAS, BA, HEH, IN, LC, N, NYP, UC, UM, UP, UV, Y
New York City; contemporary.

1649 ——— Amelia; or, A Young Lady's Vicissitudes . . . Philadelphia: Carey and Hart, 1848. 86 p. 8vo   AAS, N, UP, Y
LC has a title page, deposited Aug. 21, 1848.

——— The Batson Cottage. In A. Corbin, Mneomi (1847),
No. 765.

1650 ——— Kitty's Relations, and Other Pencil Sketches . . . Phila-
delphia: Carey and Hart, 1847. 97 p. 8vo   B, UP, Y
Contents: Kitty's Relations—The Escorted Lady—The People That Did
Not Take Boarders—A Pic-nic at the Seashore—The Tenth Passenger.

1651 ——— Laura Lovel: A Sketch—for Ladies Only . . . Lowell:
Franklin bookstore, 1834. 64 p. 24mo   AAS, H, HEH, UP, Y
Massachusetts; contemporary.

1652 ——— Leonilla Lynmore, and Mr. and Mrs. Woodbridge; or,
A Lesson for Young Wives. Also, Dudley Villiers . . . Philadelphia: Carey and Hart, 1847. 118 p. 8vo   AAS, BP, H, UP, Y

1653 ——— Mr. and Mrs. Woodbridge, with Other Tales... Providence: Isaac H. Cady, 1841. 180 p. 12mo

AAS, B, HEH, N, NYP, UM, Y

Also contains: Mark Meriden, by Mrs. H. E. B. Stowe—Gentility, by T. S. Arthur—The Soft Answer, by T. S. Arthur.

1654 ——— Mrs. Washington Potts, and Mr. Smith . . . Philadelphia: Lea and Blanchard, 1843. 63 p. 8vo

AAS, HEH, NYP, UC, UP, Y

1655 ——— Pencil Sketches; or, Outlines of Character and Manners . . . Philadelphia: Carey, Lea & Blanchard, 1833. 274 p. 12mo   AAS, B, BA, BP, CLS, HEH, IN, LC, N, NYS, UC, UP, UV, Y

Contains: The Escorted Lady—A Pic-nic at the Seashore—The Miss Vanlears—Country Lodgings—Sociable Visiting—Frank Finlay—The Traveling Tinman—Mrs. Washington Potts—Uncle Philip.

1656 ——— ——— 2d Ser. Philadelphia: Carey, Lea & Blanchard, 1835. 281 p. 12mo

AAS, B, BA, BP, CLS, H, HEH, LC, LCP, N, NYP, NYS, UC, UP, Y

Contents: The Wilson House; or, Village Gossip—The Album—The Reading Parties—The Set of China—Laura Lovel—John W. Robertson—A Tale of a Cent—The Ladies' Ball.

1657 ——— ——— 3d Ser. Philadelphia: Carey, Lea and Blanchard, 1837. 283 p. 12mo

AAS, B, BA, BP, CLS, HM, IN, LC, LCP, N, NYP, NYS, UM, UP, Y

Contents: The Red Box; or, Scenes at the General Wayne—Constance Allerton; or, The Mourning Suits—The Officers: A Story of the Last War—The Serenades—The Old Farm House—That Gentleman; or, Pencillings on Ship-board—Chase Loring: A Story of the Revolution—Alphonsine.

1658 LETTERS FROM THE ALMS-HOUSE, on the Subject of Temperance. By a Drunkard. Lowell: Brown and Colby, publishers and printers, 1841. 75 p. 16mo   BP

1659 LEWIS, HENRY CLAY. Odd Leaves from the Life of a Louisiana "Swamp Doctor" . . . By Madison Tensas, M.D. [pseud.] . . . Philadelphia: A. Hart, 1850. 203 p., illus. 12mo   LC, UPI, Y

According to a note in the LC Catalogue, Vol. 87, p. 498, under the [1858] ed., that ed. was "a reissue of the 1843 edition (published by Carey & Hart; Collins printer)." Sabin 94822 n. states "beside the undated issue of 'Odd Leaves' with the copyright date 1843, there is another undated issue copyrighted in 1846, found separately, NYP." I saw a copy of the latter at UC, with imprint: "Philadelphia: T. B. Peterson and Brothers [cop. 1846]." The firm of Peterson Brothers was not publishing, however, until about 1859.

1660 LEWIS, JOHN. Young Kate; or, The Rescue. A Tale of the Great Kanawha ... [anon.]. New York: Harper & Brothers, 1844. 2 vols. in 1. 12mo   IN, LC, UM, UP, Y
West Virginia frontier.

1661 ———— ———— New York: Harper & Brothers, 1845. 2 vols. in 1. 12mo   AAS, Y

1662 LIFE AND ADVENTURES of Charles Anderson Chester, the Notorious Leader of the Philadelphia "Killers" . . . Philadelphia: Printed for the publishers, 1850. 36 p., illus. 8vo
                                    AAS, HEH, LC, NYP, Y

1662a LIFE AND ADVENTURES of the Accomplished Forger and Swindler, Colonel Monroe Edward. New York: H. Long & Brother, 1848. 152 p., illus. 8vo   AAS, H, N, NYP, Y
Printed in double cols.
This has been attributed to George Wilkes.

1663 THE LIFE AND SUFFERINGS of Cecelia Mayo, Founded on Incidents in Real Life. Boston: M. Aurelius, 1843. 36 p., illus. 12mo
                                   AAS, HEH, LC, N, UP, Y

1664 LIFE IN A WHALE SHIP; or, The Sports and Adventures of a Leading Oarsman. Written by an American Author, and Based upon the Cruise of an American Whale Ship in the South Atlantic and Indian Oceans, during the Years 1836-7-8 . . . Boston: J. N. Bradley & Co., at the office of the Daily Mail and Universal Yankee Nation [1841?]. Nos. 1-4, 7-8, illus. 8vo   AAS, Y
Advert. states that it will be published weekly for six months, forming a book of 500 pp.
At head of title: "Price 6¼ Cents."
Paged continuously.

1665 ———— Boston: Redding & Co., 1846. Cover titles, 4 pts., illus. 8vo   AAS, BP, H(pt. 1)
Title reads: *Romance of the Deep! or, The Cruise of the Aeronaut.*
Pt. IV imprint: "Published by Thomas Drew, Jr., Worcester, 1846."
Paged continuously.

1666 LIFE IN TOWN; or, The Boston Spy. Being a Series of Sketches Illustrative of Whims and Women in the "Athens of America." By an Athenian ... Boston: Redding and Company, 1844. 3 pts., illus. 8vo   AAS, BA, BP, H, HEH(pt.3), LC, UM, Y

Preface dated, "Boston, January 1, 1844."
On cover: "In Twelve Monthly Numbers, Each Complete in Itself . . ."
Apparently only 3 nos. were issued: the second with cover title, ". . . No. 2
Popular Lectures"; and the third with cover title, ". . . No. 3. Fancy Fairs."

1667 ———— [3d ed.] Boston: Redding & Co., 1844. 56 p., illus.
8vo BP, H

Cover title: "Pills for the People. A Dose for Three. To Be Taken Immediately . . . Illustrated by Straitshanks."
The Preface, dated "Cambridge, April 1, 1844," states, "As the first two editions of the numbers already published are exhausted, it was thought expedient to issue a third in the present form."

1668 THE LIFE OF ELEANOR MORELAND, in a Letter to Her Niece . . .
Cambridge: Printed by Hilliard and Metcalf, Jan., 1822. 64 p.
12mo AAS, BP, HEH, LC, Y

1669 THE LIFE OF MISS FANNY BELL and the Female Hermit. Part II.
The Indian Girl; or, The Father's Revenge. Complete in One
Number. Boston: For sale by travelling agents through the
United States, 1849. Cover title, 32 p., illus. 8vo Y
At head of cover title: "The Golden Prize. Part I."

1670 ———— Boston: For sale by travelling agents through the United
States, 1849. Cover title, 32 p., illus. 8vo AAS, BP, N, UP
Another issue of No. 1669. Cover title reads: "Remarkable Narrative of the
Female Hermit. And Teloula, the Indian Girl."

1671 THE LIFE OF MISS MARION SMITH, Being a Faithful Narrative,
Written by Her Niece. Boston, 1844. 12 p. 12mo AAS, LC

1672 LIGHTS AND SHADOWS of Domestic Life, and Other Stories. By
the Author of Rose and Her Lamb; The Two New Scholars . . .
Boston: Ticknor, Reed and Fields, 1850. 267 p. 8vo
AAS, HEH, LC, UP, Y
Also contains: The Secret of Happiness—Laura Seymour—The Intimate
Friends—Shadows and Realities—Sketches of Character; or, Who Is Free?

1673 LINDMARK, JOHN. The Vigilant Farmers: A Western Tale; and
The Magic Stone: An Eastern Tale . . . New York: Published
by the author, 1832. 70 p., illus. 12mo LC, Y

1674 LINDO, F. Revenge; or, The Robber of Guatemala . . . Cincinnati: Robinson & Jones, 1848. 104 p. 8vo LC, NYP
Printed in double cols.

1675   LINN, JOHN BLAIR. Miscellaneous Works, Prose and Poetical. By a Young Gentleman of New York . . . [anon.]. New York: Printed by Thomas Greenleaf, 1795. 353 p. 12mo

AAS, B, BP, H, HEH, IN, LC, N, NYH, NYP, UC, UM, UP, Y

Contains: History of Elvira—Augustus and Aurelia.

1675a   LIPPARD, GEORGE. Adrian, the Neophyte . . . Philadelphia: I. R. & A. H. Diller, 1843. 13 p. 8vo   UV

1676   ——— The Battle-Day of Germantown . . . Philadelphia: A. H. Diller, 1843. 34 p., illus. 8vo

AAS, HEH, IN, LC, LCP, NYP, UV, Y

At head of title: "Original Revolutionary Chronicle."
Printed in double cols.
Lippard titles credited for the most part to LCP, are shelved next door in the Historical Society of Pennsylvania. See BAL for Lippard bibliographical information.

1677   ——— 'Bel of Prairie Eden: A Romance of Mexico . . . Boston: Hotchkiss & Co., 1848. 88 p. 8vo

AAS, HEH, LC, LCP, UP, UV, Y

Printed in double cols.
Sabin 41399 lists a Philadelphia 1845 ed. which is in error.

1678   ——— Blanche of Brandywine; or, September the Eleventh, 1777 . . . Philadelphia: G. B. Zieber & Co., 1846. 351 p., illus. 8vo   AAS, H, HEH, LC, N, NYP, UC, UP(pts.1-2), Y
Issued in three parts.
Census does not distinguish between copies in pts. or bound as one vol.

1679   ——— ——— Philadelphia: G. B. Zieber & Co., 1847. 351 p., illus. 8vo   AAS, Y

1680   ——— ——— Philadelphia: T. B. Peterson, No. 98 Chestnut Street [cop. 1846]. 351 p. 8vo   AAS, B, H, IN, Y

1681   ——— The Empire City; or, New York by Night and Day . . . New York: Stringer & Townsend, 1850. 2 vols. (100 p., 2 p.l., [101]-203 p.). 8vo   AAS(V.1), UP, UV, Y(V.1)
Printed in double cols.

1681a   ——— The Entranced; or, The Wanderer of Eighteen Centuries . . . Philadelphia: Joseph Severns and Company, 1849. 92 p. 8vo
Not seen. See BAL 11790.

1682 ———— Herbert Tracy; or, The Legend of the Black Rangers. A Romance of the Battle-field of Germantown . . . Philadelphia: R. G. Berford, 1844. 168 p. 12mo   AAS, H, NYH, NYP, Y

1682a ———— The Killers: A Narrative of Real Life in Philadelphia . . . By a Member of the Philadelphia Bar [anon.]. Philadelphia: Hankinson and Bartholomew, 1850. 50 p. 8vo   LCP, UV
Printed in double cols.

1683 ———— The Ladye Annabel; or, The Doom of the Poisoner. A Romance by an Unknown Author . . . [anon.]. Philadelphia: R. G. Berford, 1844. 133 p. 8vo   LCP, Y
Printed in double cols.

1683a ———— ———— 3d ed. Philadelphia: G. B. Zieber & Co., 1845. 133 p. 8vo
Title reads: *The Ladye Annabel: A Romance of the Alembic, the Altar, aud [sic] the Throne.*
Printed in double cols.
Not seen. See BAL 11774.

1683b ———— ———— Philadelphia: T. B. Peterson, 1849.
Title reads: *Ladye Annabel; or, The Child of Aldarin.*
Not seen. See BAL 11785.

1684 ———— Legends of Mexico . . . Philadelphia: T. B. Peterson, 1847. 136 p. 8vo   AAS, B, HEH, LC, N, NYP, UM, UP, Y
Contents: The Battles of Taylor (The Crusade of the Nineteenth Century—The Camp in the Wilderness—The Dead Woman of Palo Alto—Palo Alto—Resaca de la Palma—Monterey—Buena Vista).

1684a ———— ———— Philadelphia: T. B. Peterson, 1848. 136 p. 8vo   AAS
Title reads: *Legends of Mexico; or, The Battles of Old Rough and Ready.*
At head of cover title: "Tenth Edition."

1685 ———— The Man with the Mask: A Sequel to the Memoirs of a Preacher. A Revelation of the Church and the Home . . . Philadelphia: Jos. Severns and Company, No. 72 Chesnut Street [1849]. 106 p., 1 l. 8vo   HEH, UV, Y
Last leaf: "A word before we part," informs the reader that *The Empire City; or, New York by Night and Day*, is in preparation.
Printed in double cols.

1685a ———— Memoirs of a Preacher: A Revelation of the Church and the Home . . . Philadelphia: Jos. Severns and Company, 72 Chesnut Street [1849]. 94 p., illus. 8vo   UV
"Second Edition" on front cover.

1686 —————— The Nazarene; or, The Last of the Washingtons. A Revelation of Philadelphia, New York, and Washington, in the Year 1844 ... Philadelphia: G. Lippard and Co., 1846. 5 pts. (240 p.). 8vo   BP, LC, LCP(pt. 1), NYP, Y

1687 —————— Paul Ardenheim, the Monk of Wissahikon ... Wissahikon, Penn., 1848. 536 p. 8vo   Y
This is a made-up copy of a set of Peterson sheets with a fabricated title leaf. Retained herein as a curio.

1688 —————— —————— Philadelphia: T. B. Peterson, No. 98 Chesnut Street [cop. 1848]. 536 p. 8vo
AAS, B, BP, H, HEH, LC, LCP, N, UP

1689 —————— The Quaker City; or, The Monks of Monk-Hall. A Romance of Philadelphia Life, Mystery and Crime [anon.]. Philadelphia: G. B. Zeiber and Co., 1844. 494 p., illus. 8vo
LCP
Partly printed in double cols.
Issued in ten pts. comprising four books. Book the First: Mary, the Merchant's Daughter; Book the Second: The Forger; Book the Third: Mabel; Book the Fourth: Ravoni, the Sorcerer.
HEH copy has "No. 4 ... Second Edition" on original front paper cover and collates: cover title, pp. 145-206, ii. Advert. on p. i announces that *Paul Ardenheim* is "to be published in not more than twelve numbers. ... First number to be issued, January 1st, 1845." No copy found with this date.

1690 —————— —————— Philadelphia: Published by the author, 1845. 494 p., illus. 8vo   AAS, B, N, Y
Partly printed in double cols.

1691 —————— —————— Philadelphia: Published by the author, 1846. 2 vols., illus. 8vo   LC
Paged continuously (494 p.) and partly printed in double cols.
On cover: "Sixteenth Edition."

1692 —————— —————— Philadelphia: Published by the author, 1847. 2 vols. in 1, illus. 8vo   AAS, UP, Y
Paged continuously (494 p.) and partly printed in double cols.

1693 —————— —————— Philadelphia: Published by the author [1849]. 2 vols. 8vo   AAS, B, H
Paged continuously (494 p.) and partly printed in double cols.
The "Preface to the Twenty-Seventh American Edition" is dated Feb. 22, 1849.

1694   ——— The Rose of Wissahikon; or, The Fourth of July, 1776. A Romance, Embracing the Secret History of the Declaration of Independence . . . Philadelphia: G. B. Zieber & Co., 1847. 70 p. 12mo   AAS, BP, HEH, LC, LCP, N, NYP, UM, UV, Y

1695   ——— Washington and His Generals; or, Legends of the Revolution . . . Philadelphia: G. B. Zieber and Co., 1847. 4 pts. in 3 (538 p.).

      AAS, B, BP, H, HEH, IN, LC, N, NYH (pt.1), NYP, UC, UM, UP, Y

Contents: The Battle of Germantown—Wissahikon—Benedict Arnold—The Battle of Brandywine—The Fourth of July, 1776—Romance of the Revolution.

Two printings: 8vo and 12mo. Census does not distinguish between the formats.

1695a   ——— Washington and His Men: A New Series of Legends of the Revolution . . . Philadelphia: Jos. Severns and Company, 72 Chesnut Street, between Second and Third [cop. 1849]. 70 p., illus. 8vo   HEH, UV

Contents: The Last of the Washingtons—The Mother's Prayer—The Youth of Washington—The Boy and the Book—The Challenge—The Duel; or, Courage That Is Not Afraid of the Name of "Coward"—The Hunter of the Alleghanies—The Battle of Monongahela—Washington in Love—The Death of Braddock—The King and the Planter—Washington's Christmas: A Legend of Valley Forge.

Printed in double cols.

1696   ——— ——— New York: Stringer & Townsend, 1850. 184 p., illus. 8vo   HEH, LC, LCP, NYH

Two legends are added to this ed.: The Fourth of July, 1776—Herbert Tracy; or, The Legend of the Black Rangers.

Printed in double cols.

1697 LIPPINCOTT, SARA JANE (CLARKE). Greenwood Leaves: A Collection of Sketches and Letters. By Grace Greenwood [pseud.]. Boston: Ticknor, Reed and Fields, 1850. 406 p. 12mo   AAS, B, BP, H, HEH, LC, LCP, N, NYH, UC, UP, Y

Contains: Sophie Norton's Way of Heading a Conspiracy against Her Peace—Sly Peeps into the Heart Feminine—The Society of Four—My First Hunting and Fishing—Heart Histories—A Night of Years—Destiny in a Rose-bud—A Sketch from Life—The Irish Daughter—Atalanta upon Skates —The Rose-Wreathed Cross—The Alliance—A Spring Flower Faded— Love and Loyalty—Kate Richmond's Betrothal—A Dream of Death—The Error and Its Expiation—Parting under a Cloud—Falling in Love: A Bundle of Other People's Experiences.

1698 ——— ——— 2d ed. Boston: Ticknor, Reed and Fields, 1850.
406 p. 12mo AAS, H, NYP, Y

1699 LITTLE, GEORGE. The American Cruiser; or, The Two Mess-
mates. A Tale of the Last War . . . [anon.]. Boston: Waite,
Peirce and Company, 1846. 408 p., illus. 12mo
AAS, B, HEH, IN, UP

1700 ——— ——— Boston: Wm. J. Reynolds and Company, 1847.
390 p., illus. 12mo
AAS, BA, BP, H, HEH, HM, IN, LC, N, NYP, UC, UM, Y
Title reads: *The American Cruiser: A Tale of the Last War . . .*

1700a ——— ——— Boston: Charles H. Peirce, 1848. 390 p., illus.
12mo AAS
Title reads: *The American Cruiser: A Tale of the Last War . . .*

1700b ——— ——— New York: Nafis & Cornish, 1849. 390 p., illus.
12mo AAS
Title reads: *The American Cruiser's Own Book.*

1701 LIVERMORE, HARRIET. A Wreath from Jessamine Lawn; or, Free
Grace the Flower That Never Fades . . . Philadelphia: Printed
for the authoress, 1831. 2 vols. 12mo LC, LCP, Y
England.

1702 LIVING MANNERS; or, The True Secret of Happiness. A Tale.
Philadelphia: Anthony Finley, 1822. 108 p. 12mo
AAS, BA, LCP
Hudson River.

1703 LIVING ON OTHER PEOPLE'S MEANS; or, The History of Simon
Silver. Boston: Weeks, Jordan & Co., 1837. 72 p. 12mo
AAS, BP, HEH, NYP, UP, Y
Massachusetts; contemporary.

1704 ——— 3d ed. Boston: Weeks, Jordan & Co., 1837. 72 p.
12mo H, Y

LOCKE, CHARLES HENRY, *jt. au. See* P's and Q's (1831), No. 2083.

1704a LOCKE, RICHARD ADAMS. A Complete Account of the Late Dis-
coveries in the Moon [anon.]. [New York? 1835?] Caption
title, 11 p. 8vo LC
First published in the New York *Sun*, Aug. 1835.
At head of first column: "From a Supplement to the Edinburgh Journal."
Printed in double cols.

1705 LOCKWOOD, RALPH INGERSOLL. The Insurgents: An Historical Novel . . . [anon.]. Philadelphia: Carey, Lea & Blanchard, 1835. 2 vols. 12mo

AAS, B, BA, BP, H, HEH, IN, LC, N, NYP, UM, UP, Y

Massachusetts; 1786.

1706 —— Rosine Laval: A Novel. By Mr. Smith [pseud.]. Philadelphia: Carey, Lea & Blanchard, 1833. 300 p. 12mo

AAS, BP, HEH, LC, NYP, UC, UP, UV, Y

Rockville; 1823.

LONGCLIFFE, HARRY. The Disguised Maiden: A Tale of the Colombian Rebellion. In M. M. Ballou, Red Rupert (1848), No. 248.

LONGFELLOW, HENRY WADSWORTH. The Bald Eagle. In Tales of Humor (1840), Nos. 1242, 2533.

For discussion of authorship see BAL 7574.

1707 —— Hyperion: A Romance . . . [anon.]. New York: Samuel Colman, 1839. 2 vols. 12mo

AAS, B, BA, BP, H, HEH, IN, LC, LCP, N, NYP, NYS, UC, UM, UP, Y

Switzerland and Germany.

1708 —— —— 2d ed. Cambridge: John Owen, 1845. 370 p. 8vo

AAS, BP, CLS, H, HEH, IN, LC, Y

Some copies do not have "Second Edition" on title page.

1709 —— —— 3d ed. Cambridge: John Owen, 1846. 370 p. 8vo

AAS, H, LCP, Y

1710 —— —— 4th ed. Boston: William D. Ticknor & Co., 1847. 370 p. 8vo

BP, NYP, Y

1711 —— —— 5th ed. Boston: William D. Ticknor & Co., 1848. 370 p. 8vo

UM

1712 —— —— 7th ed. Boston: William D. Ticknor & Co., 1850. 370 p. 8vo

CLS, HEH, Y

1713 —— —— 8th ed. Boston: Ticknor, Reed & Fields, 1850. 370 p. 8vo

AAS, UC, Y

1714 —— Kavanagh: A Tale . . . Boston: Ticknor, Reed and Fields, 1849. 188 p. 8vo

AAS, B, BA, BP, CLS, H, HEH, IN, LC, LCP, N, NYH, NYP, NYS, UC, UM, UP, Y

For differences in issues see Livingston.

New England; contemporary.

1715   ——— Outre-Mer: A Pilgrimage beyond the Sea. No. I . . . [anon.]. Boston: Hilliard, Gray & Co., 1833. 107 p. 8vo
BA, BP, H, HEH, IN, N, UP, Y

1716   ———— ———— No. II. Boston: Lilly, Wait and Company, 1834. 208 p. 8vo   AAS, BA, BP, H, HEH, IN, N, UP, Y

1717   ———— ———— New York: Harper & Brothers, 1835. 2 vols. 12mo
AAS, B, BA, BP, H, HEH, HM (v.2), IN, LCP, N, NYP, UC, UP, UV, Y

1718   ———— ———— 2d ed. Boston: William D. Ticknor & Co., 1846. 374 p. 8vo   AAS, B, BP, H, LC, UPI, Y

1719   ———— ———— 3d ed. Boston: William D. Ticknor & Co., 1848. 374 p. 8vo   AAS, B, BA, LC, LCP, UM, Y

1720   ———— ———— 4th ed. Boston: Ticknor, Reed and Fields, 1850. 374 p. 8vo   AAS, BA, CLS, HEH, LC, Y

1721 LONGSTREET, AUGUSTUS BALDWIN. Georgia Scenes, Characters, Incidents, &c., in the First Half Century of the Republic. By a Native Georgian [anon.]. Augusta: Printed at the S. R. Sentinel office, 1835. 235 p. 12mo
AAS, CLS, H, HEH, IN, LC, N, NYP, UC, UP, UV, Y

1722   ———— ———— 2d ed. New York: Harper & Brothers, 1840. 214 p., illus. 12mo   AAS, B, BA, BP, CLS, HEH, IN, LC, N, UP, Y
HM and Y have copies of a 2d ed.–New York: Harper & Brothers [n.d.], with copyright notice dated 1840. Pagination as above.

1723   ———— ———— 2d ed. New York: Harper & Brothers, 1842. 214 p., illus. 12mo   LC

1724   ———— ———— 2d ed. New York: Harper & Brothers, 1843. 214 p., illus. 12mo   UC

1725   ———— ———— 2d ed. New York: Harper & Brothers, 1844. 214 p., illus. 12mo   HM

1726   ———— ———— 2d ed. New York: Harper & Brothers, 1845. 214 p., illus. 12mo   BP, CLS, UPI

1727   ———— ———— 2d ed. New York: Harper & Brothers, 1846. 214 p., illus. 12mo   LC

1728 —————— ————— 2d ed. New York: Harper & Brothers, 1847. 214 p., illus. 12mo   AAS, NYP, Y

1728a —————— ————— 2d ed. New York: Harper & Brothers, 1848. 214 p., illus. 12mo   Y

1729 —————— ————— 2d ed. New York: Harper & Brothers, 1850. 214 p., illus. 12mo   AAS, B, HEH, LC, NYP, Y

1730 LORRAINE, A. M. Donald Adair: A Novel by a Young Lady of Virginia ... [anon.]. Richmond: Peter Cottom, 1828. 2 vols. 12mo   H, HEH (V.1), UP, Y
American Revolution.

1731 —————— ————— 2d ed. Richmond: Peter Cottom, 1841. 2 vols. 12mo   UV

1732 —————— ————— New York: Published by the author, 1848. 2 vols. in 1. 12mo   UV

1733 THE LOTTERY TICKET: An American Tale . . . Cambridge: Printed by Hilliard and Metcalf, Feb. 1822. 51 p. 12mo
AAS, BA, BP, H, HEH, LC, LCP, NYP, UC, UV, Y
New Hampshire; contemporary.

1734 —————— To Which Is Added: The Destructive Consequences of Dissipation and Luxury. Hartford: D. F. Robinson & Co., 1827. 105 p., illus. 12mo   AAS, H, LC, UP, Y

1734a LOVE OF ADMIRATION; or, Mary's Visit to B-----. A Moral Tale. By a Lady ... New Haven: A. H. Maltby. Sold by Hilliard, Gray, Little and Wilkins, and Crocker and Brewster, Boston; also by Jonathan Leavitt and J. P. Haven, New York, 1828. 160 p. 12mo   HEH, NYP, UP, Y

1735 THE LOVE OF PRAISE and the Love of Virtue . . . By an American Lady. Hudson: Wm. E. Norman, 1821. 23 p. 24mo
AAS, N, Y
England; contemporary.

1736 LUCRETIA AND HER FATHER: A Narrative Founded on Fact. By a Clergyman of New England . . . Second Edition. Hartford: D. F. Robinson & Co., 1828. 96 p., illus. 12mo
AAS, HEH, LC, Y
LC cover imprint dated 1829.

LUDLOW, CHARLES. The Dream of Love. *In* J. T. Parker, *comp.*, The American Legendary (1830), No. 1991.

1737 LUFF, LORRY, *pseud.* Antonita, the Female Contrabandista: A Mexican Tale of Land and Water. By Lorry Luff [pseud.]. New York: Williams Brothers, 1848. 95 p. 8vo   LC
Also contains: The Breach of Promise.
Printed in double cols.

1738 ———— ———— New York: W. F. Burgess, 1850. 96 p. 8vo   LC
Title reads: *The Texan Captain and the Female Smuggler.*
Also contains: The Breach of Promise.
Printed in double cols.

———— The Texan Captain. *See* preceding entry.

1739 LUKE LOVELL, the Widow's Son; or, The Adventures of a Young Gentleman from the State of Maine, Who Went to Seek His Fortune in Boston. By the Author of "Lucy Lane" ... Boston: W. R. Davis, 1848. Cover title, 32 p., illus. 8vo   LC, Y
Printed in double cols.

1740 LUMMUS, AARON. The Life and Adventures of Dr. Caleb, Who Migrated from Egypt, and Afterwards Practised Physic in the Land of Canaan and Elsewhere ... Boston: Printed for the author by Lincoln & Edmands, 1822. 230 p. 16mo
AAS, B, BP, HEH, LC, UP, Y

1740a LUTYENS, G. N. The Life and Adventures of Moses Nathan Israel ... Containing an Account of His Birth, Education and Travels through Parts of Germany, Italy, and the United States ... Easton [Pa.]: Printed by Christian J. Hutter, 1815. 12mo
"First American novel in which Jewish characters appear"—Parke-Bernet catalog 2769:74.

LUZEE, HENRIETTA. More Scared than Hurt: A Bear Story. *In* M. M. Ballou, Albert Simmons (1849), No. 229.

1741 M'CABE, JOHN COLLINS. Scraps... Richmond: Printed by J. C. Walker, 1835. 192 p. 12mo AAS, B, BP, H, HEH, LC, NYP, UP, Y
Contains: Wylie Woodward: A Tale of Fancy—The Broken-hearted—Legend of the Mississippi—The Visionary—The Stone House.

1742 —————— ————— 2d ed. Richmond: Printed by J. C. Walker, 1835. 192 p. 12mo   B

McCall, John Cadwalader. The Witch of New England (1824). *See* No. 2751 for title entry which is now identified as by McCall.

1743 M'Clintock, William L. John Beedle's Sleigh Ride, Courtship, and Marriage. Attributed to Capt. M'Clintock of the U.S. Army. New York: C. Wells, 1841. 44 p., illus. 12mo
                                    AAS, HEH, LC, UP, UV, Y
Also attributed to John Neal.

1744 McClung, John Alexander. Camden: A Tale of the South . . . [anon.]. Philadelphia: Carey & Lea, 1830. 2 vols. 12mo
                                    AAS, LC, UC, UM(V.1), UP, Y
American Revolution.

1745 McConnel, John Ludlum. Grahame; or, Youth and Manhood . . . [anon.]. New York: Baker and Scribner, 1850. 385 p. 12mo   AAS, B, BP, HEH, LC, LCP, N, NYP, UP, Y

1746 —————— Talbot and Vernon . . . [anon.]. New York: Baker and Scribner, 1850. 513 p. 12mo
                    AAS, B, BA, BP, HEH, IN, LC, LCP, N, UC, UM, UP, Y

1746a McDermott, William. The Twins; or, Edward and the Indian Protege. A Tale of the Early Settlement of Western New-York . . . Syracuse, Onondaga Co., N.Y., 1845. 48 p. 8vo
                                                                      Y
Cover imprint: "Syracuse: N. M. D. Lathrop, printer, 1846."

1747 McDougall, Frances Harriet (Whipple) Green. The Mechanic . . . Providence: Burnett & King, 1842. 219 p. 12mo
                                    AAS, B, BA, H, HEH, IN, LC, N, UM, UP, Y

1748 McDowell, J. R. Henry Wallace; or, The Victim of Lottery Gambling . . . [anon.]. New York: Printed and published by Wilson & Swain, 1832. 108 p. 18mo
                                    AAS, BA, HEH, LC, NYP, UP, UV, Y
New York City; early 19th cent.

M'Farland, John, *attrib. au. See* Quipes, *Father, pseud.*

1749 McHenry, James. The Betrothed of Wyoming . . . [anon.]. Philadelphia: Sold by the principal booksellers, 1830. 231 p. 12mo   AAS, HEH, LC, LCP, N, NYP, UC, UP, Y
Wyoming, Pa.; 1778.

1750 ———— ———— 2d ed. Philadelphia: Sold by the principal booksellers, 1830. 231 p. 12mo   AAS, BP, H, LC, UP, Y

1751 ———— ———— 3d ed. Philadelphia: Sold by the principal booksellers, 1830. 231 p. 12mo   AAS, LC, N, NYP, UC, UM, UP, Y

1752 ———— The Hearts of Steel: An Irish Historical Tale of the Last
Century . . . [anon.]. Philadelphia: A. R. Poole, 1825. 2 vols.
12mo   AAS, IN, LC, NYP, UC

1753 ———— Meredith; or, The Mystery of the Meschianza. A Tale
of the American Revolution . . . [anon.]. Philadelphia: Sold
by the principal booksellers, 1831. 260 p. 12mo
        AAS, BA, BP, H, HEH, HM, IN, LC, LCP, N, NYP, UC, UM, UP, UV, Y

1754 ———— ———— 2d ed. Philadelphia: Sold by the principal booksellers, 1831. 260 p. 12mo   AAS, BP, LC, LCP, UP, Y

1755 ———— O'Halloran; or, The Insurgent Chief. An Irish Historical Tale of 1798 . . . [anon.]. Philadelphia: H. C. Carey and
I. Lea, 1824. 2 vols. 12mo   H, HEH, NYP, NYS, UP, Y

1756 ———— The Spectre of the Forest; or, Annals of the Housatonic.
A New England Romance . . . [anon.]. New York: E. Bliss
and E. White, 1823. 2 vols. 12mo   AAS, H, IN, LC, LCP, NYP, Y
Late 17th cent.

1757 ———— The Wilderness; or, Braddock's Times. A Tale of the
West . . . [anon.]. New York: E. Bliss and E. White, 1823. 2
vols. 12mo   AAS, B, BP, H, HEH, IN, NYP, UC, UM, UP, Y

1758 ———— ———— Pittsburgh: M. P. Morse, 1848. 2 vols. in 1.
12mo   AAS, IN, LC, N, NYP, UP, UPI, Y
The same sheets were later issued with a prefatory note dated 1876. AAS, HEH

1759 McINTOSH, MARIA JANE. Charms and Counter-charms . . . New
York: D. Appleton & Company, 1848. 400 p. 12mo
                                     AAS, HEH, LCP, N, UC, UP, Y

1760 ———— ———— 3d ed. New York: D. Appleton & Company,
1848. 400 p. 12mo   B, HEH, LCP

1761 ———— ———— 5th ed. New York: D. Appleton & Company,
1849. 400 p. 12mo   AAS, IN, NYP, Y

1762 ———— Conquest and Self-conquest; or, Which Makes the Hero . . . [anon.]. New York: Harper & Brothers, 1843. 216 p. 12mo   AAS, BP, LCP, N, UP, Y
Washington, New Orleans, etc.

1762a ———— ———— New York: Harper & Brothers, 1844. 216 p. 12mo   AAS

1763 ———— ———— New York: Harper & Brothers [cop. 1839]. 216 p. 12mo   UM

1764 ———— The Cousins: A Tale of Early Life . . . [anon.]. New York: Harper & Brothers, 1845. 205 p. 12mo   AAS, BP, LC, N, UM, UP, Y
Georgia and New York.

1765 ———— ———— New York: Harper & Brothers, 1846. 205 p. 12mo   AAS, Y

1766 ———— ———— New York: Harper & Brothers [cop. 1845]. 205 p. 12mo   AAS, Y

1767 ———— Praise and Principle; or, For What Shall I Live . . . [anon.]. New York: Harper & Brothers, 1845. 252 p. 12mo   AAS, BA, HEH, Y
Meadows, Mass.; contemporary.

1768 ———— ———— New York: Harper & Brothers, 1847. 252 p. 12mo   AAS, H, Y

1769 ———— ———— New York: Harper & Brothers, 1848. 252 p. 12mo   AAS, NYP

1770 ———— ———— New York: Harper & Brothers [cop. 1845]. 252 p. 12mo   LCP

1771 ———— Two Lives; or, To Seem and To Be . . . New York: D. Appleton & Co., 1846. 318 p. 12mo   AAS, B, BP, HEH, LC, LCP, NYP, UM, UP, Y
New York City; contemporary.

1772 ———— ———— 2d ed. New York: D. Appleton & Company, 1847. 262 p. 12mo   AAS, IN, LC, N, UP, Y

1773 ———— ———— 7th thousand. New York: D. Appleton & Company, 1849. 262 p. 12mo   AAS, HM

1774 ——— Woman an Enigma; or, Life and Its Revealings . . . [anon.]. New York: Harper & Brothers, 1843. 238 p. 12mo

AAS, BA, HEH, LC, N, UP, Y

Paris.

1775 ——— ——— New York: Harper & Brothers, 1844. 238 p. 12mo

AAS, N, Y

1776 ——— ——— New York: Harper & Brothers, 1848. 238 p. 12mo

AAS, UP, Y

1777 MACK, THOMAS C. The Priest's Turf-Cutting Day. An Historical Romance, by T. C. M. New York: The author, 1841. 82 p. 12mo

AAS, B, H, HEH, LC, NYP, UC, Y

1778 McLELLAN, ISAAC, JR. The Gold Demon and the Poor Cobler [sic] of Boston: A Romance of the Revolution . . . Boston: D. Ruggles, 1845. 59 p. 8vo

BP, Y

LC has a title page, deposited Oct. 3, 1845.

1779 MacLELLAN, RUFUS CHARLES. The Story Reader's Garland: A Cluster of Tales . . . Baltimore: Printed by John D. Toy, 1849. 82 p. 12mo

B, LC

1780 McSHERRY, JAMES. Pere Jean; or, The Jesuit Missionary. A Tale of the North American Indians . . . Baltimore: Printed and published by J. Murphy, 1847. 256 p., illus. 12mo

LC, UV

Canada; 1642.

1781 MALLORY, DANIEL. Short Stories and Reminiscences of the Last Fifty Years. By an Old Traveller . . . [anon.]. New York: Daniel Mallory, 1842. 2 vols. 12mo

AAS, BP, HEH, IN, LC(V.2), LCP, N, NYH, UP, Y(V.1)

1782 ——— ——— 3d ed. New York: Daniel Mallory, 1842. 2 vols. 12mo

AAS, LC(V.1)

1783 ——— ——— 4th ed. New York: Daniel Mallory, 1842. 2 vols. 12mo

NYH(V.2), UP

1783a ——— ——— New York: Robert P. Bixby & Co., No. 3 Park Row [1845?]. 2 vols. in 1, illus. 12mo

UP

Title reads: *The Iris; or, Annual Visitory for 1844. Edited by Daniel Mallory.*

A reprint of his *Short Stories.*

1784 MAN, GEORGE FLAGG. The Geranium Leaf: An Original Tale. By Luom del Valchiusa [pseud.]. Boston: Marsh, Capen, Lyon & Webb, 1840. 69 p. 12mo AAS, BP, H, HEH, LC, N, UM, Y

THE MAN IN THE CLARET-COLORED COAT, *pseud.* *See* Gould, Edward Sherman

1785 MANCUR, JOHN HENRY. Alda Grey: A Tale of New Jersey . . . New York: William H. Colyer, 1843. Cover title, pp. [133]-191. 8vo AAS, N, NYH
At head of cover title: "Tales of the Revolution," No. 3.

1786 ——— Christine: A Tale of the Revolution . . . New York: William H. Colyer, 1843. Cover title, pp. [13]-60. 8vo
AAS, HEH, IN, LC, N, NYP, UP, Y
At head of cover title: "Price, One Shilling."
No. 1 of "Tales of the Revolution."

1787 ——— Constance; or, The Debutante . . . Philadelphia: E. Ferret & Co. [cop. 1846]. 112 p. 8vo B

1788 ——— The Deserter: A Legend of Mount Washington . . . [New York]: William H. Colyer, 1843. Cover title, pp. [61]-132. 8vo AAS, HEH, IN, LC, UP
At head of cover title: "No. 2. Tales of the Revolution. Price One Shilling."

1789 ——— Everard Norton . . . New York: William H. Colyer, 1844. Cover title, pp [257]-317. 8vo AAS, UP
At head of cover title: "No. 5. Tales of the Revolution."

1790 ——— Henri Quatre; or, The Days of the League . . . New York: Harper & Brothers, 1834. 2 vols. 12mo
AAS, BA, H, HEH, LCP, N, NYP(V.2), NYS, Y
France.

1790a ——— ——— 2d ed. New York: Harper & Brothers, 1847. 2 vols. 12mo Y

1791 ——— Jasper Crowe . . . New York: William H. Colyer, 1843. Cover title, pp. [193]-256. 8vo AAS, H, Y
No. 4 of "Tales of the Revolution."

1792 ———— La Meschianza ... New York: William H. Colyer, 1844. Cover title, pp. [319]-374. 8vo   NYP

At head of cover title: "No. 6. Tales of the Revolution. Price One Shilling." Mr. Kirk Bryan of Norristown, Pa., informed me that his copy contains two leaves preceding the above title leaf: a general title "Tales of the Revolution ... New York: William H. Colyer, 1844"; and a "Contents" leaf which lists "Christine, p. 13, The Deserter, p. 61, Alda Grey, p. 133, Jasper Crowe, p. 193, Everard Norton, p. 257, La Meschianza, p. 319."

1793 ———— The Palais Royal: An Historical Romance . . . New York: William H. Colyer, 1845. 252 p. 12mo   H, LC, NYP

France; 1650.

1794 ———— Tales of the Revolution . . . New York: William H. Colyer, 1844. 374 p. 8vo   Y

Contents: Christine—The Deserter—Alda Grey—Jasper Crowe—Everard Norton—La Meschianza.

These tales were separately issued with their own cover titles. No. 6, *La Meschianza*, was issued with a general title page and table of contents.

1795 ———— Wilfred Lovel: A Revolutionary Romance . . . Philadelphia: A. J. Rockafellar, 1843. 62 p. 8vo

      AAS, H, HEH, NYH, NYP, UM, UP, Y

Printed in double cols.

New York City; late 17th cent.

1796 MANDELL, D. J. The Adventures of Search for Life: A Bunyanic Narrative, as Detailed by Himself. By D. J. Mandell, Pastor of the First Universalist Society in Westbrook, Me. Portland: S. H. Colesworthy, 1838. 90 p. 16mo   LC, NYP, Y

1797 THE MANIAC BEAUTY; or, Love at Nahant . . . [anon.]. Boston: F. Gleason, 1844. Cover title, 66 p. 8vo   AAS, BP, HEH, Y

Written by Osgood Bradbury.

1798 MANNERING, GUY, *pseud.* Rosalvo Delmonmort: A Tale by Guy Mannering [pseud.]. Boston: Thomas G. Bangs, 1818. 196 p. 12mo   BA, H, IN, NYP, NYS, UV, Y

Loshe indicates Mannering as a pseud.

England.

MANNING, G. H. Henry Wilber; or, A Short Chapter from the Book of Life. *In* M. M. Ballou, Red Rupert (1848), No. 248.

1799 THE MANUSCRIPT of Diedrich Knickerbocker, Jun. . . . New York, 1824. 75, [1] p. 8vo   BP, NYS, Y
Sometimes ascribed to Washington Irving.

1800 MANVILL, MRS. P. D. Lucinda; or, The Mountain Mourner. Being Recent Facts, in a Series of Letters, from Mrs. Manvill, in the State of New York, to Her Sister in Pennsylvania. Johnstown [N.Y.]: Printed and sold by W. & A. Child, 1807. 150 p. 12mo   AAS, HEH, NYP, Y
Contains 30 letters.
Saratoga County, N.Y.; contemporary.

1801 ——— ——— 2d ed. Ballston Spa, N.Y.: Printed and sold by William Child, 1810. 168 p. 12mo   AAS, IN, UC, Y
Contains 31 letters.

1802 ——— ——— 3d ed. Ballston Spa: Printed by J. Comstock, 1817. 180 p. 12mo   AAS, B, HEH, LC, N, UP, Y
Contains 31 letters.

1802a ——— ——— 4th ed. Waterloo: Printed and sold by William Child, 1824. 168 p. 8vo   HEH
Contains 31 letters.

1802b ——— ——— 7th ed. Erie, Pa.: Rufus Clough, 1831. 119 p., illus. 12mo   AAS
Contains 30 letters.

1803 ——— ——— 5th ed. Ithaca: Mack, Andrus & Woodruff, 1836. 192 p. 12mo   AAS, H, HEH, LC, NYP, Y
Pages [173]-192 "The Stranger," by Henry G. Bell, an English author.
Contains 31 letters.

1804 ——— ——— 5th ed. Mobile: J. S. Kellogg & Co., 1836. 192 p. 12mo   AAS
Contains 31 letters.

1805 ——— ——— 5th ed. Ithaca: Mack, Andrus & Woodruff, 1839. 191 p. 12mo   AAS, Y
Contains 31 letters.

1806 THE MARAUDER: An Original Tale of the Seventeenth Century. New Bedford: Melcher & Rogers, 1823. 124 p. 8vo   B, LC, Y

1807　MARGARETTA; or, The Intricacies of the Heart . . . Philadelphia: Samuel F. Bradford, 1807. 419 p. 12mo　　　　AAS, H, NYS
Written in a series of letters.
Philadelphia and Baltimore; contemporary.

1808　——— Charleston: Edmund Morford, 1807. 419 p. 12mo
　　　　　　　　　　　　　　　　　　　　　　　　　　　LC
MARIA, *pseud.* *See* Weston, Mrs. Maria D.

MARIA DEL OCCIDENTE, *pseud.* *See* Brooks, Maria (Gowen)

1809　MARION AND HIS MEN: An Historical Novel. By the Author of "Paul Jones," "The Old Loyalist," "Hastings," &c. . . . New York: William H. Graham, 1846. 95 p. 8vo　　　　AAS, Y
Printed in double cols.

1810　MARION RAYMOND; or, The Wife with Two Husbands! A Romance of the Heart. Boston: H. L. Williams, 1845. 50 p., illus. 8vo　　　　BP, Y
Ireland.

1811　MARION'S MEN: A Romance of the Revolution. By the Author of "The Old Loyalist," "The Southern Whig" . . . Philadelphia: A. J. Rockafellar, 1843. 56 p. 8vo
　　　　　　　　　　　　　AAS, H, HEH, LC, N, UP, Y
Printed in double cols.

1812　MARITIME SCRAPS; or, Scenes in the Frigate United States during a Cruise in the Mediterranean . . . By a Man-of-War's-Man. Boston: Printed and published for the author, 1838. 108 p. 12mo　　　　AAS, BA, BP, HEH, IN, LC, Y
C. T. Harbeck, *A Contribution to the Bibliography of the History of the United States Navy* (1906), p. 121, enters under Harry Rivers.

1813　MARKOE, PETER. The Algerine Spy in Pennsylvania; or, Letters Written by a Native of Algiers on the Affairs of the United States in America, from the Close of the Year 1783 to the Meeting of the Convention . . . [anon.]. Philadelphia: Printed and sold by Prichard & Hall, 1787. 129 p. 12mo
　　　　AAS, BA, BP, HEH, IN, JCB, LC, LCP, N, NYH, NYP, UP, UV, Y

1814　MARSH, JOHN. Hannah Hawkins, the Reformed Drunkard's Daughter . . . New York: American Temperance Union, 1844. 72 p., illus. 12mo　　　　AAS, BA, H, HEH, IN, UP, Y
Baltimore; contemporary.

1814a ——— ——— 2d ed. New York: American Temperance Union, 1845. 72 p., illus. 12mo   AAS, HEH

1815 ——— ——— 4th ed. New York: American Temperance Union, 1846. 72 p., illus. 12mo   AAS, N, NYP

1815a ——— ——— 5th ed. New York: American Temperance Union, 1846. 72 p., illus. 12mo   Y

1815b ——— ——— 5th ed. New York: American Temperance Union, 1847. 72 p., illus. 12mo   AAS

1815c ——— ——— 6th ed. New York: American Temperance Union, 1847. 72 p., illus. 12mo   AAS, Y

1816 ——— ——— 7th ed. New York: American Temperance Union, 1848. 72 p., illus. 12mo   AAS, Y

1817 ——— ——— 8th ed. New York: American Temperance Union, 1849. 72 p., illus. 12mo   AAS, HEH

1818 ——— ——— 9th ed. New York: American Temperance Union [n.d.]. 72 p., illus. 12mo   UM

1819 MARTIN, JOSEPH, *comp.* Select Tales: Being a Compilation of Singular, Interesting, Remarkable, and Authentic Narratives, Ancient and Modern. Selected Principally from the Most Esteemed and Popular Literary Works, European and American, the Greater Part of Which Have Never Before Been Offered to the Public in Book Form. Charlottesville [Va.]: Joseph Martin, 1833. 424 p. 12mo   AAS, HEH, UP, UV, Y

Contains: The Boat on the Ocean—Juridical Recollections: The Trial, Sentence, and Premature Death of Rebecca Harmon—The Cavern of Death: A Narrative of Border Warfare—The First and Last Sacrifice: An Adventure at Murder Creek.

William Runge of the University of Virginia Library informs me that there are two issues, "distinguished from one another by a note 'To Subscribers' at the end of 'The Preface', p. 4."

1819a ——— ——— 2d ed. Charlottesville [Va.]: Joseph Martin, 1834. 424 p. 12mo   UV

MARTINGALE, HAWSER, *pseud. See* Sleeper, John S.

MARVEL, IK, *pseud. See* Mitchell, Donald Grant

1820　MARVEL, MARK, *pseud*.　The Slave of the Mine; or, The Stolen Heir.　By Mark Marvel [pseud.].　Boston: Gleason's Publishing Hall, 1845.　58 p.　8vo　　　AAS, B, BP, HEH, N, NYP, UP, Y
LC has a title page, deposited Dec. 29, 1845.

1821　MARY BEACH; or, The Fulton Street Cap Maker.　New York: W. F. Burgess, 1849.　97 p.　8vo　　　AAS
Printed in double cols.

1822　MARY WILSON: A Tale of New England . . .　Boston: Waite, Peirce and Company, 1845.　157 p., illus.　12mo
AAS, B, HEH, Y
Contemporary.

1823　———　Boston: Waite, Peirce and Company, 1846.　157 p., illus. 12mo
N, Y

1824　———　Boston: Waite, Peirce and Company, 1847.　157 p., illus. 12mo
AAS, BP

1825　———　Boston: Charles Waite, 1847.　157 p., illus.　12mo
B, BP, Y

1826　———　Boston: Strong & Brodhead, 1848.　157 p., illus.　12mo
AAS, Y

1827　MATHEWS, CORNELIUS.　Behemoth: A Legend of the Mound-Builders [anon.].　New York: J. & H. G. Langley, 1839.　192 p.　12mo
AAS, B, BP, H, HEH, IN, LC, N, NYH, NYP, UC, UM, UP, UV, Y
Sabin 46828 lists an 1843 ed.
Mississippi Valley.

1828　———　Big Abel and the Little Manhattan . . .　New York: Wiley and Putnam, 1845.　93 p.　8vo
AAS, B, BP, H, HEH, LC, N, NYH, NYP, UC, UP, UV, Y
Sabin 46829 lists an 1847 ed.
New York City.

1829　———　The Career of Puffer Hopkins . . .　New York: D. Appleton and Co., 1842.　319 p., illus.　8vo
AAS, BP, H, HEH, IN, NYH, NYP, NYS, UC, UM, UP, Y
New York City; contemporary.

1830　———　Chanticleer: A Thanksgiving Story of the Peabody Family [anon.].　Boston: B. B. Mussey & Co., 1850.　155 p.　12mo
AAS, B, H, HEH, IN, LCP, N, NYP, UC, UM, UP, Y

1831 —— —— 2d ed. Boston: B. B. Mussey & Co., 1850. 155
p. 12mo   AAS, H, IN, LC, LCP, NYP, Y

1832 —— Moneypenny; or, The Heart of the World. A Romance
of the Present Day . . . [anon.]. New York: Dewitt & Davenport, 1849. 155 p., illus. 8vo   AAS, B, IN, NYH, Y

1833 —— —— New York: Dewitt & Davenport, 1849-50. 2 pts.
8vo   NYP
Each part has its own cover title; paged continuously (270 p.).
At head of cover title, Pt. I: "Second Edition." Author's name printed on
cover title of Pt. II.

1834 —— —— New York: Dewitt & Davenport, 1850. 270 p.
8vo   AAS, BP, H, N, NYH, NYS, UP

1835 —— The Motley Book: A Series of Tales and Sketches. By
the Late Ben. Smith [pseud.] . . . New York: J. & H. G. Langley, 1838. 190 p., illus. 8vo AAS, B, BP, H, LC, NYH, NYP, UP, Y
Contents: Beelzebub and His Cart—Potter's Field—Greasy Peterson—The
Adventures of Sol Clarion—The Vision of Dr. Nicholas Grim—The Melancholy Vagabond—The Merry-makers: Exploit No. 1—The Great Charter
Contest in Gotham—The Witch and the Deacon—Dinner to the Honour-
able Abimelech Puffer—The Druggist's Wife—First Anniversary of the
N. A. Society for the Encouragement of Imposture—The Merrymakers: Ex-
ploit No. II—Disasters of Old Drudge—The Unburied Bones—Parson
Huckins's First Appearance.

1835a —— —— New Ed. New York: J. & H. G. Langley, 1838.
190 p., illus. 8vo   HEH, Y

1836 —— —— 3d ed. New York: Benj. G. Trevett, 1840. 190
p., illus. 8vo   AAS, B, BP, HEH, IN, LC, N, UC, UM, UP, Y

1837 —— The Various Writings . . . New York: Harper & Brothers, MDCCCLXIII [i.e., 1843]. 370 p. 8vo
                        AAS, B, H, HEH, LC, N, NYH, NYP, UC, UP, Y
Printed in double cols.

1838 MATTSON, MORRIS. Paul Ulric; or, The Adventures of an Enthusiast . . . [anon.]. New York: Harper & Brothers, 1835. 2
vols. 12mo   AAS, BP, H, HEH, LC, N, NYP, UC, UP, Y
England; contemporary.

1839 MATURIN, EDWARD. Benjamin, the Jew of Granada: A Romance
. . . New York: Richards and Company, 30 Ann Street [cop.
1847]. 80 p. 8vo   AAS, HEH, Y
Printed in double cols.

1840 ———— Eva; or, The Isles of Life and Death. New York: Stringer & Townsend, 1848. 2 vols.
Title from Appleton.

1841 ———— Montezuma; or, The Last of the Aztecs . . . New York: Paine & Burgess, 1845. 2 vols. 12mo
AAS, B, BP, H, HEH, IN, LC, N, NYP, NYS, UC, UM, UP, UV, Y

1842 ———— Sejanus, and Other Roman Tales . . . [anon.]. New York: F. Saunders, 1839. 220 p. 12mo
AAS, HEH, N, NYP, UM, UP, Y

1843 ———— ———— New York: Printed by Jared W. Bell, 1839. 220 p. 12mo
Y

1844 MAULE, MRS. RACHEL. Zimluko; or, The Hag of the Beetling Cliff. A Romance . . . Philadelphia: J. H. Jones, printer, 1849. 216 p. 8vo
HEH, LC, UM

1845 MAUREN, FRANK. Isadore Merton; or, The Reverses of Fortune. A Story of Real Life . . . Boston: F. Gleason, 1847. 50 p. 8vo
H, Y
LC has a title page, deposited Sept. 23, 1847.

1845a MAYO, SARAH CARTER (EDGARTON). Ellen Clifford; or, The Genius of Reform . . . [anon.]. Boston: A. Tompkins and B. B. Mussey, 1838. 142 p. 12mo
HEH, Y

1846 ———— The Palfreys: A Tale. By a Lady [anon.]. Boston: Abel Tompkins, 1838. 69 p. 12mo   AAS, H, HEH, N, NYP, UP, Y

1846a ———— The Poetry of Woman . . . [anon.]. Boston: A. Tompkins and B. B. Mussey, 1841. 180 p. 12mo
Y
Contents: The Flower of the Parsonage—The Step-Mother—Cousin Edith—Our Minister's Wife—Lallaree—Josephine—The Poetess—The Missionary—The Martyr.

1847 ———— Selections from the Writings of Mrs. Sarah C. Edgarton Mayo. With a Memoir by Her Husband . . . Boston: A. Tompkins, 1849. 432 p., illus. 12mo
AAS, B, BP, HEH, IN, LC, N, NYP, UC, UP, Y
Contains: Annette Lee—The Martyr—Eleonora, the Shakeress—The Rustic Wife—The Gossipings of Idle Hours—Debby Lincoln—The Deformed Boy—Lydia Vernon—Esther.

1848 ———— ———— Boston: A. Tompkins, 1850. 432 p. 12mo
AAS, Y

1849   MAYO, WILLIAM STARBUCK. The Berber; or, The Mountaineer of the Atlas. A Tale of Morocco... New York: Geo. P. Putnam, 1850. 454 p. 12mo
AAS, IN, LC, LCP, N, NYP, UC, UM, UP, UV, Y

1850   ———— ———— 2d ed. New York: Geo. P. Putnam, 1850. 454 p. 12mo   AAS, H, IN, NYH, NYP, NYS, UP, Y

1851   ———— ———— 3d ed. New York: Geo. P. Putnam, 1850. 454 p. 12mo   AAS, B, HEH

1852   ———— Kaloolah; or, Journeyings to the Djébel Kumri. An Autobiography of Jonathan Romer. Edited by W. S. Mayo, M.D. New York: George P. Putnam, 1849. 514 p., illus. 12mo   AAS, BP, IN, LCP, N, NYP, UM, UP, UV, Y

1853   ———— ———— 2d ed. New York: George P. Putnam, 1849. 514 p., illus. 12mo   AAS, B, BP, H, UM, UP, Y

1854   ———— ———— 3d ed. New York: George P. Putnam, 1850. 514 p. 12mo   AAS, BA, BP, H, HEH, NYP, Y

1855   ———— ———— 5th ed. New York: George P. Putnam, 1850. 185 p. 8vo   AAS, H, NYP, Y
Printed in double cols.

1856   MEADOWS, JOHN. The Brinley Shell; or, The Miser and His Niece. A Thrilling Tale of Love, Witchcraft, and Mystery ... Boston: F. Gleason [cop. 1848]. 100 p. 8vo   AAS, B, BP
Also contains: The Escape; or, The Officer's Bride—The Nymph of Nahant; or, Pride and Punishment.
Printed in double cols.

1857   MEANS WITHOUT LIVING ... Boston: Weeks, Jordan & Co., 1837. 72 p. 12mo   AAS, BP, H, N, NYP, UP, Y
At head of title: "New Experiments."
AAS has a 2d copy, with a variant title page.

     MEDINA, LOUISA H. The Sister of Charity. *In* The Romantic Historian (1834), No. 2154.

1858   MEEKS, HOWARD. Stories of the Fountain Rock: A New Series of Political Temperance Tales ... Philadelphia: T. Stokes, 1846. 80 p. 12mo   AAS, H, NYP, Y

243

1858a MELLEN, GRENVILLE. The First Glass, by Grenville Mellen. And The Intemperate, by Mrs. Sigourney. Southwark, Philadelphia: [Wm. F. Geddes, printer, No. 9 Library St.], 1834. Caption title, 8 p. 4to

Title at head of first column: "The Wedding and the First Glass, by Grenville Mellen. Extracted from the *Token* for 1834."
"The Intemperate" was extracted from the *Religious Souvenir* for 1834.
Printed in double cols.
A copy is owned by Roger Butterfield of New York City.

———— The Palisadoes. *In* N. P. Willis, *ed.*, The Legendary (1828), No. 2739.

1859 ———— Sad Tales and Glad Tales, by Reginald Reverie [pseud.] ... Boston: S. G. Goodrich, 1828. 185 p. 12mo

AAS, B, BA, BP, H, HEH, IN, LC, NYP, UC, UM, UP, UV, Y

Contains: The Palisadoes—The Spy and the Traitor—The Meeting of the Planets—The Presidency of the Republic in 1825, Argued by the Gods, and Settled by Jove, in the Supreme Council Chamber of Olympus—The Tale of an Aeronaut; and His Reflections on the Moral Character of a Balloon: In a Grave Letter from Gilbert Gas, Esq., to Mice Mundanus.

1860 MELVILLE, HERMAN. Mardi and a Voyage Thither ... New York: Harper & Brothers, 1849. 2 vols. 12mo AAS, B, BA, BP, H, HEH, IN, LC, LCP, N, NYP, NYS, UC, UM, UP, UPI, UV, Y

For complete bibliographical description of this title and the others by Melville, see Minnigerode.

1861 ———— Omoo: A Narrative of Adventures in the South Seas ... New York: Harper & Brothers, 1847. 389 p., illus. 12mo

AAS, BP, H, HEH, HM, IN, LC, LCP, N, NYP, NYS, UC, UM, UP, UV, Y

1862 ———— ———— 3d ed. New York: Harper & Brothers, 1847. 389 p., illus. 12mo AAS, B, IN, LC, N, NYP, UC, Y

1863 ———— ———— 5th ed. New York: Harper & Brothers, 1847. 389 p., illus. 12mo AAS, BA, BP, LC, N, Y

1864 ———— ———— 6th ed. New York: Harper & Brothers, 1850. 389 p., illus. 12mo AAS, H, Y

1865 ———— Redburn: His First Voyage ... New York: Harper & Brothers, 1849. 390 p. 12mo

AAS, B, BA, BP, H, HEH, IN, LC, LCP, N, NYP, UC, UM, UP, UV, Y

1866 ———— ———— New York: Harper & Brothers, 1850. 390 p. 12mo AAS, H, LC, N, NYP, NYS, UC, UM, Y

1867 ———— Typee: A Peep at Polynesian Life . . . New York: Wiley and Putnam, 1846. 325 p., illus. 12mo

AAS, BA, BP, CLS, H, HEH, IN, LC, LCP, N, NYP, UC, UP, Y

In 2 pts., each with a title page.

1868 ———— ———— Revised ed. with a Sequel . . . New York: Wiley and Putnam, 1846. 307 p., illus. 12mo

AAS, B, BP, H, LC, N, NYP, NYS, UC, UP, Y

In 2 pts., each with a title page.
The sequel is "The Story of Toby."

1869 ———— ———— Revised ed. with a Sequel . . . New York: Wiley and Putnam, 1847. 307 p., illus. 12mo

AAS, B, BP, H, IN, LC, N, NYH, NYP, UC, UM, Y

Y has a variant 2d copy: map not included in pagination, and dedication "To" Lemuel Shaw.

1869a ———— ———— Revised ed. with a Sequel. New York: Wiley and Putnam, 1848. 307 p., illus. 12mo   AAS, N, Y

1870 ———— ———— Revised ed. with a Sequel . . . New York: Harper & Brothers, 1849. 307 p., illus. 12mo

AAS, B, BA, BP, H, LC, LCP, N, NYP, UC, UP, Y

1871 ———— White-Jacket; or, The World in a Man-of-War . . . New York: Harper & Brothers, 1850. 465 p. 12mo   AAS, B, BA

BP, H, HEH, HM, IN, LC, LCP, N, NYP, NYS, UC, UM, UP, UV, Y

1872 MELVILLE, J., *pseud.* The Buckskin; or, The Camp of the Besiegers. A Tale of the Revolution, by the Author of "Ethan Allen," "Master of Langford," "Fatal Legacy" . . . [anon.]. New York: William H. Graham, 1847. 98 p. 8vo

AAS, B, HEH, LC, N, NYP, UC, UP, Y

Printed in double cols.
It has been determined that J. Melville was the pseudonym of Josiah A. Fraetas. See Nos. 1006a-b for new titles entered under his name.

1873 ———— Ethan Allen; or, The King's Men. An Historical Novel, by the Author of "The Master of Langford" . . . [anon.]. New York: William H. Graham, 1846. 108 p. 8vo

AAS, HEH, UP, Y

Printed in double cols.
Written by Josiah A. Fraetas.

1874 ——— The Master of Langford; or, The Treacherous Guest. A Tale of Passion . . . New York: William H. Graham, 1845. 100 p. 8vo   HEH, Y
Printed in double cols.
Written by Josiah A. Fraetas.

1875 MEMOIRS OF ALCOHOL. Written by Himself. Including Biographical Sketches of His Sons Brandy, Rum, and Whiskey, and of His Daughter Gin. Hartford: Robinson & Pratt, 1834. 36 p. 12mo   H, Y

1875a THE MEMOIRS OF LAFITTE; or, The Barritarian Pirate. A Narrative Founded on Fact. Providence, R.I.: William S. Spear, 1826. 125 p., illus. 18mo   AAS, Y
G. H. Orians notes a New York: J. M. Danforth, 1828 ed., in *American Literature*, IX (1937-38), 352, with the above title.
For later eds. see Nos. 1598-1602.

MERRICK, S. C., *pseud.* See Burleigh, George Shepard

1876 METCALFE, M. CHRISTINA. Eldorus, the Prince of Rovers; or, The Venetian Minstrel's Prophecy. A Tale of Venice, the Forest, and the Sea . . . Boston: F. Gleason, 1850. 100 p., illus. 8vo   AAS, B
Printed in double cols.

1877 THE METEOR; or, The Cutter of the Ocean. A Sea Story of the Days of '76. By an Old Salt. New York: William B. Smith & Co., 1847. 99 p. 8vo   AAS, NYH, Y

MILFORD, EVA. The Monks of St. Nicholas the Old. *In* J. H. Robinson, Angela (1850), No. 2128.

1878 MILLS, HELEN P. Francisco Gerardo; or, The Pirate's Lieutenant . . . Boston: Star Spangled Banner office [1850]. 100 p., illus. 8vo   AAS, Y
Also contains: Rinaldo, the Terrible—Harry Halyard's Ruin. A True Tale for the Intemperate to Read, by Ned Buntline [pseud.].
Cover imprint: "Boston: Jones's publishing House; New York: H. Long & Brother; Detroit: P. Homans, 1850."

1878a MIRANDA; or, The Discovery. A Tale. To Which Are Added, Chariessa; or, A Pattern for Her Sex. Also, an Original Story, Founded on a Fact. Being a Pleasing Companion for Young Gentlemen and Ladies. Norwich [Ct.]: Printed by J. Trumbull, 1800. 108 p. 12mo   AAS, HEH, Y
Sig. B canceled but no loss of text.

1879   MISS ELIZA ROSSELL.   A Tale of the Unfortunate Female.   Written by a Friend.   Boston: Z. D. Montague, 1845.   36 p., illus. 8vo   AAS, B, BP, HEH, N, NYP, Y
LC has a title page, deposited Dec. 11, 1844.

1880   MITCHELL, AGNES (WOODS).   The Smuggler's Son, and Other Tales and Sketches . . .   By A. W. M.   Philadelphia: Herman Hooker, 1842.   300 p.   12mo   AAS, B, HEH, N, NYP, UP, Y
Contains: The Bride of Hawthorn Glen—A Covert from the Tempest—Frederic Gordon—Anna Gray—The Heiress.

1881   MITCHELL, DONALD GRANT.   A Bachelor's Reverie . . .   By Ik Marvel [pseud.].   Wormsloe [Ga.], 1850.   40 p.   4to
H, NYP, Y

1882   ———   The Lorgnette; or, Studies of the Town by an Opera Goer [anon.].   New York, 1850.   24 nos.   12mo
AAS(1,7,11-14,18,20), H, HEH, NYH, UP, Y
Imprint, Nos. 1-13: Henry Kernot; Nos. 14-24: Stringer & Townsend.

1883   ——— ———   2d ed.   New York: Stringer and Townsend [1850].   2 vols., illus.   12mo
AAS, BA, BP, H, HEH, LC, LCP, N, NYP, NYS, UC, UM, UP, Y

1884   ——— ———   3d ed.   New York: Stringer and Townsend [1850].   2 vols.   12mo
AAS(V.2), LCP(V.2), UM(V.2), Y(V.2)

1885   ———   Reveries of a Bachelor; or, A Book of the Heart.   By Ik Marvel [pseud.] . . .   New York: Baker & Scribner, 1850.   298 p., illus.   12mo
AAS, BP, CLS, H, HEH, IN, LC, LCP, N, NYP, NYS, UP, UV, Y

MITCHELL, ISAAC.   Alonzo and Melissa.   *See* The Asylum; or, Alonzo and Melissa, No. 1886.
Edward B. Reed's letter to the *Nation*, Dec. 8, 1904, p. 458, discusses the authorship of *Alonzo.*

1886   ———   The Asylum; or, Alonzo and Melissa.   An American Tale, Founded on Fact . . .   Poughkeepsie: Joseph Nelson, 1811.   2 vols., illus.   12mo
AAS, B, BP, H, HEH, IN, LC, N, NYH, NYP, NYS, UC, UP, UV, Y
Later eds. appeared with Daniel Jackson, Jr., as the author.
Connecticut and Long Island Sound; 1760-85.

1887 —————— ————— Plattsburgh, N.Y.: Printed for the proprietor, 1811. 218 p. 8vo   AAS, B, HEH, IN, LC, N, UP, Y
Title reads: *A Short Account of the Courtship of Alonzo & Melissa.*
Some copies have "By Daniel Jackson, Jun." stamped or printed on the title page.

1888 —————— ————— Brattleboro: Holbrook and Fessenden, 1824. 240 p. 12mo   AAS, B, H, HEH, LC, N, Y
Title of this ed. and all of the following eds. reads: *Alonzo and Melissa.*

1889 DELETE.

1890 —————— ————— Exeter: Abel Brown, 1828. 240 p. 12mo
AAS, B, BP, HEH, LCP, UC, Y

1891 —————— ————— Philadelphia: Abel Brown, 1830. 256 p. 16mo
AAS, BP, H, IN, LC, UP, Y

1892 —————— ————— [Exeter]: A. R. Brown, 1830. 256 p. 16mo
AAS, HEH, NYP, Y

1893 —————— ————— Castleton, Vt.: Printed and published by George Collingwood Smith, 1831. 254 p. 24mo   AAS, LC, Y

1894 —————— ————— Concord: Luther Roby, 1831. 253 p. 24mo
AAS, Y

1895 —————— ————— Exeter: A. R. Brown, 1831. 256 p. 16mo
AAS, B, BP, HEH, IN, UC, UV, Y

1896 —————— ————— Sandbornton: D. V. Moulton, 1832. 253 p. 24mo   AAS, B, BP, HEH, N, UC, UM, UP, Y

1897 —————— ————— Boston: Published at the Water Street Bookstore, 1833. 256 p. 12mo   AAS, HEH, Y

1897a —————— ————— Sandbornton, 1834. 253 p. 24mo   HEH

1898 —————— ————— Sandbornton, 1835. 253 p. 24mo
AAS, LCP, UP, Y

1899 —————— ————— Sandbornton, 1836. 253 p. 24mo
AAS, B, BP, HEH, NYP, NYS, Y

1900 —————— ————— Boston: Charles Gaylord, 1836. 187 p., illus. 12mo   AAS, NYP, Y

1901 —————— ————— Portland, 1837. 141 p., illus. 12mo   AAS, Y

1902 —————— ————— Boston: E. Littlefield, 1839. 256 p. 16mo
AAS, B, BA, Y

1903 —————— ————— Sandbornton, N.H.: Charles Lane, 1839. 253 p.
24mo AAS, UC, UP, Y

1904 —————— ————— Boston: Lewis & Sampson, 1842. 256 p. 16mo
AAS, B, IN, Y

1905 —————— ————— Hartford: S. Andrus and Son, 1844. 253 p.
24mo AAS

1906 —————— ————— Hartford: S. Andrus and Son, 1846. 253 p.
24mo AAS, HEH, Y

1906a —————— ————— Boston: Phillips & Sampson, 1847. 256 p. 12mo
AAS, Y

1907 —————— ————— Waterford: Williams & Co., 1848. 187 p., illus.
12mo AAS, NYP, Y

1907a —————— ————— Hartford: S. Andrus and Son, 1849. 253 p.
24mo HEH

1908 —————— ————— New York: Nafis & Cornish [n.d.]. 250 p.
16mo AAS, B, NYP, Y

1909 —————— ————— New York: Richard Marsh, No. 374 Pearl Street
[n.d.]. 250 p. 16mo   AAS, B, BP, HEH, IN, Y
HEH copy in original binding issued with No. 21.

————— A Short Account of the Courtship of Alonzo & Melissa.
See No. 1887

1909a THE MODERATE DRINKER. By a Friend of Temperance. Boston:
Ford and Damrell, 1834. 31 p. 16mo   AAS, UV

1910 MOODY, RICHARD. Otiska; or, The First and the Last Love . . .
[anon.]. Rochester, 1832. 123 p. 16mo   HEH, NYH
Western New York.

1911 MOORE, HORATIO NEWTON. Fitzgerald and Hopkins; or, Scenes
and Adventures in Theatrical Life . . . Philadelphia: S. G.
Sherman, 1847. 166 p., illus. 8vo   BA, BP, H, LC

1912 ————— Mary Morris and Other Tales . . . Philadelphia: G. B.
Zieber and Co., 1845. 161 p. 12mo   UC, Y
Also contains: Theodore and Julia—Samuel Q. Johnson.

249

1913 MOORE, JOHN MCDERMOTT. The Adventures of Tom Stapleton; or, 202 Broadway ... New York: W. F. Burgess, 1850. 120 p., illus. 8vo   AAS, HEH, NYP, Y
Printed in double cols.

1914 —— Lord Nial: A Romance ... By J. M. M. .... New York: John Doyle, 1834. 276 p. 12mo AAS, BP, HEH, N, UP, Y
First 24 p. a prose tale.

MORAGNE, MARY ELIZABETH. *See* Davis, Mary Elizabeth (Moragne)

1915 MORELAND VALE; or, The Fair Fugitive. By a Lady of the State of New York, Author of Henry Villars. New York: Printed by L. Nichols & Co., 1801. 184 p. 12mo
AAS, B, BP, H, HEH, IN, N, NYP, UP, UV, Y
New York State.

1916 —— Newark: Printed by J. Wallis, 1805. 200 p. 12mo
LC, UC, Y

MORGAN, JANE, *pseud. See* Cooper, James Fenimore

MORGAN, MRS. L. F. *See* Morgan, Susan Rigby (Dallam)

1917 MORGAN, SUSAN RIGBY (DALLAM). The Haunting Shadow, by Mrs. L. F. Morgan ... Baltimore: Cushing and Brother, 1848. 180 p. 12mo   B

1918 —— The Polish Orphan; or, Vicissitudes ... [anon.]. Baltimore: Armstrong & Berry, 1838. 2 vols. 12mo   B, HEH, Y

1919 —— The Swiss Heiress; or, The Bride of Destiny ... [anon.]. Baltimore: J. Robinson, 1836. 2 vols. 12mo
AAS, B, HEH, IN, NYP, UP, UV, Y

1920 MORGANIANA; or, The Wonderful Life and Terrible Death of Morgan. Written by Himself. Illustrated with Gritholaphic Plates, by Hassan Straightshanks, Turkey. First American Edition, Translated from the Original Arabic Manuscript. By Baron Munchausen, Jr. ... Boston: Printed and published by the proprietors, 1828. 92 p., illus. 8vo AAS, HEH, LC, Y

1921 MORRIS, GEORGE POPE. The Little Frenchman and His Water Lots, with Other Sketches of the Times ... Philadelphia: Lea & Blanchard, 1839. 155 p., illus. 12mo
AAS, BP, H, HEH, IN, LC, N, NYH, NYP, UC, UM, UP, Y

Also contains: The Monopoly and the People's Line—Letters from the Springs—A Letter and a Poem—Leaves from an Editor's Portfolio—Mr. Beverley Lee; or, The Days of the Shin-plasters.

————— Sketches from the Springs. *In* The Atlantic Club-Book (1834), Nos. 195-196.

1922 MORRISON, JOHN B. An Original Tale: Isabella of Brooke, Contrasting the Manners and Customs of the Early Settlers of Pennsylvania and Virginia with the Polished Refinements of the Present Age . . . By a Pennsylvanian [anon.]. Pittsburgh: Published by the author, 1830. 118 p. 12mo AAS, NYP, UPI, Y

1923 MORTIMER, CHARLOTTE B. Morton Montagu; or, A Young Christian's Choice. A Narrative Founded on Facts in the Early History of a Deceased Moravian Missionary Clergyman . . . New York: D. Appleton & Company, 1850. 255 p. 12mo
AAS, BA, BP, H, HEH, LC, N, NYP, UP, Y

1924 MORTON: A Tale of the Revolution . . . Cincinnati: Printed and published by Hatch, Nichols and Buxton, 1828. 331 p. 12mo
LC, NYP

1925 THE MORTON FAMILY. By a Young Lady. Boston: James Munroe and Company, 1845. 71 p. 8vo   AAS, HEH, UP, UV, Y
LC has a title page, deposited Dec. 27, 1844.

1926 MOTLEY, JOHN LOTHROP. Merry-mount: A Romance of the Massachusetts Colony . . . [anon.]. Boston and Cambridge: James Munroe and Company, 1849. 2 vols. 12mo
AAS, B, BA, BP, H, HEH, IN, LC, N, NYP, UC, UM, UP, UV, Y
HEH has page proofs of the title page of Vol. I, dated 1848, and the text of both vols.

1927 ————— Morton's Hope; or, The Memoirs of a Provincial . . . [anon.]. New York: Harper & Brothers, 1839. 2 vols. 12mo
AAS, B, BA, BP, H, HEH, IN, LC, LCP, N, NYP, NYS, UC, UP, UV, Y
Massachusetts and Europe; last quarter of 18th cent.

MOULTON, MARY. A Simple Sketch of Simple Things. *In* J. S. Appleton, *ed.*, Voices from the Kenduskeag (1848), No. 39.

1927a MT. HOLYOKE; or, The Travels of Henry and Maria. A Tale. Amherst, Mass.: J. S. and C. Adams, and S. C. Carter, 1828. 70 p. 24mo   BP, NYP

Mowatt, Anna Cora (Ogden). *See* Ritchie, Anna Cora (Ogden) Mowatt

1927b Munroe, Charlotte (Bellamy). Is It a Small Thing? or, Individual Reform. By Mrs. N. T. Munroe. Boston: Abel Tompkins, 1847. 146 p. 12mo   AAS, HEH

1927c ———— ———— Boston: Abel Tompkins, 1849. 146 p. 12mo
             AAS

Murgatroyd, Matthew, *pseud*. *See* Jones, James Athearn

1928 Murphy, Francis, *comp.* Tales of an Evening. Founded on Facts . . . Norristown [Pa.]: Printed by J. Winnard, 1815. 143 p. 12mo   AAS, LC, LCP, NYP, Y
Contents: The Beautiful Alcade of Gadara—Fame and Pleasure—The Misanthrope—The Trials and Triumphs of Friendship—The Dreamer—The Jack Boots; or, Covetousness Its Own Punishment—Historical Scrap.

1929 Murphy, John S. The Somerby Family: A Total Abstinence Tale . . . Boston: Theodore Abbot, 1843. 115 p. 8vo H, HEH

Murray, *Lieut.*, *pseud.* *See* Ballou, Maturin Murray

1930 Murray, W. W. Isadore; or, The Captives of the Norridgwocks. A Tale of Real Life . . . Boston: J. Carrick, 1846. 37 p., illus. 8vo   AAS, HEH, NYP, Y
Cover imprint dated 1847.
Printed in double cols.
New Hampshire; early 18th cent.

1931 ———— Robert and Jane; or, The Village Dress-maker, and the Rejected Son Restored. A Tale of Real Life . . . Lowell: H. P. Huntoon, 1849. Cover title, 31 p., illus. 8vo   AAS, HEH

1931a My Native Village: Sketches from Real Life, Designed to Aid the Temperance Cause. New York: Dayton and Saxton, 1841. 209 p. 12mo   HEH
Of Quaker interest.

1932 Myers, Peter Hamilton. Ellen Welles; or, The Siege of Fort Stanwix. A Tale of the Revolution [anon.]. Rome [N.Y.]: W. O. M'Clure, 1848. 48 p. 8vo   Y

1933 ———— The First of the Knickerbockers: A Tale of 1673 . . . [anon.]. New York: George P. Putnam, 1848. 221 p. 12mo
AAS, B, BA, BP, H, HEH, IN, LC, LCP, N, NYH, NYP, NYS, UC, UM, UP, UV, Y

1934 ——— ——— 2d ed. New York: George P. Putnam, 1849. 222
p. 12mo   AAS, H, IN, LC, NYH, NYP, UC, Y
Sabin 51636 notes an 1850 ed.

1935 ——— The King of the Hurons . . . [anon.]. New York:
George P. Putnam, 1850. 319 p. 12mo
AAS, B, BP, H, HEH, LC, LCP, N, NYH, NYP, UC, UM, UP, Y
Early 18th cent.

1936 ——— The Young Patroon; or, Christmas in 1690. A Tale of
New York . . . [anon.]. New York: George P. Putnam, 1849.
142 p. 12mo
AAS, B, BA, BP, H, HEH, IN, LC, N, NYH, NYP, UC, UM, UP, Y

MYRTHE, A. T., *pseud. See* Ganilh, Anthony

1937 THE MYSTERIES OF NASHUA; or, Revenge Punished and Constancy
Rewarded . . . Nashua: C. T. Gill, 1844. 40 p., illus. 8vo
H, LC, NYP, Y
Printed in double cols.

1938 MYSTERIES OF NEW YORK. Boston: Published at the "Yankee"
office, 1845. Cover title, 64 p., illus. 8vo   AAS, BP, HEH, Y

1939 MYSTERIES OF PHILADELPHIA; or, Scenes of Real Life in the Quaker
City . . . By an Old Amateur. Philadelphia, 1848. 80 p. 8vo
H, Y

1940 NACK, JAMES. Earl Rupert, and Other Tales and Poems . . .
With a Memoir of the Author, by P. M. Wetmore. New York:
George Adlard, 1839. 220 p. 12mo
AAS, B, BP, H, HEH, IN, LC, N, NYH, NYP, NYS, UC, UM, UP, Y
Contains: My Cousin; or, The Amusements of a Rainy Day.

——— Keeping It Up. *In* T. S. Arthur, Our Children (1849),
No. 133a.

——— The Problem. *In* T. S. Arthur, Our Children (1849),
No. 133a.

1941 NAHANT; or, "The Floure of Souvenance." Philadelphia: H. C.
Carey and I. Lea, 1827. 31 p. 8vo
AAS, B, BP, H, HEH, LC, UC, Y
Written by Jeanette M. Hart.
Atlantic Coast.

1941a NALE, JIM, *Gent., pseud.* Fimbleton Fumbleton, Esq.; or, The
Nobleman Incog. A Mixtum, Catherun, Omnium, in Twenty
Chapters of Foolscap. By "Jim Nale, Gent." [pseud.], Author
of Nothing. Hanover, Pa.: Printed by Joseph S. Gitt, 1844.
266, 6 p. 8vo   UV
Philadelphia.

1942 NARRATIVE AND CONFESSIONS of Lucretia P. Cannon, Who Was
Tried, Convicted, and Sentenced to Be Hung at Georgetown,
Delaware, with Her Two Accomplices. Containing an Ac-
count of Some of the Most Horrible and Shocking Murders . . .
Ever Committed by One of the Female Sex. New York:
Printed for the publishers, 1841. 24 p., illus. 8vo
                                    AAS, H, HEH, LC, NYH, NYP, UM

NEAL, ALICE B. *See* Haven, Alice Emily (Bradley) Neal

1943 NEAL, JOHN. Authorship: A Tale . . . [anon.]. Boston: Gray
and Bowen, 1830. 267 p. 12mo
                    AAS, B, BP, H, HEH, HM, IN, LC, N, NYP, UC, UM, UP, UV, Y
England.

1944 ——— The Down-Easters . . . New York: Harper & Brothers,
1833. 2 vols. 12mo
            AAS, B, BP, H, HEH, IN, LC, N, NYH, NYP, UC, UM, UP, UV, Y

1945 ——— Errata; or, The Works of Will. Adams . . . [anon.]. New
York: Published for the proprietors, 1823. 2 vols. 12mo
            AAS, B, H, HEH, LC, N, NYP, NYS, UM, UP, UV(V.2), Y
Massachusetts; contemporary.

1946 ——— Keep Cool: A Novel. Written in Hot Weather, by
Somebody, M.D.C. [pseud.] . . . Baltimore: Joseph Cushing,
1817. 2 vols. 12mo   H, HEH, IN, LC, LCP, NYP, NYS, UP, UV, Y
New York City; contemporary.

1947 ——— Logan: A Family History . . . [anon.]. Philadelphia:
H. C. Carey & I. Lea, 1822. 2 vols. 12mo
                    AAS, B, H, IN, LC, NYH, NYP, UP, UV, Y
Colonial period.

1948 ——— Rachel Dyer: A North American Story . . . Portland:
Shirley and Hyde, 1828. 276 p. 12mo
            AAS, B, BA, BP, H, HEH, IN, LC, N, NYH, NYP, UC, UM, UP, UV, Y
Salem; late 17th cent.

1949 —— Randolph: A Novel . . . [anon.]. [Baltimore?]: Published for whom it may concern, 1823. 2 vols. 12mo
AAS, H, HEH, IN, LC, NYP, NYS, UP, UV, Y
Written in a series of letters.

1950 —— Seventy-six . . . [anon.]. Baltimore: Joseph Robinson, 1823. 2 vols. 12mo
B, H, HEH, IN, LC, UP, UV, Y

1951 NEAL, JOSEPH CLAY. Charcoal Sketches; or, Scenes in a Metropolis . . . Philadelphia: E. L. Carey and A. Hart, 1838. 222 p., illus. 12mo
AAS, BP, HEH, LC, N, NYP, UP, UV, Y

1952 —— —— 2d ed. Philadelphia: E. L. Carey and A. Hart, 1838. 222 p., illus. 12mo
AAS, IN, NYH, UC, UP, Y

1953 —— —— 3d ed. Philadelphia: E. L. Carey and A. Hart, 1839. 222 p., illus. 12mo
UP, Y

1954 —— —— 4th ed. Philadelphia: E. L. Carey and A. Hart, 1839. 222 p., illus. 12mo
AAS, HEH, IN, UM, UP, Y

1955 —— —— 5th ed. Philadelphia: E. L. Carey and A. Hart, 1840. 222 p., illus. 12mo
AAS, HM, Y

1956 —— —— 6th ed. Philadelphia: E. L. Carey and A. Hart, 1841. 222 p., illus. 12mo
AAS, BP, LC, Y

1957 —— —— Philadelphia: Carey & Hart, 1843. 222 p., illus. 12mo
AAS, B, H, NYS, UPI, Y

1958 —— —— Philadelphia: Carey & Hart, 1844. 222 p., illus. 12mo
AAS, LCP, Y

1959 —— —— Philadelphia: Carey & Hart, 1845. 222 p., illus. 12mo
AAS, NYH, Y

1959a —— —— Philadelphia: Carey & Hart, 1846. 222 p., illus. 12mo
AAS, Y

1959b —— —— New York: Stringer and Townsend, 1849. 222 p., illus. 12mo
AAS, HEH

1960 —— —— 2d Ser. New York: Burgess, Stringer & Company, 1848. 192 p., illus. 8vo
AAS, BP, N, NYP, UC, UP, Y

1961 —— —— 2d Ser. New York: Stringer and Townsend, 1850. 192 p., illus. 8vo
AAS, HEH, Y

1962 —— Peter Ploddy and Other Oddities . . . Philadelphia: Carey & Hart, 1844. 181 p., illus. 12mo
AAS, B, BP, H, HEH, IN, LC, LCP, N, NYH, UP, UV, Y
Contents: Peter Ploddy's Dream—The Black Maria—Slyder Downehylle—Highways and Holidays—The Newsboy—Gossip about Gossiping—Shiverton Shakes—The Boys That Run with the Engine—Jack Spratt's Revenge—Corner Loungers.

NELSON, S. The Rescued Maiden. *In* O. Bradbury, Isabelle (1848), No. 380.

THE NEW PYGMALION: A Novel. To Which Is Added: Amelia; or, The Faithless Briton . . . Northampton: Printed by Andrew Wright, 1798.
Issued with *A Collection of Moral . . . Stories* (1798), No. 563.

1963 NEWELL, CHARLES MARTIN. The Cruise of the Graceful; or, The Robbers of Carraccas. By Captain Barnacle, U.S.N. [pseud.]. Boston: "Star Spangled Banner" office, 1847. 50 p., illus. 8vo
AAS, B, H, Y
At head of title: "$100 Prize Tale."
Printed in double cols.

—— The Fair and the Brave: A Sea Tale. *In* J. Jones, The Belle of Boston (1849), No. 1483.

—— A Sailor's Love; or, The Dangers of the Sea. *In* M. A. Clough, Paolina (1849), No. 552.

1963a THE NEWEST KEEPSAKE for 1840. Containing the Best Account of the March of Mind. Together with the Speeches, Circumstances and Doings of the Trundle-Bed Convention, in Session at the Marlboro Chapel, January 8, 1840. Norwch [sic]: M. B. Young, 1840. 207 p. 12mo HEH
Verso of title page: "S. Adams, printer, 59 Gold-St. New-York."
This is a satire, not an annual.

1964 NICHOLS, MARY SARGEANT (NEAL) GOVE. Agnes Morris; or, The Heroine of Domestic Life . . . [anon.]. New York: Harper & Brothers, 1849. 143 p. 12mo AAS, B, LC, UP, Y
New England.

1965 —— The Two Loves; or, Eros and Anteros . . . [anon.]. New York: Stringer and Townsend, 1849. 112 p. 8vo AAS, NYP, Y
Printed in double cols.

1965a —— Uncle John; or, "It Is Too Much Trouble." By Mary Orme [pseud.] ... New York: Harper & Brothers, 1846. 179 p. 12mo   AAS, N, NYP, UV, Y
Manners and morals; Massachusetts.

1966 NICHOLS, THOMAS LOW. Ellen Ramsay; or, The Adventures of a Greenhorn, in Town and Country ... New York: For sale by booksellers, 1843. 61 p., illus. 8vo   AAS, HEH, Y
At head of title: "Stories of American Life. Nichols's Monthly Series—Number One."
Printed in double cols.
New York City; contemporary.

1967 —— The Lady in Black: A Story of New York Life, Morals, and Manners... New York: Sold by the principal booksellers, 1844. 44 p. 8vo   AAS, BP, HEH, N, Y
Printed in double cols.

1968 —— Raffle for a Wife ... New York: Burgess, Stringer & Co., 1845. 72 p. 12mo   H, UP, Y
New York City; contemporary.

1969 NICK BIGELOW, and the Female Burglar, and Other Leaves from a Lawyer's Diary ... New York: Burgess, Stringer and Company, 1846. 88 p., illus. 8vo   AAS, B, BP, H, Y
Contents: A City Scene—The Loafer's Story—Darius Touchitt—The Mechanic's Daughter—Nick Bigelow—The Last Will of Robert Selden—Luke Merton; or, The Game of Roulette—The Divorce—Peggy Foster, the Attorney General—My Fellow Student—The Proscribed—Bess Bradshaw, the Female Burglar.

NOLAND, CHARLES FENTON MERCER. Jones's Fight: A Story of Kentucky, by an Alabamian. In W. T. Porter, ed., The Big Bear of Arkansas, and Other Sketches (1845), Nos. 2061-62.

—— Old Sense, of Arkansas. By "N" of That Ilk. In W. T. Porter, ed., The Big Bear of Arkansas, and Other Sketches (1845), Nos. 2061-62.

—— A Quarter Race in Kentucky. In W. T. Porter, ed., A Quarter Race in Kentucky, and Other Sketches (1847), Nos. 2063-64.

1970 NORVEL HASTINGS; or, The Frigate in the Offing. A Nautical Tale of the War of 1812. By a Distinguished Novelist ... Philadelphia: A. Hart, 1850. 143 p. 12mo   HEH, LC, Y

1971 NOTT, HENRY JUNIUS. Novellettes of a Traveller; or, Odds and Ends from the Knapsack of Thomas Singularity [pseud.] ... Edited by Henry Junius Nott ... New York: Harper & Brothers, 1834. 2 vols. 12mo

AAS, B, CLS, H, LC, N, NYH, NYP, NYS, UM, UP, Y

Contents: Biographical Sketch of Thomas Singularity—The Andalusian Rope-dancer—The Solitary—Cock Robin—The Shipwreck—The Counterfeiters—The French Officer.

1972 NOURSE, JAMES. Uncle Hugh; or, "Twenty Years Ago." A Temperance Story ... Philadelphia: T. E. Chapman, 1841. 122 p. 12mo

AAS, LC

1973 NOURSE, JAMES DUNCAN. The Forest Knight; or, Early Times in Kentucky ... New York: E. Ferrett, 1846. 86 p. 8vo H
Printed in double cols.

1974 —— Levenworth: A Story of the Mississippi and the Prairies ... Louisville: Geo. W. Noble, 1848. 143 p. 8vo H, LC, Y

NUGATOR, *pseud.* See Carter, St. Leger Landon

1974a NUNES, JOSEPH A. Aristocracy; or, Life in the City. By a Member of the Philadelphia Bar ... [anon.]. Philadelphia: S. G. Sherman, No. 3, Hart's Building, Sixth Street, 2d door above Chesnut [cop. 1848]. 2 vols. in 1. 8vo AAS, HEH, UV
Paged continuously (256 p.).
Printed in double cols.

1975 —— —— Philadelphia: T. B. Peterson, No. 98 Chesnut Street [cop. 1848]. 2 vols. in 1. 8vo BP, HM, LC, UP, Y
Title reads: *Aristocracy; or, Life among the "Upper Ten." A True Novel Founded on the Fashionable Society of Philadelphia.*
Paged continuously (256 p.).
Printed in double cols.

1976 OAKLEY, E. Eliza Atwood; or, The Resemblance. An Authentic Tale ... New York: Samuel Raynor, 1848. 163 p. 12mo

AAS, N, NYP, Y

LC has a title page, deposited June 11, 1848.

OAKWOOD, OLIVER, *pseud.* See Potts, Stacy Gardner

1977 O'FLARRITY, PADDY, *pseud.* The Life of Paddy O'Flarrity, Who, from a Shoe Black, Has by Perseverance and Good Conduct Arrived to a Member of Congress ... Written by Himself. [Washington, D.C.], 1834. 56 p. 12mo AAS, LC
Cover title: "A Spur to Youth; or, Davy Crockett Beaten."

1978 OLD FORT DUQUESNE: A Tale of the Early Toils, Struggles and Adventures of the First Settlers at the Forks of the Ohio, 1754 . . . Pittsburgh: Cook's Literary Depot, 1844. 79 p. 8vo

AAS, H, HEH, LC, NYP, Y

Cover imprint: "Philadelphia: R. G. Berford, 1844."
Printed in double cols.

1979 OLD FRIENDS. A Remembrancer of Beloved Companions, and Years Bygone . . . New York: Bliss, Wadsworth and Co., 1835. 327 p. 12mo

H, LC, Y

OLD 'UN, *pseud.* *See* Durivage, Francis Alexander

OLDSTYLE, JONATHAN, *Gent., pseud.* *See* Irving, Washington

1980 OLIVER, SAMUEL CLARKE. Onslow; or, The Protégé of an Enthusiast. An Historical Traditionary Tale of the South. By a Gentleman of Alabama . . . [anon.]. Philadelphia: G. B. Zieber & Co., 1844. 222 p. 8vo

HEH, UP, UV, Y

Printed in double cols.

OLIVIA, *pseud.* *See* Briggs, Emily Edson

ONESIMUS, *Captain, pseud.* *See* Hewson, John

1981 ORAN, the Outcast; or, A Season in New York . . . New York: Peabody & Co., 1833. 2 vols. 12mo

IN, LC, N, NYH, NYP, UC, UP, UV, Y

Written by Charles James Cannon.

ORME, MARY, *pseud.* *See* Nichols, Mary Sargeant (Neal) Gove

1982 ORMSBY, AUGUSTUS B. F. Will Brockman; or, The Smugglers. A Tale by a Country Curate. To Which Is Added: The Murder in the Wilderness . . . [anon.]. Syracuse: A. B. F. Ormsby, 1846. 37 p. 8vo

The Union Catalogue at LC locates a copy in the University of Syracuse Library.
LC has a title page, deposited July 4, 1846.

1983 THE ORPHAN SEAMSTRESS: A Narrative of Innocence, Guilt, Mystery, and Crime. New York: W. F. Burgess, 1850. 72 p., illus. 8vo

HEH, Y

Printed in double cols.

1983a THE ORPHAN STRANGER: A Tale for the Lyceum Fair . . . Cambridge: Metcalf, Torry and Ballou, 1839. 94 p. 12mo

AAS, BP, H, HEH, Y

New England, France, England.

1984 THE ORPHANS: An American Tale. Addressed Chiefly to the Young. New York: Collins & Hannay, 1825. 123 p. 12mo

AAS, B, H, HEH, N, UC, UM, UP, Y

1984a ORR, MRS. NATHANIEL. The Belle Heiress. By Mrs. N. Orr, of N. J. Written Expressly for Charles S. Brown of Oswego, N. Y. Auburn: Printed by Henry Oliphant, 1849. 89 p. 8vo

AAS, H, HEH

ORTON, J. T. Doctor Gray and His Daughter. *In* The Fountain and the Bottle (1850), No. 996.

1985 OSBORN, LAUGHTON. Confessions of a Poet . . . [anon.]. Philadelphia: Carey, Lea & Blanchard, 1835. 2 vols. 12mo

AAS, B, BP, H, IN, LC, N, NYH, NYP, UP, Y

England.

1986 ———— The Dream of Alla-Ad-Deen. From the Romance of "Anastasia," by Charles Erskine White, D.D. [pseud.]. New York: S. White, 1838. 32 p. 8vo NYP

W. Cushing, *Initials and Pseudonyms* [1885], notes an 1831 ed.

1987 ———— Sixty Years of the Life of Jeremy Levis . . . [anon.]. New York: G. & C. & H. Carvill, 1831. 2 vols. 12mo

AAS, B, BA, BP, H, HEH, IN, LC, N, NYH, NYP, UC, UP, UPI, Y

Late 18th cent.

OUDENARDE, DOMINIE NICHOLAS AEGIDIUS, *pseud. See* Paulding, James Kirke

P., C. A., *of Kentucky*. A Millerite Miracle. *In* W. T. Porter, *ed.*, A Quarter Race in Kentucky (1847), Nos. 2063-64.

PACKARD, CLARISSA, *pseud. See* Gilman, Caroline (Howard)

1988 PANOLA; or, The Indian Sisters. Scenes in Forest Life. New York: W. F. Burgess, 1849. 96 p. 8vo UC

Printed in double cols.

Maine; late 17th cent.

1989 THE PARENT'S COUNSELLOR; or, The Dangers of Moroseness. A Narrative of the Newton Family. Philadelphia: E. Bacon, 1825. 188 p. 12mo   AAS, BP, H, LC
Rev. Benjamin Allen, attrib. au.

1990 PARKER, HENRY WEBSTER. Poems . . . Auburn: J. M. Alden, 1850. 238 p. 12mo   AAS, B, H, LC, N, NYH, NYP, UC, UM, UP, Y
Contains: Travels in a Dew-Drop—Von Blitzen's Experiment—Legend of the Lone Island.

1991 PARKER, JONATHAN T., *comp.* The American Legendary: Consisting of Original and Select Tales. Series I, Volume I . . . Rutland: Printed by E. Maxham, 1830. 298 p. 12mo
AAS, HEH, UP, UV, Y
Contents: The Haunted Fortress—Ingratitude, by E. C. Purdy—Henry and Caroline—Education—Henry Rosalvan—The Dream of Love, by Charles Ludlow—The Midnight Attack—The Dying Warrior—A Tale of Susquehanna—The Soldier's Son, by Mrs. Dumont—The Foraging Party—Emily: A Country Scene—The Wild Rose of the Valley—The Reclaimed, by the compiler—Theodore Harland, by Mrs. Dumont—The Strawberry Girl—The Pet Lamb—The Village Ball; or, Ella's Birthday—The Power of Woman—A Tale of Lake Erie, by George W. Thompson—Laurel Hill—The Blue Ribbon—The First Error—The Golden Chain, by O. Oakwood, pseud.—The Broken Vow—The Ringlet—Lucy Gay—The Noble Youth, by the compiler.

PARTICULAR, PERTINAX, *pseud.* *See* Watkins, Tobias

1992 THE PATRIOTIC SAILOR; or, Sketches of the Humors, Cares, and Adventures of Naval Life. By a Thoroughbred Seaman . . . Partially Founded on Facts . . . [anon.]. Baltimore: H. W. Bool, Jr., 1829. 2 vols. 12mo   AAS, IN, NYP

1993 PATTERSON, MRS. The Unfortunate Lovers and Cruel Parents: A Very Interesting Tale, Founded on Fact . . . Seventeenth Edition. Printed at Random, by T. Johnson & J. Callendar, 1797. 27 p. 12mo   H
Boston; late 18th cent.

1994 ——— ——— 18th ed. New Haven: Printed by Read & Morse, 1799. 23 p. 12mo   NYP, Y

1995 ——— ——— Springfield: Printed and sold by T. Ashley, 1800. 23 p. 12mo   AAS, B

1995a ——— ——— 18th ed. New York, 1803. 36 p. 12mo   B
PATTERSON, EDWARD HOWARD NORTON. Aztec Revelations (1849). *See* No. 215 for title entry which is now identified as by Patterson.

PATTERSON, ROBERT.   Old Singletire, the Man That Was Not Annexed.   *In* W. T. Porter, *ed.*, A Quarter Race in Kentucky (1847), Nos. 2063-64.

—— *jt. au.*   Stoke Stout of Louisiana.   *In* W. T. Porter, *ed.*, The Big Bear of Arkansas (1845), Nos. 2061-62.

1996   PAUL JONES: A Tale of the Sea.   By the Author of "Marion's Men," "Ernest Harcourt," "Eveline Trevor" . . .   Philadelphia: A. J. Rockafellar, 1843.   64 p.   8vo   AAS, HEH, NYP, UP, Y
Printed in double cols.

1997   PAULDING, JAMES KIRKE.   The Book of Saint Nicholas.   Translated from the Original Dutch of Dominie Nicholas Aegidius Oudenarde [pseud.].   New York: Harper & Brothers, 1836.   237 p.   12mo
AAS, B, BP, HEH, IN, LC, N, NYH, NYP, UM, UP, UV, Y
For contents see Herold; for collation see Wegelin's *Paulding.*

—— Childe Roeliff's Pilgrimage: A Travelling Legend.   *In* W. C. Bryant, *ed.*, Tales of Glauber-Spa (1832), Nos. 439-441.

1998   —— Chronicles of the City of Gotham . . . [anon.].   New York: G. & C. & H. Carvill, 1830.   270 p.   12mo
AAS, B, BP, H, HEH, IN, LC, LCP, N, NYH, NYP, NYS, UC, UP, UV, Y

1999   —— The Diverting History of John Bull and Brother Jonathan.   By Hector Bull-Us [pseud.].   New York: Inskeep & Bradford, 1812.   135 p.   12mo
AAS, B, BP, H, HEH, IN, LC, NYH, NYP, NYS, UP, UV, Y

2000   —— —— 2d ed.   New York: Inskeep & Bradford, 1813.   132 p., illus.   12mo   AAS, LC, N

2001   —— —— 3d ed.   Philadelphia: M. Carey & Son, 1819.   144 p., illus.   12mo   BP, Y

2002   —— —— 3d ed.   Philadelphia: Robert Desilver, 1827.   114 p., illus.   12mo   AAS, H, NYP, Y

2003   —— —— New York: Harper & Brothers, 1835.   193 p.   12mo   AAS, B, CLS, IN, LC, N, NYP, NYS, UC, UM, UP, Y
Also contains: The History of Uncle Sam and His Boys: A Tale for Politicians.

2004 ——— The Dutchman's Fireside ... [anon.]. New York: J. & J. Harper, 1831. 2 vols. 12mo
  AAS, B, BA, H, HEH, IN, LC, LCP(V.1), N, NYP, NYS, UM, UP, UV, Y
  At head of title: "Harper's Stereotype Edition."
  New York; mid-18th cent.

2005 ——— ——— New York: J. & J. Harper, 1831. 2 vols. 12mo
                  IN, N, UM, Y
  At head of title: "Third Edition."

2006 ——— ——— New York: J. & J. Harper, 1831. 2 vols. 12mo
                 LCP, NYP, UC, Y
  At head of title: "Fourth Edition."

2007 ——— ——— New York: J. & J. Harper, 1833. 2 vols. 12mo
                 AAS, HEH, HM
  At head of title: "Fourth Edition."

2008 ——— ——— 5th ed. New York: Harper & Brothers, 1837.
 2 vols. 12mo   AAS, LC, NYP, UP, Y
  Sabin 59196 notes an 1838 ed.

2009 ——— ——— 5th ed. New York: Harper & Brothers, 1845.
 2 vols. 12mo   BP, NYP

2010 ——— John Bull in America; or, The New Munchausen [anon.]. New York: Charles Wiley, 1825. 226 p. 12mo
  AAS, B, BP, HEH, IN, LC, N, NYP, NYS, UC, UM, UP, Y

2011 ——— ——— 2d ed. New York: Charles Wiley, 1825. 228 p.
 12mo   AAS, BA, BP, H, LCP, NYH, UC, Y

 ——— Jonathan's Visit to the Celestial Empire. *In* The Atlantic Club-Book (1834), Nos. 195-196.

 ——— Knickerbocker Hall; or, The Origin of the Baker's Dozen. *In* The Atlantic Club-Book (1834), Nos. 195-196.

2012 ——— Koningsmarke, the Long Finne: A Story of the New World ... [anon.]. New York: Charles Wiley, 1823. 2 vols.

 12mo   AAS, BP, H, HEH, IN, LC, LCP, NYP, UP, UV, Y
  Delaware; mid-17th cent.

2013 ——— ——— New York: Harper & Brothers, 1834-35. 2 vols.
 12mo   AAS, LC(V.2), LCP, N(V.1), Y

2014 —————— ——— New York: Harper & Brothers, 1836. 2 vols.
12mo   AAS, HEH(V.1), N(V.2), NYP, UC, UP, Y

2015 ——— ——— The Merry Tales of the Three Wise Men of Gotham ...
[anon.]. New York: G. & C. Carvill, 1826. 324 p. 12mo
    AAS, B, BA, BP, H, HEH, IN, LC, N, NYH, NYP, UC, UM, UP, Y
Contents: The Man Machine; or, The Pupil of "Circumstances"—Story of
the Second Wise Man of Gotham: The Perfection of Reason—Story of the
Third Wise Man of Gotham: The Perfection of Science.

2016 —————— ——— New York: Harper & Brothers, 1839. 236 p.
12mo   AAS, BP, H, HM, IN, LC, N, NYP, UC, UM, Y

2017 ——— The New Mirror for Travellers, and Guide to the
Springs. By an Amateur ... [anon.]. New York: G. & C.
Carvill, 1828. 292 p. 12mo
    AAS, B, BP, H, HEH, IN, LC, N, NYH, NYP, NYS, UC, UM, UP, Y

2018 ——— The Old Continental; or, The Price of Liberty ...
[anon.]. New York: Paine and Burgess, 1846. 2 vols. 12mo
    AAS, B, H, HEH, IN, LC, LCP, N, NYH, NYP, NYS, UC, UM, UP, UV, Y
New York; American Revolution.

2019 ——— The Puritan and His Daughter ... New York: Baker
and Scribner, 1849. 2 vols. 12mo
    AAS, B, BA, BP, H, HEH, IN, LC, LCP, N, NYP, NYS, UC, UM, UP, UV, Y
Virginia and New England; mid-17th cent.

2020 —————— ——— New York: Baker and Scribner, 1850. 2 vols.
12mo   AAS, B, NYP, Y

——— Selim, the Benefactor of Mankind. *In* W. C. Bryant,
ed., Tales of Glauber-Spa (1832), Nos. 439-441.

2021 ——— A Sketch of Old England, by a New-England Man ...
[anon.]. New York: Charles Wiley, 1822. 2 vols. 12mo
    AAS, B, BP, H, HEH, IN, LC, N, NYH, NYP, NYS, UC, UP, Y

2022 ——— Tales of the Good Woman. By a Doubtful Gentleman
... [anon.]. New York: G. & C. & H. Carvill, 1829. 367 p.
12mo   AAS, B, BA, BP, CLS, H, HEH, IN, LC, NYH, NYP, UP, UV, Y
Contains: The Yankee Roué—The Drunkard—Dyspepsy—Old Times in the
New World.

2023 —————— ——— New York: Harper & Brothers, 1836. 2 vols.
12mo   AAS, BP, LC, N, NYP, NYS(V.1), UC, UM, UP, Y

2024 —————— Westward Ho! . . . [anon.]. New York: Printed and published by J. & J. Harper, 1832. 2 vols. 12mo   AAS, B, BA, BP, H, HEH, IN, LC, LCP, N, NYH, NYP, NYS, UC, UM, UP, UV, Y
Kentucky frontier.

2025 ————— ————— New York: Printed by J. & J. Harper, 1833. 2 vols. 12mo   AAS, UP

2026 ————— ————— New York: Harper & Brothers, 1845. 2 vols. 12mo   NYP, Y

PAYNE, JOHN HOWARD. Benefactors. *In* The Atlantic Club-Book (1834), Nos. 195-196.

2027 PEABODY, ELIZABETH (PALMER). Holiness; or, The Legend of St. George. A Tale from Spencer's Faerie Queene, by a Mother [anon.]. Boston: E. R. Broaders, 1836. 182 p. 12mo   AAS, B, BA, BP, H, HEH, LC, N, NYP, UP, Y

2028 —————— The Water Spirit . . . [anon.]. Boston: Stimpson & Clapp, 1833.
Ed. from sales catalog.

2029 ————— ————— 2d ed. Boston: Stimpson & Clapp, 1833. 59 p. 12mo   H, N, NYP, UV, Y

2030 PECK, GEORGE WASHINGTON. Aurifodina; or, Adventures in the Gold Region. By Cantell A. Bigly [pseud.]. New York: Baker and Scribner, 1849. 103 p. 12mo   AAS, B, H, HEH, IN, LC, LCP, N, NYH, NYP, UC, UP, Y

2031 PEIRCE, ISAAC. The Narraganset Chief; or, The Adventures of a Wanderer. Written by Himself . . . [anon.]. New York: J. K. Porter, 1832. 195 p. 12mo   AAS, B, BP, IN, LC, N, NYP, UC, Y

2032 PENCHANT, PHILIP, *pseud.?* The Mysteries of Fitchburg, by Philip Penchant, Author of "White Lantern," "Spectre Horseman." Fitchburg: Charles Shepley, 1844. 28, [4] p. 8vo   AAS, Y

2033 PENCIL, MARK, *pseud.* The White Sulphur Papers; or, Life at the Springs of Western Virginia. By Mark Pencil [pseud.]. New York: Samuel Colman, 1839. 166 p. 12mo   AAS, BA, BP, H, HEH, IN, LC, N, NYH, NYP, UM, UP, Y
Contains: Journal of a Lady during the Season at the White Sulphur—The Story of a Crutch—Sketches of Character at the Springs.

PENFEATHER, AMABEL, *pseud.*　*See* Cooper, Susan Fenimore

PEPPERGRASS, PAUL, *pseud.*　*See* Boyce, John

PETERS, JEREMY, *pseud.*　*See* Smith, Thomas Lacy

2034　PETERSON, CHARLES JACOBS.　Agnes Courtenay: A Tale of the Old Dominion ... Amherst, Mass.: H. B. Nims, 1847. 35 p. 8vo
AAS

2035　────── The Algerine and Other Tales. By Harry Danforth [pseud.]. Boston: Gleason's Publishing Hall, 1846. 100 p. 8vo　　　　　　　　　　　　　　　　　　HEH, NYH, Y
Also contains: Paoli—The Wrecker—The Autumn Storm—The Host's Tale —Popping the Question—The Union Jack—The Meteor Career—Passing the Straits—The Widow's Loss—What Must Be Must—The Cousins.

2036　────── Cruising in the Last War ... Philadelphia: T. B. Peterson, No. 98 Chesnut Street [cop. 1850]. 2 pts. 8vo
AAS, B(pt.1), BP(pt. 1), H, IN, LCP(pt.1), N, UP, Y
Paged continuously (228 p.).
War of 1812.

2037　────── Grace Dudley; or, Arnold at Saratoga ... Philadelphia: T. B. Peterson, No. 98 Chesnut Street [cop. 1849]. 111 p., illus. 8vo　　　　　　　　　AAS, H, HEH, LC, N, NYP, UP, Y
Printed in double cols.

2038　────── The Oath of Marion. A Story of the Revolution ... Boston: F. Gleason, 1847. 50 p. 8vo　　　　　　AAS, Y

2039　────── The Valley Farm; or, The Autobiography of an Orphan. Edited by Charles J. Peterson ... Philadelphia: T. B. Peterson, No. 98 Chesnut Street [cop. 1850]. 104 p. 8vo
AAS, HEH, Y

2040　PHASES OF LIFE; or, The Mysteries of Catskill. In Two Volumes. Catskill: J. H. Van Gorden, 1845. 59 p. 8vo　　　　NYH
Vol. I only published?

2041　PHELPS, ALMIRA (HART) LINCOLN.　Ida Norman; or, Trials and Their Uses ... Baltimore: Cushing & Brother, 1848. 272 p. 12mo　　　　　　　　　　　AAS, HEH, LC, LCP, N, Y
New York City.

2042 PHILLIPS, JONAS B. Tales for Leisure Hours ... [anon.]. Philadelphia: Atkinson & Alexander, printers, 1827. 162 p. 12mo
LCP, Y

Contents: Naseby: A Tale of the Reign of King Charles—The Only Daugh-
ter; or, The Rose of the Isle—The Indian of the Falls Valley; or, The Found-
ling Maid—The Wanderer's Legacy; or, The Warlock of Rotherglen—
Fergus Bane; or, The Sybil of Linlithglen—The Border Chieftain; or, The
Lily of Comrie—Neal Gordon; or, Indian Love: A Tale of the Revolution—
The Pride of Inverhale—The Volunteer: A Tale of the Revolution—The
Valley of Glencoe: A Tale of the 17th Century—The Settler's Last Child:
A Tradition of the West.

2043 THE PHILOSOPHICAL EMPEROR: A Political Experiment; or, The
Progress of a False Position. Dedicated to the Whigs, Conserv-
atives, Democrats, and Loco Focos, Individually and Collec-
tively, of the United States. New York: Harper & Brothers,
1841. 112 p. 12mo   AAS, H, LC, N, UM, UP, Y

PHLOGOBOMBOS, TERENTIUS, *pseud.* *See* Judah, Samuel Benjamin
Herbert

2044 PICKARD, HANNAH MAYNARD (THOMPSON). Procrastination; or,
Maria Louisa Winslow. By a Lady [anon.]. Boston: D. S.
King, 1840. 115 p. 12mo   AAS, B, H, UP, Y

2045 PIKE, ALBERT. Prose Sketches and Poems, Written in the West-
ern Country... Boston: Light & Horton, 1834. 200 p. 12mo
AAS, B, BP, H, HEH, IN, LC, NYH, UP, UPI, Y
Contains: A Mexican Tale—The Inroad of the Navajo—Refugio.

PILLS FOR THE PEOPLE. *See* Life in Town (1844), No. 1667.

2045a PIPER, A. G. The Lady Imogen; or, The Wreck and the Chase.
A Tale of Block Island and the Sound. By F. Clinton Barring-
ton [pseud.] ... Boston: F. Gleason, 1850. 100 p. 8vo   Y
Printed in double cols.

2046 THE PIRATE BOY; or, Adventures of Henry Warrington. A Story
of the Sea. By the Author of The Cabin Boy; Ambrose and
Eleanor; Valley of the Mohawk ... New York: Nafis & Cornish, 267 Pearl Street [cop. 1844]. 122 p., illus. 12mo
AAS, HEH, UP

2047 PISE, CHARLES CONSTANTINE. Father Rowland: A North American Tale ... [anon.]. Baltimore: Fielding Lucas, Jr., 1829.
190 p. 12mo   AAS, HEH, IN, UV, Y
Late 18th cent.

2048 —————— 2d ed. Baltimore: Fielding Lucas, Jr. [cop. 1831]. 195 p. 12mo   AAS, LC, NYH, UP, Y

2048a —————— Baltimore: Fielding Lucas, Jr. [cop. 1841]. 195 p. 12mo   N, UP, Y

2049 —————— The Indian Cottage: A Unitarian Story . . . [anon.]. Baltimore: F. Lucas, Jun. [cop. 1831]. 171 p. 12mo   Y Virginia.

2050 —————— Baltimore: F. Lucas, Jun. [cop. 1831]. 159 p. 12mo   AAS, LC

2051 —————— Zenosius; or, The Pilgrim Convert . . . New York: E. Dunigan & Brother, 1845. 279 p., illus. 12mo   HEH, LC

Piso, Lucius M., *pseud.* See Ware, William

2052 Poe, Edgar Allan. The Narrative of Arthur Gordon Pym of Nantucket. Comprising the Details of a Mutiny and Atrocious Butchery on Board the American Brig Grampus, on Her Way to the South Seas, in the Month of June, 1827 . . . [anon.]. New York: Harper & Brothers, 1838. 201 p. 12mo
AAS, BA, BP, H, HEH, IN, LC, LCP, NYP, UC, UP, UV, Y
For additional bibliographical information on Poe's works see Heartman & Canny.

2053 —————— The Prose Romances . . . No. 1. Containing the Murders in the Rue Morgue, and The Man That Was Used Up. Philadelphia: William H. Graham, 1843. 48 p. 8vo
HEH, IN, LC, NYP, UC, Y
No more published.

2054 —————— Tales . . . New York: Wiley and Putnam, 1845. 228 p. 12mo   BP, H, HEH, IN, N, NYP, UP, Y
For contents see Robertson.

2055 —————— New York: John Wiley, 1849. 228 p. 12mo
AAS, NYP, UP, Y

2056 —————— Tales of the Grotesque and Arabesque . . . Philadelphia: Lea and Blanchard, 1840. 2 vols. 12mo
B, BA, BP, H, HEH, HM, IN, LC, LCP, N, NYP, UP, UV, Y
For contents see Robertson.

2057 —————— The Works . . . New York: J. S. Redfield, 1850. Vols. I-II. 12mo
AAS, B, BA, HEH, IN, LC, LCP, N, NYP, NYS(v.2), UC(v.2), UM, UP, Y

——— X-ing a Paragrab. *In* J. H. Ingraham, The Spanish Galleon (1849), No. 1352.

2058 THE POLISH CHIEFS: An Historical Romance, by the Author of Sketches of Character . . . New York: J. K. Porter, 1832. 2 vols. 12mo   AAS, B, H, HEH, LC, N, UP, UV, Y
Written by Samuel L. Knapp.
American Revolution.

2059 POPE, MRS. ELIZA. Henry and Julietta; or, Virtue Rewarded. A Tale Founded on Fact. By a Young Lady [anon.]. New York: Printed for the author by J. T. Murden, 1818. 188 p. 12mo
UV
England, Italy; end of 13th cent.

PORTER, CALVIN. The Deformed: A Story of the Green Mts. in 1848. *In* M. M. Ballou, Albert Simmons (1849), No. 229.

2060 ——— Leslie Wilmot; or, Witchcraft . . . Boston: F. Gleason, 1848. 50 p. 8vo   LC
Also contains: Shopping with a Country Cousin: A Sketch of City Life.

2061 PORTER, WILLIAM TROTTER, *ed.* The Big Bear of Arkansas, and Other Sketches, Illustrative of Characters and Incidents in the South and South-west . . . Philadelphia: Carey & Hart, 1845. 181 p., illus. 12mo   IN, LC, UP, Y
Contents: The Big Bear of Arkansas, by T. B. Thorpe—Jones's Fight: A Story of Kentucky, by an Alabamian [C. F. M. Noland]—The Great Kalamazoo Hunt: A Story of Michigan, by a New Yorker—That Big Dog Fight at Myers's: A Story of Mississippi, by a Mississippian [Phillip B. January]—How Simon Suggs "Raised Jack": A Georgia Story, by an Alabamian [J. J. Hooper]—Swallowing an Oyster Alive: A Story of Illinois, by a Missourian [J. S. Robb]—A Texan Joker "in a Tight Place"—Billy Warrick's Courtship and Wedding: A Story of "The Old North State," by a Country Court Lawyer—A Bully Boat and a Brag Captain: A Story of Steamboat Life on the Mississippi, by Sol. Smith—Letter from Billy Patterson Himself—A Swim for a Deer: A Mississippi Story, by the "Turkey Runner"—Chunkey's Fight with the Panthers: A Thrilling Hunting Story of Mississippi—A Yankee That Couldn't Talk Spanish, by John A. Stuart, Esq., of South Carolina—"Old Sense" of Arkansas, by "N" of That Ilk [C. F. M. Noland]—Stoke Stout of Louisiana, by Thorpe and Patterson—Life and Manners in Arkansas, by an Ex-Governor of a Cotton-growing State—Anecdotes of the Arkansas Bar, by a Backwoods Lawyer—Hoss Allen of Missouri—Pulling Teeth in Mississippi, by Uncle Johnny—The Way "Lige" Shaddock "Scared Up a Jack"—Cousin Sally Dilliard: A Legal Sketch in the "Old North State" [by H. C. Jones].

2062 ——— ——— Philadelphia: Carey & Hart, 1847. 181 p., illus. 12mo   HEH

2063 ────── *ed.* A Quarter Race in Kentucky, and Other Sketches Illustrative of Scenes, Characters, and Incidents Throughout "the Universal Yankee Nation". . . Philadelphia: Carey and Hart, 1847. 203 p., illus. 12mo   H, LC, LCP, N

Contents: A Quarter Race in Kentucky, by a North Alabamian [C. F. M. Noland]—A Shark Story, by "J. Cypress, Jr.", (the Late Wm. P. Hawes, Esq., of New York)—Lanty Oliphant in Court, by Maj. Kelly of Louisiana—Bill Morse on the City Taxes, by "Baggs" of Boston, Mass.—Ance Veasy's Fight with Reub. Sessions by "Azul" of Mississippi—The Fastest Funeral on Record, by F. A. Durivage, Esq.—Going to Bed before a Young Lady, by Judge Douglass of Illinois [actually about him, not by him]—A Millerite Miracle, by C. A. P. of Kentucky—Old Singletire, the Man That Was Not Annexed, by the late Robert Patterson, Esq., of Louisiana—"Running a Saw" on a French Gentleman, by "Ginsangandson" of Philadelphia—Breaking a Bank, by Sol Smith—Taking the Census [J. J. Hooper]—Dick Harlan's Tennessee Frolic, by "S————l" of Tennessee [G. W. Harris]—"Falling off a Log" in a Game of Seven-up, by a Virginian in Mississippi—French without a Master, by "Straws" (Joseph M. Field)—A Rollicking Dragoon Office, by "the Man in the Swamp"—The Georgia Major in Court, by a Tennessee Editor—Uncle Billy Brown—"Glorious!" by "Rambler" of the N. O. "Picayune" [J. B. Cobb]—Old Tuttle's Last Race, by "Buckeye" of Ohio—Bill Dean, the Texan Ranger, by Geo. W. Kendall, Esq.—The Steamboat Captain Who Was Averse to Racing, by "The Young 'Un" [G. P. Burnham]—Bob Herring, the Arkansas Bear Hunter, by T. B. Thorpe—McAlpin's Trip to Charleston, by the Author of Cousin Sally Dilliard [H. C. Jones]—India Rubber Pills, by "Cheval" of Philadelphia—A Murder Case in Mississippi, by an Associate Editor of the N. O. "Delta"—Kicking a Yankee, by Jos. M. Field—A "Down East" Original, by "De Nogby" of Boston—Somebody in My Bed, by W. J. Jones, Esq., of Harrisburg, Pa.—A Day at Sol Slice's, by "Nat Slocum" of South Carolina—Cupping on the Sternum, by H. C. L. of Mississippi—A Bear Story, by the Late Wm. P. Hawes—Playing "Poker" in Arkansas, by a Resident of That "Neck of Timber."

2064 ────── ────── Philadelphia: A. Hart, 1850. 203 p., illus. 12mo
    BP, H

2065 PORTRAITS OF THE PEOPLE; or, Illustrations and Sketches of American Character, by Popular Artists and Authors. New York: Herrick, West & Ropes, 1841. 58 p., illus. 8vo   BP, HEH
Contains: The Heiress [not T. S. Arthur's].
HEH copy in original parts.

POSTL, KARL. *See* Sealsfield, Charles

2065a POTTER, CHANDLER EASTMAN. Mysteries of Manchester: A Tale. [anon.]. Manchester: J. P. Emery. Jordon & Co., Hotchkiss & Co., Redding & Co., Boston, 1844. 40 p. 4to   AAS, HEH

POTTS, STACY GARDNER. The Golden Chain, by O. Oakwood [pseud.]. *In* J. T. Parker, *comp.*, The American Legendary (1830), No. 1991.

2066 ——— Village Tales; or, Recollections of By-past Times. By Oliver Oakwood [pseud.] ... Trenton, N.J.: Joseph Justice, 1827. 252 p. 12mo AAS, B, H, HEH, IN, LC, N, UC, UP, Y

POWELL, C. FRANK. The Indian Bride. *In* Thrilling Tales (1843), No. 2599a.

2066a ——— Romantic History of Dhoondiah, an Oriental Bandit and the Greatest Robber the World Ever Knew ... Was Finally Pursued with a Large Army and Killed by the Duke of Wellington ... New York: Burgess, Stringer and Co., 1846. 114 p. 8vo AAS

2067 THE POWER OF THE PLEDGE: A Sequel to the History of the Bottle ... New York: Oliver & Brother, 1848. 32 p., illus. 8vo
AAS, HEH, NYP, Y
On cover: "New-York Organ Temperance Tales, No. 2."
Printed in double cols.
New York City; contemporary.

2068 ——— 2d ed. New York: Oliver & Brother, 1848. 32 p., illus. 8vo AAS, H, N
On cover: "New-York Organ Temperance Tales, No. 2."
Printed in double cols.

2068a ——— 3d ed. New York: Oliver & Brother, 1848. 32 p., illus. 8vo UM
On cover: "New-York Organ Temperance Tales, No. 2."
Printed in double cols.

2069 PRAY, ISAAC CLARKE. Prose and Verse from the Port Folio of an Editor ... Boston: Russell, Shattuck and Co., 1836. 186, [2] p. 12mo
AAS, B, BA, BP, H, HEH, IN, LC, N, NYH, NYP, UC, UM, UP, Y
Contains: The Pledge: A Legend of the Rhine—The Oath: From a Bequeathed Manuscript—Maleena: A Story of the Indians—The Brigand—Diary of the Abused: A Bequeathed Manuscript—Lady ——'s Soiree.

2069a PRESTON, LYMAN. Stories for the Whole Family, Young and Old, Male and Female ... New York: J. M. Elliott, printer, 1833. 108 p., illus. 12mo Y

2069b —— —— New Haven: Printed by J. Peck, 1836. 152 p.,
illus. 12mo
Y

2070 —— —— Rochester: William Alling, 1841. 222 p., illus.
12mo
HEH, NYH, NYP, Y

2071 —— —— New York: Huntington & Savage, 1844. 230 p.
12mo
AAS, B, HEH, N, UP, Y

2072 PRICE, WILLIAM. Clement Falconer; or, The Memoirs of a
Young Whig . . . [anon.]. Baltimore: N. Hickman, 1838. 2
vols. 12mo
AAS, B, BP, H, HEH, LC, UC, UM, UP(V.1), UV, Y
Maryland, and Washington, D.C.; contemporary.

2073 —— —— Baltimore: Printed by J. Young, 1844. 2 vols.
in 1. 12mo
NYP, Y

2074 THE PRICE of a Glass of Brandy . . . By a Lady of Baltimore.
Baltimore: Printed by Robert Neilson, 1841. 24 p. 8vo NYP

2075 PRIEST, JOSIAH. A History of the Early Adventures of Washington among the Indians of the West; and the Story of His Love
of Maria Frazier, the Exile's Daughter; with an Account of the
Mingo Prophet . . . Albany: J. Munsell, printer, 1841. Cover
title, [64] p., illus. 8vo   AAS, BA, HEH, NYP, UPI, Y
Printed in double cols.

2076 —— The Robber; or, The Narrative of Pye and the High-
wayman. Being a Detailed and Particular Account of an At-
tempted Robbery of the Inn of John Pye, between the Cities of
Albany and Troy, in 1808 . . . Together with a History of the
Old Men of the Mountain, the Gold Hunters of Joes Hills . . .
Albany: Printed by Stone and Munsell, 1836. 32 p., illus. 8vo
AAS, BP, HEH, LC, NYH

2077 —— —— Albany: Printed by Hoffman & White, 1839.
32 p., illus. 8vo
AAS, NYP

2078 —— Stories of Early Settlers in the Wilderness: Embracing
the Life of Mrs. Priest, Late of Otsego County, N.Y. . . . The
First Raftsmen of the Susquehannah; A Short Account of Brant,
the British Indian Chief; and of the Massacre of Wyoming . . .
Albany: Printed by J. Munsell, 1837. 40 p., illus. 8vo
AAS, BP, HEH, N, NYP, Y

2079 —— Stories of the Revolution. With an Account of the Lost Child of the Delaware; Wheaton and the Panther ... Albany: Printed by Hoffman & White, 1836. 32 p., illus. 8vo

AAS, H, HEH, LC, LCP, N, NYH

Contents: The Captive Boys of Rensselaerville—The Feats and Intrepidity of Colonel Harper—The Escape of Cowley and Sawyer from the Indians—The Escape of the British Indians When Burgoyne Was Taken—The Escape of McKean's Scouting Party in Otsego County—The Story of the Hessian Woman in the Camp of Burgoyne—The Five Prisoners of Brandt at the Massacre of Cherry Valley—The Wonderful Preservation of Mrs. Moore, When a Prisoner among the Indians—The Lost Child of the Delaware—Wheaton and the Panther—La Fayette and the Indian Girl of Illinois—The Contest between the Indians and One White Man.

2080 —— —— Albany: Printed by Hoffman & White, 1836. 32 p., illus. 8vo

AAS, BP, H, HEH, LC, N, NYH, NYP, Y

Another ed. with one new story added: "Massacre of Fourteen Prisoners by Esther an Indian Queen, at the Battle of Wyoming, during the Revolution."

2081 —— —— Albany: Printed by Hoffman & White, 1838. 32 p., illus. 8vo

AAS, B, BA, H, HEH, NYH, NYP, UP, Y

Contents same as No. 2080.

2082 THE PRIZE ARTICLES Contributed to Richards' Weekly Gazette ... Athens, Georgia: William C. Richards, 1849. 38 p. 8vo

HEH, NYH

Contains: Percy; or, The Banished Son, by Mrs. Caroline Hentz—The New Aria: A Tale of Trial and Trust, by J. M. Legaré.

Cover title reads: "Percy; or, The Banished Son: A Prize Tale, by Mrs. Caroline Lee Hentz. And Other Prize Articles Contributed to Richards' Weekly Gazette."

Printed in double cols.

2083 P's AND Q's ... Boston: Bowles & Dearborn, 1828. 200 p., illus. 16mo

AAS, B, BA, H, NYP, UC

Contains: The Barber's Letter—A Horrible Adventure—A Wanderer's Life —The Hanging—The Hot-Tongs Society: An Angler's Adventure—An Advertisement—The Troubles of Courtship: A Thanksgiving Story—Punishments—The Adventurer's Tale—The Last of the Blacklegs—The Midshipman to the Schoolmaster—Good and Evil: From the Persian—Blue Devils—Jeremy Gumm: A Tale of Macedonia.

Cushing credits a Boston, 182- ed. to Charles Locke, Joseph H. and Edwin Buckingham, and Silas P. Holbrook. "The Last of the Blacklegs" is in Holbrook's *Sketches by a Traveller* (1830), No. 1221.

2084 —— 2d ed. Hingham [Mass.]: C. & E. B. Gill, 1831. 200 p. 16mo

AAS, HEH, LC, NYP

2084a PUNKIN, JONATHAN, *pseud.* Downfall of Freemasonry, Being an Authentic History of the Rise, Progress, and Triumph of Anti-masonry. Also of the Origin and Increase of Abolition. Together with a Faithful Account of the Travels . . . and Escapes of the Governor from the Cut-Throats of the Lodge . . . All Carefully Revised by Punkin's Shorthander, Worked by Steam from Blabberlips. By Jonathan Punkin, Esq. [pseud.]. [Harrisburg, Pa.]: Published for the editor, near the Council Chambers, Unction Room, 1838. 48 p., 1 l., v, [13]-159 p., illus. 8vo   AAS, HEH, N, NYP, Y

Second pagination begins with half title: "Book the Second. Governor's Correspondence."

2085 THE PUPIL of Raphael . . . New York: Wiley & Putnam, 1843. 2 vols. 12mo   B, H, LC, NYH
Italy; 1513.

PURDY, E. C. Ingratitude. *In* J. T. Parker, *comp.*, The American Legendary (1830), No. 1991.

2085a QUACKENBOS, GEORGE PAYN. St. Jean's Evening; or, Crime and Mystery . . . New York: E. Winchester, 1846. 45 p. 8vo
                                                            HEH
At head of cover title: "American Tale for the Fireside."
Printed in double cols.

2086 QUINCY, SAMUEL M. The Fair Penitent; or, The Unknown Stranger. A Tale of the Eighteenth Century. Founded on Fact . . . [N.p., cop. 1833.]
LC has a title page, deposited Nov. 1, 1833.

2087 QUIPES, *Father, pseud.* The Life and Travels of Father Quipes, Otherwise Dominick O'Blarney. Written by Himself. Carlisle [Pa.]: Printed for the purchaser, 1820. 32 p., illus. 12mo
                                                            LC
John MacFarland, attrib. au.

QUOD, JOHN, *pseud.* *See* Irving, John Treat

R., M. K. Croghan; or, The Hero of Fort Sandusky. *In* The Romantic Historian (1834), No. 2154.

2088 RAMON, THE ROVER OF CUBA. The Personal Narrative of That Celebrated Pirate. Translated from the Original Spanish. Boston: Richardson, Lord and Holbrooke, 1829. 162 p. 12mo
                                      AAS, BP, HEH, LC, UC, UM, Y

2089 —— And Other Tales, by the Author of "Evenings in Boston" ... New York: Nafis & Cornish, 1843. 295 [i.e., 293] p., illus. 12mo   H, HEH, LC, NYP, UP, Y
Also contains: The Brazilian—The Montero of Cuba.

2090 —— 30th ed. New York: Nafis & Cornish, 1849. 295 [i.e., 293] p., illus. 12mo   AAS, Y
Also contains: The Brazilian—The Montero of Cuba.

2091 —— New York: Nafis & Cornish, 278 Pearl Street [cop. 1843]. 295 [i.e., 293] p., illus. 12mo   AAS, HEH, LC, N, Y
Also contains: The Brazilian—The Montero of Cuba.

2092 RANSOM, JAMES BIRCHETT. Osceola; or, Fact and Fiction. A Tale of the Seminole War. By a Southerner ... [anon.]. New York: Printed by Harper & Brothers, 1838. 150 p., illus. 12mo
       AAS, B, BA, BP, HEH, LC, N, NYP, UM, UP, UV, Y

2093 RAUX, EUGENE. The Wandering Christian; or, Lost and Found. A Romance of the Western Continent ... Philadelphia: National Publishing Company, 1846.
LC has a title page, deposited Nov. 18, 1846.

2093a RAY, WILLIAM. Sophia; or, The Girl of the Pine Woods. A Tale Founded Principally on Fact. By Walter Walpole, Esq. [pseud.] ... To Which Are Added a Few Select Poems by William Ray. Geneva, N.Y.: Printed by H. Leavenworth, 1823. 120 p. 12mo   AAS
A typescript of an article by William S. Kable, yet to be published, presents a good case for Ray's authorship of *Sophia*.

2093b —— Paterson, N.J.: David Burnett, 1834. 96 p., illus. 16mo   Y
Also contains: The Golden Eagle.
For the 1838 ed. see title entry, No. 2479.

2094 RAYBOLD, GEORGE A. The Fatal Feud; or, Passion and Piety ... New York: T. Mason and G. Lane, 1838. 156 p. 12mo   AAS

2095 —— New York: Lane & Scott, 1850. 156 p. 12mo
       LC

2096 —— Paul Perryman; or, The Unhappy Death. A Fact ... New York: T. Mason and G. Lane; J. Collord, printer, 1838. 32 p. 16mo   NYH

2097 —————— New York: T. Mason and G. Lane; J. Collord, printer, 1840. 32 p. 16mo   BP

2097a —————— New York: G. Lane & P. P. Sandford. James Collord, printer, 1841. 32 p. 16mo   AAS

2098 READ, MRS. MARTHA. Monima; or, The Beggar Girl. A Novel, in One Volume, Founded on Fact. By an American Lady . . . [anon.]. New York: Printed by P. R. Johnson, 1802. 465 p. 12mo   NYS, UV, Y
France, West Indies, and Philadelphia; contemporary.

2099 —————— New York: T. B. Jansen & Co., 1803. 465 p. 12mo   AAS, NYP

2100 —————— Philadelphia: Printed by Eaken & Mecum, 1803. 458 p. 12mo   LC, LCP, N, UM

2101 —————— Philadelphia: J. H. Gould, 1847. 109 p. 8vo   NYP
Title reads: *Monima; or, The Beautiful French Girl in Philadelphia. A Tale of Thrilling Interest Founded on Facts. By H. Haydn.*

2102 READ, THOMAS BUCHANAN. Paul Redding: A Tale of the Brandywine . . . Boston: A. Tompkins & B. B. Mussey, 1845. 136 p. 8vo   AAS, B, BA, BP, HEH, IN, N, UP, UV, Y

2103 —————— 2d ed. New York: E. Ferrett & Co., 1845. 136 p. 8vo   LC, NYP, UC

2104 REALITIES OF LIFE: Sketches Designed for the Improvement of the Head and Heart. By a Philanthropist. New Haven: S. Babcock, 1839. 197 p. 12mo   AAS, H, LC, Y

2105 RECOLLECTIONS OF THE UNITED STATES ARMY. A Series of Thrilling Tales and Sketches, by an American Soldier. Written during a Period in "The Service," since 1830. Boston: James Munroe and Company, 1845. 167 p., illus. 12mo
                                                AAS, BA, H, HEH, LC, UP, Y
Contents: Corporal Tim—The Officer and Soldier; or, The Sergeant's Revenge—The Woodman's Wife—The Deserters—The Lieutenant's Tale of the Condemned Soldier's Last Hour—The Soldier's Death—The Soldier's Burial—The Officer and Duellist; or, The Insult—Charley Clifton's Last Picnic—The Express Rider—Ned Stanley's Death—The Disinterment of the Right Honorable Lord Edward Stanley—The Fate of a Military Tyrant—Frank Morton's Escape.

2106 —— 2d ed. Boston: James Munroe and Company, 1845. 167 p., illus. 12mo   AAS, N, NYP, Y

2107 RED MARY; or, The Mariner of the Pacific. By the Author of "The Mysteries of New York." Boston: Edward Philip Williams, 1844. 32 p., illus. 8vo   AAS, B, Y

2108 REES, JAMES. Mysteries of City Life; or, Stray Leaves from the World's Book. Being a Series of Tales, Sketches, Incidents, and Scenes, Founded upon the Notes of a Home Missionary . . . Philadelphia: J. W. Moore, 1849. 408 p. 12mo
AAS, HM, LC, LCP, N, NYP, UM, UP, Y

2109 REFLECTIONS AND TALES. By a Lady of Philadelphia. Philadelphia: Published by the authoress, 1830. 108 p. 12mo
AAS, LC, LCP
Contains: Rosalia—Teresa.

2110 RELF, SAMUEL. Infidelity; or, The Victims of Sentiment. A Novel in a Series of Letters . . . [anon.]. Philadelphia: Printed by W. W. Woodward, 1797. 190 p. 12mo   AAS, IN, LC, UC, UV
Philadelphia; contemporary.

THE REMARKABLE NARRATIVE OF CORDELIA KRATS. *See* The Female Wanderer (1846), No. 950.

REMARKABLE NARRATIVE OF THE FEMALE HERMIT. *See* Life of Miss Fanny Bell, and the Female Hermit, No. 1670.

2111 REQUIER, AUGUSTUS JULIAN. The Old Sanctuary: A Romance of the Ashley . . . Boston: Redding & Company, 1846. 197 p. 12mo   BA, H
LC has a title page, deposited May 18, 1846.
Carolinas; prior to American Revolution.

2112 RETRENCHMENT; or, Ways and Means. Family Sketches in the Nineteenth Century . . . Boston: Whipple & Damrell, 1841. 106 p. 12mo   AAS, LC, Y

2113 RETROPROGRESSION. Being an Account of a Short Residence in the Celebrated Town of Jumbleborough. Boston: James Burns, 1839. 83 p. 12mo   AAS, H, HEH

2114 REVELATIONS OF ASMODEUS; or, Mysteries of Upper Ten-dom. Being a Spirit Stirring, a Powerful and Felicitous Expose of the Desolating Mystery, Blighting Miseries, Atrocious Vices and Paralyzing Tragedies Perpetrated in the Fashionable Pandemoniums of the Great Empire City. New York: C. G. Graham & Co., 1849. 96 p. 8vo   HEH
Printed in double cols.

REVERIE, REGINALD, *pseud*. *See* Mellen, Grenville

2115 REYNOLDS, ELHANAN WINCHESTER. The New Doctrine; or, Teachings and Tendencies . . . Fredonia, N.Y.: Printed at the Censor office, 1848. 144 p. 8vo   BP, LC
Pennsylvania.

2116 RHODES, JOHN W. Melini; or, The Victim of Guilt. A Historical Tale of the "Good Old Colony Times". . . Boston: John M. L. Babcock & Silvanus B. Weston, 1844. 48 p. 8vo
AAS, BP
Cover imprint: "Boston: Brainard and Company, 1844."
Printed in double cols.

2117 RICHARD WHITE; or, One Eyed Dick of Massachusetts. A Tale for the Young . . . Boston: George W. Light, 1841. 106 p., illus. 12mo   AAS, HEH, LC, N, NYP, UP, Y
American Revolution.

2118 ——— 2d ed. Boston: James French, 1845. 107 p., illus. 12mo   AAS, HEH, Y

2118a RICHMOND, JAMES COOK. A Midsummer's Day-Dream: Libellous; or, A Little Book of the Vision of Shawmut. By Admonish Crime [pseud.] . . . Boston: Jordan & Wiley. New York: Burgess, Stringer & Co., August, 1847. 24 p., illus. 8vo
H, HEH, N, NYP, Y
Satire on Boston.

2119 ——— Nothing, by Nobody . . . [anon.]. Philadelphia: E. Littell, 1827. 222 p. 12mo   H, HEH, NYP, UC, UP, Y

2119a RIDDELL, JOHN LEONARD. Orrin Lindsay's Plan for Aerial Navigation, with a Narrative of His Explorations in the Higher Regions of the Atmosphere, and His Wonderful Voyage Round the Moon! Edited by J. L. Riddell, M.D. New Orleans: Rea's Power Press office, 1847. 33 p. 8vo   HEH, LC, NYP, Y

2119b —— —— Louisville: J. C. Noble's Book and Job Printing office, 1847. 24 p. 8vo
Union Catalog locates a copy at the University of Michigan Library.

RIGMAROLE, CRAYON, *Esq., pseud.* *See* Sims, Alexander Dromgoole

RINGBOLT, *Captain, pseud.* *See* Codman, John

2120 RITCHIE, ANNA CORA (OGDEN) MOWATT. Evelyn; or, A Heart Unmasked. A Tale of Domestic Life . . . Philadelphia: G. B. Zieber and Company, 1845. 2 vols. 12mo
AAS, BP, H, NYP(V.1), UC, UP, Y
Written in a series of letters.
New York City; contemporary.

2121 —— The Fortune Hunter; or, The Adventures of a Man about Town. A Novel of New York Society, by Mrs. Helen Berkeley [pseud.] . . . New York: J. Winchester, New World Press, 30 Ann Street [cop. 1844]. 108 p. 8vo
AAS, B, H, HEH, NYH, NYP, UP, Y

2122 —— —— New York: William Taylor [1844?]. 108 p. 8vo
B, NYP

2123 —— —— Philadelphia: T. B. Peterson, No. 98 Chesnut Street [cop. 1848]. 108 p. 8vo AAS, HEH, NYH, UC, Y

2124 RIVES, JUDITH PAGE (WALKER). Tales and Souvenirs of a Residence in Europe. By a Lady of Virginia . . . [anon.]. Philadelphia: Lea & Blanchard, 1842. 301 p. 8vo
AAS, B, BP, HEH, IN, LC, LCP, N, UP, Y
Contents: A Tale of Our Ancestors—Fragments of a Journal—The Soldier's Bride: A Tale—The Valley of Goldau: A Tale—A Ballad.

2125 ROBB, JOHN S. Kaam; or, Daylight. The Arapahoe Half-breed: A Tale of the Rocky Mountains . . . Boston: "Star Spangled Banner" office, 1847. 42 p., illus. 8vo AAS, HEH, NYP, Y
At head of title: "Great American Prize Romance."
Cover imprint of HEH copy reads: "Jones, Publisher, 82 Washington St.; H. Long & Brother, 32 Ann St., New York; T. B. Peterson, 98 Chesnut St., Philadelphia, 1847." Cover imprint of a copy formerly owned by Mr. Thomas W. Streeter, of New Jersey, reads: "Boston: Jones's Publishing House, 82 Washington Street; H. Long & Brother, 32 Ann St., New York; T. B. Peterson, 98 Chesnut St., Philadelphia, 1848."
Printed in double cols.

2126 —— Streaks of Squatter Life, and Far-West Scenes . . . Philadelphia: Carey and Hart, 1847. 187 p., illus. 12mo
AAS, BA, HEH, IN, LC, UP, Y

—— Swallowing an Oyster Alive: A Story of Illinois, by a Missourian. *In* W. T. Porter, *ed.*, The Big Bear of Arkansas (1845), Nos. 2061-62.

2127 THE ROBBER; or, Sons of a Night. A True Story. Weathersfield [Conn.]: L. Roberson, 1816. 32 p., illus. 32mo   Y

2128 ROBINSON, JOHN HOVEY. Angela; or, The Convent of Santa Clara. A Tale of Portugal ... New York: Samuel French, 151 Nassau [1850?]. 100 p., illus. 8vo   AAS, HEH, UP, Y
Also contains: Wilson MacFarland, by Lieut. E. Curtiss Hine—The Monks of St. Nicholas the Old, by Eva Milford.
Printed in double cols.

2129 —— The Black Knight; or, The Wandering Bohemian. A Romance of the Days of Chivalry ... Boston: F. Gleason, 1849. 100 p. 8vo   AAS, HEH, UP, Y
Also contains: The Count and the Prima Donna, by F. A. Durivage.
Printed in double cols.

2130 —— The Boston Conspiracy; or, The Royal Police. A Tale of 1773-75 ... Boston: Dow & Jackson, 1847. 110 p. 12mo
AAS, B, BP, LC, LCP, UC, Y

—— Cecelia; or, Woman's Love. *In* M. A. Clough, Annie Merrivale [1850], No. 551a.

2131 —— The Child of the Sierra; or, The Gipsey Brigand! A Romance of Sunny Spain ... Boston: F. Gleason [cop. 1848]. 100 p. 8vo   AAS, H, Y
Also contains: Kate Hovey's Party—Florence Darnley—Blanche; or, The Baron's Vow.
Printed in double cols.

2132 —— Ella Montfield; or, The Three Disguises. A Tale of Boston ... Boston: Purdy & Bradley, 1846. 42 p. 8vo BP, NYH
LC has a cover title, deposited Feb. 12, 1846.

2133 —— Father Ildefonso; or, The Priests of St. Omer ... New York: Williams Brothers, 1847. 100 p. 8vo   LC, Y

2134 ——— The Fingers of Fate; or, The Astrologer's Daughter. A Tale of 1770 ... Boston: Page & Davis, 1846. 78 p., illus. 8vo
UM, Y
Printed in double cols.
LC has a title page, deposited Nov. 10, 1846.

2135 ——— The Isadore; or, The Fated Barque. A Story of New England. Founded on Fact . . . Boston: Warren W. Page, 1847. 50 p. 8vo
Y
Printed in double cols.

2136 ——— Kosato, the Blackfoot Renegade . . . Boston: Yankee Nation office, 1850. 48 p. 8vo
HEH, NYP
Contains: An Appeal to Heaven, by H. G. Chipman.
Printed in double cols.

2137 ——— The Lady's Dream; or, The Fortune Teller of Copp's Hill. A Legend of Boston . . . Boston: W. W. Page, 1846. Cover title, 48 p. 8vo
BP
Printed in double cols.

2138 ——— ——— Boston: W. W. Page, 1848. Cover title, 48 p. 8vo
H
H lacks pp. 47-48.
Printed in double cols.

2139 ——— Marietta; or, The Two Students. A Tale of the Dissecting Room and "Body Snatchers"... Boston: Jordan & Wiley, 1846. 46 p., illus. 8vo
AAS, Y
Printed in double cols.

2140 ——— Silver-Knife; or, The Hunter of the Rocky Mountains. A Romance of the Wild West . . . Boston: Hotchkiss & Company, 1850. 103 p. 8vo
Y
Printed in double cols.

2141 ROBINSON, MRS. JOHN HOVEY. Evelyn, the Child of the Revolution. A Romance of Real Life . . . Boston: Hotchkiss & Company, 1850. 104 p. 8vo
BP, LC, Y
Printed in double cols.
Boston.

2142 ROBINSON, THERESE ALBERTINE LOUISE (VON JAKOB). Heloise; or, The Unrevealed Secret. A Tale by Talvi [pseud.]. New York: D. Appleton & Company, 1850. 264 p. 8vo
AAS, BA, HEH, LC, N, NYP, UC, UP, Y
Europe.

2143 RODDAN, JOHN T. John O'Brien; or, The Orphan of Boston. A Tale of Real Life ... Boston: Patrick Donahoe, 1850. 264 p. 12mo   AAS, BP, HEH, UP, Y

2144 ROE, AZEL STEVENS. James Montjoy; or, I've Been Thinking ... New York: D. Appleton & Company, 1850. 327 p. 12mo
          AAS, BA, H, HEH, IN, LCP, N, NYP, UP, Y
Eastern seaboard; early 19th cent.

2145 ROGERS, GEORGE. Adventures of Elder Triptolemus Tub: Comprising Important and Startling Disclosures Concerning Hell ... To Which Is Added: The Old Man of the Hill-side [anon.]. Boston: Abel Tompkins, 1846. 197 p., illus. 12mo
          AAS, B, LC, NYP, UC, UP, Y

2146 ————— ———— Boston: Abel Tompkins, 1848. 197 p., illus. 12mo   AAS, H

2147 ——— The Pro and Con of Universalism ... Utica, N.Y.: Published for the author, by A. B. Grosh & Co., 1840. 356 p. 12mo   HEH
Contains: Alice Sherwood; or, The Pennsylvania Valley: A Tale.

2148 ————— ———— Boston: A. Tompkins, 1842. 356, 24, [2] p. 12mo   BP, Y
Contains: Alice Sherwood; or, The Pennsylvania Valley: A Tale.
The appended 26 p. is a story entitled: "Revelations from Hell, by a Damned Spirit."

2149 ————— ———— 6th ed. Cincinnati: Published by the author, 1843. 356 p. 12mo   NYP, Y
Contains: Alice Sherwood; or, The Pennsylvania Valley: A Tale.

2150 ————— ———— 6th ed. Erie: O. D. Spafford, 1846. 356 p. 12mo   H, N
Contains: Alice Sherwood; or, The Pennsylvania Valley: A Tale.

2150a ——— Tales from Life, Designed to Illustrate Certain Religious Doctrines and Practices Which Prevail at the Present Day ... Boston: A. Tompkins and B. B. Mussey, 1841. 180 p. 12mo
          AAS, B, H, HEH
Contains: An Old Settler's Narrative—Parson Stubbleton; or, Sanford Settlement Revisited, Being a Sequel to the "Narrative"—A Pleasant Rencontre; or, The Report of an Incident and Conversation as They Occurred—Truman Troth's Experience.

ROGERS, JAMES, *pseud.* *See* Sands, Robert Charles

2151 THE ROMAN EXILE; or, The Times of Aurelius. Boston: John
G. Jones, 1843. 186 p. 12mo
Ed. from sales catalog.

2152 —— 2d ed. Boston: John G. Jones, 1843. 186 p. 12mo
AAS, B, BA, H, HEH, N, Y

2153 —— 3d ed. Great Falls, N.H.: John G. Jones, 1850. 32 p.
8vo   Y

ROMANCE OF THE DEEP! or, The Cruise of the Aeronaut. *See*
Life in a Whale Ship, No. 1665.

2154 THE ROMANTIC HISTORIAN. A Series of Lights and Shadows,
Elucidating American Annals. Philadelphia: Hogan & Thomp-
son, 1834. 315 p. 16mo   B, LC, UC, UP, Y
Contents: A Midnight Tramp in the Jerseys—The Sister of Charity, by L.
H. Medina—The Martyrs: A Tale of the Revolution, by H. A. L. of Phila-
delphia—The Battle of Lexington, by J. F.—The Deserter—Preparatory Re-
marks to the Moravian Indians: A Tale—A Midnight Scene, during the Rev-
olution—The Victims of Revenge, by M. A. B.—A Tale of St. Domingo, by
B. B.—Wacousta—Croghan; or, The Hero of Fort Sandusky, by M. K. R.—
The Italian Bride, by E. C. S.

2155 ROSA; or, American Genius and Education. New York: Printed
for the author by Isaac Riley, 1810. 263 p. 12mo
AAS, H, LC, NYH, UP, Y
Baltimore; late 18th cent.

2156 ROSE-HILL. A Tale of the Old Dominion, by a Virginian. Phil-
adelphia: Key & Biddle, 1835. 208 p. 12mo   H, IN, N, UC, Y
Attributed to T. T. Tabb by Sabin.
American Revolution.

2157 ROSEWOOD, EMMA. Alford and Selina; or, The Mystery Dis-
closed, and the Reputed Orphan Restored to a Father's Embrace.
A Tale of Real Life ... Boston: Dow & Jackson, 1845. 30 p.
8vo   AAS, BP, H, LC, Y
Massachusetts; contemporary.

2158 —— The Virtuous Wife; or, The Libertine Detected. A
Tale of Boston and Vicinity. Containing a Warning to Girls
from the Country, and an Example for City Ladies ... Boston:
Dow and Jackson, 1845. 32 p. 8vo   NYP
LC has a cover title, deposited Mar. 25, 1845.

2159   ROWSON, SUSANNA (HASWELL).   Charlotte: A Tale of Truth . . .
Philadelphia: Printed by D. Humphreys, 1794. 2 vols.   12mo
AAS, B, H, HEH, IN, JCB, LC, NYH, NYP, UV, Y
Vail 2.

For bibliographical descriptions of Rowson's works appearing in this bibliography with a Vail number, and for other copies not appearing in this
census, see Vail.

2160   ———— ———— 2d ed.   Philadelphia, 1794.
AAS, H, IN, NYH, UC, UP, UV, Y
Vail 3.

2161   ———— ———— 3d ed.   Philadelphia, 1797.   AAS, LC, UV, Y
The title of this ed. and of the following eds., unless otherwise specified,
reads: *Charlotte Temple: A Tale of Truth.*
Vail 4.

2162   ———— ———— 4th ed.   Harrisburgh, Penns., 1801.   AAS, Y
Vail 5.

2163   ———— ———— Hartford, 1801.   AAS, NYH, Y
Title reads: *The History of Charlotte Temple.*
Vail 6.

2164   ———— ———— New Haven, 1801.   AAS, N, NYH, UP, Y
Title reads: *The History of Charlotte Temple.*
Vail 7.

2165   ———— ———— Philadelphia, 1801.   NYP, UP, Y
Vail 8.

2166   ———— ———— 5th ed.   Harrisburgh, Pennsyl., 1802.
AAS, HEH, IN, LC, NYP, UC, UV, Y
Vail 10.

2167   ———— ———— 6th ed.   Alexandria, 1802.   AAS, NYP, Y
Vail 9.

2168   ———— ———— New   York: Printed for Hugh M. Griffith
[1802?].   AAS, NYP, Y
Vail 11.

2169   ———— ———— New York: Printed by John Swain [1802?].
AAS, HEH, JCB, NYH, NYP, Y
Vail 12.

2170   ———— ———— Danbury, 1803.   AAS, Y
Vail 12a.

2171 —————— ————— Hudson, 1803.   AAS, NYH, Y
  Title reads: *The History of Charlotte Temple.*
  Vail 13.

2172 —————— ————— New York: Printed by Lazarus Beach, for J. Harrison, 1803.   AAS, HEH, NYP, UP, Y
  Vail 14.

2173 —————— ————— New York: Printed by Lazarus Beach, for John
  Tiebout, 1803.   NYP, Y
  Vail 15.

2174 —————— ————— [New Haven]: Printed for Increase Cooke and
  Co., 1805.   AAS, Y
  Title reads: *The History of Charlotte Temple.*
  Vail 16.

2175 —————— ————— Chambersburg, 1807.   AAS, Y
  Vail 17.

2175a —————— ————— Washington: Printed for Joseph Israel, 1807.
  176, [4] p.   12mo   HEH
  Not in Vail.

2176 —————— ————— Hudson, 1808.   AAS, LC, NYP, Y
  Title reads: *The History of Charlotte Temple.*
  Vail 18.

2177 —————— ————— New Haven, 1808.   AAS, Y
  Vail 19.

2178 —————— ————— Philadelphia, 1808.   AAS, NYH, Y
  Vail 20.

2179 —————— ————— Philadelphia, 1809.   AAS, NYP, UC, Y
  Vail 21.

2180 —————— ————— Boston, 1811.   AAS, Y
  Vail 22.

2181 —————— ————— Hartford, 1811.   AAS, NYH, NYP, Y
  Vail 23.

2182 —————— ————— [New Haven]: Printed for Increase Cooke & Co.,
  1811.   AAS, NYP, Y
  Title reads: *The History of Charlotte Temple.*
  Vail 24.

2183 —— —— Philadelphia, 1812.   AAS, NYH, Y
Vail 25.

2184 —— —— Windsor, 1812.   AAS, IN, NYP, Y
Vail 26.

2185 —— —— Brattleborough (Ver.), 1813.   AAS, HEH, Y
Vail 27.

2186 —— —— New Haven, 1813.   AAS, NYP, Y
Vail 28.

2187 —— —— Hudson: Printed by A. Stoddard, 1814.   141 p.
16mo   AAS, Y
Title reads: *The History of Charlotte Temple.*
Vail 29.

2188 —— —— New York: Samuel A. Burtus, 1814.
          AAS, H, NYP, UC, UM, Y
Title reads: *The History of Charlotte Temple.*
Vail 30.

2189 —— —— New York: Evert Duyckinck, 1814.
          AAS, LCP, NYP, Y
Vail 31.

2190 —— —— Concord, N.H., 1815.
          AAS, B, H, HEH, IN, NYH, NYP, UC, Y
Vail 32.

2191 —— —— Windsor, 1815.   AAS, BP, H, HEH, IN, LC, NYP, Y
AAS has a 2d copy with cover imprint dated 1826.
Vail 33.

2192 —— —— Brookfield, 1816.   AAS, UC, Y
Vail 34.

2193 —— —— New York, 1816.   AAS, HEH
Vail 35.

2194 —— —— Walpole, N.H., 1816.   AAS, Y
Vail 36.

2194a —— —— Wilmington: Printed by R. Porter, 1816.   107 p.
12mo   AAS
Not in Vail.

2195 —— —— New Haven, 1818.   AAS, HEH, Y
Vail 37.

2196	———— ————	Philadelphia: J. Carson, 1818.	AAS, Y
	Vail 38.		
2197	———— ————	Philadelphia: Benjamin Warner, 1818.	AAS, H, Y
	Vail 39.		
2198	———— ————	Baltimore, 1819.	H
	Vail 40.		
2199	———— ————	Poughkeepsie, 1819.	AAS, LC, Y
	Vail 42.		
2200	———— ————	Philadelphia, 1820.	AAS, Y
	Vail 43.		
2201	———— ————	Boston, 1824.	AAS, B, BP, Y
	Vail 45.		
2202	———— ————	Hartford, 1825.	AAS, IN, UM, Y
	Vail 46.		
2203	———— ————	New York, 1826.	AAS, NYH, Y
	Vail 47.		
2204	———— ————	Philadelphia, 1826. 142 p.	AAS, HEH, NYP, Y
	Vail 48.		
2205	———— ————	Philadelphia: John Grigg, 1826. 144 p.	AAS, LCP, NYP, Y
	Vail 49.		

2206 ———— ———— Cincinnati: Published by Wm. Hill Woodward, No. 210 Main St., near the Upper Market, 1827.   186, [2] p. 12mo   AAS, Y
Not in Vail.

2207	———— ————	Hartford, 1827.	AAS, HEH, Y
	Vail 51.		
2208	———— ————	New York: R. Hobbs, 1827.	AAS, Y

AAS has a 2d copy with cover imprint: "New York: W. Whale, 1828."
AAS has a 3d copy with cover imprint: "New York: George G. Sickels, 1828."
AAS has a 4th copy with cover imprint: "Stereotyped by T. Seward. New York: George G. Sickels, 1829."
Vail 52.

2209 ———— ———— Hartford, 1828.   AAS, NYP, Y
        Vail 53.

2210 ———— ———— Hartford, 1829.   AAS, HEH, LC, NYH, Y
        Vail 55.

2211 ———— ———— New York: John Lomax, 1830.
        Vail 57.

2212 ———— ———— New York: George G. Sickels, 1830.
                                        AAS, NYP, UM, Y
        Vail 58.

2213 ———— ———— Cincinnati, 1831.   AAS, Y
        Vail 59.

2214 ———— ———— Hartford: Silas Andrus, 1831.   138 p.   12mo
                                                        AAS, Y
        Not in Vail.

2215 ———— ———— New York, 1831.   AAS, BA, HEH, NYP, Y
        Some copies have an added title dated 1832, which is repeated on the cover.
        Vail 60.

2216 ———— ———— Hartford, 1832.   AAS, Y
        Vail 61.

2217 ———— ———— Baltimore, 1833.   LC
        Vail 64.

2218 ———— ———— Hartford, Ct.: Andrus and Judd, 1833.   NYP, Y
        Vail 65.

2218a ———— ———— Cincinnati: U. P. James, 1833.   139 p., illus.
        12mo   AAS, IN, Y
        Not in Vail.

2219 ———— ———— Hartford, Ct.: Andrus and Judd [1833-36?].
                                          AAS, NYP, Y
        Vail 66.

2219a ———— ———— Cincinnati: U. P. James, 1834.   139 p., illus.
        12mo   AAS, Y
        Not in Vail.

2219b ———— ———— Baltimore: Stereotyped for the booksellers, 1834.
        156 p.   16mo   AAS
        Not in Vail.

2220	—— ——	Concord, N.H., 1834.	AAS, Y
	Vail 67.		
2221	—— ——	Trenton, 1834.	AAS, LCP, NYH, Y
	Vail 68.		
2222	—— ——	Hartford, Ct., 1835.	AAS, UC, Y
	Vail 69.		
2223	—— ——	Cincinnati, 1836.	Y
	Vail 72.		
2223a	—— ——	Cincinnati: J. A. James, 1837. 129 p., illus.	
	12mo		Y
	Not in Vail.		
2224	—— ——	Baltimore, 1837.	
	Vail 73.		
2225	—— ——	Hartford, 1837.	AAS, B, HEH, NYP, Y
	Vail 74.		
2226	—— ——	Philadelphia: Published by A. I. Dickinson, 223	
	Arch Street, 1837. 143 p. 12mo		AAS, UP, Y
	Not in Vail.		
2227	—— ——	Cincinnati: Published by U. P. James, 1839. 139	
	p. 12mo		AAS, IN, Y
	Not in Vail.		
2228	—— ——	Hartford, 1839.	NYH
	Vail 75.		
2229	—— ——	New York, 1839.	AAS, NYP, Y
	Vail 76.		
2230	—— ——	New York, 1840.	AAS, LC, LCP, NYP, Y
	Vail 77.		
2231	—— ——	Philadelphia: John B. Perry [1840?].	
	Vail 78.		
2232	—— ——	Ithaca, N.Y., 1841.	AAS, NYP, Y
	Vail 79.		
2233	—— ——	New York, 1842.	AAS, NYP, Y
	Vail 80.		

2234 ———— ———— New York: Nafis & Cornish [1842-50].

AAS, NYP, Y

Vail 81.

2235 ———— ———— Concord, N.H., 1843.   AAS, HEH, IN, NYP, Y

Vail 82.

2236 ———— ———— Ithaca, N.Y., 1843.   AAS, HEH, NYH, NYP, Y

Vail 83.

2237 ———— ———— Boston, 1845.   AAS, B, H, Y

Vail 84.

2238 ———— ———— Ithaca, N.Y., 1846.   AAS, Y

Vail 85.

2239 ———— ———— Philadelphia: Published by Richard Magee, Turner & Fisher, Philadelphia, New York, and Boston.   J. B. Keller, Baltimore, 1847.   119 p., illus.   12mo   AAS, HEH, NYP
Not in Vail.

2240 ———— ———— Waterford, 1848.   AAS, HEH, Y

Vail 86.

2241 ———— ———— Ithaca, N.Y.: Andrus, Gauntlett & Co., 1850.
138 p.   12mo   AAS
Not in Vail.

2242 ———— Charlotte's Daughter; or, The Three Orphans.   A Sequel to Charlotte Temple ...   Boston: Richardson & Lord, 1828.
184 p.   12mo

AAS, B, BA, BP, H, HEH, LC, N, NYH, NYP, UC, UM, UP, UV, Y

Vail 164.

2243 ———— ———— New York: Nafis & Cornish [1842-48].   179 p.
12mo   AAS, B, NYP, UP, Y
Title reads: *Lucy Temple: One of the Three Orphans.*
Vail 165.

2244 ———— ———— Philadelphia: Richard Magee, 1848.   129 p.
12mo   AAS, N, Y
Title reads: *Lucy Temple: One of the Three Orphans.*
Not in Vail.

2245 ———— The Fille de Chambre ...   Philadelphia: Printed for H. & P. Rice, 1794.   207 p.   12mo   AAS, H, IN, LCP, UV, Y
Vail 186.

2246 ——— ——— Baltimore: Printed by James Angell, 1794.
    Vail 187.

2247 ——— ——— Baltimore: Printed by S. & J. Adams, 1795. 256
    p. 12mo   AAS, UC
    Vail 188.

2248 ——— ——— Baltimore: Printed for Thomas E. Clayland,
    1795. 256 p. 12mo   H
    Vail 189.

2249 ——— ——— Boston: R. P. & C. Williams, 1814. 249 p. 12mo
                        AAS, H, IN, LC, NYP, NYS, UC, Y
    Title reads: *Rebecca; or, The Fille de Chambre.*
    Vail 202.

2250 ——— ——— Boston: Printed for the booksellers, 1831. 288
    p. 12mo   AAS, NYH, UC, UP, Y
    Title reads: *Rebecca; or, The Fille de Chambre.*
    Cover imprint date 1832.
    Vail 203.

 ——— The History of Charlotte Temple. *See* Charlotte Temple

2251 ——— The Inquisitor; or, Invisible Rambler ... Philadelphia:
Printed and sold by William Gibbons, 1793. 3 vols. in 1. 12mo
                        AAS, BA, IN, NYH, UV
    Vail 192.

2252 ——— ——— Philadelphia: Mathew Carey, 1794. 3 vols. in 1.
    12mo
           AAS, B, BP, H, HEH, IN, JCB, LC, N, NYP, UC, UM, UP, UV, Y
    Vail 193.

 ——— Lucy Temple: One of the Three Orphans. *See* Charlotte's Daughter; or, The Three Orphans, Nos. 2243-44.

2253 ——— Mentoria; or, The Young Lady's Friend ... Philadelphia: Robert Campbell, 1794. 2 vols. in 1. 12mo
           AAS, B, H, IN, LC, LCP, N, NYP, UP, UV, Y
    Vail 197.

 ——— Rebecca; or, The Fille de Chambre. *See* The Fille de Chambre, Nos. 2249-50.

2254 —— Reuben and Rachel; or, Tales of Old Times . . . Boston: Printed by Manning & Loring, 1798. 2 vols. in 1. 12mo
AAS, B, BA, BP, H, HEH, IN, LC, NYH, NYP, NYS, UC, UM, UP, UV, Y
Vail 205.

2255 —— Sarah; or, The Exemplary Wife . . . Boston: Charles Williams, 1813. 270 p. 24mo
AAS, BP, H, HEH, LC, NYH, NYP, UC, UP, UV, Y
Written in a series of letters.
Vail 207.

2256 —— Trials of the Human Heart . . . Philadelphia: Printed for the author, 1795. 4 vols. 12mo
AAS, BA, H, HEH, IN, LCP, N, NYP(V.1-2), NYS, UC, UP, UV, Y
Vail 212.

2257 ROYALL, ANNE (NEWPORT). The Tennessean: A Novel, Founded on Facts . . . New Haven: Printed for the author, 1827. 372 p. 12mo AAS, BA, BP, H, IN, LC, LCP, N, NYH, NYP, UP, UPI, UV, Y
Boston and New Orleans.

ROYCE, ASHLEY ALLEN, pseud. See Hawthorne, Nathaniel

2258 ROYSTON, SAMUEL WATSON. The Enemy Conquered; or, Love Triumphant . . . New Haven: T. H. Pease, 1845. 31 p. 12mo
AAS, BP, H, Y
Georgia.

2259 RURAL LIFE in New England: A Domestic Romance. By the Author of "Lights and Shadows of Factory Life." New York: J. Winchester, New World Press, 30 Ann Street [cop. 1844]. 114 p. 8vo AAS, B, H, HEH, LC, NYP, Y
On cover: "New World Library of Fiction—No. 20."
Written by Eliza Jane Cate.

2260 RUSH, CAROLINE E. Robert Morton; or, The Step-mother. A Book Founded on Fact. Containing: Edmund and Ione; Letters from the South . . . Philadelphia: Published for the authoress by Crissy & Markley, 1850. 191 p., illus. 12mo
AAS, BP, H, HEH, LC, N, NYP, UP, Y

2261 RUSH, REBECCA. Kelroy: A Novel. By a Lady of Pennsylvania [anon.]. Philadelphia: Bradford and Inskeep, 1812. 301 p. 12mo AAS, BA, H, HEH, LC, LCP, N, NYP, UM, UP, UV, Y
Philadelphia; contemporary.

2262 RUTER, P. S. Reminiscences of a Virginia Physician ... Louisville: Ben Casseday & Co., 1849. 2 pts. 8vo

AAS, B, H, HEH(pt. 2), LC, NYH, NYP, UM

Paged continuously (278 p.).

Contents: Scenes in 1811: A Night with an Earthquake—Hydrophobia—Body-Snatching—The Burned Ship—The Presentiment—The Too Early Marriage—Mary Landon—The Old Bachelor—Circumstantial Evidence—Keeping Up the Family Name—The Clergyman's Story—Crime and Punishment—The Drunkard's Son.

S., E. C. The Italian Bride. *In* The Romantic Historian (1834), No. 2154.

2263 S., J. S. Barbara Howard; or, The Belle of Allensville ... [anon.]. Boston: Sleeper, Dix and Rogers, 1841. 106 p. 8vo

AAS, HEH, UP, Y

2264 SABIN, ELIJAH ROBINSON. The Life and Reflections of Charles Observator, in Which Are Displayed the Real Characters of Human Life ... Boston: Printed by Rowe & Hooper, 1816. 271 p. 12mo   AAS, B, BA, BP, H, IN, LC, LCP, N, UC, UM, UP, Y
New England.

2265 ST. CLAIR, A. S. Senora Ines; or, The American Volunteers. A Tale of the Mexican War ... Boston: F. Gleason [cop. 1848]. 100 p. 8vo   AAS, H, UC, Y
Printed in double cols.
LC has a title page, deposited Dec. 1848.

2266 ST. CLAIR, HENRY, *comp.* Tales of Terror; or, The Mysteries of Magic. A Selection of Wonderful and Supernatural Stories, Translated from the Chinese, Turkish, and German ... Boston: Printed and published by Charles Gaylord, 1833. 2 vols. in 1, illus. 12mo   Y
Contains: Peter Rugg, the Missing Man, by William Austin.

2267 ————— ——— Boston: Printed and published by Charles Gaylord, 1835-33. 2 vols. in 1, illus. 12mo   AAS, HEH, NYP, UM
Contains: Peter Rugg, the Missing Man, by William Austin.

2268 ————— ——— Philadelphia: J. Harding, 1848. 2 vols. in 1, illus. 12mo   LC, NYP, UP
Contains: Peter Rugg, the Missing Man, by William Austin.

2269 ST. HERBERT: A Tale. By an American Lady. Windsor: Printed by Thomas M. Pomroy, 1813. 105 p. 12mo   AAS, B, NYP, Y
New York City.

2270 ST. HUBERT; or, Mistaken Friendship. District of Columbia: W. W. Wood, 1800. 36 p. 8vo   NYP

2271 ST. ROSALIE; or, The Mysterious Casket. Boston: "Star Spangled Banner" office [1849]. 100 p. 8vo   NYP, UP
At head of title: "A Tale of Thrilling Interest."

2272 THE SALEM BELLE: A Tale of 1692. Boston: Tappan & Dennet, 1842. 238 p. 12mo
AAS, B, BP, H, HEH, IN, N, NYH, NYP, UC, UP, UV, Y

2273 ——— Boston: John M. Whittemore, 1847. 238 p. 12mo
AAS, IN, LC, UM, Y
Title reads: *The Salem Belle: A Tale of Love and Witchcraft in the Year 1692.*

2274 SALEM WITCHCRAFT; or, The Adventures of Parson Handy from Punkapog Pond. Second Edition with Corrections. New York: Elam Bliss, 1827. 71 p. 12mo   BP, LC
Possibly the 1st ed. in book form.

SAMPSON-SHORT-AND-FAT, *pseud. See* Kettell, Samuel

2275 SAN BLAS, CAESARIO, *pseud.* A Voyage to the Island of Philosophers, by Caesario San Blas [pseud.], Bachelor. Part 1st: Containing an Account of the Island and Its Inhabitants... [N.p.], 1830. 53 p. 8vo   AAS

SANDS, ROBERT CHARLES. Boyuca. *In* W. C. Bryant, *ed.,* Tales of Glauber-Spa (1832), Nos. 439-441.

2275a ——— The Executioner, Being a True, Impartial, and Most Extraordinary Account of What Happened to the Man Who Burnt the Rev. John Rogers, as Related by His Son James Rogers [pseud.]. Philadelphia: Wm. Beastall, No. 507 Market Street [183-?]. 62 p., illus. 18mo   H, HEH, NYP, UV
Included in No. 2276 under title, "The Man Who Burnt John Rogers."

——— Mr. Green. *In* W. C. Bryant, *ed.,* Tales of Glauber-Spa (1832), Nos. 439-441.

2276 ——— The Writings of Robert C. Sands... New York: Harper & Brothers, 1834. 2 vols., illus. 8vo
AAS, B, BA, BP, HEH, IN, LC, N, NYH, NYP, NYS, UC, UM, UP, Y
Contains: The German's Story—The Man Who Burnt John Rogers—A Simple Tale—Boyuca—Mr. De Viellecour and His Neighbours—Scenes at Washington—Ghosts on the Stage.

2277 ——— ——— 2d ed. New York: Harper & Brothers, 1835. 2 vols., illus. 8vo   AAS, H, HEH, LC, NYP, Y(V.1)
Sabin 76442 lists an 1836 ed.

SANFORD, EDWARD. A Charcoal Sketch of Pot Pie Palmer. *In* The Atlantic Club-Book (1834), Nos. 195-196.

2278 SANFORD, EZEKIEL. The Humours of Eutopia: A Tale of Colonial Times. By an Eutopian ... [anon.]. Philadelphia: Carey, Lea & Carey, 1828. 2 vols. 12mo
AAS, B, BA, BP, H, HEH, LC, UP, Y
LC also has a title page dated 1827, deposited Dec. 17, 1827.
Connecticut.

2278a SANFORD, RUFUS BISHOP. Allington; or, The Stolen Child. A Tale of Novel Interest ... Hartford: Printed by J. Gaylord Welk, 1846. 353 p. 16mo   B, LC

2279 SANSAY, LEONORA (MARY HASSALL?). Laura. By a Lady of Philadelphia ... [anon.]. Philadelphia: Bradford & Inskeep, 1809. 181 p. 12mo
AAS, H, HEH, IN, LC, LCP, N, NYH, NYP, UP, UV, Y
The Preface is dated "Philadelphia, Feb. 14th, 1809."
LCP 2d copy, shelved in the Pennsylvania Historical Society, has Preface dated "New York, February 15th, 1809."
The compiler acknowledges his indebtedness to Louis Aguilar Eyre and Miss Suzanne Webb for information indicating that this and the following title are by the same author.
Philadelphia; late 18th cent.

2280 ——— Secret History; or, The Horrors of St. Domingo, in a Series of Letters, Written by a Lady at Cape Francois to Colonel Burr, Late Vice-President of the United States, Principally during the Command of General Rochambeau [anon.]. Philadelphia: Bradford & Inskeep, 1808. 225 p. 12mo AAS, B, BA, BP, H, HEH, HM, IN, LC, LCP, N, NYH, NYP, NYS, UP, UV, Y

2281 SARGENT, CHARLES LENOX. The Life of Alexander Smith, Captain of the Island of Pitcairn, One of the Mutineers on Board His Majesty's Ship Bounty, Commanded by Lieutenant William Bligh. Written by Smith Himself, on the Above Island, and Bringing the Accounts from Pitcairn, Down to the Year 1815 [anon.]. Boston: Printed by Sylvester T. Goss, 1819. 240 p. 12mo   BA, BP, H, LC, N, NYP, Y

2282 SARGENT, EPES. Fleetwood; or, The Stain of Birth. A Novel of American Life [anon.]. New York: Burgess, Stringer and Company, 1845. 238 p. 12mo   AAS
Reviewed in the *Broadway Journal*, I, No. 23 (June 7, 1845).

2283 ———— Wealth and Worth; or, Which Makes the Man? . . . New York: Harper & Brothers, 1842. 204 p., illus. 12mo
AAS, H, HEH, LC, UP, Y

2284 ———— ———— New York: Harper & Brothers, 1843. 204 p., illus. 12mo   AAS, N, Y

2284a ———— ———— New York: Harper & Brothers, 1845. 204 p., illus. 12mo   HEH, Y

2284b ———— What's to Be Done? or, The Will and the Way . . . [anon.]. New York: Harper and Brothers, 1842. 232 p. 12mo   Y

2284c ———— ———— New York: Harper and Brothers, 1846. 232 p. 12mo   AAS

2285 SARGENT, LUCIUS MANLIUS. As a Medicine. Founded on Fact ... [anon.]. Boston: Whipple & Damrell, 1839. 155 p. 12mo
AAS, H, HEH, LC, Y
At head of title: "Number Eighteen."
As the majority of Sargent's temperance tales ran to many eds., and the eds. were usually made up of the same sheets with new title pages or cover titles, the various eds. are listed under the first entry in this bibliography.
2d thousand, 1839. AAS
3d thousand, 1839. Y
4th thousand, 1839. Y
5th thousand, 1839. AAS, N, Y
7th thousand, 1840. AAS, NYP

2286 ———— Diary of the Rev. Solomon Spittle ... [anon.]. Boston: W. S. Damrell, 1847. 54 p. 12mo   AAS, BP, HEH, LC, Y

2287 ———— Fritz Hazell. Founded on Fact [anon.]. Boston: William S. Damrell, 1835. 98 p. 16mo   HEH
At head of title: "Number Seven."
4th ed., 1835. HEH
5th ed., 1835. N, Y
6th ed., 1835. AAS, BA, HEH
7th ed., 1836. AAS
8th ed., 1837. Y
8th ed., 1838. AAS, NYP
10th ed., 1838. AAS
11th thousand, 1839. AAS, HEH, Y
12th thousand, 1839. AAS, Y
13th thousand, 1839. NYP

2288 ———— Groggy Harbor; or, A Smooth Stone from the Brook. And A Shepherd's Sling [anon.]. Boston: Ford and Damrell, 1834. 76 p. 12mo   BP, HEH, NYP, Y
At head of title: "Number Five."
3d ed., 1834. AAS
4th ed., 1835. AAS, BP
6th ed., 1835. HEH, Y
8th ed., 1835. B, HEH
8th ed., 1836. HEH
9th ed., 1836. AAS, BP
9th ed., 1837. AAS, BA, Y
10th thousand, 1839. AAS
11th thousand, 1839. AAS, Y
12th thousand, 1840. AAS, NYP
12th thousand, 1843. AAS

2289 ———— I Am Afraid There Is a God! Founded on Fact . . . [anon.]. Boston: Ford and Damrell, 1833. 47 p. 16mo
                              AAS, BA, BP, HEH, IN, Y
At head of title: "Number Three."
3d ed., 1833. AAS, BP, Y
7th ed., 1835. AAS, B, H, HEH, LC
11th ed., 1836. AAS, BP, Y
12th ed., 1837. AAS, Y
13th ed., 1839. Y
14th thousand, 1839. AAS, Y
15th thousand, 1840. AAS, H, N, NYP
15th thousand, 1843. AAS

2290 ———— An Irish Heart. Founded on Fact [anon.]. Boston: William S. Damrell, 1836. 158 p. 16mo   HEH
At head of title: "Number Eleven."
3d ed., 1836. BA
4th ed., 1836. Y
5th ed., 1836. AAS, BP, N
7th ed., 1837. AAS, Y
7th ed., 1838. NYP, Y
8th thousand, 1839. AAS
9th thousand, 1840. AAS, H
9th thousand, 1843. AAS, UC

2291 ———— Kitty Grafton. Founded on Fact [anon.]. Boston: Whipple and Damrell, 1837. 130 p. 16mo
                              AAS, HEH, N, NYP, UP. Y
At head of title: "Number Fourteen."
2d ed., 1838.
7th thousand, 1839. AAS, HEH, Y
8th thousand, 1840. NYP
8th thousand, 1843. AAS

2292 ——— The Legal Remedy; or, The Beauties of Going to Law. As Illustrated in the Famous Case of Pilkington vs. Popsquirt . . . [anon.]. Boston: Redding and Company, 1849. 24 p., illus. 12mo AAS, NYP, Y

2293 ——— The Life-Preserver. Founded on Fact [anon.]. Boston: Whipple & Damrell, 1838. 132 p. 16mo BP, HEH
At head of title: "Number Seventeen."
3d ed., 1839. AAS
4th thousand, 1839. Y
5th thousand, 1839. AAS, N, UP, Y
6th thousand, 1839. AAS
7th thousand, 1840. AAS, NYP

2294 ——— Margaret's Bridal. Founded on Fact . . . [anon.]. Boston: Whipple & Damrell, 1839. 86 p. 16mo
AAS, BP, H, HEH, LC, N, Y
At head of title: "Number Twenty."
4th thousand, 1839. Y

2295 ——— My Mother's Gold Ring . . . Boston: Ford and Damrell, 1833. 24 p. 16mo BA, IN
At head of title: "Number One."
2d ed., 1833. AAS
3d ed., 1833. AAS, BP
4th ed., 1833. NYP
5th ed., 1833. AAS, BP, Y
6th ed., 1833. AAS, BP, Y
7th ed., 1833. AAS, NYP, Y
8th ed., 1833. Y
9th ed., 1833. AAS, BP
10th ed., 1833. AAS
12th ed., 1833. AAS, HEH
13th ed., 1833. AAS, NYP
14th ed., 1833. NYP
15th ed., 1833. AAS, BP, HEH, UP, Y
16th ed., 1833. AAS, BP, HEH, NYP, Y
17th ed., 1833. AAS, HEH, N, Y
18th ed., 1833. AAS, NYP
19th ed., 1833. AAS
20th ed., 1834. BP
22d ed., 1834. AAS, BA, Y
24th ed., 1834. HEH
25th ed., 1834. AAS
28th ed., 1834.
31st ed., 1835. AAS, B, H, HEH
31st ed., 1836. Y
110th ed., 1836. AAS, BP, Y
111th ed., 1837. AAS, Y

112th thousand, 1839. AAS
113th thousand, 1839. AAS
114th thousand, 1840. NYP
114th thousand, 1843. AAS

2296 ——— Nancy Le Baron. Founded on Fact [anon.]. Boston: William S. Damrell, 1837. 89 p. 16mo   AAS, BP, HEH, Y
At head of title: "Number Thirteen."
5th ed., 1837. AAS
5th ed., 1838. B, NYP
6th thousand, 1839. AAS, Y
7th thousand, 1839. AAS, Y
8th thousand, 1840. NYP
8th thousand, 1843. AAS, BP

2297 ——— The Prophets! Where Are They? Founded on Fact [anon.]. Boston: Whipple & Damrell, 1839. 36 p. 16mo
AAS, H, HEH, LC, N, UP, Y
At head of title: "Number Nineteen."
6th thousand, 1839. Y
7th thousand, 1840. AAS
9th thousand, 1840. AAS, NYP

2298 ——— Right Opposite. Founded on Fact [anon.]. Boston: William S. Damrell, 1835. 64 p. 16mo   HEH, NYP
At head of title: "Number Six."
4th ed., 1835. AAS, Y
6th ed., 1835. AAS, BA, HEH, N, Y
7th ed., 1835. HEH
8th ed., 1835. NYP, Y
10th ed., 1835. UP, Y
10th ed., 1838. AAS
11th thousand, 1839. HEH, Y
12th thousand, 1840. NYP

2299 ——— A Sectarian Thing [anon.]. Boston: Ford and Damrell, 1834. 48 p. 16mo   BA, BP, IN, UP, Y
At head of title: "Number Four."
2d ed., 1834. AAS, UP, Y
3d ed., 1834. AAS
4th ed., 1834. AAS, BP, N
6th ed., 1835. AAS
7th ed., 1835. AAS, B, H, HEH
7th ed., 1836. HEH
8th ed., 1836. AAS, BP
9th ed., 1837. AAS, NYP, Y
10th thousand, 1839. AAS
11th thousand, 1839. AAS, Y
12th thousand, 1840. AAS, NYP

2300 ———— Seed Time and Harvest. Founded on Fact . . . [anon.].
Boston: William S. Damrell, 1835. 24 p. 16mo

AAS, HEH, IN, Y

At head of title: "Number Ten."
7th ed., 1835. AAS, BA, HEH
8th ed., 1836. AAS, N
9th ed., 1837. Y
9th ed., 1838. AAS, NYP
10th thousand, 1839. AAS, HEH, Y
11th thousand, 1840. NYP

2301 ———— The Stage-coach. Founded on Fact [anon.]. Boston:
Whipple & Damrell, 1838. 288 p. 12mo B, HEH, IN, N, UV, Y
At head of title: "Number Sixteen."
2d ed., 1838. AAS, HEH, UP, Y
3d ed., 1838. HEH, UC
4th ed., 1838. LC, UC
5th thousand, 1839. AAS
6th thousand, 1839. AAS
7th thousand, 1840. AAS, NYP
9th thousand, 1843. AAS, H

2302 ———— The Temperance Meeting in the Village of Tattertown.
Founded on Fact [anon.]. Boston: William S. Damrell, 1843.
232 p. 16mo H, HEH, IN, LC
At head of title: "Number Twenty-One."

———— Temperance Tales. Boston [various dates]. 6 vols.
16mo
These tales are Sargent's separately issued titles, collected and issued with
general title pages.

2303 ———— Too Fast and Too Far; or, The Cooper and the Currier.
Founded on Fact [anon.]. Boston: Whipple & Damrell, 1837.
34 p. 16mo AAS, HEH, UP, Y
At head of title: "Number Fifteen."
—1838. BP, NYP
5th thousand, 1839. AAS, Y
6th thousand, 1839. AAS
7th thousand, 1840. AAS, NYP
7th thousand, 1843. AAS

2303a ———— Well Enough for the Vulgar. Founded on Fact [anon.].
Boston: William S. Damrell, 1836. 99 p. 16mo HEH

2304 ———— ———— 2d ed. Boston: Whipple & Damrell, 1836. 99
p. 16mo Y

At head of title: "Number Twelve."
3d ed., 1836.   AAS, BP, HEH, N
7th ed., 1837.   AAS
7th ed., 1838.   AAS, NYP, Y
8th thousand, 1839.
9th thousand, 1840.   NYP
14th thousand, 1843.   AAS, UC

2305   —— What a Curse! or, Johnny Hodges, the Blacksmith. Founded on Fact [anon.].   Boston: William S. Damrell, 1835. 32 p.   16mo   BA, HEH
At head of title: "Number Eight."
4th ed., 1835.   AAS, BA, HEH, Y
5th ed., 1836.   AAS, N
6th ed., 1837.   Y
6th ed., 1838.   NYP
8th thousand, 1839.   AAS, HEH, Y
9th thousand, 1840.   NYP

2306   —— Wild Dick and Good Little Robin [anon.].   Boston: Ford & Damrell, 1833.   41 p.   16mo   AAS, BA, IN, UP, Y
At head of title: "Number Two."
2d ed., 1833.   AAS, NYP
3d ed., 1833.   AAS
4th ed., 1833.   AAS, HEH, N, Y
5th ed., 1833.   AAS, BP
5th ed., 1834.   AAS
6th ed., 1834.   AAS, HEH, LC
8th ed., 1835.   AAS, B
9th ed., 1836.   HEH
23d ed., 1836.   AAS, BP, Y
24th ed., 1837.   AAS, UM, Y
25th thousand, 1839.   AAS
26th thousand, 1839.   AAS, Y
27th thousand, 1840.   AAS, NYP
27th thousand, 1843.   AAS

2307   —— A Word in Season; or, The Sailor's Widow.   Founded on Fact . . . [anon.].   Boston: William S. Damrell, 1835.   36 p. 16mo   AAS, B
At head of title: "Number Nine."
2d ed., 1835.   AAS
7th ed., 1835.   AAS, B, BA, HEH, Y
7th ed., 1836.   AAS, HEH, LC
8th ed., 1836.   AAS, N
9th ed., 1837.   AAS, Y
9th ed., 1838.   AAS, NYP, Y
10th thousand, 1839.   AAS, HEH, Y
11th thousand, 1839.   AAS
12th thousand, 1840.   NYP

2308 SAVAGE, SARAH. The Factory Girl. By a Lady . . . [anon.]. Boston: Munroe, Francis & Parker, 1814. 112 p. 12mo

AAS, B, HEH, Y

Hampton; contemporary.

2309 ———— ———— 2d ed. Boston: Munroe and Francis, 1824. 105 p. 12mo

Y

2310 ———— Filial Affection; or, The Clergyman's Granddaughter. A Moral Tale . . . [anon.]. Boston: Cummings and Hilliard, 1820. 162 p. 12mo

AAS, BA, H, Y

2311 ———— James Talbot . . . [anon.]. Cambridge: Hilliard and Metcalf, Nov., 1821. 37 p. 12mo

AAS, B, BA, Y

2312 ———— ———— Boston: Christian Register Office, John B. Russell, printer, 1824. 35 p. 12mo

AAS, BA, HEH, LC, Y

2313 ———— James Talbot, and The Suspected Boy . . . Boston: Wm. Crosby and H. P. Nichols, 1845. 127 p. 12mo

AAS

2314 ———— Trial and Self-Discipline . . . [anon.]. Boston and Cambridge: James Munroe and Company, 1835. 100 p. 12mo

AAS, BA, H, HEH, LC, N, UM, UP, Y

Included in *Scenes and Characters Illustrating Christian Truths*. No. I. (1835).

2315 SAVAGE, TIMOTHY, B.C., *pseud.?* Amazonian Republic, Recently Discovered in the Interior of Peru. By Ex-Midshipman Timothy Savage, B.C. [pseud.?] . . . New York: Samuel Coleman, 1842. 177 p. 12mo

AAS, BA, BP, H, HEH, LC, N, NYP, UC, UM, UP, Y

2316 SAWYER, CAROLINE MEHETABEL (FISHER). The Merchant's Widow and Other Tales . . . New York: P. Price, 1841. 192 p. 12mo

AAS, B, HEH, N, NYP, UP, Y

Also contains: The Unequal Marriage—The Lonely Burial—The Valley of Peace.

2317 ———— ———— Boston: A. Tompkins, 1841. 192 p. 12mo

AAS, Y

Also contains: The Unequal Marriage—The Lonely Burial—The Valley of Peace.

2317a ———— ———— New York: Hallock & Lynn, 1849. 192 p. 12mo

AAS

Also contains: The Unequal Marriage—The Lonely Burial—The Valley of Peace.

2318 SAWYER, LEMUEL. Printz Hall: A Record of New Sweden . . . [anon.]. Philadelphia: Carey & Hart, 1839. 2 vols. 12mo
AAS(v.1), LC, N, NYH, UP, Y

SCENES AND CHARACTERS Illustrating Christian Truths (1835). *See* Nos. 966, 1612, 2314, and 2341.

2319 SCENES AT WASHINGTON: A Story of the Last Generation. By a Citizen of Baltimore. New York: Harper & Brothers, 1848.
197 p. 12mo   AAS, B, BP, HEH, LC, N, NYP, UC, UM, UP, Y

2320 SCHNAP, JULIUS, *pseud.* Old Times and New; or, A Few Raps over the Knuckles of the Present Age. By Julius Schnap [pseud.] and Hans van Garretson [pseud.], the Orange Blossoms of Niew Amsterdam. New York: Printed for the publishers, 1846. 93 p. 12mo   AAS, H, LC, LCP, NYP, Y
New York City.

2321 SCOTT, JULIA H. (KINNEY). The Blind Widow and Her Family. Written for the Evangelical Magazine and Gospel Advocate . . . Hudson: Printed by Ashbel Stoddard, 1837. 24 p. 16mo
AAS, H, LC, Y
At head of title: "Prize Tale."

2322 ———— The Sacrifice: A Clergyman's Story. By Julia H. Kinney . . . Hudson: Printed by Ashbel Stoddard, 1837. 24 p. 16mo   AAS, LC, Y
At head of title: "Prize Tale."

2323 SCOTT, RAPHAEL. The Voyages, Adventures, and Miraculous Escapes of Raphael Scott . . . Philadelphia: E. E. Barclay, 1850.
47 p., illus. 8vo   AAS, HEH, NYP

2324 THE SCOTTISH EXILES, Rendered into Prose, from Sir Walter Scott's "Lady of the Lake." By a Lady of Philadelphia. Philadelphia: J. Field, 1828. 180 p. 12mo   B, LCP, UM, UP, Y

2325 THE SCRAP TABLE, for MDCCCXXXI. Boston: Carter, Hendee & Babcock, 1830. 184 p. 12mo
AAS, B, BA, BP, H, HEH, NYH, NYP, UM, UP, Y
Contents: The Hermit of Drooninggarde—Voyage of Mary Queen of Scots —The Decree in Chancery—The Arlingtons: A Sketch—A Sketch of the Olden Time—The Exile—The Hon. Mrs. Napier—All for Love, All for Honor—Ascot Heath: A Tale of the Olden Time.

2326 SEABORN, *Captain* ADAM, *pseud.* Symzonia: A Voyage of Discovery. By Captain Adam Seaborn [pseud.]. New York: Printed by J. Seymour, 1820. 248 p., illus. 12mo
AAS, B, BA, BP, H, HEH, IN, LC, LCP, NYH, NYP, NYS, UC, UP, UV, Y
J. O. Bailey, "An Early American Utopian Fiction," *American Literature*, XIV (Durham, N.C., 1942), 285-293, suggests that John Cleves Symmes was the author.

2327 SEALSFIELD, CHARLES. The Cabin Book; or, Sketches of Life in Texas. By Seatsfield . . . New York: J. Winchester, 1844. 155 p. 8vo
AAS, BA, H, HEH, HM, LC, LCP, NYP(pt. 3), UC, UP, Y
Printed in double cols.
Issued in 3 pts.
Author born Karl Anton Postl.

2328 ——— ——— Philadelphia: Colon and Adriance, 1845. Cover title, 155 p. 8vo LC, Y
Title reads: *Life in Texas.*
At head of title: "Price Twelve and a Half Cents."
Printed in double cols.
Issued in 3 pts.

——— Life in Texas. *See* The Cabin Book, No. 2328.

2329 DELETE.

2330 ——— Life in the New World; or, Sketches of American Society. By Seatsfield ... New York: J. Winchester, New World Press, XXX Ann Street [cop. 1844]. 7 pts. (349 p.) 8vo
AAS, B, BA, BP, H, HEH, HM, IN, LC, N, NYP, NYS, UC, UM, UP, Y
Cover titles of the pts. extend the above title as follows: Pt. I, The Courtship of George Howard, Esq. . . . ; Pt. II, Containing the Completion of the Courtship of George Howard, Esq., and The Courtship of Ralph Doughby, Esq.; Pt. III, Containing the Completion of the Courtship of Ralph Doughby, Esq., and The Life of a Planter . . . ; Pt. IV, Containing the Life of a Planter . . . ; Pt. V, Containing Scenes in the South-West . . . ; Pt. VI, Containing the Squatter Chief; or, The First American in Texas . . . ; Pt. VII, Containing the Completion of the First American in Texas.
Advert. on back cover of Pt. VII: "Now complete in seven numbers—price twelve and-a-half cents each, or one dollar bound."
Copyright notice on verso of title page in three lines. Second printing? in two lines.
Printed in double cols.

——— A Night on the Banks of the Tennessee. *In* The Atlantic Club-Book (1834), Nos. 195-196.

2331 ———— North and South; or, Scenes and Adventures in Mexico. By Seatsfield ... New York: J. Winchester, 30 Ann Street [cop. 1844]. 118 p. 12mo

AAS, H, HEH, HM, LC, NYP, UC, UP, Y

Printed in double cols.

2332 ———— Rambleton: A Romance of Fashionable Life in New York during the Great Speculation of 1836. By Seatsfield ... New York: J. Winchester, 30 Ann Street [cop. 1844]. 285 p. 12mo

AAS, BA, H, LC, N, UP, Y

Printed in double cols.

2333 ———— ———— New York: William Taylor, No. 2 Astor House [1846]. 285 p. 12mo H, HEH, N, NYP, UC, Y

Cover title: "Flirtations in America; or, High Life in New York and Saratoga. New York, 1846."
Printed in double cols.
H has a 2d copy with cover imprint dated 1847.

2334 ———— Tokeah; or, The White Rose ... [anon.]. Philadelphia: Carey, Lea & Carey, 1829. 2 vols. 12mo LC(V.1), NYP, UC

Georgia frontier; early 19th cent.

2335 ———— ———— 2d ed. Philadelphia: Lea and Blanchard, 1845. 98 p. 8vo B, BP, N

Printed in double cols.

SEATSFIELD. *See* Sealsfield, Charles

SEAWORTHY, GREGORY, *pseud. See* Throop, George Higby

SECONDTHOUGHTS, SOLOMON, *pseud. See* Kennedy, John Pendleton

SEDGWICK, CATHARINE MARIA. Le Bossu. *In* W. C. Bryant, *ed.,* Tales of Glauber-Spa (1832), Nos. 439-441.

2336 ———— The Boy of Mount Rhigi ... [anon.]. Boston: Chas. H. Peirce, 1848. 252 p., illus. 12mo

AAS, BA, BP, H, HEH, IN, N, UC, UP, Y

Western Massachusetts.

2337 ———— ———— Boston: William Crosby and H. P. Nichols, printers, 1849. 252 p., illus. 12mo AAS, IN, N, UC, Y

2338 ———— ———— Boston: William Crosby and H. P. Nichols, printers, 1850. 252 p., illus. 12mo AAS, B, IN, Y

2339 —————— Clarence; or, A Tale of Our Own Times . . . [anon.].
Philadelphia: Carey & Lea, 1830. 2 vols. 12mo
AAS, B, BA, BP, HEH, IN, LC, LCP, N, NYP, NYS, UC, UP, UV, Y
New York City.

2340 ————— ————— New York: George P. Putnam, 1849. 515 p.,
illus. 12mo   AAS, BP, H, HEH, LC, LCP, NYP, NYS, UC, UM, UP, Y

2341 ————— Home . . . [anon.]. Boston: James Munroe and Company, 1835. 158 p. 12mo   AAS, B, BA, BP, HEH, UP, Y
New York City; contemporary.
Included in *Scenes and Characters Illustrating Christian Truths.* No. III
(1835).

2342 ————— ————— 3d ed. Boston: James Munroe and Company,
1835. 158 p. 12mo   AAS, Y

2343 ————— ————— Boston: James Munroe and Company, 1837.
158 p. 12mo   AAS, IN, UC, Y
No ed. number.

2344 ————— ————— 12th ed. Boston: James Munroe and Company,
1837. 158 p. 12mo   BA, BP, NYP

2345 ————— ————— 15th ed. Boston: James Munroe and Company,
1839. 158 p. 12mo   AAS, H, IN, Y

2345a ————— ————— 15th ed. Boston: James Munroe and Company,
1840. 158 p. 12mo   AAS

2345b ————— ————— 15th ed. Boston: James Munroe and Company,
1841. 158 p. 12mo   AAS, Y

2346 ————— ————— 15th ed. Boston: James Munroe and Company,
1845. 158 p. 12mo   NYH

2347 ————— ————— 20th ed. Boston: James Munroe and Company,
1846. 158 p. 12mo   BP, Y

2347a ————— ————— 20th ed. Boston: James Munroe and Company,
1850. 158 p. 12mo   Y

2348 ————— Hope Leslie; or, Early Times in the Massachusetts . . .
[anon.]. New York: White, Gallaher and White, 1827. 2
vols. 12mo
AAS, B, BA, H, HEH, IN, LC, LCP, N, NYP, UC, UM, UP, UV, Y
Early 17th cent.

2349 ——— ——— New York: Harper & Brothers, 1842. 2 vols.
12mo   AAS, BA, H, HEH(V.2), IN, LC, LCP, N, NYP, NYS

2350 ——— The Linwoods; or, "Sixty Years Since" in America . . .
[anon.]. New York: Harper & Brothers, 1835. 2 vols. 12mo
AAS, B, BA, BP, H, HEH, IN, LC, LCP, N, NYP, NYS, UC, UM, UP, UV, Y
New York City.

2350a ——— ——— New York: Harper & Brothers, 1836. 2 vols.
12mo   Y

2351 ——— Live and Let Live; or, Domestic Service Illustrated . . .
[anon.]. New York: Harper & Brothers, 1837. 216 p. 12mo
AAS, B, BA, BP, H, HEH, IN, LC, LCP, N, NYH, NYP, NYS, UC, UM, UP,
UV, Y
New York City; 182-.

2352 ——— ——— New York: Harper & Brothers, 1838. 216 p.
12mo   AAS, Y

2353 ——— ——— New York: Harper & Brothers, 1841. 216 p.
12mo   AAS

2353a ——— ——— New York: Harper & Brothers, 1842. 216 p.
12mo   AAS

2354 ——— Mary Hollis: An Original Tale . . . [anon.]. New York:
New-York Unitarian Book Society. Printed by Van Pelt and
Spear, 1822. 22 p. 8vo   HEH, Y

2355 ——— ——— Concord, N.H., 1834. 23 p. 12mo
AAS, H, N, Y

2356 ——— A New-England Tale; or, Sketches of New-England
Character and Manners . . . [anon.]. New York: E. Bliss & E.
White, 1822. 277 p. 12mo
B, BP, H, HEH, IN, LC, NYH, NYP, NYS, UM, UP, UV, Y

2357 ——— ——— 2d ed. New York: E. Bliss & E. White, 1822.
285 p. 12mo   AAS, BA, BP, H, HEH, IN, N, UC, Y

2358 ——— The Poor Rich Man and the Rich Poor Man . . . [anon.].
New York: Harper & Brothers, 1836. 186 p. 12mo
AAS, B, BA, BP, H, HEH, IN, NYS, UC, UP, UV, Y
New York City.

2359 ——— ——— New York: Harper & Brothers, 1837. 186 p.
12mo   AAS, BA, BP, H, HEH, IN, LCP, N, UM, Y

2360 —— —— New York: Harper & Brothers, 1838. 186 p.
12mo   AAS, Y

2361 —— —— New York: Harper & Brothers, 1839. 186 p.
12mo   AAS, HEH, Y

2362 —— —— New York: Harper & Brothers, 1840. 186 p.
12mo   AAS, H

2362a —— —— New York: Harper & Brothers, 1841. 186 p.
12mo   AAS, HEH

2363 —— —— New York: Harper & Brothers, 1842. 186 p.
12mo   AAS, Y

2364 —— —— New York: Harper & Brothers, 1843. 186 p.
12mo   NYP

2364a —— —— New York: Harper & Brothers, 1845. 186 p.
12mo   AAS

2365 —— —— New York: Harper & Brothers, 1847. 186 p.
12mo   AAS, CLS

2366 —— Redwood: A Tale . . . [anon.]. New York: E. Bliss and
E. White, 1824. 2 vols. 12mo
            AAS, B, BP, H, HEH, IN, LC, N, NYH, NYP, UC, UP, UV, Y
New England; contemporary.

2367 —— —— New York: George P. Putnam, 1850. 457 p.
12mo   AAS, B, BA, H, LCP, NYP, NYS, UM, Y

—— Romance in Real Life. *In* N. P. Willis, *ed.*, The Legendary (1828), No. 2739.

2368 —— Tales and Sketches . . . Philadelphia: Carey, Lea and
Blanchard, 1835. 285 p. 12mo
            AAS, BP, HEH, IN, LC, LCP, N, NYP, UC, UM, UP, UV, Y
Contents: A Reminiscence of Federalism—The Catholic Iroquois—The
Country Cousin—Old Maids—The Chivalric Sailor—Mary Dyre—Cacoethes
Scribendi—The Eldest Sister—St. Catharine's Eve—Romance in Real Life—
The Canary Family.

2369 —— —— 2d Ser. New York: Harper & Brothers, 1844.
396 p. 12mo
            AAS, B, BA, BP, H, HEH, IN, N, NYP, NYS, UC, UM, UP, Y
Contents: Wilton Harvey—Cousin Frank—A Day in a Railroad Car—The
Irish Girl—Daniel Prime—A Huguenot Family—The Postoffice—A Vision—
Second Thoughts Best—Our Burial Place.

2370 ———— Tales of City Life: I, The City Clerk; II, Life Is Sweet
... Philadelphia: Hazard Mitchell, 1850. 91 p., illus. 16mo
B

2371 ———— The Travellers: A Tale, Designed for Young People ...
[anon.]. New York: E. Bliss and E. White, 1825. 171 p.
12mo   AAS, BA, BP, H, HEH, LCP, N, UM, UP, Y

2372 DELETE.

2373 SEDGWICK, SUSAN ANNE LIVINGSTON (RIDLEY). Alida; or, Town
and Country ... [anon.]. New York: Henry G. Langley, 1844.
176 p. 8vo   AAS, B, BA, BP, HEH, LCP, N, NYP, NYS, Y
Printed in double cols.
Brookside, Mass.

2374 ———— Allen Prescott; or, The Fortunes of a New England Boy
... [anon.]. New York: Harper & Brothers, 1834. 2 vols.
12mo
     AAS, B, BA, BP, H, HEH, HM, IN, LC, LCP, N, NYP, UC, UM, UP, Y

2375 ———— The Young Emigrants: A Tale Designed for Young Persons ... [anon.]. Boston: Carter and Hendee, 1830. 240 p.
12mo   AAS, B, BA, BP, HEH, LCP, N, NYP, UC, UM, Y
Ohio; late 18th cent.

2376 THE SEVEN BROTHERS of Wyoming; or, The Brigands of the Revolution. New York: H. Long & Brother [cop. 1850]. 114 p.
8vo   H, LC, N, Y
Written by M. M. Huet.

2377 SHECUT, JOHN LEWIS EDWARD WHITRIDGE. Ish-Noo-Ju-Lut-
Sche; or, The Eagle of the Mohawks. A Tale of the Seventeenth Century ... [anon.]. New York: P. Price, 1841. 2 vols.
12mo   AAS, B, H, HEH, IN, LC, N, NYH, NYP, UC, UM, UP, UV, Y

2378 ———— The Scout; or, The Fast of Saint Nicholas. A Tale of
the Seventeenth Century ... [anon.]. New York: C. L. Stick-
ney, 1844. 312 p. 12mo   AAS, B, HEH, IN, LC, Y
New York.

SHELTON, FREDERIC WILLIAM. Peter Cram; or, The Row at Tinnecum. A Sketch of Long Island. *In* L. G. Clark, *ed.*, The
Knickerbocker Sketch-book (1846), No. 545.

2379 ——— Salander and the Dragon: A Romance of the Hartz Prison . . . New York: Samuel Hueston, 1850. 184 p., illus. 12mo   AAS, H, HEH, LC, NYP, Y

2380 SHEPARD, ISAAC FITZGERALD. Scenes and Songs of Social Life . . . Boston: Saxton & Kelt, 1846. 336 p., illus. 12mo
                                    AAS, B, BA, BP, HEH, LC, NYP, UP, Y
Contains: The Trial and Triumph of Genius—The Profane Swearer—Woman's Love—The Forest Bride—Records of a Bachelors' Club: Session the First: The Rumseller's Death-bed—Records of a Bachelors' Club: Session the Second: Married for a Dinner—The First and Last Visit—Stella Lea, the Orphan Girl—A Stranger's Tale—The Betrayed—The Broken Heart—The Skipper's Daughter of Marblehead—The Sabbath Breakers.

2380a ——— ——— Boston: Phillips, Sampson & Co., 1850. 336 p., illus. 12mo   Y
Added engraved title page in Y copy dated 1851.

2380b SHEPHARD, MRS. The Invisible Monitor; or Memoirs of the D'Alvara Family . . . Philadelphia: Printed for Conrad Seyfert. John Bioren, printer, 1816. 8vo
Parke-Bernet catalog 2769:97.

2381 SHERBURNE, GEORGE ANN HUMPHREYS. Imogine; or, The Pirate's Treasure. The Demon's Cave . . . Washington, D.C.: William Fischer, 1839. 180 p. 12mo   H, LCP, NYP
Paper label on original binding reads: "Tales by Miss Sherburne."

2382 SHERBURNE, HENRY. The Oriental Philanthropist; or, True Republican . . . Portsmouth, N.H.: Wm. Treadwell & Co., 1800. 215, [1] p. 12mo   AAS, B,
       BA, BP, H, HEH, IN, JCB, LC, LCP, N, NYP, NYS, UC, UM, UP, UV, Y
LC 2d copy has pp. 113-115 reprinted.

2382a SHERIDAN, MRS. ELIZA. Ellen Fenton; or, The Miser of the North End . . . Boston: Jones's Publishing House, 1847. 50 p. 8vo
                                                                    AAS
Cover title: "Ellen Fenton, and The Secret Poisoner."
Printed in double cols.

2382b ——— The Gunsmith of Orleans; or, The Dead Woman's Secret. A Romance in Real Life . . . Boston: Jones's Publishing House. New York: H. Long & Brothers, 1847. 48 p. 8vo
Also contains: Viola of Venice; or, A Father's Marriage.
Information from LC card for copy withdrawn from circulation.

2382C ——— The Market Queen; or, The Wife's Stratagem. A Romance in Real Life . . . Boston: "Star Spangled Banner" office, 1848. 42 p., illus. 8vo   N
Also contains: The Two Captains; or, The Orphan Brothers.
Printed in double cols.

SHERWOOD, GRACE. James Blair; or, Love in the Valley of the Juniata. *In* The Fountain and the Bottle (1850), No. 996.

2383 SHINDLER, MARY STANLEY BUNCE (PALMER) DANA. Charles Morton; or, The Young Patriot. A Tale of the American Revolution. By Mary S. B. Dana. New York: Dayton & Newman, 1843. 236 p. 12mo   AAS, HEH, LC, N, UC, Y

2384 ——— Forecastle Tom; or, The Landsman Turned Sailor. By Mary S. B. Dana . . . New York: Harper & Brothers, 1846. 216 p. 12mo   AAS, BA, HEH, LC, UP, Y

2385 ——— The Young Sailor. A Narrative Founded on Fact. By Mary S. B. Dana . . . New York: Harper & Brothers, 1843. 190 p. 12mo   AAS, N, UP, Y

2386 ——— ——— New York: Harper & Brothers, 1844. 190 p. 12mo   AAS, HEH, Y

2387 ——— ——— New York: Harper & Brothers, 1846. 190 p. 12mo   HEH

2388 SHINNING IT: A Tale of a Tape-Cutter; or, The Mechanic Turned Merchant. By One Who Knows. New York: M. Y. Beach, 1844. Cover title, 32 p. 8vo   H

SHORT AND FAT, SAMPSON, *pseud. See* Kettell, Samuel

2389 SHORTFELLOW, TOM, *pseud.* Annie, the Orphan Girl of St. Mary; or, The Golden Marriage . . . By Shortfellow [pseud.] . . . Boston: Gleason's Publishing Hall, 1846. 100 p., illus. 8vo
                                                         AAS, B, HEH, UP, UV, Y
Printed in double cols.
Boston; 18--.

2390 ——— Eva Labree; or, The Rescued Chief. A Tale of the City and Forest. By Tom Shortfellow [pseud.] . . . Boston: Gleason's Publishing Hall, 1845. 66 p., illus. 8vo
                                                     AAS, BP, HEH, NYP, UC, UV, Y

2391 ———— Evelyn of Alleyne Cliff; or, The Two Lovers. A Romance of the Highlands. By Tom Shortfellow [pseud.]. Boston: Gleason's Publishing Hall, 1845. 42 p. 8vo
B, NYP, UP, UV, Y
New York.

2392 ———— Mary Kale; or, Big Thunder! Chief of the Anti-Renters. By Tom Shortfellow [pseud.] . . . Boston: F. Gleason, 1845. 56 p., illus. 8vo   AAS, BP, HEH, IN, NYP, UC, UM, UP, UV, Y
New York.

2392a ——— ——— Boston: F. Gleason, 1849. 100 p., illus. 8vo
AAS, Y
Title reads: *Big Thunder, Chief of the Anti-Renters: A Tale of the City and Forest.*
Also contains: Eva Labree—the Sequel.
Printed in double cols.

SHORTFIELD, LUKE, *pseud.* *See* Jones, John Beauchamp

2392b SIDDONS, LEONORA, *pseud.* The Female Warrior: An Interesting Narrative of the Sufferings . . . of Miss Leonora Siddons, Who, Led On by Patriotism, Joined the Texian [sic] Army under General Houston . . . New York: Printed for and published by E. E. Barclay, 1843. 23 p., illus. 8vo   LC

2392c ——— ——— New York: Printed for and published by E. E. & G. Barclay, 1843. 23 p., illus. 8vo   Y

2392d ——— ——— New York: Printed for and published by E. E. Barclay, 1844. 23 p., illus. 8vo   HEH, UC
"Texian" in title changed to "Texan."

SIDNEY, EDWARD WILLIAM, *pseud.* *See* Tucker, Nathaniel Beverley

2393 SIGOURNEY, LYDIA HOWARD (HUNTLEY). The Intemperate and The Reformed. Showing the Awful Consequences of Intemperance, and the Blessed Effects of the Temperance Reformation [anon.]. Boston: Seth Bliss, 1833. 48 p. 12mo
BA, BP, NYP, Y
First story also in No. 1858a.
Ohio frontier.

2394 ——— ——— Boston: Seth Bliss, 1834. 48 p. 12mo AAS, NYP

2395 ——— Myrtis: With Other Etchings and Sketchings... New
York: Harper & Brothers [cop. 1846]. 292 p. 12mo
AAS, B, BP, HEH, LC, LCP, NYS, UC, UM, UP, Y
Also contains: The Emigrant Bride—Lady Arabella Johnson—Mary Rice—
Fall of the Pequod—The Yankee—A Legend of Pennsylvania—The Lady of
Mount Vernon—A Tale of Poland—The Alms-house—The Plough and the
Sword—The Reverse—The Lost Children.

2396 ——— Sketch of Connecticut, Forty Years Since ... [anon.].
Hartford: Oliver D. Cooke & Sons, 1824. 278 p. 12mo
AAS, B, BA, H, HEH, LC, N, NYH, NYP, UM, UP, UV, Y

2397 ——— Sketches... Philadelphia: Key & Biddle, 1834. 216 p.,
illus. 12mo
AAS, B, BA, BP, H, HEH, IN, LC, LCP, N, NYH, NYP, UC, UP, Y
Contents: The Father—Legend of Oxford—The Family Portraits—Oriana—
The Intemperate—The Patriarch.

2398 ——— ——— Philadelphia: Edward C. Biddle, 1836. 216 p.,
illus. 12mo
AAS, BP

2399 ——— ——— Amherst: J. S. & C. Adams, 1839. 216 p., illus.
12mo
AAS, B, NYH, UM, Y

2400 ——— ——— Amherst: J. S. & C. Adams, 1840. 216 p., illus.
12mo
AAS, HEH, NYH, UC, Y

2401 ——— ——— Amherst: J. S. & C. Adams, 1842. 216 p., illus.
12mo
AAS, HEH, IN, Y

2402 ——— ——— Amherst: J. S. & C. Adams, 1844. 216 p., illus.
12mo
AAS, IN, NYP, Y

——— The Twins. The Patriarch and the Vine. And The
Apples of Sodom. *In* M. A. Denison, Gertrude Russel (1849),
No. 849a.

2403 ——— Water-Drops... New York: Robert Carter, 1848. 275
p. 12mo
AAS, B, BP, H, HEH, IN, LC, N, UM, UP, Y
Prose and verse.

2403a ——— ——— 2d ed. New York: Robert Carter & Brothers,
1849. 275 p. 12mo
AAS, Y

2404 ——— ——— 3d ed. New York: Robert Carter & Brothers,
1850. 275 p., illus. 12mo
NYP

2405　SILVER, MRS.　The Lover's Pilgrimage and A Trial of Affection
. . .　Boston: Printed by Freeman and Bolles, 1846.　336 p.
12mo　　　　　　　　　　　　　　　　　　　AAS, B, HEH, Y

2406　SIMMS, JEPTHA ROOT.　The American Spy; or, Freedom's Early
Sacrifice.　A Tale of the Revolution, Founded upon Fact . . .
Albany: Printed by J. Munsell, 1846.　63 p.　12mo
AAS, BP, H, HEH, IN, LC, N, NYH, UP, Y

2407　SIMMS, WILLIAM GILMORE.　Beauchampe; or, The Kentucky
Tragedy.　A Tale of Passion . . . [anon.].　Philadelphia: Lea
and Blanchard, 1842.　2 vols.　12mo
AAS(V.1), HEH, HM(V.1), IN, LC, N, NYP, UC, UP(V.1), UV, Y

2408　——　The Book of My Lady: A Melange.　By a Bachelor
Knight . . . [anon.].　Philadelphia: Key & Biddle, 1833.　334
p.　12mo　　　　　　　　　　　　　　　　　　　UP, Y
Contains: Ponce de Leon—The Venetian Bridal—A Story of the Sea— Haig-
lar: A Story of the Catawba—Missouri: The Captive of the Pawnee—La
Pola—The Children of the Sun—A Legend of the Pacific—A Scene of the
Revolution—The Choctaw Criminal—The Festival of Isis—The Last of the
Yemassees—The Opportunity.

2409　——　——　Boston: Allen & Ticknor, 1833.　334 p.　12mo
B, BP, H, LC

2410　——　Border Beagles: A Tale of Mississippi . . . [anon.].　Philadelphia: Carey and Hart, 1840.　2 vols.　12mo
AAS, B, BA, BP, H, HEH, IN, LC, N, NYH, NYP, UC, UP, UV, Y

2411　——　Carl Werner, an Imaginative Story: With Other Tales of
Imagination . . . [anon.].　New York: George Adlard, 1838.　2
vols.　12mo
AAS, CLS, H, HEH, IN, LC, N, NYH, NYP, UC, UP, UV, Y
Contents: Carl Werner— Ipsistos—The Star Brethren—Onea and Anyta—
Conrade Weickhoff—Logoochie; or, The Branch of Sweet Water: A Leg-
end of Georgia—Jocassée—The Cherokee Embassage.

2412　——　——　Boston: F. Gleason, 1846.　58 p.　8vo　　AAS, Y
Title reads: *Matilda; or, The Spectre of the Castle. An Imaginative Story.*

2413　——　Castle Dismal; or, The Bachelor's Christmas.　A Domestic Legend . . . [anon.].　New York: Burgess, Stringer & Co.,
1844.　192 p.　12mo　　　　　　　　　　　　　　BP, HEH, LC
South Carolina; contemporary.

2414 —— —— New York: Burgess, Stringer & Co., 1845. 192
p. 12mo   NYH, NYP, Y

2415 —— Confession; or, The Blind Heart. A Domestic Story
. . . [anon.]. Philadelphia: Lea and Blanchard, 1841. 2 vols.
12mo   AAS, BP, CLS, H, HEH, IN, LC, N, UP, Y

2416 —— Count Julian; or, The Last Days of the Goth . . . [anon.].
Baltimore: William Taylor & Co., 1845. 201 p. 8vo
          AAS, B, CLS, H, HEH, NYP, UP, Y
Spain; 8th cent.

2417 —— The Damsel of Darien . . . [anon.]. Philadelphia: Lea
and Blanchard, 1839. 2 vols. 12mo   AAS, B, BA(V.1),
      BP, CLS, H, HEH, HM, IN, LC, N, NYP, UC, UM, UP, UV, Y
Early 16th cent.

2418 —— Father Abbot; or, The Home Tourist. A Medley . . .
Charleston, S.C.: Printed by Miller & Browne, 1849. 235 p.
16mo   CLS, H, HEH, LC, NYP, UP, Y

2419 —— Flirtation at the Moultrie House: In a Series of Letters,
from Miss Georgiana Appleby to Her Friends in Georgia,
Showing the Doings at the Moultrie House, and the Events
Which Took Place at the Grand Costume Ball, on the 29th Au-
gust, 1850; with Other Letters [anon.]. Charleston: Printed by
Edward C. Councell, 1850. 46 p. 12mo   CLS, H, NYP, UP, Y

2420 —— Guy Rivers: A Tale of Georgia . . . [anon.]. New York:
Harper & Brothers, 1834. 2 vols. 12mo
   AAS, B, BA, BP, H, HEH, IN, LC, N, NYP(V.1), NYS, UC, UP, UV, Y

2421 —— —— 2d ed. New York: Harper & Brothers, 1835-34.
2 vols. 12mo   AAS, HEH(V.1), UP, Y

2422 —— —— 3d ed. New York: Harper & Brothers, 1837. 2
vols. 12mo   Y

2423 —— —— 3d ed. New York: Harper & Brothers, 1846. 2
vols. in 1. 12mo   AAS, NYH, Y

2423a —— —— 3d ed. New York: Harper & Brothers, 1847. 2
vols. in 1. 12mo   UM

2424 —— Helen Halsey; or, The Swamp State of Conelachita. A
Tale of the Borders . . . New York: Burgess, Stringer & Co.,
1845. 216 p. 12mo   BP, H, HEH, IN, LC, NYH, NYP, UP, UV, Y

2425 —— The Kinsmen; or, The Black Riders of Congaree . . . [anon.]. Philadelphia: Lea and Blanchard, 1841. 2 vols. 12mo   AAS, BA, BP, CLS, H, HEH, IN, LC, N, NYP, UP, UV, Y
South Carolina; American Revolution.

2426 —— The Lily and the Totem; or, The Huguenots in Florida. A Series of Sketches, Picturesque and Historical, of the Colonies of Coligni, in North America, 1562-1570 . . . [anon.]. New York: Baker and Scribner, 1850. 470 p. 12mo
AAS, B, BA, BP, H, HEH, IN, LC, LCP, N, NYH, NYP, UM, UP, UV, Y

2427 —— —— 2d ed. New York: Baker and Scribner, 1850. 470 p. 12mo   AAS, HM, LC, N, NYP, UC, Y

2428 —— Martin Faber: The Story of a Criminal . . . [anon.]. New York: J. & J. Harper, 1833. 189 p. 12mo
AAS, BA, BP, H, LC, NYH, NYP, UP, UV, Y

2429 —— —— And Other Tales. New York: Harper & Brothers, 1837. 2 vols. 12mo
AAS, BA, CLS, H, HEH, IN, N, NYP, UP, Y
Also contains: Sweet William: A Tale of Faerie—The Mental Prism—The Sins of Typography—The Spirit Bridegroom—A Passage of Arms in '76—The Plank: A Story of the Sea—Major Rocket—Chatelar, the Poet—A Passage from History—Juan Ponce de Leon.

—— Matilda; or, The Spectre of the Castle. *See* Carl Werner, No. 2412.

2430 —— Mellichampe: A Legend of the Santee . . . [anon.]. New York: Harper & Brothers, 1836. 2 vols. 12mo
AAS, B, BP, CLS, H, HEH, IN, LC, N, NYP, UC, UM, UP, UV, Y
South Carolina; American Revolution.

2431 —— The Partisan: A Tale of the Revolution . . . [anon.]. New York: Harper & Brothers, 1835. 2 vols. 12mo
AAS, B, BP, H, HEH, HM, IN, LC, N, NYP, UC, UP, UV, Y
South Carolina.

2432 —— Pelayo: A Story of the Goth . . . [anon.]. New York: Harper & Brothers, 1838. 2 vols. 12mo
AAS, BA, BP, CLS, H, HEH, IN, LC, N, NYP, UC, UM, UP, Y
Spain; 8th cent.

2433 —— The Prima Donna: A Passage from City Life . . . Philadelphia: Louis A. Godey, 1844. 24 p. 8vo   AAS, H, UP, Y
New York City.

2434 —— Richard Hurdis; or, The Avenger of Blood. A Tale of Alabama . . . [anon.]. Philadelphia: E. L. Carey & A. Hart, 1838. 2 vols. 12mo

AAS, BP, H, HEH, HM, IN, N, NYH, NYP, UV, Y

2435 —— —— 2d ed. Philadelphia: E. L. Carey & A. Hart, 1838. 2 vols. 12mo

AAS, Y

—— A Sea Piece. *In* The Atlantic Club-Book (1834), Nos. 195-196.

2436 —— The Wigwam and the Cabin . . . First Series [anon.]. New York: Wiley & Putnam, 1845. 233 p. 12mo

AAS, B, BA, BP, H, HEH, IN, LC, N, NYH, NYP, UC, UP, Y

Contents: Grayling; or, Murder Will Out—The Two Camps: A Legend of the Old North State—The Last Wager; or, The Gamester of the Mississippi —The Arm-chair of Tustenuggee: A Tradition of the Catawba—The Snake of the Cabin—Oakatibbe; or, The Choctaw Sampson—Jocassée: A Cherokee Legend.

2437 —— —— 2d Ser. New York: Wiley and Putnam, 1845. 238 p. 12mo

AAS, B, BP, H, HEH, IN, LC, N, NYH, NYP, UC, UP, Y

Contents: The Giant's Coffin; or, The Feud of Holt and Houston: A Tale of Reedy River—Sergeant Barnacle; or, The Raftsman of the Edisto—Those Old Lunes! Or, Which Is the Madman?—The Lazy Crow: A Story of the Cornfield—Caloya; or, The Loves of the Driver—Lucas de Ayllon: A Historical Nouvellette.

2438 —— The Yemassee: A Romance of Carolina . . . [anon.]. New York: Harper & Brothers, 1835. 2 vols. 12mo

BA, BP, CLS, H, HEH, HM(V.1), IN, LC, N, NYP, NYS, UC, UP, UV, Y 1715.

2439 —— —— 2d ed. New York: Harper & Brothers, 1835. 2 vols. 12mo

AAS, LC(V.1), UP, Y

2440 —— —— New York: Harper & Brothers, 1843. 2 vols. 12mo

AAS, BP, NYH, NYP, Y

2441 —— —— New York: Harper & Brothers, 1844. 2 vols. in 1. 12mo

AAS, N, Y

SIMMUNS, JEEMES, *pseud.?* Fox Hunt. *In* Afloat and Ashore (1848), No. 7g.

SIMPLE, SAM, *pseud.* *See* Wilburn, George T.

2442 SIMS, ALEXANDER DROMGOOLE. Bevil Faulcon: A Tradition of the Old Cheraw. By Crayon Rigmarole, Esq. [pseud.]. Columbia, S.C.: I. C. Morgan, printer & publisher, 1842. 310, [1] p. 12mo   BP, CLS, N, NYP

SINCLAIR, SYDNEY, *pseud.* *See* Weld, Gilbert Cumming

SINGULARITY, THOMAS, *pseud.* *See* Nott, Henry Junius

2442a SIX MONTHS in a House of Correction; or, The Narrative of Dorah Mahony, Who Was under the Influence of the Protestants about a Year, and an Inmate of the House of Correction, in Leverett St., Boston, Massachusetts, Nearly Six Months . . . Boston: Benjamin B. Mussey, 1835. 201 p. 12mo   B, HEH, Y
Parody on *Six Months in a Convent* by Rebecca T. Reed.

2443 SKETCHES OF DOMESTIC LIFE. By an Observer . . . Portland [Me.]: Shirley, Hyde and Company, 1831. 339 p. 12mo
LC, Y

Contents: The Twin Sisters—Aunt Ruth's Jewels—The Orphan—The Broken Stage-coach—The Mother.

2444 SKETCHES OF TROJAN LIFE. Drawn with a Free Pencil, by an Amateur. Troy: L. Willard, 1847. 44 p. 8vo
AAS, HEH, LC, NYP, UP, Y

Contains: The Condemned: A Chapter from Our City Prison: A Tale of Truth and Horror.

2445 SLEEPER, JOHN SHERBURNE. Tales of the Ocean, and Essays for the Forecastle: Containing Matters and Incidents Humorous, Pathetic, Romantic, and Sentimental . . . by Hawser Martingale [pseud.]. Boston: Printed and published by S. N. Dickinson, 1841. 431 p., illus. 12mo   AAS, H, Y

2446 ———— ———— Boston: Printed and published by S. N. Dickinson, 1842. 431 p., illus. 12mo   AAS, N

2447 ———— ———— Boston: William J. Reynolds, 1845. 431 p., illus. 12mo   Y

2448 ———— ———— Boston: William J. Reynolds, 1846. 431 p., illus. 12mo   AAS, HEH, Y

2448a ———— ———— Boston: William J. Reynolds, 1847. 431 p., illus. 12mo   AAS

2448b ———— ———— Boston: William J. Reynolds, 1848. 431 p., illus.
    12mo   AAS, Y

SLEEPER, MARTHA G. (QUINCY). The Two Wards. *In* J. N. T. Tucker, Theresa (1846), No. 2611a.

SLICK, JONATHAN, *Esq., pseud.* *See* Stephens, Ann Sophia (Winterbotham)

SLOCUM, NAT, *pseud.?* A Day at Sol Slice's, by Nat Slocum, of South Carolina. *In* W. T. Porter, *ed.*, A Quarter Race in Kentucky (1847), Nos. 2063-64.

2449 SLY, COSTARD, *pseud.* Sayings and Doings at the Tremont House in the Year 1832. Extracted from the Note-book of Costard Sly [pseud.] . . . and Edited by Dr. Zachary Philemon Vangrifter. Boston: Allen and Ticknor, 1833. 2 vols. 12mo
    AAS, B, BA, BP, H, HEH, LC, N, NYH, NYP, UC, UM, UP, Y

SMITH, MR., *pseud.* *See* Lockwood, Ralph Ingersoll

SMITH, BEN, *pseud.* *See* Mathews, Cornelius

2450 SMITH, ELIZABETH OAKES (PRINCE). Riches without Wings; or, The Cleveland Family. By Mrs. Seba Smith . . . Boston: George W. Light, 1838. 162 p. 12mo
    AAS, BP, H, LC, NYP, UM, UP, Y
New England; contemporary.

2451 ———— ———— 3d ed. Boston: George W. Light, 1839. 160 p.
    12mo   AAS, H, Y

2452 ———— ———— 4th ed. Boston: James B. Dow, 1844. 156 p.
    12mo   AAS, Y

2453 ———— The Salamander: A Legend for Christmas. Found amongst the Papers of the Late Ernest Helfenstein [pseud.] . . . Edited by E. Oakes Smith. New York: George P. Putnam, 1848. 149 p., illus. 12mo
    AAS, B, BP, H, HEH, IN, LC, N, NYH, NYP, UC, UM, UP, Y
New York.

2454 ———— ———— 2d ed. New York: George P. Putnam, 1849.
    149 p., illus. 12mo   AAS, IN, LC, NYH, NYP, Y

2455 SMITH, HAMILTON. The Forest Maid: A Tale . . . Penn-Yan, N.Y.: Printed for the author, by H. Gilbert, 1832. 32 p. 8vo
AAS, B, H, UV, Y
Great Lakes country.

2456 SMITH, I. ANDERSON. Blanche Vernon, the Actress! A Romance of the Metropolis . . . New York: For sale by all the principal booksellers, 1846. 56 p. 8vo   AAS, NYP, Y
New York City; contemporary.

2456a SMITH, J. HENRY. The Green Family; or, The Veil Removed. Comprising the Most Thrilling Incidents in the Lives of the Members of the Green Family . . . and the Shortcomings and Iniquities of Persons in Both High and Low Life . . . Springfield, Mass.: Smith & Jones, 1849. 120 p. 8vo   AAS, Y

SMITH, JOHN, *pseud*. *See* Smith, Seba

2457 SMITH, MARGARET (BAYARD). What Is Gentility? A Moral Tale . . . [anon.]. City of Washington: Pishey Thompson, 1828. 257 p. 12mo   AAS, B, IN, LC, N, UC, UP, UV, Y
Washington; contemporary.

2458 ———— A Winter in Washington; or, Memoirs of the Seymour Family . . . [anon.]. New York: E. Bliss & E. White, 1824. 2 vols. 12mo   AAS, BP, H, IN, LC, N, NYP, UP, UV, Y
Allibone notes an 1827 ed.
Contemporary.

2459 SMITH, MICHAEL. The Lost Virgin of the South: A Tale of Truth, Connected with the History of the Indian War in the South, in the Years 1812-13-14 and 15 . . . By Don Pedro Casender [pseud.] . . . Tallahassee: M. Smith, 1831. 327 p. 12mo   AAS

2460 ———— ———— 2d ed. Courtland, Alabama: M. Smith, 1833.
Dedication, to Andrew Jackson, signed and dated, "The author and publisher, Courtland, Al., 4th Nov., 1833." Information about this ed., which is located in the University of Texas Library, was furnished by Mr. Vail.

2460a SMITH, MOSES. Naval Scenes in the Last War; or, Three Years on Board the Frigate Constitution, and the Adams. Including the Capture of the Guerriere. Being the True Narrative of Moses Smith, a Survivor of the "Old Ironsides" Crew. Boston: Gleason's Publishing Hall, 1846. 50 p., illus. 8vo   N, NYP, Y
Verisimilitude account.

2461 SMITH, RICHARD PENN. The Actress of Padua, and Other Tales
. . . [anon.]. Philadelphia: E. L. Carey & A. Hart, 1836. 2
vols. 12mo   AAS, B, H, HEH(V.2), IN, LC, NYP, UC, UP, UV, Y
Also contains: The Campaigner's Tale—The Last of His Tribe—The Old
Story—Retribution—Madness—The Sea Voyage—The Leper's Confession—
The First Born—Prediction—The Man with a Nose—Apologue—The Appa-
rition—The Emigrant's Daughter—The Daughter—A Tale of Hard Scrabble
—The Pauper and His Dog—The Old Maid's Legacy.

2462 —— The Forsaken: A Tale . . . [anon.]. Philadelphia: John
Grigg, 1831. 2 vols. 12mo   AAS, BA, HEH, N, NYP, UM, UP, Y
Philadelphia; American Revolution.

2463 SMITH, SARA (HENDERSON). Alice Singleton; or, The Fashion of
This World Passeth Away . . . New York: John Wiley, 1850.
86 p. 12mo   LC

2464 SMITH, SEBA. John Smith's [pseud.] Letters, with "Picters" to
Match . . . New York: Samuel Colman, 1839. 139 p., illus.
12mo   AAS, B, BA, H, HEH, IN, LC, LCP, N, NYP, UC, UM, UP, Y

2465 —— Letters Written during the President's Tour "Down
East," by Myself, Major Jack Downing [pseud.], of Downingville . . . Down East [Cincinnati], 1833. 69 p., illus. 12mo
    AAS, HEH, LC, NYH, Y

2466 —— —— Cincinnati: U. P. James, 1838. 72 p., illus.
12mo   LC

2467 —— The Life and Writings of Major Jack Downing [pseud.],
of Downingville, Away Down East in the State of Maine.
Written by Himself . . . Boston: Lilly, Wait, Colman & Holden, 1833. 260 p., illus. 12mo
    AAS, BP, CLS, H, HEH, IN, LC, LCP, NYH, NYP, NYS, UP, Y

2468 —— —— 2d ed. Boston: Lilly, Wait, Colman & Holden,
1834. 260 p., illus. 12mo   AAS, H, HEH, IN, N, NYP, UC, UM, Y
The first two eds. contain 70 letters; the following eds. contain 71 letters.

2469 —— —— 3d ed. Boston: Lilly, Wait, Colman & Holden,
1834. 288 p., illus. 12mo
    AAS, BP, H, HEH, IN, LC, LCP, NYP, UM, UP, Y

2470 —— —— 3d ed. Albany, N.Y., 1834. 288 p., illus. 12mo
Ed. from Sabin 84149.

2471 —— —— 8th ed. Boston: Lilly, Wait, Colman & Holden,
1834. 288 p., illus. 12mo   AAS, Y

2472 ——— ——— 9th ed. Boston: Lilly, Wait, Colman & Holden, 1835. 288 p., illus. 12mo   AAS, B

2473 ——— May-Day in New York; or, House-Hunting and Moving; Illustrated and Explained in Letters to Aunt Keziah. By Major Jack Downing [pseud.]. New York: Burgess, Stringer and Company, 1845. 120 p. 12mo   AAS, B, HEH, LC, N, UP, Y

2474 ——— The Select Letters of Major Jack Downing [pseud.] . . . Philadelphia: Printed for the publishers, 1834. 212 p., illus. 12mo   AAS, H, HEH, IN, LC, N, UC, UM, UP, UV, Y

SMITH, MRS. SEBA. *See* Smith, Elizabeth Oakes (Prince)

SMITH, SOLOMON FRANKLIN. Breaking a Bank. *In* W. T. Porter, *ed.*, A Quarter Race in Kentucky (1847), Nos. 2063-64.

——— A Bully Boat and a Brag Captain: A Story of Steamboat Life on the Mississippi. *In* W. T. Porter, *ed.*, The Big Bear of Arkansas (1845), Nos. 2061-62.

2475 SMITH, THOMAS LACEY. Chronicles of Turkeytown; or, The Works of Jeremy Peters [pseud.], First Series. Containing: The History of a Dreadful Catastrophe; The Amours of Dr. Post and Mrs. Peweetle; and The History of a Tatterdemalion . . . Philadelphia: R. H. Small, 1829. 238 p. 12mo
                        AAS, BP, HEH, IN, LC, LCP, N, NYH, NYP, UP, Y
New Jersey.

SMOKING 'EM OUT; or, The Yankee Schoolmaster Out West, by the Green Mountain Bard. *In* M. M. Ballou, Albert Simmons (1849), No. 229.

2476 SNELLING, MRS. ANNA L. Kabaosa; or, The Warriors of the West. A Tale of the Last War . . . New York: Printed for the publisher by D. Adee, 1842. 320 p., illus. 12mo
                        AAS, B, BA, BP, HEH, LC, N, NYH, NYP, UC, UP, Y
Great Lakes country; War of 1812.

2477 SNELLING, WILLIAM JOSEPH. Tales of the Northwest; or, Sketches of Indian Life and Character. By a Resident beyond the Frontier . . . [anon.]. Boston: Hilliard, Gray, Little and Wilkins, 1830. 288 p. 12mo
                        AAS, BA, H, HEH, IN, LC, LCP, N, NYP, UM, UP, Y
Contents: The Captive—The Hoharp—The Devoted—Payton Skah—Charles Hess—The Bois Brule—Weemokhenchah Wandeeteekah—La Butte des Morts—Pinchon—The Lover's Leap.

2478 THE SOLDIER'S ORPHAN: A Novel... New York: Printed by C. S. Van Winkle, 1812. 188 p. 12mo

AAS, B, BA, BP, HEH, IN, NYS, UM, UP, UV, Y

John Finch, attrib. au.
Massachusetts; late 18th cent.

SOMEBODY, *M.D.C., pseud.* *See* Neal, John

2479 SOPHIA; or, The Girl of the Pine Woods. To Which Is Added: Lafitte; or, The Barratarian Chief. An American Tale. Dansville, N.Y.: A. Stevens, 1838. 174 p. 16mo

AAS, H, HEH, UP, Y

Written by William Ray. See No. 2093a for 1st ed.

2480 SOUTHWORTH, EMMA DOROTHY ELIZA (NEVITTE). The Deserted Wife ... New York: D. Appleton & Co., 1850. 176 p. 8vo

AAS, H, HEH, UP, Y

Printed in double cols.
Maryland.

2481 ——— Retribution; or, The Vale of Shadows. A Tale of Passion ... New York: Harper & Brothers, 1849. 108 p. 8vo

AAS, B, H, HEH, N, NYP, UM, Y

Printed in double cols.
Washington, D.C.

2482 SPAFFORD, HORATIO GATES. The Mother-in-Law; or, Memoirs of Madam De Morville. By Maria-Ann Burlingham [pseud.]. Boston, 1817. 190 p., illus. 12mo AAS, BP, H

2483 SPECULATION; or, Making Haste to Be Rich. The Story of William Wilson, the Whistling Shoemaker. Boston: George W. Light, 1840. 80 p. 12mo AAS, LC, UP, Y

Last quarter of 18th cent.

2484 SPERRY, J. AUSTIN. Fothergill; or, The Man of Enterprise. By J. Austin Sperry, M.D., Author of "Seaton Seevers," "Morgan," "The Man with the Moustache," etc. Cincinnati: Printed at "The Great West" office, 1850. 118 p. 8vo AAS, LC, Y

Printed in double cols.
Ohio; 18--.

2485 SPOFFORD, HARRY. The Mysteries of Worcester; or, Charley Temple and His First Glass of Liquor. A Temperance Tale ... Worcester: H. J. Copp, 1846. 36 p. 8vo AAS, H, NYP, UP

2486 SPRING, SAMUEL. Giafar al Barmeki: A Tale of the Court of Haroun al Raschid . . . [anon.]. New York: Harper & Brothers, 1836. 2 vols. 12mo

AAS, B, BP, H, HEH, LC, N, NYP, UC, UP, Y

2487 ———— ———— 2d ed. New York: Harper & Brothers, 1847. 2 vols. in 1. 12mo   LC
Title reads: *The Rose of Persia; or, Giafar al Barmeki.*

2488 ——— The Monk's Revenge; or, The Secret Enemy. A Tale of the Later Crusades. New York: Williams Brothers, 1847. 240 p. 8vo   UP, Y

——— The Rose of Persia; or, Giafar al Barmeki. *See* Giafar al Barmeki, No. 2487.

2489 SPROAT, P. W. The Savage Beauty . . . By a Wild American [anon.]. Philadelphia: Printed by S. Roberts, 1822. 136 p. 12mo   AAS, BA, BP, H, LC, NYH, NYP, UC, UP, Y
Some copies have the author's name on the title page and a two-page "Key to The Savage Beauty" at end.

2490 SQUINTS THROUGH AN OPERA GLASS. By a Young Gent Who Hadn't Any Thing Else to Do. New York: Merchant's Daybook, 1850. 46 p. 12mo   AAS, H, NYP
A series of character sketches.

2491 STANWOOD, AVIS A. (BURNHAM). Fostina Woodman, the Wonderful Adventurer . . . Boston: Redding and Company, 1850. 60 p., illus. 8vo   BP, H, HEH, LC, N, NYP
Massachusetts; contemporary.

2492 THE STAR OF FREEDOM. New York: William S. Dorr, printer, [184-?]. 96 p. 12mo   AAS, B, LC

2493 THE STARTLING, THRILLING, & INTERESTING NARRATIVE of the Life, Sufferings, Singular and Surprising Adventures of Fanny Templeton Danforth . . . Philadelphia: E. E. Barclay, 1849. 36 p., illus. 8vo   LC

2493a ——— Philadelphia: E. E. Barclay, 1850. 36 p., 1 l., illus. 8vo
AAS, UP, Y

2494 STEPHEN MORELAND: A Novel . . . Philadelphia: Key & Biddle, 1834. 2 vols. 12mo   B, LC, UM, Y
Written by Jesse Conard.

2495 STEPHENS, ANN SOPHIA (WINTERBOTHAM). Alice Copley: A Tale of Queen Mary's Time . . . Boston: "Yankee" office, 1844. 48 p. 8vo   AAS, LC, NYP
Printed in double cols.

2496 —— David Hunt, and Malina Gray . . . Philadelphia: George R. Graham & Co., 1845. 98 p. 8vo   UP, Y
At head of title: "Cabinet of American Literature, No. 1."
NYP has only "Malina Gray," pp. [55]-98.

2497 —— The Diamond Necklace, and Other Tales . . . Boston: Gleason's Publishing Hall, 1846. 100 p. 8vo   N, NYP, Y
Also contains: The Step-son—Sybil Floyd—The Freshet—The Judge's Charge—Retribution; or, The Three Chimneys—The Saxon's Daughter: A Tale of Old England.
Printed in double cols.

2497a —— Henry Longford; or, The Forged Will. A Tale of New York City . . . Boston: F. Gleason, 1847. 50 p. 8vo   AAS

2498 —— High Life in New York. By Jonathan Slick, Esq. [pseud.] . . . New York: Edward Stephens, 1843. Cover title, 48 p. 8vo   AAS, H, NYP, UP, Y
At head of title: "Price Twelve and a Half Cents."
Printed in double cols.

2499 —— —— 2d ed. New York: Edward Stephens, 1843-44. 3 pts. 8vo   LCP(pt.2), NYP
Paged continuously (136 p.), each part having its own cover title.
Imprints of Pts. II-III read: "New York: Burgess, Stringer & Co. . . . . 1844."
Printed in double cols.

2500 —— —— Complete in One Number. New York: Burgess, Stringer & Co., 1845. Cover title, 136 p. 8vo
                               AAS, BP, H, HEH, NYP
At head of cover title: "Complete for 25 Cents."
Printed in double cols.

2501 —— The Tradesman's Boast . . . Boston: Gleason's Publishing Hall, 1846. 66 p. 8vo   AAS, LC, NYP, Y
England; late 15th cent.

—— The Wife. *In* M. Woodruff, *ed.*, A Drop from the Bucket (1847), No. 2759.

2502 STERLING, CHARLES F. Buff and Blue; or, The Privateers of the Revolution. A Tale of Long Island Sound . . . New York: Wm. H. Graham, 1847. 128 p. 8vo   AAS, BA, H, LC, N, UP, Y
Printed in double cols.

2503 ——— The Red Coats; or, The Sack of Unquowa. A Tale of the Revolution . . . New York: Williams Brothers, 1848. 111 p. 8vo   BP, LC
Printed in double cols.

2504 STEVENS, HARRY. The Child of the Wreck: A Tale of the Nineteenth Century . . . Philadelphia: Burgess & Zieber, 1843. 32 p. 4to   HEH, UP, Y
On cover: "American Novelist's Library, No. 4."
Printed in double cols.
New York state.

2505 STIMSON, ALEXANDER LOVETT. Poor Caroline, the Indiaman's Daughter; or, All's Well That Ends Well. A Tale of Boston and Our Own Times [anon.]. Boston: The author, 1845. 64 p. 8vo   AAS, B, BP, LC, Y

2506 STONE, DAVID M. Frank Forrest; or, The Life of an Orphan Boy . . . New York: M. W. Dodd, 1850. 143 p., illus. 12mo   HEH, Y

2507 STONE, WILLIAM LEETE. Mercy Disborough: A Tale of New England Witchcraft [anon.]. Bath, N.Y.: R. L. Underhill & Co., 1844. 98 p., illus. 16mo   AAS, UV
The first story in his *Tales and Sketches* (1834), published separately in 1837 with title: *The Witches: A Tale of New England.*

2508 ——— Tales and Sketches . . . New York: Harper & Brothers, 1834. 2 vols. 12mo
AAS, B, H, HEH, IN, LC, LCP, N, NYH, NYP, NYS, UC, UM, UP, UV, Y
Contents: Mercy Disborough: A Tale of the Witches—A Romance of the Border—Lake St. Sacrament—The Withered Man: A Legend of the Highlands—The Dead of the Wreck—The Grave of the Indian King—The Murdered Tinman—A Sparkling Vision—The Mysterious Bridal—Setting the Wheels in Motion—The Skeleton Hand—A Night of Peril—The Drowned Alive.

2509 ——— ——— 2d ed. New York: Harper & Brothers, 1847. 2 vols. in 1. 12mo
Ed. from sales catalog.

———— Uncle Zim and Deacon Pettibone. *In* The Atlantic Club-Book (1834), Nos. 195-196.

2510 ———— Ups and Downs in the Life of a Distressed Gentleman . . . [anon.]. New York: Leavitt, Lord & Co., 1836. 225 p. 12mo   AAS, B, BA, BP, H, HEH, IN, LC, N, NYH, NYP, UC, UM, UP, Y

2511 ———— The Witches: A Tale of New England . . . [anon.]. Bath [N.Y.]: R. L. Underhill, 1837. 72 p., illus. 16mo
AAS, B, H, HEH, LC, Y

2512 STORIES FROM REAL LIFE: Compiled with a View to the Moral Improvement of All Classes. Fitchburg: S. & C. Shepley, 1848. 158 p., 1 l., illus. 24mo   AAS, H, HEH, LC, NYP, UC, UP, Y

Contents: The Foundling; or, Industry and Perseverance Move Mountains —The Dove of the Storm—Our Jessie; or, The Exclusives, by Mrs. Emma C. Embury—The Savoyard: An Incident from Real Life—The Miller's Maid— Family Quarrels.

Sabin 92210 notes variations of imprints. AAS also has: Worcester: J. Grout, Jr., 1848.

STOWE, HARRIET ELIZABETH (BEECHER). Mark Meriden. *In* E. Leslie, Mr. and Mrs. Woodbridge (1841), No. 1653.

2513 ———— The Mayflower; or, Sketches of Scenes and Characters among the Descendants of the Pilgrims . . . New York: Harper & Brothers, 1843. 324 p. 12mo
AAS, BA, BP, H, HEH, IN, LC, N, NYH, NYP, NYS, UC, UP, Y

Contents: Love versus Law—The Tea Rose—Trials of a Housekeeper—Little Edward—Let Every Man Mind His Own Business—Cousin William—Uncle Tim—Aunt Mary—Frankness—The Sabbath: Sketches from a Note-book of an Elderly Gentleman—So Many Calls—The Canal-Boat—Feeling—The Sempstress—Old Father Morris.

2514 ———— ———— 2d ed. New York: Harper & Brothers, 1844. 324 p. 12mo   AAS, B, HM, IN, NYP, UC, UPI, Y

2515 ———— ———— New York: Harper & Brothers, 1846. 324 p. 12mo   AAS, BP, H, NYP, Y

2516 ———— ———— New York: Harper & Brothers [cop. 1843]. 324 p. 12mo   H, Y

2517 ———— A New England Sketch . . . Lowell: Alfred Gilman, 1834. 52 p. 16mo   HEH, N, NYP, UC, UP, Y
At head of title: "Prize Tale."
Contemporary.

2518 STRANGE, ROBERT. Eoneguski; or, The Cherokee Chief. A Tale of Past Wars. By an American . . . [anon.]. Washington, D.C.: Franck Taylor, 1839. 2 vols. 12mo

HEH, IN, LC, N, NYP, Y

North Carolina.

2519 STRANGER OF THE VALLEY; or, Louisa and Adelaide. An American Tale . . . by a Lady . . . New York: Collins and Hannay, 1825. 2 vols. 12mo

AAS, HEH, IN, LC, UP, Y

2520 STRATTON, NED. A Romantic Tale of High American Life; or, Excursion to Montauk, First and Last Time . . . Providence: John F. Moore, printer, 1847. 32 p., illus. 8vo

B, LC, Y

STROCK, DANIEL, JR. [Author of the stories listed in note below.] *In* The Fountain and the Bottle (1850), No. 996.

Charles Clifford—The Last Interview—The Raftman's Oath.

STUART, C. The Mysterious Countess. *In* The Atlantic Club-Book (1834), Nos. 195-196.

STUART, JOHN A. A Yankee That Couldn't Talk Spanish, by John A. Stuart, Esq., of South Carolina. *In* W. T. Porter, *ed.*, The Big Bear of Arkansas (1845), Nos. 2061-62.

2521 STUBBS, STEPHEN. Agnes; or, The Power of Love. A Tale of Missouri. Founded on Fact . . . Boston: Gleason's Publishing Hall, 1845. 50 p. 8vo

AAS, B, HEH, Y

SUMMERFIELD, CHARLES, *pseud.* *See* Arrington, Alfred W.

2522 SUMNER, ALBERT W. The Sea Lark; or, The Quadroone of Louisiana. A Thrilling Tale of the Land and Sea . . . Boston: F. Gleason, 1850. 100 p. 8vo

AAS, Y

Printed in double cols.
War of 1812.

2523 SUSAN PIKE; or, A Few Years of Domestic Service. A Tale, by a Lady. New York: C. S. Francis, 1839. 66 p. 24mo

BP

2524 SUTHERLAND, THOMAS JEFFERSON. Loose Leaves from the Port Folio of a Late Patriot Prisoner in Canada . . . [anon.]. New York: Printed for the publisher, by Sackett & Sargent, 1839. 216 p. 12mo

IN, NYP

Contains: Advertisement—A Sketch—The Cotillon Party—Appendix to the Captive Patriot—The Patron of Buble Port—Bejazet's Cage—A Fragment—

Incidents of a Stage Coach—The Mistaken Bride—The Lawyer's Apology—
Luck and Ill Luck.
Issued in pts.; see Sabin 93966.

2525 ———— ———— New York: William H. Colyer, printer, 1840.
216 p. 12mo   H, LC, NYH, NYP
NYP has a second copy with cover title dated 1844.

SYR, *pseud.*   *See* Allen, Samuel Adams

2526 TALBOT, MARY ELIZABETH.   Rurality: Original Desultory Tales
. . . Providence: Marshall and Hammond, printers, 1830.   196
p., illus.   12mo   AAS, B, BP, H, HEH, LC, N, UC, UM, UP, Y
Contents: Reminiscences—Albert and Loise—The Duel—The Shipwreck—
The Ball—The Rivals.
MS note in B copy states, "Mary Eliz. Talbot, maiden name, married Seth K.
Gifford, clerk for Goodhue jewelers."

2527 A TALE, FOUNDED ON FACTS.   Modern Quixotism.   Improve Your
Conduct.   Confessions of Saint Martin.   Soliloquy.   (To Be
Continued.) [N.p.], 1832.   11 p.   12mo   AAS

2528 THE TALE OF A NEW YORKER.   By a Known Author . . .   New
York: George Roberts & Co., 1835.   45 p.   12mo
B, H, NYH, Y

2529 TALES AND SKETCHES by a Christmas Fireside.   By the Author of
"Rose Graham" . . .   Boston: A. Tompkins and B. B. Mussey,
1838.   72 p.   12mo   AAS, B, HEH, LC, N, UP, Y
Contents: The Old Man's Tale—The Governess—A Character.

2530 TALES FOR THE TIMES: Being a Selection of Interesting Stories . . .
New York: Nafis & Cornish, 278 Pearl Street [cop. 1840].   192
p., illus.   12mo   AAS, BA, H, IN, Y
Contents: The Lame Pig—A Night's Adventure—From the Journal of an
Odd Fellow—Madame Brillante—Rumpelstilzchen—The Furlough—Lord
Vaporcourt—The Magic Spinning-Wheel—A Rill from the Town Pump
[by N. Hawthorne]—London Omnibusses—The Coach Wheel—The Piper
of Neisse—Too Handsome for Any Thing—The Good-natured Couple—
The First Time of Asking—A Legend of Tom Thumb—A Chapter on Ears
—Lesson in Biography—Horrors of a Head-dress—The Last of the Serpents
—Mr. Higginbotham's Catastrophe [by N. Hawthorne]—The Elopement—
The Dilemma.
At bottom of p. 192: "End of Volume II." Contents same as Vol. II of *Tales
of Humor* (Boston, 1840), No. 2533.
S. G. Goodrich denied authorship in his *Recollections of a Lifetime* (1857),
II, 550, but he probably edited the collection.

2531 TALES FOR YOU: A Collection of Original and Selected Literature, from Celebrated English and American Authors. Philadelphia: J. J. Sharkey, 1841. 240 p. 12mo AAS, LC, NYP, Y

Contents: The Lover's Leap—The Merchant's Daughter—The Threefold Destiny: A Fairy Legend, by Ashley Allen Royce [i.e., Nathaniel Hawthorne]—Kate Connor, by Mrs. C. Hall—The Mountain of the Two Lovers —The Knight of Sheppey—The Wood Demon—Married by Mistake—The Spectre's Voyage—The Wyandot's Story—An Incident at Algiers—A Legend of Charlemagne, by Miss E. B. Clarke—The Abbey Garden; or, The Confession of Edward Walden—First Love—Reconciliation.

2532 TALES OF AN AMERICAN LANDLORD: Containing Sketches of Life South of the Potomac ... New York: W. B. Gilley, 1824. 2 vols. 12mo

AAS, H, HEH, IN, LC, N, NYH, NYP(V.1), NYS, UC, UP, UV, Y

2533 TALES OF HUMOR ... Boston: E. Littlefield, 1840. 2 vols. 12mo AAS, BA, BP, N, UP(V.1), Y(V.1)

Contents: (Vol. I), The Bashful Man—Jim Soolivan—Mrs. Bullfrog [by N. Hawthorne]—The Bald Eagle [by H. W. Longfellow]—The Captain's Lady—The Yellow Domino—The Haunted Quack [by N. Hawthorne]—A Ghost Story—The Height of Impudence—Grasso Legnaiuolo; or, Who Am I?—The Magician—Hans in Luck—Reflections in the Pillory—The Village Musician—The Lying Servant—Measure for Measure—The Storm. For contents of Vol. II see Tales for the Times, No. 2530.

S. G. Goodrich denied authorship in his Recollections of a Lifetime (1857), II, 550, but he probably edited the collection.

2534 TALES OF THE EMERALD ISLE; or, Legends of Ireland. By a Lady of Boston, Author of "Tales of the Fireside" and "Stories for Children" ... New York: W. Borradaile, Nov., 1828. 258 p. 12mo AAS, B, H, HEH, LC, UP, Y

Contents: Tradition; or, Saint Kevin's Bed—Carol More O'Daly; or, The Constant Lover—Humble Life; or, The Sycamore-Tree: A True Story— Retribution—The Victim—Mystery: A Modern Story—Bran, the Bloodhound; or, The Heir of De Burgo.

2535 TALES OF THE FIRESIDE. By a Lady of Boston ... Boston: Hilliard, Gray, Little and Wilkins, 1827. 225 p. 12mo

AAS, B, BA, BP, H, HEH, IN, LC, N, UC, UP, Y

Contents: The Fortune Teller: A Tale of the Eighteenth Century, Founded on Fact—The House on the Heath: A Tale of Real Life—The Miniature Picture; or, Love at First Sight—The Battle of Monmouth; or, The Fair Quaker: A Tale of the American Revolution—Rose Bradshaw; or, The Curate of St. Mark's—The Emigrants; or, Aspasia de Nemours, Founded on Fact.

2536 TALES OF THE REVOLUTION, and Thrilling Stories, Founded on Facts. By the Author of "Indian Wars." Methuen, Mass.: James Jasper Henderson, 1837. 62+ p. 16mo   HEH

2537 TALES OF THE REVOLUTION: Being Rare and Remarkable Passages of the History of the War of 1775. New York: Harper & Brothers, 1835. 216 p. 12mo   AAS, BP, NYP, Y
Written by Benjamin Bussey Thatcher.

2538 —— New York: Harper & Brothers, 1839. 216 p. 12mo
AAS, BP, UC, Y

2539 —— New York: Harper & Brothers, 1841. 216 p. 12mo
LC, Y

2540 —— New York: Harper & Brothers, 1844. 216 p. 12mo   LC

2541 TALES OF THE REVOLUTION. By a Young Gentleman of Nashville ... Nashville: Hunt, Tardiff and Co., 1833. 179 p. 12mo
LC

Contents: The Two Friends—Ransom Livingston: A Tale of the South—The Hermit of the White Cliff.

TALETELL, GEORGE, F.Y.C., pseud. See Holmes, Isaac Edward

TALVI, pseud. See Robinson, Mrs. Therese

2541a TASISTRO, LOUIS FITZGERALD. Fitzhenry; or, A Marriage in High Life. A Story of the Heart. Founded on Events in the Life of a Fashionable English Lady of High Rank ... [anon.]. Boston: F. Gleason, 1847. 100 p. 8vo   Y
Printed in double cols.

2542 TAYLOR, F. Ella V- - -; or, The July Tour. By One of the Party ... [anon.]. New York: D. Appleton & Co., 1841. 219 p. 12mo   AAS, B, H, HEH, LC, N, NYH, UP, Y
Massachusetts; contemporary.

2543 TAYLOR, JAMES WICKES. The Victim of Intrigue: A Tale of Burr's Conspiracy ... Cincinnati: Robinson & Jones, 1847. 120 p. 8vo   AAS, LC, Y
Cover imprint: "Philadelphia: T. B. Peterson, 98 Chesnut Street ... 1847."

2544 TEFFT, BENJAMIN FRANKLIN. The Shoulder-knot; or, Sketches of the Three-fold Life of Man. A Story of the Seventeenth Century ... New York: Harper & Brothers, 1850. 305 p. 12mo   AAS, B, BP, H, HEH, LC, LCP, N, UC, UP, Y

2545 THE TEMPLAR. To Which Is Added the Tales of Passaic. By a Gentleman of New York. Hackensack, N.J.: J. Spencer and E. Murden, 1822. 127 p. 8vo   H, NYH, UP, Y

TEMPLETON, JOSIAH, *pseud.* *See* Warfield, Susanna

2546 THE TEMPTATION; or, Henry Thornton. By a Minister ... Boston: D. S. King, 1841. 106 p., illus. 12mo   AAS, HEH, UP, Y

2546a ———— Revised by D. P. Kidder. New York: Lane & Tippett, 1846. 90 p., illus. 12mo   Y

2547 TENNEY, TABITHA (GILMAN). Female Quixotism, Exhibited in the Romantic Opinions and Extravagant Adventures of Dorcasina Sheldon ... [anon.]. Boston: Printed by I. Thomas and E. T. Andrews, June, 1801. 2 vols. in 1. 12mo   AAS, IN, UV
Philadelphia; contemporary.

2548 ———— ———— 2d ed. Newburyport: Thomas & Whipple, 1808. 2 vols. in 1. 12mo   AAS, H, LCP, Y

2549 ———— ———— Boston: J. P. Peaslee, 1825. 2 vols. 12mo
AAS(V.2), BA, H, NYP, NYS, UP

2550 ———— ———— Boston: J. P. Peaslee, 1829. 2 vols. 12mo
AAS, LC, NYP, Y

2551 ———— ———— Boston: George Clark, 1841. 3 vols. 12mo
AAS, B, H, HEH, LC(V.1), N, UM, Y

TENSAS, MADISON, *M.D., pseud.* *See* Lewis, Henry Clay

THATCHER, BENJAMIN BUSSEY. *See* Nos. 2537-40 for title entries which are now identified as by Thatcher.

2552 THAYER, CAROLINE MATILDA (WARREN). The Gamesters; or, Ruins of Innocence. An Original Novel, Founded in Truth. By Caroline Matilda Warren ... Boston: Thomas & Andrews, 1805. 304 p. 12mo
AAS, BA, HEH, IN, LC, N, NYS, UC, UP, UV, Y

2553 ———— ———— Boston: J. Shaw, 1828. 300 p. 16mo
AAS, BP, H, HEH, IN, LC, NYP, UC, UM, UP, Y

2554 THAYER, MRS. J. The Drunkard's Daughter ... Boston: William S. Damrell, 1842. 94 p., illus. 8vo   B, NYP, Y
At head of title: "Picnic Tales, Number Three."

2555 ——— ——— Boston: Isaac Tompkins, 1844. 94 p., illus. 8vo
B, Y

2556 ——— Passion, and Other Tales . . . Boston: James French, 1846. 252 p. 12mo AAS, B, HEH, LC, Y
Also contains: The Belle—Enthusiasm—Flora Devere.

2557 ——— The Widow's Son . . . Boston: William S. Damrell, 1843. 112 p., illus. 8vo AAS, Y
At head of title: "Picnic Tales, Number Five."

2557a ——— ——— Boston: Isaac Tompkins, 1844. 112 p., illus. 8vo
At head of title: "Pic-Nic Tales."
Copy located at Barnard College.

2558 THEODORE AND MATILDA; or, The Fatal Plot, and Foul Deeds Detected. In Which Are Displayed the Triumphs of Virtue and the Punishment of Vice. A Touching and Thrilling History. To Which Is Added: Cruelty Disarmed and the Lonely Man . . . Boston: Dow and Jackson, 1845. 29 p., illus. 8vo LC
Printed in double cols.

2559 THOMAS, FREDERICK WILLIAM. Clinton Bradshaw; or, The Adventures of a Lawyer . . . [anon.]. Philadelphia: Carey, Lea & Blanchard, 1835. 2 vols. 12mo AAS, HEH, IN, LC, N, UP, Y

2560 ——— ——— Cincinnati: Robinson and Jones, 1847. 2 vols. in 1. 8vo AAS, LC, Y
Printed in double cols.

2561 ——— East and West . . . [anon.]. Philadelphia: Carey, Lea & Blanchard, 1836. 2 vols. 12mo
AAS, B, BP, H, HEH, HM, IN, LC, N, NYP, NYS, UM, UP, Y

2562 ——— Howard Pinckney . . . [anon.]. Philadelphia: Lea and Blanchard, 1840. 2 vols. 12mo
AAS, B, HEH, LC, N, NYP, UP, Y

2563 ——— Sketches of Character, and Tales Founded on Fact . . . Louisville: The Chronicle of Western Literature and Art, 1849. 117 p. 8vo AAS, H, LC, N, UC, UP, Y
Contents: Boarding-School Scenes; or, A Frolic among the Lawyers—The Unsummoned Witness—William Wirt—The Last of the Pioneers—Simon Kenton—Mary McIntire Has Arrived—John Randolph.

2564　THOMAS, J. B.　The Incarnation, and Miscellaneous Poems. Also, Infidelity: A Tale of the Revolution ...　Covington, Ky.: R. C. Langdon, printer, 1844.　96 p.　8vo

AAS, HEH, LC, N, NYH

2565　THOMAS, JOSIAH LORD.　My Dear Arabella: A Touching Tale of Tenderness [anon.].　[Portland, Me.? 1849.]　Caption title, 15 p.　8vo

AAS, H

Cover title reads: "The rejected $1000 Prize Tale Written for the Flag of Our Union ... By the Editor of the Portland Genius."
Printed in double cols.

2566　THOMPSON, DANIEL PIERCE.　The Adventures of Timothy Peacock, Esquire; or, Freemasonry Practically Illustrated ...　By a Member of the Vermont Bar [anon.].　Middlebury: Knapp and Jewett, printers, 1835.　218 p.　12mo

AAS, B, H, NYP, UP, UV, Y

New England; early 19th cent.

2567　——— The Green Mountain Boys: A Historical Tale of the Early Settlement of Vermont ... [anon.].　Montpelier: E. P. Walton and Sons, publishers and printers, 1839.　2 vols.　12mo

AAS, B, BP, H, HEH, IN, LC, N, NYH, NYP, UP, Y

2568　——— ——— Montpelier, 1840.　2 vols.　12mo
Ed. from Sabin 95478.

2568a　——— ——— Burlington: C. Goodrich & S. B. Nichols, 1848. 2 vols. in 1.　12mo

HEH

2569　——— ——— Boston: Benjamin B. Mussey and Company, 1848. 2 vols. in 1.　12mo

AAS, BP, IN, LCP, UC

2570　——— ——— Boston: Benjamin B. Mussey and Company, 1849. 2 vols. in 1.　12mo

AAS, Y

2571　——— ——— Boston: Benjamin B. Mussey and Company, 1850. 2 vols. in 1.　12mo

Y

2572　——— Locke Amsden; or, The Schoolmaster ... [anon.].　Boston: Benjamin B. Mussey and Co., 1847.　231 p.　12mo

AAS, B, BA, BP, HEH, HM, N, NYP, UC, UM, UP, Y

HM copy has "Second Edition" on wrappers.

2573　——— ——— Boston: Benjamin B. Mussey and Co., 1848.　231 p.　12mo

AAS, BP, HEH, IN, UC, Y

2574 ———— ———— Boston: Benjamin B. Mussey and Co., 1850. 231 p. 12mo
AAS, HEH, UC, Y

2575 ———— Lucy Hosmer; or, The Guardian and Ghost. A Tale of Avarice and Crime Defeated . . . Burlington: C. Goodrich & S. B. Nichols, 1848. 88 p. 8vo
AAS, B, BP, H, HEH, IN, NYH, UM, UP, Y

Also contains: Julia Grayson; or, The Sailor in Love—The Old Soldier's Story.

2576 ———— May Martin; or, The Money Diggers. A Green Mountain Tale . . . Montpelier: E. P. Walton and Son, 1835. 231 p. 12mo
AAS, BP, H, IN, N, UP, UV, Y

2576a ———— ———— Bath, N.Y.: R. L. Underhill & Co.; Charles Adams, printer, 1838. 192 p. 16mo
HEH

2576b ———— ———— [Montpelier, Vt.?]: Printed for the Proprietor, 1842. Cover title, 37 p. 8vo
Y
Printed in double cols.

2577 ———— ———— Boston: Gleason's Publishing Hall, 1846. 66 p. 8vo
AAS, BP, H
BP copy does not have a date in the imprint.

2578 ———— ———— Burlington: Chauncey Goodrich, 1848. 156 p. 12mo
AAS, BP, HM, N, NYP, UC, UP, Y

2579 ———— ———— Canandaigua, N.Y.: H. Underhill, 1849. 171 p. 12mo
AAS, NYH, Y

2580 ———— ———— 3d ed. Burlington: Chauncey Goodrich, 1850. 156 p. 12mo
AAS, HEH, Y

2581 ———— The Shaker Lovers, and Other Tales . . . Burlington: C. Goodrich & S. B. Nichols, 1848. 88 p. 8vo
AAS, BP, H, HEH, IN, LC, NYH, UM, UP, Y

Also contains: Ethan Allen and the Lost Children—A Vermonter in a Fix; or, A New Way to Collect an Old Debt—An Indian's Revenge—The Bravo Husband: A Tale of Italy.
AAS cover imprint dated 1849.

2581a THOMPSON, GEORGE. Adventures of a Pickpocket; or, Life at a Fashionable Watering Place. By Himself [anon.]. New York: Printed for the publisher [n.d.]. 100 p., illus. 8vo UV
Cover imprint: "Boston: Berry & Co., No. 27 Devonshire Street."

335

2582 ——— City Crimes; or, Life in New York and Boston. A Volume for Everybody: Being a Mirror of Fashion, a Picture of Poverty, and a Startling Revelation of the Secret Crimes of Great Cities. By Greenhorn [pseud.], Author of "The House-breaker," "Dissipation," "Venus in Boston," "The Gay Deceiver" . . . Boston: William Berry & Co., publishers, 27 Devonshire Street [cop. 1849]. 192 + p., illus. 8vo HM, N
Printed in double cols.
LC has cover titles for Pts. I-IV, deposited Mar. 5, 6, and Oct. 18, 19, 1849.
N has Pts. I and II in original paper covers: Pt. I, 1 p.l., [7]-116 p.; Pt. II, 1 p.l., 99-162 p.

2583 ——— The Countess; or, Memoirs of Women of Leisure. Being a Series of Intrigues with the Bloods, and a Faithful Delineation of the Private Frailities of Our First Men . . . [anon.]. Boston: Berry & Wright, publishers, No. 27 Devonshire Street [1849]. 100 p., illus. 8vo Y
Printed in double cols.

2584 ——— The House Breaker; or, The Mysteries of Crime. By Greenhorn [pseud.] . . . Boston: W. L. Bradbury, 1848. 48 p., illus. 8vo NYP

2584a ——— Jack Harold; or, The Criminal's Career. A Story with a Moral. By Greenhorn [pseud.]. Boston: William Berry & Co., 27 Devonshire Street [cop. 1850]. 201 p., illus. 8vo LC
Printed in double cols.

2585 ——— Venus in Boston: A Romance of City Life . . . By Greenhorn [pseud.], Author of Dissipation, House Breaker, Radcliff, City Crimes . . . New York: Printed for the publishers [1849]. 100 p., illus. 8vo Y
Printed in double cols.

THOMPSON, GEORGE W. A Tale of Lake Erie. *In* J. T. Parker, *comp.*, The American Legendary (1830), No. 1991.

2586 THOMPSON, WILLIAM TAPPAN. Chronicles of Pineville: Embracing Sketches of Georgia Scenes, Incidents, and Characters . . . [anon.]. Philadelphia: Carey & Hart, 1845. 186 p., illus. 12mo AAS, HEH, HM, IN, Y

2587 ——— ——— Philadelphia: Carey and Hart, 1849. 186 p., illus. 12mo H, HEH
HEH cover imprint: "New York: Burgess, Stringer & Co. . . ., 1845."

2588 ——— John's Alive; or, The Bride of a Ghost [anon.]. Balti-more: Taylor, Wilde and Company, 1846. 50 p., illus. 8vo

AAS, BA, NYP, Y

2589 ——— Major Jones's [pseud.] Courtship . . . Madison, 1843.
Mr. H. P. Miller states in his "The Background and Significance of Major Jones's Courtship," in *The Georgia Historical Quarterly*, XXX (Dec. 1946), 267-296, that the only extant copy of the first ed. is in the Duke University Library. He cites references to nine eds. prior to 1850.

2590 ——— Major Jones's [pseud.] Courtship: Detailed, with Other Scenes, Incidents, and Adventures, in a Series of Letters, by Himself. Second Edition . . . Philadelphia: Carey & Hart, 1844. 200 p., illus. 12mo   BA, H, LC, Y

2590a ——— ——— 7th ed. Philadelphia: Carey & Hart, 1846. 200 p., illus. 12mo   HEH, Y

2590b ——— ——— With Additional Letters... Philadelphia: Carey & Hart, 1847. 217 p., illus. 12mo   Y

2591 ——— ——— 9th ed. Philadelphia: Carey & Hart, 1849. 217 p., illus. 12mo   AAS

2592 ——— Major Jones's [pseud.] Sketches of Travel, Comprising the Scenes, Incidents, and Adventures in His Tour from Geor-gia to Canada . . . Philadelphia: Carey & Hart, 1848. 192 p., illus. 12mo   AAS, BA, LC, LCP, Y

2593 ——— ——— Philadelphia: Carey & Hart, 1850. 192 p., illus. 12mo   BP, Y

THORPE, THOMAS BANGS. The Big Bear of Arkansas. *In* W. T. Porter, *ed.*, The Big Bear of Arkansas, and Other Sketches (1845), Nos. 2061-62.

——— Bob Herring, the Arkansas Bear Hunter. *In* W. T. Por-ter, *ed.*, A Quarter Race in Kentucky (1847), Nos. 2063-64.

2594 ——— The Mysteries of the Backwoods; or, Sketches of the Southwest . . . Philadelphia: Carey and Hart, 1846. 190 p., illus. 12mo

AAS, B, BA, BP, H, HEH, HM, IN, LC, N, NYH, NYP, UC, UM, UP, Y

Contents: Traits of the Prairies—A Piano in "Arkansaw"—Piscatory Arch-ery—Place de la Croix: A Romance of the West—Wit of the Woods—The Water Craft of the Backwoods—Pictures of Buffalo Hunting—Scenes on the Mississippi—The Disgraced Scalp-Lock; or, Incidents on the Western Wa-

ters—Alligator Killing—A Grizzly Bear Hunt—Concordia Lake—A Frontier
Incident—The Mississippi—The American Wild-cat—Tom Owen, the Bee-
Hunter.

———— Stoke Stout, of Louisiana, by Thorpe and Patterson. *In*
W. T. Porter, *ed.*, The Big Bear of Arkansas (1845), Nos. 2061-
62.

2595   THREE DEGREES OF BANKING; or, The Romance of Trade ... Bos-
ton: Weeks, Jordan and Company, 1838.   134 p.   16mo
AAS, BA, HEH, N, UC, Y
On wrapper of BA copy: "Second Edition."

2596   THREE EXPERIMENTS IN DRINKING; or, Three Eras in the Life of
an Inebriate.   Boston: Otis Broaders & Co.; Cassady & March,
1837.   72 p.   12mo   H, HEH

2596a ———— 2d ed.   Boston: Otis Broaders & Co.; Cassady & March,
1837.   72 p.   12mo   Y

2596b ———— 3d ed.   Boston: Otis Broaders & Co.; Cassady & March,
1837.   72 p.   12mo   AAS

2597   THE THREE WIDOWS; or, The Various Aspects of Gotham Life.
By a Member of the New York Bar.   New York: W. F. Burgess,
1849.   96 p.   8vo   B, NYP
Printed in double cols.

2598   THE THRILLING AND ROMANTIC STORY of Sarah Smith and the
Hessian: An Original Tale of the American Revolution.   To
Which Is Added: Female Heroism Exemplified—an Interesting
Story, Founded on Fact ...   Philadelphia, 1844.   24 p., illus.
12mo   LC

2599   ———— Philadelphia, 1845.   32 p., illus.   8vo
AAS, BP, HEH, LC, NYP, UC, UP, Y

2599a THRILLING TALES and Passages from Distinguished Authors.
New York: Adee & Estabrook, 1843.   216 p.   12mo   HEH
Contains: The Pilot's Dream—Texian Traits, by G. W. Kendall—The Fiend
Lover: A Tale—The Fever of '93: A Sketch, by H. J. Van Dyke—The In-
dian Bride, by C. F. Powell—The High Resolve—Scenes of Female Life—
The Gambler.

THROOP, GEORGE HIGBY.   Nag's Head; or, Two Months among
"The Bankers" ...   By Gregory Seaworthy [pseud.].   *See*
No. 1070, where it is erroneously entered under James Gregory.

THWACKIUS, HERMAN, *pseud.* *See* Clopper, Jonas

TITTERWELL, TIMO., *pseud.* *See* Kettell, Samuel

TOBY, *Uncle, pseud.* *See* Trask, George

2600 TODD, CHARLES W. Woodville; or, The Anchoret Reclaimed . . . [anon.]. Knoxville, T.: Printed for the author by F. S. Heiskell, 1832. 278 p. 12mo   BP, LC, Y

2601 TOMLIN, JOHN. Tales of the Caddo . . . Cincinnati: Printed at the office of "The Great West," 1849. 110 p. 8vo   LC, Y
Contents: Jack Faraday—Curators and Regulators—Dick Haverhill's Revenge—The Corsair of the Caddo—The Reformed Freebooter—Rose Larkin—Don Pedro's Island—An Attack by Wolves—Mike Story's Revenge—The Emigrant's Daughter—Fighting Jim.
Printed in double cols.

2602 TORREY, CHARLES TURNER. Home; or, The Pilgrims' Faith Revived . . . Salem: John P. Jewett and Company, 1845. 255 p. 12mo   BA, HEH, N, UP, Y
Massachusetts.

2602a ———— ———— 2d ed. Salem: John P. Jewett and Company, 1845. 256 p. 12mo   AAS, B

TRALL, RUSSELL THACHER. The Angel Tempter. *In* M. Woodruff, *ed.*, A Drop from the Bucket (1847), No. 2759.

TRASK, GEORGE. Not an Invitation to Tea; or, What's Trumps? A Scene in the New York Custom House, by Uncle Toby [pseud.]. *In* J. Jones, The Belle of Boston (1849), No. 1483.

TRAVERS, HENRY. [Author of the stories listed in note below.] *In* The Fountain and the Bottle (1850), No. 996.
The Man Who Enjoyed Himself—The Man Who Made a Beast of Himself—Paying for Sport—Twelve o'Clock.

2603 THE TREASON OF ARNOLD, and Other Tales. Boston: F. Gleason [n.d.]. 100 p. 8vo   LC
Also contains: The Miller of Knupfen—The Newspaper Borrower—The Southern Belle; or, The Shaker Girl of Lebanon—Mary Moxon; or, The Avengers—The Wedding—An Old Man's Whim—The Wish—Kate Hovey's Party—Florence Darnley—Blanche; or, The Baron's Vow—The Wrecker of Barnegat—Christmas Eve—Bad Luck—New Year's Eve.
Printed in double cols.

2604 TREMAYNE, MRS. S. C. H.   Florence Dalbiac, and Other Tales . . .
New York: Printed by S. W. Benedict, 1840.   234 p.   12mo
AAS, B, HEH, LC, NYP, UP, Y
Also contains: The Three Widows—A Sail in Sight; or, The Rescue—The
Escape: A Tale Founded on Facts.

2605 THE TRIAL, Wonderful Escapes and Final Deliverance of Miss
Sophia Thompson.   Founded on Facts.   Boston: Evan's Power
Press Print, 1836.   32 p.   12mo   AAS

2606 TRIUMPH OF RELIGION.   By a Young Lady . . .   Savannah: S. C.
& J. Schenk, 1825.   152 p.   12mo   AAS
Written in a series of letters.

2607 ——— 2d ed.   Charleston: W. Riley, 1829.   194 p.   12mo AAS

TROWBRIDGE, JOHN TOWNSEND.   The Adopted Son; or, The Reward of Charity.   By Paul Creyton [pseud.].   *In* M. M. Ballou, Albert Simmons (1849), No. 229.

2607a ——— Kate the Accomplice; or, The Preacher and the Burglar.
By Paul Creyton [pseud.].   Boston: Jones' Publishing House,
1849.
Cited by Jacob Blanck in *Antiquarian Bookman*, II (July 1948), 123.

2608 TRUESDELL, MARY (VAN HOGEL).   Tippecanoe: A Legend of
the Border . . . [anon.].   [N.p.], 1840.   64 p.   8vo
BA, BP, H, IN, Y

2609 TUCKER, GEORGE.   The Valley of Shenandoah; or, Memoirs of
the Graysons . . . [anon.].   New York: Charles Wiley, 1824.
2 vols.   12mo   BA, H, LC, N, UP, Y
Early 19th cent.

2610 ——— ——— 2d ed.   New York: Orville A. Roorbach, 1828.
2 vols.   12mo   HEH, LC

2611 ——— A Voyage to the Moon.   With Some Account of the
Manners and Customs, Science and Philosophy, of the People
of Morosofia, and Other Lunarians.   By Joseph Atterley
[pseud.] . . .   New York: Elam Bliss, 1827.   264 p.   12mo
AAS, B, BP, H, HEH, IN, LC, N, NYP, NYS, UM, UP, UV, Y

2611a TUCKER, J. N. T.   Theresa; or, The Chief Hyadata's Fall.   A
Legendary Romance of Onondaga Valley . . .   Boston: Glea-
son's Publishing Hall, 1846.   50 p.   8vo   HEH, Y
Also contains: The Two Wards, by Mrs. M. G. Sleeper.

2611b ——— The Two Brides; or, Romance at Saratoga . . . Boston: Cochran, Cole & Company, 1846. 32 p. 8vo   AAS, NYP
Also contains: The Dreamer: An Original Tale, by Mrs. Charlotte Hilborn —The First Bow.
Printed in double cols.

2612 TUCKER, NATHANIEL BEVERLEY. George Balcombe . . . [anon.]. New York: Harper & Brothers, 1836. 2 vols. 12mo
AAS, B, H, HEH, IN, LC, N, NYP, UC, UP, UV, Y
Virginia and Missouri; contemporary.

2613 ——— The Partisan Leader: A Tale of the Future. By Edward William Sidney [pseud.] . . . Printed for the publishers, by James Caxton, 1856 [i.e., Washington, 1836]. 2 vols. 12mo
AAS, BP, HEH, IN, LC, N, NYH, NYP, UP, UV, Y
Virginia.

2614 TUCKERMAN, HENRY THEODORE. Isabel; or, Sicily. A Pilgrimage . . . Philadelphia: Lea and Blanchard, 1839. 230 p. 12mo
AAS, B, BA, BP, H, HEH, LC, LCP, N, NYP, UM, UP, UV, Y

2615 ——— The Italian Sketch Book . . . By an American [anon.]. Philadelphia: Key & Biddle, 1835. 216 p. 12mo
AAS, BA, H, HEH, LC, LCP, N, NYS, UC, UM, Y
Contains: The Florentine.

2616 ——————— 2d ed. Boston: Light & Stearns, 1837. 272 p., illus. 12mo   AAS, B, BA, BP, H, HEH, UP, Y
Contains: The Disclaimer: A Tale of Rome—The Sad Bird of the Adriatic—The Rose-colored Packet—The Florentine.

2617 ——————— 3d ed. New York: J. C. Riker, 1848. 424 p., illus. 12mo   AAS, BA, BP, H, HEH, LC, N, NYP, UC, UM, UP, Y
Contains: The Vetturino: A Tale of the Road-side—The Disclaimer—The Rose-colored Packet—The Florentine—Harry Clinton: A Tale of the Promenade—The Sad Bird of the Adriatic.

2618 ——— Rambles and Reveries . . . New York: James P. Giffing, 1841. 436 p. 12mo
AAS, BA, BP, H, HEH, LC, N, NYP, NYS, UC, UM, UP, Y
Contains: The Bachelor Reclaimed: A Sketch from Real Life.

2619 TUDOR, WILLIAM. Gebel Teir . . . [anon.]. Boston: Carter & Hendee, 1829. 158 p. 12mo
AAS, B, BA, BP, H, HEH, IN, LC, N, NYH, NYP, UC, UM, UP, UV, Y

2620 TUEL, JOHN E. The Prisoner of Perote: A Tale of American Valor and Mexican Love ... Boston: F. Gleason, 1848. 50 p., illus. 8vo   AAS, LC

2621 ——— St. Clair; or, The Protegé. A Tale of the Federal City. By J. T. E. . . . New York: William Taylor & Co., 1846. 142 p. 8vo   LC, Y

2622 TUFTS, MARSHALL. Shores of Vespucci; or, Romance without Fiction . . . [anon.]. Lexington: M. Tufts, 1833. 240 p. 12mo   AAS, B, BP, H, HEH, LC, N, NYH, NYP, Y

2623 TUTHILL, LOUISA CAROLINE (HUGGINS). Anything for Sport ... Boston: Wm. Crosby & H. P. Nichols, 1846. 130 p., illus. 12mo   AAS, UP, Y

2623a ——— ——— 3d ed. Boston: Wm. Crosby and H. P. Nichols, 1847. 130 p., illus. 12mo   HEH

2623b ——— ——— 4th ed. Boston: Wm. Crosby and H. P. Nichols, 1849. 130 p., illus. 12mo   HEH

2624 ——— The Belle, The Blue, and The Bigot; or, Three Fields for Woman's Influence . . . [anon.]. Providence: Samuel C. Blodget, 1844. 322 p. 12mo   AAS, B, BA, H, HEH, N, NYP, UC, UP, Y
Contents: The Belle; or, Woman's Influence in Society—The Blue; or, Woman's Influence in Literature—The Bigot; or, Woman's Influence in Religion.

2625 ——— My Wife ... Boston: William Crosby and H. P. Nichols, 1846. 171 p. 8vo   AAS, B, HEH, LC, N, NYP, UP, Y

2626 ——— Onward! Right Onward! . . . 2d ed. Boston: Wm. Crosby and H. P. Nichols, 1845. 169 p. 12mo
AAS, BA, HEH, LC, N, Y
New York City.

2626a ——— ——— 3d ed. Boston: Wm. Crosby and H. P. Nichols, 1846. 169 p. 12mo   Y

2627 ——— ——— 5th ed. Boston: Wm. Crosby and H. P. Nichols, 1846. 169 p. 12mo   AAS, B

2627a ——— ——— 6th ed. Boston: Wm. Crosby and H. P. Nichols, 1847. 169 p. 12mo   AAS

2627b ——— ——— 8th ed. Boston: Wm. Crosby and H. P. Nichols, 1849. 169 p. 12mo   B

2627c ———— ———— 9th ed. Boston: Wm. Crosby and H. P. Nichols, 1849. 169 p. 12mo   Y

2628 TYLER, ROYALL. The Algerine Captive; or, The Life and Adventures of Doctor Updike Underhill [pseud.], Six Years a Prisoner among the Algerines ... Printed at Walpole, Newhampshire, by David Carlisle, Jun., 1797. 2 vols. 12mo
            AAS, BA, BP, H, HEH, IN, LCP, N, NYP, NYS, UP, UV, Y

2629 ———— ———— Hartford: Printed by Peter B. Gleason and Co., 1816. 2 vols. in 1. 18mo
            AAS, B, HEH, IN, LC, N, NYH, UC, UM, UP, Y

2630 ———— The Yankey in London: Being the First Part of a Series of Letters Written by an American Youth, during Nine Months Residence in the City of London ... Volume I [anon.]. New York: Printed and published by Isaac Riley, 1809. 180 p. 12mo   AAS, BA, BP, H, HEH, IN, LC, LCP, N, NYP, UC, UP, UV, Y
No more published.

2631 THE TYROLESE MINSTRELS; or, The Romance of Every Day Life. By a Lady. Boston: George W. Light, 1841. 200 p., illus. 16mo   AAS, B, BA, BP, H, HEH, LC, N, NYP, UC, UM, UP, Y

2632 UNCLE SOLOMON and the Homan Family; or, How to Live in Hard Times. By a Poor Man. Boston: Printed by Cassady and March, 1837. 23 p. 12mo   AAS, H, Y
New Jersey; contemporary.

2633 ———— 3d ed. Boston: Printed by Cassady and March, 1837. 23 p. 12mo   H, NYP

UNCLE TOBY, *pseud. See* Trask, George

UNDERHILL, *Dr.* UPDIKE, *pseud. See* Tyler, Royall

2634 THE UNVEILED HEART. A Simple Story, by the Author of Early Impressions ... Boston: John Allen and Co., 1835. 262 p. 8vo   HEH, LC, N, Y

2635 THE VAIN COTTAGER; or, The History of Lucy Franklin. To Which Are Prefixed a Few Hints to Young Women in Humble Life, Respecting Decency and Propriety of Dress. From Sidney's press, New Haven, for Increase Cooke and Co., 1807. 72 p. 12mo   AAS, Y
"Larking"; contemporary.

Van Dyke, Henry Jackson. The Fever of '93: A Sketch. *In* Thrilling Tales (1843), No. 2599a.

Vangrifter, *Dr.* Zachary Philemon, *ed. See* Sly, Costard, *pseud.* Sayings and Doings at the Tremont House (1833), No. 2449.

2636 Vanvalkenburg, Sylvester. The Mysteries of Haverhill . . . Haverhill: John Scott & Co., 1844. 24 p. 8vo   AAS

2637 Van Winkle, Henry Edward. Rombert: A Tale of Carolina . . . [anon.]. New York: Charles S. Francis, 1835. 2 vols. 12mo   AAS, BA, CLS, H, HEH, HM, LC, NYH, NYP, UC, UP, Y
Early 18th cent.

2638 Vickery, Sukey. Emily Hamilton: A Novel. Founded on Incidents in Real Life. By a Young Lady of Worcester County . . . [anon.]. Worcester: Printed and sold wholesale and retail, by Isaiah Thomas, Jun., June, 1803. 249 p. 12mo
          AAS, B, BP, H, HEH, IN, LC, N, NYP, NYS, UC, UM, UP, UV, Y
Written in a series of letters.
Massachusetts; contemporary.

2639 The Victims of Gaming: Being Extracts from the Diary of an American Physician. Boston: Weeks, Jordan & Company, 1838. 172 p. 8vo   AAS, BP, HEH, LC, N, UM, UP, Y
Contents: Remarks on Play—The History of Augustine Robwood—Ezra Driver—The Forger—St. George Fallenberg—The Suicide.

2640 Victor, Frances Auretta (Fuller) Barrett. Anizetta, the Guajira; or, The Creole of Cuba. A Romance of the Spanish Isle, by Miss Frances A. Fuller . . . Boston: "Star Spangled Banner" office, 1848. 100 p., illus. 8vo   AAS, LC
At head of title: "A Splendid Original Tale."
Printed in double cols.

2641 Vide, V. V. Sketches of Aboriginal Life . . . New York: Buckland & Summer, 1846. 250 p. 12mo
          AAS, BP, H, HEH, IN, LC, N, NYH, NYP, UC, UP, Y
At head of title: "American Tableaux, No. 1."
Contents: The Aztec Princess; or, Destiny Foreshadowed—The Flight of the Katahba Chief—Monica; or, The Itean Captive—Tula; or, The Hermitess of Athabasca.

2642 VIRGINIA; or, The Lost and Found. A Tale, by the Author of "Constance; or, The Merchant's Daughter" . . . New York: Dayton & Saxton, 1842. 180 p., illus. 12mo

AAS, HEH, LC, UP, Y

Written by John Walker Brown.
Midwest; contemporary.

2643 VON DUNDERHEAD, Messrs., pseud. The Budget; or, Humble Attempts at Immortality. By Messrs. Von Dunderhead [pseud.] . . . Hallowell: Glazier, Masters & Co., 1830. 199 p. 12mo

BP, H, HEH, LC, N, UP, Y

2644 W., T. "None but Suitable Persons." Rhode-Island Temperance Tale, by a Rum-Seller. Founded on Fact [anon.]. Providence, R.I.: B. T. Albro, printer, 1839. 64 p. 16mo

AAS, H, HEH, NYP, Y

At head of title: "Number One."

2645 WALKER, AMBROSE. The Highlands: A Tale of the Hudson . . . [anon.]. Philadelphia: Printed for the author, 1826. 2 vols. 12mo   AAS, BP, UC, Y

Late 18th cent.

2646 WALKER, JESSE. Fort Niagara: A Tale of the Niagara Frontier [anon.]. Buffalo: Steele's press, 1845. 156 p. 12mo

AAS, IN, LC, NYH, UP, UV, Y

"Tales of the Niagara Frontier," Pt. II.

2647 ——— Queenston: A Tale of the Niagara Frontier [anon.]. Buffalo: Steele's press, 1845. 151 p. 12mo

AAS, IN, LC, N, NYH, NYP, UP, UV, Y

"Tales of the Niagara Frontier," Pt. I.

2648 WALLACE, HORACE BINNEY. Stanley; or, The Recollections of a Man of the World . . . [anon.]. Philadelphia: Lea & Blanchard, 1838. 2 vols. 12mo

AAS, B, BP, HEH, IN, LC, LCP, N, NYP, UC, UP, UV, Y

2649 WALN, ROBERT, JR. The Hermit in America on a Visit to Philadelphia: Some Account of the Beaux and Belles, Dandies and Coquettes . . . of That Famous City . . . Edited by Peter Atall, Esq. [pseud.]. Philadelphia: M. Thomas, 1819. 215 p. 12mo

AAS, H, LC, LCP, N, NYH, NYP, NYS, UC, UM, UP, UV, Y

2650 ——— ——— 2d ed. Philadelphia: M. Thomas, 1819. 246 p., illus. 12mo   AAS, BA, BP

2651 ———— ———— 2d Ser. Philadelphia: J. Maxwell and Moses Thomas, 1821. 228 p. 12mo   LC, LCP, NYH, NYP, Y
Title reads: *The Hermit in Philadelphia.*

WALPOLE, WALTER, *pseud. See* Ray, William

2652 WARE, HENRY. David Ellington ... Boston: Wm. Crosby and H. P. Nichols, 1846. 192 p. 12mo   AAS, BP, H, HEH, Y

2653 ——— The Recollections of Jotham Anderson [pseud.], Minister of the Gospel ... Boston: Christian Register office, 1824. 118 p. 12mo   AAS, BA, H, HEH, LC

2654 ———— ———— 2d ed. Boston: Christian Register office, 1828. 189 p. 12mo   AAS, BA, H, LC, N, UP, Y

2655 WARE, NATHANIEL A. Harvey Belden; or, A True Narrative of Strange Adventures ... [anon.]. Cincinnati: Printed for the author, 1848. 278 p. 8vo   AAS, HEH

WARE, WILLIAM. Aurelian; or, Rome in the Third Century. *See* Probus; or, Rome in the Third Century, Nos. 2667-68.

2656 ——— Julian; or, Scenes in Judea ... [anon.]. New York: C. S. Francis, 1841. 2 vols. 12mo
    AAS, B, BA, BP, H, HEH, IN, LC, N, NYP, NYS, UP, UV, Y

2657 ——— Letters of Lucius M. Piso [pseud.], from Palmyra, to His Friend Marcus Curtius at Rome ... New York: C. S. Francis, 1837. 2 vols. 12mo
    AAS, B, BP, H, HEH, IN, LC, N, NYS, UC, UM, UP, UV, Y

2658 ———— ———— New York: C. S. Francis, 1838. 2 vols. 12mo
    AAS, BP, H, HEH, LC, LCP(V.2), N, NYP, UC, Y
Title reads: *Zenobia; or, The Fall of Palmyra.*

2659 ———— ———— New York: C. S. Francis, 1839. 2 vols. 12mo
    AAS, B, BA, Y
Title reads: *Zenobia; or, The Fall of Palmyra.*

2660 ———— ———— New York: C. S. Francis, 1842. 2 vols. in 1. 12mo   LCP, UM, Y
Title reads: *Zenobia; or, The Fall of Palmyra.*

2661 ———— ———— New York: C. S. Francis & Co., 1843. 2 vols. 12mo   AAS, HEH, Y
Title reads: *Zenobia; or, The Fall of Palmyra.*
HEH original paper labels on spines: Vol. I, "Fifth Edition"; Vol. II, "Fourth Edition."

2662 —————— 6th ed. New York: C. S. Francis & Co., 1846. 2
vols. 12mo   AAS, LCP, NYP, Y
Title reads: *Zenobia; or, The Fall of Palmyra.*

2663 —————— 7th ed. Boston: James Munroe and Company,
1846. 2 vols. 12mo   AAS, H
Title reads: *Zenobia; or, The Fall of Palmyra.*

2664 —————— 7th ed. New York: C. S. Francis & Co., 1848.
2 vols. 12mo   AAS, B, HEH, Y
Title reads: *Zenobia; or, The Fall of Palmyra.*

2665 —————— 8th ed. New York: C. S. Francis & Co., 1850.
2 vols. 12mo   BP, NYP
Title reads: *Zenobia; or, The Fall of Palmyra.*

2666 ———— Probus; or, Rome in the Third Century. In Letters of
Lucius M. Piso [pseud.], from Rome, to Fausta, the Daughter
of Gracchus, at Palmyra . . . New York: C. S. Francis, 1838.
2 vols. 12mo
AAS, B, BA, BP, H, HEH, IN, LC, LCP, N, NYP, NYS, UC, UM, UP, UV, Y

2667 —————— New York: C. S. Francis & Co., 1848. 2 vols.
12mo   AAS, B, LC, NYS, UP, Y
Title reads: *Aurelian; or, Rome in the Third Century.*

2668 —————— New York: C. S. Francis & Co., 1849. 2 vols.
12mo   AAS, H, HEH(V.1), NYH, NYP
Title reads: *Aurelian; or, Rome in the Third Century.*

———— Zenobia; or, The Fall of Palmyra. *See* Letters of Lucius
M. Piso, from Palmyra, Nos. 2658-65.

2669 WARFIELD, SUSANNA. Illorar de Courcy: An Auto-biographical
Novel. By Josiah Templeton, Esq. [pseud.]. Baltimore: William and Joseph Neal, 1835. 2 vols. 8vo
Sabin 101419 states that "it was suppressed."
Mr. Francis J. Dallett, librarian, informs me that the Athenaeum of Philadelphia has a copy.

2670 WARLAND, JOHN H. The Plume: A Tuft of Literary Feathers . . .
Boston: Benjamin B. Mussey, 1847. 311 p., illus. 12mo
AAS, B, BP, H, HEH, LC, N, NYH, NYP, UM, UP, Y

2671 WARREN, GREENLIFFE. The Flying Cloud: A Romance of the Bay of New York . . . Boston: H. L. Williams, 1845. 82 p., illus. 8vo AAS, BP, Y

Printed in double cols.

LC has a title page, deposited Nov. 6, 1845.

2672 ———— Olph; or, The Wreckers of the Isle of Shoals. A Romance of Sixty Years Ago . . . Boston: H. L. Williams, 1846. 93 p., illus. 8vo AAS, B, BP, UP, Y

An advert. of a title, *Olph; or, The Wreckers*, gave J. H. Ingraham as the author.

2672a ———— ———— New York: W. F. Burgess, 1849. 93 p., illus. 8vo HEH

2673 WATERHOUSE, BENJAMIN. A Journal of a Young Man of Massachusetts, Late a Surgeon on Board an American Privateer, Who Was Captured at Sea by the British, in May, Eighteen Hundred and Thirteen . . . Written by Himself . . . [anon.]. Boston: printed by Rowe and Hooper, 1816. 228 p., illus. 12mo

AAS, B, BP, H, HEH, HM, IN, LC, LCP, N, NYH, NYP, NYS, UP, UV, Y

The *Journal* somewhat parallels the known facts about the American privateer "Enterprise" and her surgeon, Amos G. Babcock (see H. R. Viets, "A Journal . . ." in *Yale Journal of Biology and Medicine*, XII [New Haven, 1940], 105-622). That Babcock furnished the facts for the narrative is conjecture, as he has not been identified nor his acquaintance with Waterhouse established.

2674 ———— ———— 2d ed. Boston: Printed by Rowe & Hooper, 1816. 240 p., illus. 12mo AAS, B, BA, BP, HEH, LCP, UC, UM, Y

2675 ———— ———— Printed by Rowe & Hooper, Boston. Milledgeville (Geo.): Reprinted by S. & F. Grantland, 1816. 228 p., illus. 12mo H, UPI

A reissue of the 1st ed. with a new title page.

2676 ———— ———— Milledgeville (Geo.): Reprinted by S. & F. Grantland, 1816. 240 p., illus. 12mo AAS, BP, H

A reissue of the Boston 2d ed. with a new title page.

2677 ———— ———— Lexington (Ky.): Reprinted by Worsley & Smith, 1816. 240 p., illus. 12mo AAS, HEH, NYP

A reissue of the Boston 2d ed. with a new title page.

2678 WATERSTON, ROBERT CASSIE. Arthur Lee and Tom Palmer; or, The Sailor Reclaimed [anon.]. Boston: James Munroe & Company, 1839. 78 p. 12mo LC, Y

2678a ——— ——— 2d ed. Boston: James Munroe & Company, 1839.
78 p. 12mo   Y

2679 ——— ——— 3d ed. Boston: James Munroe & Company, 1839.
78 p. 12mo   BP

2680 WATKINS, TOBIAS. Tales of the Tripod; or, A Delphian Evening.
By Pertinax Particular [pseud.]. Baltimore: Fielding Lucas,
Jr., 1821. 162 p. 12mo   AAS, B, BP, H, HEH, IN, LC, NYP, UP, Y
Contents: Sylvester Eve; or, The Adventures of a Watchman—The Surprise
—The Influence of Names.

2680a WATMOUGH, EDMUND CARMICK. Scribblings and Sketches, Dip-
lomatic, Piscatory, and Oceanic. By a Fisher in Small Streams
[anon.]. Philadelphia: Printed for the publishers, 1844. 66 p.
8vo   H, N, Y
Written in a humorous vein.

2680b ——— ——— 2d ed. Philadelphia: C. Sherman, printer, 1844.
189 p. 8vo   AAS, B, H, LC, N, NYH, NYP, Y

2681 WATTERSTON, GEORGE. Glencarn; or, The Disappointments of
Youth . . . Alexandria: Printed by Cottom & Stewart, 1810.
2 vols. in 1. 12mo   H, LC, NYH, NYP, NYS, UV
Paged continuously.

2682 ——— The L - - - Family at Washington; or, A Winter in the
Metropolis [anon.]. Washington: Printed and published by
Davis and Force, 1822. 159 p. 12mo
                   AAS, B, BA, BP, H, HEH, IN, LC, LCP, N, NYH, NYP, UC, Y
Written in a series of letters.
Contemporary.

2683 ——— The Lawyer; or, Man as He Ought Not to Be . . . [anon.].
Pittsburgh: Zadok Cramer, 1808. 236 p., illus. 12mo
                            AAS, B, HEH, IN, LC, NYP, UPI, UV, Y
Maryland; contemporary.

2684 ——— ——— Charlestown: G. Davidson, 1829. 180 p. 12mo
                                              AAS, B, BP, N, Y

2685 ——— Wanderer in Washington . . . [anon.]. Printed at the
Washington Press, by Jonathan Elliot, Junior, 1827. 226 p.
16mo   AAS, H, IN, LC, LCP, NYP, Y

2686 ——— ——— 2d ed. Printed at the Washington Press and sold
by Jonathan Elliot, 1829. 226 p. 12mo   AAS, LC, Y

2687 WEBBER, CHARLES WILKINS. The Gold Mines of the Gila: A Sequel to Old Hicks the Guide ... New York: Dewitt & Davenport, 1849. 2 vols. in 1. 12mo

AAS, B, BA, H, HEH, IN, LC, LCP, N, NYP, UM, Y

Paged continuously (263 p.).

2688 ———— Jack Long; or, Shot in the Eye. A True Story of Texas Border Life [anon.]. New York: W. H. Graham, 1846. 30 p. 8vo

HEH, Y

2689 ———— ———— Elizabethtown, N.J.: James S. Drake [printer], 1847. 24 p. 8vo

Y

Title reads: *The Shot in the Eye. A True Story of Texas Border Life.*

2690 ———— Old Hicks the Guide; or, Adventures in the Camanche Country in Search of a Gold Mine ... New York: Harper & Brothers, 1848. 2 pts. 12mo

AAS, B, BA, H, HEH, IN, LC, LCP, N, NYP, UP, Y

Paged continuously (356 p.).

———— The Shot in the Eye. *See* Jack Long; or, Shot in the Eye, No. 2689.

2691 WEIR, JAMES. Lonz Powers; or, The Regulators. A Romance of Kentucky, Founded on Facts ... Philadelphia: Lippincott, Grambo & Co., 1850. 2 vols. 12mo

AAS, B, BP, H, IN, LC, LCP, NYH, NYP, UC, UM, UP, Y

2692 WELD, EDWARD. On Soundings and Off; or, Tales of the Land and the Sea ... [anon.]. New York: William H. Graham, 1846. 48 p. 8vo

Y

2693 ———— The Ransomed Bride: A Tale of the Inquisition ... New York: Burgess, Stringer and Company, 1846. 86 p. 8vo.

AAS, Y

2693a WELD, GILBERT CUMMING. The Mysterious Personage; or, The Man with the Hare [sic] Life, and the False Heir. A Moral Fiction. By Sydney Sinclair [pseud.] ... Boston: Printed and published by George H. Williams, 1848. 100 p. 8vo HEH

Printed in double cols.

2694 WELD, HORATIO HASTINGS. Corrected Proofs ... Boston: Russell, Shattuck & Co., 1836. 261 p. 12mo

AAS, B, BA, BP, H, HEH, IN, LC, N, NYH, NYP, UC, UM, UP, Y

Contains: Love and Law—The Partners—A Winter in Cedarville—A Pet in a Pet—The Old Soldier—The Martyr to Science—Easy Joe Bruce—The Omnibus—Tar Brush Sketches, by Benjamin Fiferail—My Friend's Story—Boots—Wanderings of Mr. Peter Peregrinate in Search of a Boarding-house —Old Kit and His Daughters—Sir, a Secret! Most Important—The Maiden Aunt—Music Mad.

2695 ———— Fourth Experiment of Living. Living without Means ... [anon.]. Boston: Otis, Broaders & Company, 1837. 68 p. 12mo   HEH, LC, Y

2696 ——— ——— 2d ed. Boston: Otis, Broaders & Company, 1837. 68 p.   12mo   AAS, BP

2697 ——— ——— 3d ed. Boston: Otis, Broaders & Company, 1837. 68 p.   12mo
No copy located.

2697a ——— ——— 4th ed. Boston: Otis, Broaders & Company, 1837.   68 p.   12mo   AAS, Y

2698 ——— ——— 6th ed. Boston: Otis, Broaders & Company, 1837.   68 p.   12mo   AAS, NYP

2698a ——— ——— 7th ed. Boston: Otis, Broaders & Company, 1837.   68 p.   12mo   AAS

2699 ——— ——— 8th ed. Boston: Otis, Broaders & Company, 1837.   68 p.   12mo   AAS, BP

2700 ——— ——— 10th ed. Boston: Otis, Broaders & Company, 1837.   68 p.   12mo   Y

2700a ——— ——— 11th ed. Boston: Otis, Broaders & Company, 1837.   68 p.   12mo   AAS

2701 ——— ——— 13th ed. Boston: Otis, Broaders & Company, 1837.   68 p.   12mo   BA, BP, HEH, Y

2702 ——— Jonce Smiley, the Yankee Boy Who Had No Friends. By Ezekiel Jones, Esq. [pseud.], Author of Sundries. Edited by H. Hastings Weld. New York: E. Ferrett and Company, 1845. 75 p. 8vo   LC, UP, Y
On cover: "Library of American Novels, No. 3."

2703 THE WESTERN HOME MADE HAPPY. By a Lady ... Boston: James B. Dow, 1844. 72 p. 8vo   HEH, LC, UP, Y

2704 WESTON, MRS. MARIA D. The Weldron Family; or, Vicissitudes of Fortune. A Story of Real Life in New England . . . By Maria [pseud.] . . . Providence: Weeden & Peek, 1848. 304 p. 12mo   AAS, B, BA, H, HEH, N, NYP, UC, UP, Y

WHIPPLE, FRANCES HARRIET. *See* McDougall, Frances Harriet (Whipple) Green

2705 WHIPPOORWILL, TIM, *pseud.* Nelly Brown; or, The Trials, Temptations and Pleasures of College Life . . . Boston: The Yankee office, 1845. 48 p. 8vo   BP, H, HEH
Cambridge.

WHITE, CHARLES ERSKINE, *D.D., pseud.* *See* Osborn, Laughton

2706 WHITE, RICHARD GRANT. A Tale of the Hospital. New York, 1840. 8vo
Title from Foley.

2707 THE WHITE FAUN; or, Laura Ingram . . . By a Young Lady of Baltimore. Baltimore: W. Taylor, 1847. 40 p. 8vo   NYP

2708 WHITMORE, WALTER. Ella Winston; or, The Adventures of an Orphan Girl. A Romance of Cincinnati . . . Cincinnati: Lorenzo Stratton, 131 Main Street [cop. 1850]. 112 p. 8vo
                                                                    NYP
Printed in double cols.

2709 WHITTIER, JOHN GREENLEAF. Leaves from Margaret Smith's Journal in the Province of Massachusetts Bay, 1678-9 [anon.]. Boston: Ticknor, Reed and Fields, 1849. 224 p. 8vo
AAS, B, BA, BP, H, HEH, IN, LC, LCP, N, NYH, NYP, UC, UM, UP, UV, Y
For complete bibliographical description see Currier.

2710 ——— Legends of New England . . . Hartford: Hanmer and Phelps, 1831. 142 p. 12mo
                              AAS, B, BA, BP, H, HEH, LC, N, NYH, NYP, UC, UP, Y
For contents see Currier.

2710a WIGHTMAN, HENRY. The Juvenile Polyanthos; or, Fireside Company. Being a Selection of Amusing Stories . . . New York: Wightman & Wood, 1833. 105, [3] p., illus. 12mo
                                                                    NYP
Contains: Legend of the West—Fisherman's Family—Revolutionary Tale—Hunting the Elephant—Haunted Well—Lost Boy—Friendly Indian—Spanish Widow.

2710b ———— ———— Newark, N.J.: Printed and published by Benjamin Olds, 1835. 105, [3] p., illus. 12mo LC

WILBUR, ANNE T. The Godfather. *In* E. Z. C. Judson, The Red Revenger [185-?], No. 1533.

2711 WILBURN, GEORGE T. Auto-biography of Sam Simple [pseud.]: Giving an Account of the Administration of the Affairs of the Simple Family from the Year 1829 to 1837. By His Aunt Deborah Grabstick. Together with a History of Some New and Important Experiments in Government Never Before Tried ... A Political Allegory. Boston: O. Brewer, 1837. 36 p. 12mo
BP, H, LC
Satire on Andrew Jackson.

2712 WILEY, CALVIN HENDERSON. Alamance; or, The Great and Final Experiment ... [anon.]. New York: Harper & Brothers, 1847. 151 p. 8vo AAS, HEH, LC, N, NYP, UP, Y
Printed in double cols.
North Carolina; American Revolution.

2713 WILFRED MONTRESSOR; or, The Secret Order of the Seven. A Romance of Life in the New York Metropolis. By the Author of "Abel Parsons; or, The Brother's Revenge," "Florence De Lacey." New York: Charles G. Graham & Co., 1848. 2 vols., illus. 8vo AAS, H(V.1), NYP, UP

2714 WILKES, GEORGE. The Lives of Helen Jewett and Richard P. Robinson . . . [anon.]. New York: Sold by booksellers throughout the United States [cop. 1849]. 132 p., illus. 8vo
AAS, HEH, LC, NYP, Y
Cover title reads: "The Life of Helen Jewett ... Philadelphia: W. B. Zieber, Ledger Buildings."
Printed in double cols.

2715 WILKES, J. WIMPLETON. The Mysteries of Springfield: A Tale of the Times ... Springfield: William B. Brockett, 1844. 40 p. 8vo AAS, B

WILKEY, WALTER, *Major, pseud.* *See* Deming, Ebenezer

2716 WILKINSON, MRS. HENRIETTE, *ed.* The Treasure; or, Hours in Solitude ... Being a Selection of the Best Pieces from Different Good Authors ... Cincinnati: Printed by E. Morgan and Co., 1838. 211 p. 12mo AAS, HEH
Contains: Love's Martyr: A Prize Tale, by Delia S. Bacon—The Aga of the Janissaries.

2717 WILLET, W. N.   Charles Vincent; or, The Two Clerks.   A Tale of Commercial Life . . . [anon.].   New York: Harper & Brothers, 1839.   2 vols.   12mo

AAS, BP, H, HEH, LC, N, NYP, UM, UP, Y

New York City; 18--.

2718 WILLIAM COOPER and His Family; or, Christian Principle Exemplified . . .   Boston: Wait, Greene and Company, 1827.   24 p. 12mo

BA, LC

2719 WILLIAMS, CATHERINE READ (ARNOLD).   Annals of the Aristocracy: Being a Series of Anecdotes of Some of the Principal Families of Rhode-Island . . .   Providence: B. T. Albro, printer, 1845.   2 nos.   8vo   AAS, B, H, HEH, LC, NYH, NYP(no.1), UP, Y

Contents: The Somebodys—Albert, the Melancholy Man—The Assignment—The High Sheriff of the County—Mrs. Gray—Ruth Glenn—The Fascinating Stranger—Pride and Poverty—The Haunted Brook—Mr. Breeze and Mr. Brice—The Illuminated Drawing-Room—The Coffin-maker and the Grave-digger—High Life above Stairs—Hereditary Propensities—The Crushed Heart.

Printed in double cols.

No more published.

2720 —— Aristocracy; or, The Holbey Family.   A National Tale . . .   Providence: Printed by J. Knowles, 1832.   312 p.   12mo

AAS, B, BP, H, HEH, IN, LC, N, NYP, UC, UM, UP, UV, Y

New York City and Washington; 1801-9.

2721 —— Fall River: An Authentic Narrative . . . [anon.].   Boston: Lilly, Wait & Co., 1833.   198 p., illus.   12mo

AAS, B, BP, H, HEH, IN, LC, NYH, UC, UM, UP, Y

Rhode Island.

2722 —— —— Boston: Lilly, Wait & Co., 1834.   198 p., illus. 12mo

AAS, BA, H, HEH, LC, NYH, NYP, Y

2723 —— The Neutral French; or, The Exiles of Nova Scotia . . . Providence: The author [cop. 1841].   2 vols. in 1, illus.   12mo

AAS, B, BP, H, HEH, IN, LC, N, NYH, NYP, UM, UP, Y

2724 —— —— 2d ed.   Providence: The author [cop. 1841].   2 vols. in 1, illus.   12mo   AAS, B, H, IN, LC, N, NYP, NYS, UC, UM, Y

2725 —— Religion at Home: A Story Founded on Facts . . .   Providence: Marshall & Hammond, printers, 1829.   322 p.   12mo

AAS, B, BP, H, HEH, UM, Y

New England; last quarter of 18th cent.

2726 ———— ———— 2d ed. Providence: Printed by B. Cranston & Co., 1837. 312 p. 12mo AAS, B, LC, UP, Y

2727 ———— ———— 3d ed. Providence: Printed by B. Crantson & Co., 1837. 312 p. 12mo B, BP, Y

2728 ———— Tales: National and Revolutionary . . . Providence: H. H. Brown, printer, 1830. 215 p. 12mo
AAS, B, BP, H, HEH, IN, LC, N, NYH, UC, UP, UV, Y
Contents: Narrative of Rosanna Hicks—The Blind Sisters—The King's Ship —Providential Escape—Loyalty—Scott's Pond Thirty Years Ago.

2729 ———— ———— Vol. II. Providence: Cranston & Hammond, printers, 1835. 269 p. 12mo
AAS, B, BP, HEH, IN, LC, N, NYH, NYP, UC, UP, UV, Y
Contents: Life of Judge C---: A Tale of the West—The Last of the Dinsmores—A Sketch of the Brown's—The Cholera at Quebec.

2730 WILLIS, JOHN R. Carleton: A Tale of Seventeen Hundred and Seventy-six . . . [anon.]. Philadelphia: Lea & Blanchard, 1841. 2 vols. 12mo AAS, B, H, HEH, IN, LC, N, NYP, UP, UV, Y

2731 WILLIS, NATHANIEL PARKER. Complete Works . . . New York: J. S. Redfield, 1846. 895 p., illus. Fol.
AAS, BA, H, HEH, NYP, UP, Y
Printed in double cols.

2732 ———— Dashes at Life with a Free Pencil . . . New York: Burgess, Stringer & Co., 1845. 4 pts. Fol.
AAS, BA, BP, H, HM(pts.1-2), LC, LCP, NYP(pt.1), Y
Pt. I: High Life in Europe and American Life. Pt. II: Inklings of Adventure. Pt. III: Loiterings of Travel. Pt. IV: Ephemera.
Printed in double cols.

2733 ———— ———— 2d ed. New York: J. S. Redfield [n.d.]. Cover title, p. [109]-220. Fol. B
Half title: "Part III: Loiterings of Travel."
Printed in double cols.

2734 ———— ———— 3d ed. New York: J. S. Redfield, 1845. 4 pts. Fol. AAS, BP, LC, LCP, NYP, Y
Contents: High Life in Europe—Inklings of Adventure—Loiterings of Travel—Ephemera.
Printed in double cols.

2735 ———— ———— New York: William Taylor, No. 2 Astor House [cop. 1845]. 4 pts. Fol. AAS, H, LC
Half title: "Part I: High Life in Europe, and American Life."
Printed in double cols.

2736 ———— Inklings of Adventure ... [anon.]. New York: Saunders and Otley, 1836. 2 vols. 12mo AAS, B, BA, BP, CLS(V.1), H, HEH, HM, IN, LCP, N, NYH, NYP, UC, UM, UP, Y

Contents: Pedlar Karl—Niagara, Lake Ontario, the St. Lawrence—The Cherokee's Threat—F. Smith—Edith Linsey—Scenes of Fear—Incidents on the Hudson—The Gipsy of Sardis—Tom Fane and I—Larks in Vacation—A Log in the Archipelago—Miscellaneous Papers.

2737 ———— ———— 2d ed. New York: Saunders and Otley, 1836. 2 vols. 12mo AAS, NYP(V.1), Y

2738 ———— ———— 3d ed. New York, 1836. 2 vols. 12mo Y
Roorbach lists an 1837 ed.

2739 ———— *ed.* The Legendary, Consisting of Original Pieces, Principally Illustrative of American History, Scenery and Manners ... Boston: Samuel G. Goodrich, 1828. 2 vols. 12mo
AAS, B, BP, H, HEH, LC, N, NYH, NYP, NYS(V.1), UC, UM, UP, Y

Contains: The Church in the Wilderness [by L. M. Child]—The Wedding—The Rapids—Romance in Real Life [by C. M. Sedgwick]—The Palisadoes, by Grenville Mellen—The Indian Wife [by L. M. Child]—The Sisters—The Legend of Bethel Rock—The Conscript Brothers—The Frontier House [by S. J. Hale]—The Stepmother—Leaves from a Colleger's Album—The Camp Meeting—Extracts from a Sea Book, by Samuel Hazzard—The Witch —The Siege of Soleure—Elizabeth Latimer.
No more published.

2740 ———— Life, Here and There; or, Sketches of Society and Adventure at Far-Apart Times and Places ... New York: Baker and Scribner, 1850. 377 p. 12mo
AAS, BA, BP, H, HEH, HM, IN, LC, LCP, N, NYP, UC, UP, Y

Contents: Part I, Earlier Days (Edith Lindsey—Scenes of Fear—Incidents on the Hudson—Pedlar Karl—Niagara, Lake Ontario, the St. Lawrence—The Cherokee's Threat—F. Smith). Part II, Later Days; or, Sketches of Persons and Scenes of High Life in Europe (Leaves from the Heart-Book of Ernest Clay—Beauty and the Beast; or, Handsome Mrs. Titton and Her Plain Husband—Miss Jones's Son—Lady Rachel—Wigwam versus Almack's).

2741 ———— The Miscellaneous Works ... New York: J. S. Redfield, 1847. 4 pts. Fol. AAS, B, H, Y
Printed in double cols.

2742 ———— People I Have Met; or, Pictures of Society and People of Mark, Drawn under a Thin Veil of Fiction ... New York: Baker and Scribner, 1850. 357 p. 12mo
AAS, B, BA, BP, H, HEH, LC, LCP, N, NYP, UC, UP, Y

356

2743 —— Prose Works . . . Philadelphia: Carey & Hart, 1849.
798 p. 8vo   BP, HEH, HM, NYH
Printed in double cols.
Foley lists a New York, 1846 ed.

2744 —————— Philadelphia: H. C. Baird, 1850. 798 p. 8vo
                                       AAS, UM
Printed in double cols.

2745 —— Romance of Travel: Comprising Tales of Five Lands . . .
[anon.]. New York: S. Colman, 1840. 300 p. 12mo
         AAS, BA, BP, HEH, LC, LCP, N, NYH, NYP, UM, UP, Y
Contents: Lady Ravelgold—Paletto's Bride—Violanta Cesarina—Pasquali,
the Tailor of Venice—The Bandit of Austria—Oonder Hoofden; or, The
Undercliff—The Picker and Piler—Stratford-on-Avon—Charlecote.

2746 WILMER, JOHN. The Modern Vassal: A Story of Poland . . .
Boston: Published at the office of the Living Age [1849?]. 74
p. 4to   AAS, BA, HEH, LCP, NYS
Also contains: The Wedding Garment.
Printed in double cols.

2747 WILMER, LAMBERT A. The Confessions of Emilia Harrington
. . . [anon.]. Baltimore: L. A. Wilmer, 1835. 96 p. 12mo LC
New York City.

2748 WILSON, DAVID. Life in Whitehall: A Tale of the Ship Fever
Times. Written by a Citizen [anon.]. Whitehall, N.Y.: W.
S. Southmayd & H. W. Buel, 1849. 57 p. 8vo   AAS, NYP
Printed in double cols.
LC has a title page, deposited Oct. 24, 1849.

2749 WINDLE, MARY JANE. Truth and Fancy: Tales, Legendary, His-
toric, and Descriptive . . . Philadelphia: C. Sherman, printer,
1850. 303 p. 12mo   AAS, B, H, HEH, LC, N, NYP, UC, UM, UP, Y
Contents: The Huguenot—Florence de Rohan: A Fragment from the History of Napoleon—The Lady of the Rock: A Legend of New England.

2749a WINONA, THE BROWN MAID of the South: A Tale of the South.
For the South, by a Citizen of the South. Philadelphia: Printed
and published at the office of the American Citizen, 1846. 66 p.
8vo   UV
Dedication signed: "Harry Hazard." Copyrighted by "William H. Brisbane."
Printed in double cols.
Virginia.

2750 WINSOR, HENRY. Pebblebrook and the Harding Family [anon.].
Boston: Benjamin H. Greene, 1839. 207 p. 12mo
AAS, B, BA, H, HEH, LC, N, NYP, UC, UP, Y

2751 THE WITCH OF NEW ENGLAND: A Romance ... Philadelphia:
H. C. Carey & I. Lea, 1824. 217 p. 12mo
B, BP, LC, LCP, N, NYP, UC, UP, Y
Sabin 104923 lists an 1825 ed.
Written by John Cadwalader McCall.
Late 17th cent.

2751a THE WONDERFUL, ASTOUNDING, MYSTERIOUS, and Strange History
of Laura A. Marston, of Baltimore, Md. (An Autobiography)
... Together with an Account of the Shocking Murder of
Mrs. E. Williamson and Dreadful Death of the Smuggler Kent-
worth. Baltimore: Barclay & Co., 1850. 47 p., illus. 8vo
AAS

2752 WONDERFUL DISCLOSURE! The Mystery Solved!! Or, Narrative
of Dr. M. Lorner, One of the Passengers of the Steam Ship Pres-
ident! Which Vessel Left New York, Bound for Liverpool,
March 11, 1841, since Which Time, until Recently, Nothing
Has Been Heard Respecting Her Fate. New York: W. L.
Knapp & E. E. Barclay, 1845. 26 p., illus. 8vo   LC, UP

2753 WOOD, GEORGE. Peter Schlemihl in America ... [anon.]. Philadelphia: Carey and Hart, 1848. 494 p. 8vo   AAS, B,
BA, H, HEH, HM, IN, LC, LCP, N, NYH, NYP, NYS, UC, UM, UP, UV, Y

2754 WOOD, SALLY SAYWARD (BARRELL) KEATING. Amelia; or, The
Influence of Virtue. An Old Man's Story. By a Lady of Mas-
sachusetts ... [anon.]. [Portsmouth, N.H.]: Printed at the
Oracle press by William Treadwell & Co. [1802]. 143 [i.e.,
243] p. 8vo   N, UC, UV, Y
England and France.

2755 ——— Dorval; or, The Speculator. A Novel, Founded on Recent Facts. By a Lady . . . [anon.]. Portsmouth, N.H.:
Printed at the Ledger press by Nutting & Whitelock, 1801. 285
p. 12mo   AAS, BP, H, LC, N, Y
Georgia.

2756 ——— Ferdinand & Elmira: A Russian Story. By a Lady of
Massachusetts . . . [anon.]. Baltimore: Samuel Butler, 1804.
311 p. 12mo   AAS, BP, H, HEH, IN, N, NYS, UC, UP, UV, Y
1750.

2757 ——— Julia and the Illuminated Baron. A Novel Founded on Recent Facts Which Have Transpired in the Course of the Late Revolution of Moral Principles in France. By a Lady of Massachusetts . . . [anon.]. Portsmouth, New Hampshire: Printed at the United States' Oracle press, by Charles Peirce, June, 1800. 288 p. 12mo   AAS, B, BA, HEH, LCP, NYS, UV, Y

2758 ——— Tales of the Night. By a Lady of Maine . . . [anon.]. Portland: Printed and published by Thomas Todd, 1827. 74, 90 p. 12mo   AAS, LC, UV

Contents: Storms and Sunshine; or, The House on the Hill—The Hermitage; or, Rise of Fortune.

2759 WOODRUFF, MARIA, *ed.* A Drop from the Bucket, for the Sons of Temperance . . . Auburn: Alden & Markham, 1847. 178 p. 12mo   HEH, NYP, Y

Contains: The Dangers of Irresolution—The Wife, by Ann S. Stephens—The Angel Tempter, by R. T. Trall—The Poetry of Poverty, by Julia A. Fletcher—Drink and Death—A Legend of the Inner Life, by Thomas L. Harris.

WOODWORTH, FRANCIS CHANNING. Charley Randolph. *In* The Fountain and the Bottle (1850), No. 996.

2760 WOODWORTH, SAMUEL. The Champions of Freedom; or, The Mysterious Chief. A Romance of the Nineteenth Century, Founded on the War between the United States and Great Britain . . . New York: Printed and published by Charles N. Baldwin, 1816. 2 vols. 12mo   AAS, B, BP, H, HEH, IN, LC, N, NYH, NYP, NYS, UC(V.2), UM, UP, UV, Y

2761 ——— ——— New York: Printed and published by Charles N. Baldwin, 1817. 2 vols. 12mo   AAS

2762 ——— ——— New York: W. H. Graham, 1847. 126 p. 8vo   AAS, B, H, Y

Printed in double cols.

——— The Female Spy: A Domestic Tale of the Revolution. *In* R. F. Greeley, Arthur Woodleigh (1847), No. 1061.

2762a A WORD TO HUSBANDS and Wives; or, Those Who Intend to Become Such: Being the Last Legacy of a Disconsolate Old Widower. Boston: Skinner & Blanchard, 1844. 28 p. 12mo   HEH

2763 WORTHINGTON, FRANK. Phillip Moreton, the Poor Gunsmith; or, Circumstantial Evidence. A Tale of Boston in Olden Time ... Boston: R. B. Fitts & Company, 1850. 100 p. 8vo   BP, Y
Printed in double cols.
LC has a title page, deposited Feb. 14, 1850.

2764 WRIGHT, CALEB EARL. Wyoming: A Tale [anon.]. New York: Harper & Brothers, 1845. 123 p. 8vo
AAS, BP, H, HEH, N, NYP, UP, Y
Printed in double cols.
Pennsylvania; 17--.

2765 WYNDON, FRANK. Eliza Leslie; or, Separation and Re-union. A Tale of the Heart ... Boston: Gleason's Publishing Hall, 1847. 50 p., illus. 8vo   Y
Also contains: The Rescued Bridegroom—A Thrilling Narrative.
Printed in double cols.

2766 THE YANKEE IN LONDON; or, A Short Trip to America ... Philadelphia: John Carson, 1826. 107 p. 12mo
AAS, B, BA, BP, IN, LC, LCP, N, Y

2767 THE YANKEE TRAVELLER; or, The Adventures of Hector Wigler ... Concord: George Hough, 1817. 107 p. 18mo
AAS, BP, IN, LC, NYH, UC

2768 YOUNG, SAMUEL. The Orphan and Other Tales ... Pittsburgh: Printed by A. A. Anderson, 1844. 107 p. 12mo   LC
Contents: The Orphan; or, The Triumph of Virtue—The Indian Bride: A Romance of the Pequots—The Klepht's Revenge; or, The Robber of the Mountain Pass—Sandy Ballie: A Tale of the Olden Time—The Recreant Made Virtuous and Happy—An Incident.

2769 ——— The Smoky City: A Tale of Crime ... Pittsburgh: Printed by A. A. Anderson, 1845. 204 p. 8vo   LC

2770 ——— Tom Hanson, the Avenger: A Tale of the Backwoods. Embracing the History, Legends, and Romance of the "Country around the Head of the Ohio" ... Pittsburgh: J. W. Cook, 1847. 199 p. 8vo   LC

2771 THE YOUNG CLERGYMAN ... Cambridge: Hilliard and Brown, 1828. 18 p. 8vo   AAS, BP, H, Y
Massachusetts; contemporary.

YOUNG 'UN, *pseud. See* Burnham, George Pickering

2772 ZERAH, the Believing Jew ... New York: Printed by the New York Episcopal Press, 1837. 286 p. 8vo   UP, Y

CHRONOLOGICAL INDEX

CHRONOLOGICAL INDEX

Initial articles are usually omitted in this index.

Numbers refer to items.

381

TITLE INDEX

TITLE INDEX

Initial articles are usually omitted in this index.
Numbers refer to items.